THE MURDER OF MARILYN MONROE: CASE CLOSED

THE MURDER OF MARILYN MONROE: CASE CLOSED

JAY MARGOLIS AND RICHARD BUSKIN

Skyhorse Publishing

Skyhorse Publishing books may be purchased in bulk at special discounts for sales promotion, corporate gifts, fund-raising, or educational purposes. Special editions can also be created to specifications. For details, contact the Special Sales Department, Skyhorse Publishing, 307 West 36th Street, 11th Floor, New York, NY 10018 or info@skyhorsepublishing.com.

Skyhorse® and Skyhorse Publishing® are registered trademarks of Skyhorse Publishing, Inc.®, a Delaware corporation.

Visit our website at www.skyhorsepublishing.com.

10 9 8 7 6 5 4 3

Library of Congress Cataloging-in-Publication Data is available on file.

Cover design by Brian Peterson

ISBN: 978-1-62873-757-8
Ebook ISBN: 978-1-62914-126-8

Printed in the United States of America

People say I am ruthless. I am not ruthless. And if I find the
man who is calling me ruthless, I shall destroy him.

—Robert Francis Kennedy

Jack Kennedy could have been a movie star himself.
He had the charisma, the charm, that come-hither quality
that can never be duplicated. Is it any wonder he got
elected president?

—Marilyn Monroe to Lawrence Quirk

It's not what you are. It's what people think you are.

—Joseph P. Kennedy, Sr.

CONTENTS

CONTENTS

ACKNOWLEDGMENTS

First, I would like to thank Richard Buskin, the best co-author anyone could hope for. We worked really well together, and the use of his interviews with Marilyn's friends—including her stand-in Evelyn Moriarty and Twentieth Century-Fox security guard George Erengis—helped enhance this book.

I am also grateful to Michelle Morgan for granting permission to use her 1997 James Hall interview in this book; James Spada for permission to quote from several of his interviews, including the late Fred Otash; Marilyn's last professional photographer, George Barris, who has believed in me since the genesis of my first MM book; Raymond Strait, who was Jayne Mansfield's press secretary for the last ten years of her life; the late Jane Russell, Marilyn's co-star in *Gentlemen Prefer Blondes;* MM's press agent, Michael Selsman; Allan Abbott for spending several hours discussing her case with me; Devik Wiener for inviting me into his father's archives at the Hollywood Vaults in Los Angeles; eyewitnesses Don Schulman and Irene Gizzi for providing key testimony with regard to the Robert Kennedy assassination; and Schaefer Ambulance driver Edgardo Villalobos for revealing previously unknown information not just about MM, but also RFK.

Other thanks go out to Roy Turner, Gloria Romanoff, Marijane Gray, Sylvia Leib, Carl Bellonzi, Ruth Tarnowski, Rigo Chacon, Tony Plant, Mike Carlson, Robert Dambacher, Daniel Stewart, John Watkins, former FBI agent Monte Hall, the late Robert Joling, the late C. David Heymann, his widow Bea for her continued support, and both Anthony Summers and Donald H. Wolfe for their research into Marilyn's death, Shane O'Sullivan for being the first to seriously investigate CIA presence at the

Ambassador Hotel on June 5, 1968, and especially the late Professor Philip H. Melanson for mentioning three eyewitnesses who saw *both* second and third gunmen in the pantry, a major contribution to RFK assassination research.

I am indebted to Greg Schreiner, the President of the *Marilyn Remembered* fan club, for always being available to help in any way he can; Elias W. Amador, M.D., for his medical expertise with regard to MM's death; Michelle Justice, co-author of the fan newspaper *Runnin' Wild: All About Marilyn*, for permission to use James Hall's 1992 polygraph examination conducted by Donald E. Fraser; assorted confidential sources; and last, but not least, my parents and friends.

Jay Margolis, Los Angeles, March 2014

PRIVATE DETECTIVE FRED OTASH'S SOUNDMAN THE NIGHT MARILYN MONROE DIED TO JAY MARGOLIS: "What happened to the story that they were taking Marilyn to the hospital, where she was in the ambulance and Bobby Kennedy was in the ambulance with her? I remember that story from forty years ago! It's bullshit. Total bullshit. Eunice Murray has told probably a dozen fucking stories from the night that it happened."

SYLVIA LEIB, WIDOW OF AMBULANCE DRIVER MURRAY LEIB, TO JAY MARGOLIS (04/25/2012): "Marilyn had called Bobby and she was so hysterical and she was threatening to tell a lot of stuff to the *Enquirer*. And he came down to talk to her. Bobby Kennedy had been there."

SUICIDE PREVENTION TEAM MEMBER DR. ROBERT LITMAN (08/18/1962): "At least in 1960, when I went through the medical literature on this very subject (because we were encountering this problem when consulting for Dr. Curphey back then), there was no case in the medical records where it could be authenticated that someone had died of barbiturate poisoning under the circumstances that they had become so drugged that they did not know what they were doing, and they took a lethal dose."

MARILYN MONROE'S CLOSE FRIEND AND MASSEUR RALPH ROBERTS: "That last weekend, I think she was in better shape than all those years I'd been around. And she was very excited about having her own house after all. I remember her saying, 'It's so good, laughing again.' I called her at 6 o'clock [to confirm a dinner engagement with Marilyn at her house that night] and Greenson answered. He said, 'She's not here.' It could have been so easy that she was busy, which I would have accepted . . . It would be easier to believe that she committed suicide but I don't. I think somebody done her in."

AMBULANCE ATTENDANT JAMES HALL TO JAMES SPADA (06/03/1990): "Marilyn was in another room—not her own—when I arrived. Pat Newcomb was there . . . Bobby was there earlier. That's been corroborated. That's when they gave her knockout drops, I believe. That didn't kill her and she made it through until I got there . . . I know Dr. Greenson killed her . . . He stuck a needle into her chest. One minute later, she was gone . . . If we had taken her away, she'd be alive today and Bobby Kennedy would be in jail."

MARILYN MONROE
Norma Jeane Mortenson
June 1, 1926–August 4, 1962

HOW DID MARILYN MONROE REALLY DIE?

In 1983, Peter Lawford discussed his friend Marilyn Monroe at length with biographer C. David Heymann for the latter's biography on Jackie Kennedy. Apparently, out of deep guilt (he had always held himself responsible for her death), Lawford conceded to having been part of a conspiracy to murder Marilyn Monroe, labeling himself a co-conspirator along with his brother-in-law Bobby Kennedy and Marilyn's psychiatrist, Dr. Ralph Greenson. The secret was kept all these years and the public was deceived into believing that Monroe's death was accidental.

Natalie Trundy, Jacobs' twenty-one-year-old girlfriend at the time, told biographer Anthony Summers that shortly after 10:30 p.m., Arthur "went to Marilyn's house, and I don't think I saw him for two days. He had to fudge the press." Marilyn's close friend and former publicist, Rupert Allan, told biographers Peter Harry Brown and Patte Barham, "It was carefully done and beautifully executed . . . It was decided to play up the 'accidental death' scenario but none of us believed it."

Referring to August 4, 1962, Marilyn's friend, reporter George Carpozi, Jr., said, "Bobby then calls Peter Lawford and says to him, 'Okay, this time she's getting out of hand.' Peter calls up Dr. Greenson—this was all organized beforehand—and says, 'Look, doc, let's get the show on the road,' and right after that afternoon call, Greenson goes to Marilyn's." As for the months leading to her death, Peter Lawford told Heymann:

> Marilyn realized the affair [between her and Jack Kennedy] was over but couldn't accept it. She began writing these rather pathetic letters to Jack and continued calling. She threatened

to go to the press. He finally sent Bobby Kennedy out to California to cool her off . . .

He tried to explain to her that the President was an extremely busy man, that running the country was an imposing task, that while Jack cared a great deal for her, he was already married and couldn't very well simply sneak off and see a divorce lawyer.

Although it probably wasn't easy for her, she would have to accept this decision and stop calling the President. She took it pretty hard. Bobby felt for her. They met again the following day and passed the afternoon walking along the beach.

It wasn't Bobby's intention, but that evening they became lovers and spent the night in our guest bedroom. Almost immediately the affair got very heavy, and they began seeing a lot of each other. Now Marilyn was calling the Department of Justice instead of the White House . . .

Pretty soon Marilyn announced that she was in love with Bobby and that *he* had promised to marry her. It was as if she could no longer tell the difference between Bobby and Jack . . .

According to Lawford, he told Marilyn to get her act together before it messed up her career, but she couldn't accept how she'd been used by the Kennedy brothers.

Intriguingly, Norman Mailer wrote in *Marilyn* (Warner Books updated paperback edition, March 1975) how "through the generosity of Pat Newcomb, he had the opportunity to hear Marilyn talking casually on tape." Furthermore, the British actor himself claimed to have heard the tapes she recorded for her psychiatrist Dr. Ralph Greenson, in which she freely spoke her daily thoughts, and Lawford stated that these revealed her love for the Attorney General and her desire to marry him despite he and his brother "passing her around like a football."

When neither brother would any longer accept her calls, she then began calling the First Lady at the White House and Bobby's wife Ethel at their home in Hickory Hill. Talking with Heymann, Lawford mentioned something even more disturbing that he learned when listening to Marilyn's private recordings following her death:

I suppose the most surprising revelation in Marilyn's own tapes was the fact that not only did Marilyn have an affair with both Kennedys, she was also sleeping with Dr. Greenson, who appeared to be deeply in love with her.

Marilyn was a frequent houseguest in the home of Greenson and his wife, who presumably knew nothing about the affair . . . I also got hold of portions of the [Mafia-Teamster] tapes, and heard what seemed to be sounds of their lovemaking . . .

Marilyn's house was being bugged by everyone—Jimmy Hoffa, the FBI, the Mafia, even Twentieth Century-Fox. Jimmy Hoffa wanted to gather information on Monroe and the Kennedys for personal use; the FBI wanted to ascertain what Marilyn knew about Frank Sinatra's connections to the Mafia; the Mafia was curious as to what she knew about the FBI. As for Twentieth Century-Fox—her former studio [sic—] who knows what they wanted . . . ?

MM's affair with Greenson took on a far greater meaning at the time of her death. Marilyn, as everyone later discovered, had threatened Bobby with the prospect of holding a press conference at which she planned to announce her assignations with both the President and the Attorney General. Such an admission would no doubt have resulted in a major scandal.

Bobby, on hearing of Marilyn's plans—and somehow knowing of her concomitant relationship with Greenson, called the good doctor and convinced him that his star patient also intended to disclose her romantic dealings with the psychiatrist.

This would not only have terminated Greenson's career but very likely would have landed him in prison. "Marilyn has got to be silenced," Bobby told Greenson—or something to that effect. Greenson had thus been set up by Bobby to "take care" of Marilyn . . .

I certainly think Marilyn would have held a press conference. She was determined to gain back her self-esteem. She was unbalanced at the time—and Bobby was determined to shut her up, regardless of the consequences. It was the craziest thing he ever did—and I was crazy enough to let it happen.

Best friend and occasional lover, Frank Sinatra, was more than a little suspicious after learning a crucial detail from the autopsy. Sinatra's valet, George Jacobs, stated, "When the cops said it was an overdose, he had no doubt about it, nor did I . . . It was only later when the autopsy revealed no residue of pills in her system that we got curious. Mr. S began to suspect Lawford and his brothers-in-law of possible foul play."

Pat Newcomb countered to biographer Donald Spoto, "There's no way they could've done this. I resent it so much . . . I'd like to see Bobby exonerated from this. He would never do it . . . He wouldn't hurt her . . . He was in San Francisco." Former Police Chief Daryl F. Gates conceded in his autobiography, "The truth is, we knew Robert Kennedy was in town on August 4. We always knew when he was here. He was the Attorney General, so we were interested in him, the same way we were interested when other important figures came to Los Angeles." On Marilyn and Bobby, Gates continued, "Frankly, I never bought into the theory that she killed herself because he dumped her—if he did. My feelings were that she was emotional over many things; a relationship gone sour would be just one of many problems she had."

Michael Selsman, a twenty-four-year-old press agent in 1962, held a job alongside Pat Newcomb within the Arthur P. Jacobs Company. Selsman relayed to biographer Jay Margolis, "After Marilyn died, I worked at Fox and Paramount as an executive. I'm from New York. Back in the sixties, I knew of [Marilyn's acting coaches] the Strasbergs, and knew [their actress-daughter] Susan. The Strasbergs were horrible people, and Susan was, in my mind, destroyed by her mother. The parents were attention-seekers, users, preyed on weak-minded actors, and never came up with anything original. They copied Stanislavski and feasted on the notoriety of the few successful actors that happened to come up in New York at that time. There were thousands more who never amounted to anything. Those who can act, act. Those who can't, they become coaches."

Describing what it was like working with Marilyn day-to-day, Selsman relayed, "I never saw her happy. I never saw her laugh. Never heard any jokes from her. It was strictly business. All actors are shy and lonely people. That's why they are actors . . . Marilyn's concerns in the office were mainly about interviews and photo sessions. Pat was her main contact, so whatever she thought was threatening was discussed in private with Pat and sometimes Arthur . . . It was part of my job to be at the funeral. I attempted to coordinate with the reporters, photographers from around the world, and the press agents from Fox. It was a circus." Selsman was queried as to what he knew about August 4, 1962:

> MARGOLIS: Did Arthur Jacobs tell you Bobby Kennedy was at Marilyn's home the day she died either in the afternoon or in the evening?
>
> SELSMAN: Yes.
>
> MARGOLIS: Was it afternoon or evening?
>
> SELSMAN: It was the afternoon.

Regarding Peter Lawford's last full-length interview, Dean Martin's ex-wife Jeanne remarked to Margolis, "Somebody would've said something years ago. The mystery of her death, people have let up on that one ages ago." Informed that the autopsy revealed how Marilyn's stomach was empty, Mrs. Martin replied, "I never read that. I never heard that. Don't bother telling me because I wouldn't *want* to know that."

When told that many now agree Bobby Kennedy was in Los Angeles on August 4 *before* Marilyn died and *after* she died, Mrs. Martin said, "I don't care where he was. He didn't kill Marilyn. Bobby Kennedy would not kill anybody. He would *kill* somebody? It's impossible. It's such yellow journalism." After bringing to her attention that biographer Heymann had actual interview tapes of Lawford's own voice mentioning the conspiracy to murder Marilyn, Mrs. Martin responded, "I knew the Kennedys very well. I knew Peter very well. If anybody took pills, it was Peter."[1]

As for the bugging tapes he heard, Lawford told Heymann:

> You could apparently hear [on Mafia-Teamster tapes] the voices of Marilyn and JFK as well as Marilyn and RFK, in addition to MM and Dr. Ralph Greenson. In each case, you could hear the muted sounds of bedsprings and the cries of ecstasy. Marilyn, after all, was a master of her craft.

It is certainly possible that Peter Lawford obtained Mafia-Teamster recordings. In fact, as noted by Anthony Summers, Lawford tried to obtain Mafia tapes in at least one other instance, regarding gangster Mickey Cohen's female associate Juanita Dale Slusher (a.k.a. Candy Barr). This information is supported by a D.A.'s investigation into Lawford's activities in 1961.

Fred Otash recalled to biographer James Spada, "Something strange happened with Lawford one day. He came to me and said, 'Fred, have you got some means for me to make secret recordings?' I said, 'Yes, what do you need?' He would never tell me what they were. So my vibration is that he was possibly wiring up Jack Kennedy and Bobby."

Jayne Mansfield's press secretary, Raymond Strait, who knew Otash for twenty years, agreed: "I've listened to tapes in which Jayne and the President were the principal players. Lawford had copies of the tapes and once, during a bong-sharing session with Jayne in the Pink Palace, played them back for her. Later on, she prevailed upon Peter to play them for one of her lovers but he declined. Peter apparently owned quite a library of audio tapes of his famous brothers-in-law and their trysts with famous Hollywood sex symbols."

Strait told Margolis: "Otash knew conversations between me and Jayne before I even met him! He taped Jayne because, after all, she slept with both of them [Jack and Bobby Kennedy]. Wherever they were at, Otash was there a little bit ahead of them . . . The only thing that worried Fred at all was the Johnny Stompanato case [in which actress Lana Turner's brutal lover was purportedly murdered by her daughter Cheryl]. Fred was very complicit as an accessory after the fact because he removed the knife, put Cheryl's fingerprints on it and put it back in! Lana Turner killed Johnny Stompanato. Lana caught him and Cheryl in bed together. He went after her daughter, and Lana jumped in the middle and he got it. Mother and daughter love each other. 'Save my career,' so Cheryl saves Lana's career, and that's what Cheryl did."

When Jay Margolis interviewed Joe Naar, Joe said he was not only Lawford's best friend, but also a friend of the Kennedy family. According to Naar, he and Lawford repeatedly went over Marilyn's last night and Lawford blamed himself for the movie star's death.

Peter Lawford was a close friend of Marilyn Monroe for more than a decade. Never a man to make decisions on his own, as confirmed by his lawyer Milt Ebbins, the English actor was an unwilling participant in her murder. By all accounts, feeling extremely guilty for years following his friend's death, and aware of what the Kennedy brothers had done both to him and to Marilyn, Lawford confided as much to biographer C. David Heymann. A year later, Peter Lawford was dead.[2]

MARILYN'S CLOSE FRIENDS GET SUSPICIOUS

At around 7:30 in the evening of Friday, July 13, 1962, George Barris captured the final professional photograph of Marilyn Monroe during her lifetime. A freelancer for *Cosmopolitan* magazine, Barris recalled, "I said, 'Marilyn, this is the last picture I'm going to take of you.' She was sitting on the sand and we had this Scandinavian heavy sweater she was wearing. She bundled up and she had covered her knees with the blanket. She leaned forward and said, 'Alright, George, this is just for you.' She puckered her lips and threw a kiss to me. She said, 'This is for you and the world and this is the picture I want to be remembered by.'"

Now fast-forward to August 3 of that same year. "When I was in New York after I left Los Angeles and Marilyn Monroe, I was putting together the story for *Cosmopolitan*, which was to be about twelve pages and a cover," Barris remembered. "She called and asked, 'How is everything going?' 'Fine.' 'George, you must come back. I have some very important things we have to talk about. It's very important.' 'Marilyn, it's Friday. I'll try to come out by Monday if it's alright.' 'Please, promise me.' I said, 'I promise.'"

Barris told Jay Margolis he regretted not going back to California on August 4, the very next day. Margolis asked him, "Marilyn never let on that she was going to hold a press conference, right? She just said she had to talk to you about something important?" Barris confirmed, "That's all she said."

Barris reflected in his 1995 book: "She never seemed happier . . . I was very happy for her . . . She said she'd probably just relax, go out to dinner, and then maybe go over to the Lawfords' for their regular Saturday night party. Then she said, 'Love you—see you Monday.' I said I loved her, too."

During her final interview before her untimely death, Marilyn told George Barris, "The happiest time of my life is now . . . There's a future and I can't wait to get to it—it should be interesting! I feel I'm just getting started; I want to do comedy, tragedy, interspersed . . . I have no regrets, because if I made any mistakes, I was responsible . . . I like to stay here (in California) but every once in awhile I get that feeling for New York. Here all I have to do is lock the [front and back] doors and go. I like ground to stand on."

"Why would she take her life?" George Barris asked Jay Margolis. "We did photographs at Santa Monica beach near Peter Lawford's. Marilyn bought a new house in Brentwood but it wasn't furnished. She had gone to Mexico to furnish it Mexican style. She was waiting for the furniture to arrive. Marilyn said to me, 'How can we photograph there if it doesn't look right? What can we do?' 'If you want to go back where you lived with your first husband in Catalina, I'll try.' 'No, I don't want to go back.' 'My friend's home in the Hollywood Hills would be perfect. When I brought it up, he said all he wants is a picture of you and him as a souvenir. You don't have to do it if you don't want to.' 'No, it's okay.' I took a picture of him with Marilyn. All the other photos are at his home."

In 1995, using those pictures taken at Santa Monica Beach and in North Hollywood at his friend Tim Leimert's house, George Barris created a touching and tender book about Marilyn Monroe, with her own words guiding the narrative. It was a project they planned to do sometime in the future just days after they became friends in September 1954. Back then, Marilyn was making *The Seven Year Itch* in New York and Barris was photographing her. That film became his favorite Marilyn Monroe movie. "What I particularly liked about Marilyn was that she didn't act like a movie star," he wrote. "She was down to earth . . . Sure, she was beautiful and sexy, but there was an almost childlike innocence about her . . . Marilyn was always polite and friendly to everyone on the set."

Evelyn Moriarty was Marilyn's stand-in for her final three movies: *Let's Make Love* (1960), *The Misfits* (1961), and the unfinished *Something's Got to Give* (1962). Moriarty relayed to biographer Richard Buskin, "Buck Hall was the assistant director on *Something's Got to Give* and, like the rest of the production office, he hated her. He was a bastard. According to what I was told by the camera operator and Bunny Gardel, who did her body makeup, when they were working on *Bus Stop* [in 1956], Buck

Hall would ogle Marilyn. She called him a Peeping Tom and he never forgave her for that. Well, by the time of *Something's Got to Give*, the Fox executives were fed up with Marilyn. You could feel the tension when she walked on the set. Although the crew adored her, she was a piece of meat as far as those execs were concerned and they treated her like one.

"June 1 [1962] was Marilyn's thirty-sixth birthday. So, that morning I bought her a cake with candles, but [director] George Cukor and the Fox executives wouldn't let me give it to her until they got a full day's work out of her. Late in the afternoon, George finally said I could wheel out the cake and he joined in our little celebration, but the smiles were fake. Afterwards, as Marilyn was leaving, I was with her, Bunny Gardel, and [hairstylist] Agnes Flanagan, and I said, 'She's not going to be here Monday because of the way that Buck Hall and the others just treated her on the set.' Still, I didn't know she was never going to be in again."

That same Friday of Marilyn's final birthday, having worked briefly with Elizabeth Taylor in Rome, Italy, for a *Cosmo* report on the filming of *Cleopatra*, George Barris approached Marilyn on the set of *Something's Got to Give*. As he later told Jay Margolis, "When I arrived, she said, 'What are you doing here?! I heard you were in Rome with Elizabeth Taylor! So, you found a new girl, huh?' 'No, we were just doing the story. She's impossible to work with.' 'Can you imagine they're paying her a million dollars for that picture?' They later brought out the cake and we all sang 'Happy Birthday' with me at her side.

"I was supposed to meet her at the studio Monday to start on our story. She wasn't there when I got there. She called in. She was a very frail person. They sent their own studio doctor [Dr. Lee Siegel] to investigate if she was really sick. He confirmed she was *really* sick. The studio was desperate. They had all these technicians, cameramen, and actors and actresses on salary. They're paying them and they were going broke. They had paid Elizabeth Taylor on *Cleopatra* a million dollars. The studio was in bad shape financially."

Marilyn was fired from *Something's Got to Give* on June 8. She and Barris began their joint projects the following day through July 18. "I don't think anyone was ever more determined," he'd remember, "and I never encountered a model who worked as hard as she did."

"I will never believe that she took her own life," Barris wrote. "It will always be my conviction that she was murdered."

To Jay Margolis he stated, "I'll never forget her because she was kind and she was honest and she was lovable, and she was a girl who became what she was because she was determined and she had been through her whole life making everyone happy. She was always a caring person. She was a timid person but also a very lonely person. Unfortunately, her marriages were not very successful. Only if Marilyn had a child, I think that would have saved her life."

Learning of the tragic news of her passing, Barris relayed to Margolis, "When I was in the country, I was with my brother-in-law. We went to a local grocery to get some milk and bagels. I sat in the car and he went in to buy it and he came running out. And he looked at me, 'It just came over the radio.' I said, 'What are you talking about?' 'Marilyn is dead.' 'You shouldn't make jokes like that. It's not nice.' 'No, it's true. Honestly.' I couldn't believe it. I was just in a shock. I dropped him off then I drove all the way back to New York where I lived at Sutton Place. It was about a hundred miles. Luckily, I didn't get a ticket or in an accident, I was driving so fast. When I got back, the doorman told me that there was a bunch of press and photographers and reporters looking for me. 'If they come back, tell them I'm not here.' I went upstairs. I put on the television and radio. All that came over was 'Marilyn is dead. Marilyn is dead.' It was too much. I shut everything off. I couldn't take it."

Actress Jane Russell was also suspicious of the circumstances surrounding Marilyn's death. When interviewed on November 29, 2010, by Jay Margolis, Jane Russell confirmed a story about an unpleasant run-in with Robert Kennedy: "I met him one time after his brother had been killed. I was working with this organization. We called it WAIF to get kids adopted. You couldn't get them from the United States but you could from other countries. The kids would come in with the parents that had all been picked, and he happened to be there one of these times. He met other people, and he was very friendly and nice. Then he was introduced to me, and the face just went *huh!* It was not friendly at all. I thought, well boy, something's funny there. So I guess he thought I knew all about whatever went on . . . I just think there was something very strange. When the Lord gets here, we'll know exactly what happened . . . There were things that she looked forward to. The studio had said okay. There were so many things that were happening that she wanted to happen."

An intriguing article by author Wendy Leigh appeared in the United Kingdom on March 3, 2007. After interviewing Jane Russell, Leigh discovered the actress believed her friend had been murdered: "I don't think she killed herself," Russell stated. "Someone did it for her. There were dirty tricks somewhere."

"I suggest that Jack and Bobby Kennedy—both Marilyn's lovers—may have been involved, and Jane nods darkly," Leigh wrote while adding that Russell told her, "Soon after Marilyn died, I met Bobby Kennedy and he looked at me as if to say: 'I am your enemy.'"

On August 1, 1962, three days before her death, Marilyn Monroe was rehired by Twentieth Century-Fox to complete shooting on *Something's Got to Give* and signed a one-million-dollar, two-picture deal. Just over three decades later, in July 1993, her stand-in, Evelyn Moriarty, told Richard Buskin, "There's no way she killed herself. I spoke with her the Wednesday before she died and she was so excited about going back to work. She told me they'd be shooting Dean Martin's close-ups first and then placing Dean for her close-ups—she was really up. She had to finish this picture at Fox because she was going to film *I Love Louisa* at United Artists with Frank Sinatra, produced by her publicist Arthur Jacobs. She also talked about having three pictures to do in Europe; two of them with Brigitte Bardot. It was all 'We're going to do this' and 'We're going to do that'—she had battled the studio, she had won, and she was really looking forward to all of those projects."

George Erengis, a Twentieth Century-Fox security guard, relayed to Richard Buskin, "On the Monday following her death, I went into Marilyn's dressing room on the Fox lot and it had been cleared out. Nothing, not a trace of her had been left. I was shocked. She had earned that studio a fortune but they didn't waste any time trying to erase her memory."

For her part, actress Debbie Reynolds relayed to Britain's *Daily Express* newspaper how she told Marilyn to watch herself when dating the Kennedy brothers: "I saw her two days before she died and warned her to be careful. She was such a sweet and innocent girl but she was used by men. I believe she was murdered because too many people were afraid the truth would come out."

In an earlier interview, Reynolds remembered, "Her life was very sad. And the ending was very sad indeed. And those of us who knew Marilyn, always were kind of dreaming for that great white knight to arrive and really love her and not take advantage of her."

Joe DiMaggio was that great white knight. As for Marilyn's second marriage on January 14, 1954, former FBI agent Monte Hall revealed to Jay Margolis, "I was at the wedding. Marilyn was married by a judge in a San Francisco courthouse. I happened to be there at the time. I knew Joe quite well. A lot of us in the San Francisco office knew Joe DiMaggio."

Morris Engelberg (no relation to Marilyn's physician Dr. Hyman Engelberg) was one of DiMaggio's best friends and the executor of his estate. According to him, "Joe DiMaggio was in love with Marilyn Monroe until the moment he died . . . 'I'll finally get to see Marilyn,' were his last words . . . He ached at the thought of how close they had come to remarrying . . . The date of their second marriage was set: August 8, 1962."

When Engelberg asked Joe Jr. if he concurred with his father's conviction that the Kennedys were responsible for Marilyn Monroe's death, the younger DiMaggio replied, "She didn't die of natural causes, and she wasn't going to kill herself, not when she was about to remarry my father."

Jane Russell told Jay Margolis, "I think she was going to remarry Joe DiMaggio." Russell explained how she learned of the marriage plans from mutual friends shortly before Marilyn's death.

Marilyn's niece Mona Rae Miracle revealed, "Berniece's heartbreak at handling Marilyn's funeral was ameliorated by the help Joe gave her with arrangements. 'They were going to remarry,' says Berniece. 'Marilyn was thinking ahead to that.' "[3]

BOBBY KENNEDY BROUGHT ALONG ONE OF HIS TWO LONG-TIME PERSONAL BODYGUARDS TO SEDATE MARILYN IN THE AFTERNOON

Peter Lawford recalled how, at approximately two o'clock on the afternoon of August 4, 1962, he and Bobby Kennedy arrived at Marilyn Monroe's home. Lawford told biographer C. David Heymann she had set aside some Mexican food, which suggested she was expecting Bobby's visit. Heymann wrote that the buffet included "guacamole, stuffed mushrooms, spicy meatballs . . . plus a chilled magnum of her favorite beverage, champagne. Lawford poured himself a glass and went out to the swimming pool so Marilyn and Bobby could talk." An existing receipt proves she purchased this food from Briggs Delicatessen the day before in the amount of $49.07. Regarding Bobby and Marilyn, Lawford informed Heymann:

> They argued back and forth for maybe ten minutes, Marilyn becoming more and more hysterical. At the height of her anger she allowed how first thing Monday morning she was going to call a press conference and tell the world about the treatment she had suffered at the hands of the Kennedy brothers. At this point Bobby became livid. In no uncertain terms he told her she would have to leave both Jack and him alone—no more telephone calls, no letters, nothing. They didn't want to hear from her anymore. Marilyn presently lost it, screaming

obscenities and flailing wildly away at Bobby with her fists. In her fury she picked up a small kitchen knife and lunged at him. I was with them at this time, so I tried to grab Marilyn's arm. We finally knocked her down and managed to wrestle the knife away. Bobby thought we ought to call Dr. Greenson and tell him to come over. The psychiatrist arrived at Marilyn's home within the hour.

To Donald Spoto, Pat Newcomb confirmed Peter Lawford's account: "I was at her house that afternoon until three and that's when Greenson came and told me to leave. He wanted to deal with her . . . She was very upset . . . Greenson told Mrs. Murray to take her out for a walk on the beach in the car . . . And that's the last I saw of her."

When interviewed by biographer Maurice Zolotow in October 1973, Greenson stated that, when he arrived at Marilyn's in the early afternoon, "It was clear she had taken some sleeping pills during the day."

Attempting to mask why she was *really* upset, Dr. Greenson and housekeeper Eunice Murray claimed that Marilyn was mad at Pat Newcomb—who had slept over on August 3—because Pat had enjoyed a good night's sleep whereas Marilyn, typically, hadn't. "Pat had stayed overnight, and apparently had taken sleeping pills, perhaps some of Marilyn's Nembutal," Murray relayed to Rose Shade, her coauthor on the 1975 book *Marilyn: The Last Months*. "Pat was still asleep, and would sleep serenely until noon—the way Marilyn longed to sleep. Marilyn was not pleased. To sleep twelve hours in her house was like feasting in front of a starving person."

"She resented the fact that Pat Newcomb had taken some pills . . . and slept twelve hours and Marilyn had also taken pills and slept only six hours." Ralph Greenson told Maurice Zolotow. "I said that instead of Pat staying overnight, Pat should go home and Mrs. Murray remain the night. I didn't want Marilyn to be alone."

This contradicted Greenson's earlier recollection, in a letter sent to his colleague Dr. Marianne Kris just weeks after Marilyn died, that it was actually *Marilyn* who had wanted Pat to leave: "I finally asked the girlfriend to leave because this was Marilyn's request, and I asked the housekeeper to stay overnight, which she did not ordinarily do on Saturday nights."

According to that housekeeper, "Dr. Greenson asked me if I had planned on staying that night. He asked this in a rather offhand way, without any special reason for my staying at her home, for Marilyn felt secure. She often told me that staying alone was no problem with her."

What Greenson, Murray, and Newcomb didn't want to admit was that Marilyn had been really upset over her row with Bobby Kennedy. Years later, Mrs. Murray would concede to Anthony Summers that the argument was indeed over Bobby's earlier visit. In the 1985 *Say Goodbye to the President* documentary, Murray and Summers shared the following exchange regarding Marilyn's last day on August 4:

> MRS. MURRAY: Well, over a period of time, I was not at all surprised that the Kennedys were a very important part of Marilyn's life. I was not included in this information but I was a witness to what was happening.
>
> SUMMERS: And you believe that he was here?
>
> MRS. MURRAY: At Marilyn's house?
>
> SUMMERS: Yes.
>
> MRS. MURRAY: Oh, sure.
>
> SUMMERS: That afternoon?
>
> MRS. MURRAY: Yes.
>
> SUMMERS: And you think *that* is the reason she was so upset?
>
> MRS. MURRAY: Yes.

When Summers asked Mrs. Murray why she lied to the police, she conceded, "I told whatever I thought was good to tell."

As for Pat Newcomb, she told Donald Spoto, "Marilyn seemed angry that I had been able to sleep and she hadn't—but something else was behind it all."[4]

Robert Kennedy testified in a sworn deposition to Captain Edward Michael Davis that he arrived at Marilyn's home in the afternoon. Later, Davis became LAPD chief during the years 1969–1978.

In 1978, former OCID (Organized Crime Intelligence Division) detective Mike Rothmiller actually saw the statement made by Bobby Kennedy about Marilyn Monroe and his secret trip to her home on the afternoon of August 4. Additionally, Rothmiller saw a copy of Marilyn's diary, located in the OCID file rooms. Pertaining to Bobby Kennedy's statement, Rothmiller told biographers Peter Harry Brown and Patte Barham that Bobby Kennedy "said he was involved with Monroe—but he wasn't, implying a friendly relationship. He also said he had met with her several times during the summer."

On August 4, 1962, Marilyn's female next-door neighbor to the east and her friend Elizabeth Pollard were busy playing bridge with two other ladies as they did every Saturday afternoon. According to Dr. Greenson's daughter Joan, "Marilyn found out that the neighbor who you could see from her property was a professor at the university." This was UCLA professor Ralph Mosser Barnes (born October 17, 1900) from the Engineering and Production Management department. He taught at UCLA from July 1, 1949, until July 1, 1968. It was his wife Mary W. Goodykoontz Barnes (born October 25, 1904) who played hostess to that Saturday afternoon bridge party at 12304 Fifth Helena Drive the day Marilyn died. At the time, Mrs. Barnes refused to identify herself to Sgt. Clemmons, and because she passed away on March 12, 1964, her eyewitness account seemingly disappeared into the wind—until now. As for her UCLA professor husband Mr. Barnes, he died on November 5, 1984.

The four card-playing ladies, including hostess Mary W. Goodykoontz Barnes and guest Elizabeth Pollard, earlier witnessed Bobby Kennedy go into Marilyn's house and subsequently saw him leave and, shortly thereafter, reenter with one of his two long-time personal bodyguards from the LAPD, Archie Case or James Ahern. Case or Ahern gave Marilyn an intramuscular pentobarbital (Nembutal) shot in the armpit to calm her down, shortly after Lawford and Kennedy had confiscated the knife from her.

"[Pathologist Thomas] Noguchi admitted there was a needle mark under one of her armpits," says funeral director Allan Abbott, who was one of the pallbearers when Marilyn was laid to rest. "Of course, with a star like Marilyn Monroe who was taking prescription drugs—the doctors agreed to give her those injections so it wouldn't show on camera. It was very common to have shots given in the armpit."

When asked if Noguchi admitted there was a needle mark in Marilyn's armpit, Abbott replied, "That was the word I got from one of his deputies," confirming this relates to the Nembutal injection that Case or Ahern gave Marilyn during the last afternoon of her life.

A confidential source revealed, "Bobby said in his deposition that he and Peter Lawford went to Marilyn's house late in the afternoon of August 4. There was a violent argument, and Marilyn was grabbed by Bobby and thrown to the floor . . . Then she was given an injection of pentobarbital in her armpit, which settled her down . . . RFK said in his statement that the doctor [Case or Ahern] gave Marilyn the shot under her left arm. He even named the artery on the tape. He said the shot that went into her was pentobarbital."

Talking with Jay Margolis about an event that took place in 1986, George Barris recalled, "Gloria Steinem and I were signing the book we did together in Brentwood in a big book store, and a woman came up to me. She was elderly. She wanted me to autograph a book. She said, 'Mr. Barris, I was a neighbor to Marilyn. I was playing bridge with my friends, and there were people coming and going. That afternoon was Saturday. I saw someone who I believed was Bobby Kennedy and another man go into Marilyn's home and they came out a short while later.' She could see people who came and went. She didn't know who the other man was but she assumed he was a doctor and he had a little black case. Doctors carry it . . . It probably was not Greenson because the psychiatrist came later to her house."

Since the bridge party hostess Mary W. Goodykoontz Barnes and guest Elizabeth Pollard were not the only two ladies at the bridge party, there must be another neighbor of Marilyn's who spoke with George Barris in 1986. This third woman only identified herself to Mr. Barris as Marilyn Monroe's neighbor. All that is known about her is that she was a guest at the bridge party at 12304 Fifth Helena Drive that last Saturday. In addition, there must have been a fourth person as a guest or an additional neighbor because including the hostess Mrs. Barnes, it takes four people to play bridge. The names of the third and fourth guest may never be known.

It was in 1974 when Elizabeth Pollard's daughter Betty relayed her mother's story about the Saturday afternoon card party and the sighting of Bobby Kennedy. Biographers Brown and Barham wrote: "The

Attorney General and another well-dressed man [Case or Ahern] came to the house sometime late in the afternoon. Women at a card party were able to see the man from an upstairs window. One of them, referring to Kennedy, said, 'Look, girls, there he is *again*.'"

Mrs. Murray explains how an author "related sensational rumors about Bobby Kennedy's arriving at the house that afternoon with a physician, reportedly to sedate an hysterical Marilyn." Mrs. Murray continues to comment how the "story stems from reports of a card party on Fifth Helena that afternoon at which the ladies were supposed to have looked out the window and seen Kennedy walking through Marilyn's gate with a man carrying a doctor's black bag."

Anthony Summers wrote, "I tracked that story to its source, a woman called Betty Pollard. She says her mother [Elizabeth Pollard] was playing bridge at a neighbor's home that day, when her hostess drew the players' attention to a car parking outside. Kennedy, immediately recognizable, emerged from the car and went into Marilyn's house."

That afternoon, the card-playing friends saw Kennedy bring Case or Ahern. They did not see Greenson. Importantly, Greenson was not qualified to give intramuscular injections. The ladies witnessed Bobby Kennedy leave Marilyn's, then quickly return again with "another well-dressed man" [Case or Ahern] carrying a black bag. Furthermore, the unidentified neighbor who spoke with Mr. Barris said she saw "Bobby Kennedy and another man go into Marilyn's home and they came out a short while later." In fact, since Greenson arrived nearly an hour later, it simply couldn't have been him. Logistically, what the four ladies saw was Bobby retrieve Case or Ahern from the white Lincoln convertible parked out front. Bobby Kennedy borrowed the car from FBI agent William Simon whenever he visited Marilyn.

From the window of Mary W. Goodykoontz's home on 12304 Fifth Helena Drive, looking over the gates, a person could easily see cars parked up the driveway and anyone who entered or left Marilyn's house.

Kennedy instructed Case or Ahern to give Marilyn the Nembutal shot in order to stun her, while he and Lawford searched the house for her little red diary. *Goddess* author Anthony Summers wrote that a confidential source heard tapes capturing the August 4 afternoon visit by Kennedy and Lawford to Marilyn's home:

The source says both Marilyn's and Kennedy's voices were easily recognizable. Like Otash—and it is worth noting that the source and Otash do not know each other—the source says there was a heated argument.

According to Summers' confidential source, the voices of Marilyn and Bobby Kennedy increased in volume as she challenged him to explain why he was reneging on his promise to marry her while Bobby several times demanded to know where "it" was located. Following the sound of a door being slammed, Kennedy could then be heard returning with Peter Lawford. "We have to know," the highly agitated Attorney General screeched at the actress. "It's important to the family. We can make any arrangements you want, but we must find it." As Kennedy searched for "it," Lawford tried to calm him down. Meanwhile, Marilyn screamed at the men to leave. Next, there were "thumping, bumping noises, then muffled, calming sounds. It sounded as though she was being put on the bed."

"Bobby came back with Peter," Marilyn wrote in her little red diary. "Shook me until I was dizzy and threw me on the bed. Should call the doctor."

As noted earlier, it was Lawford who called Dr. Greenson to the home. However, Kennedy was looking for Monroe's diary. It was the diary that Bobby could make "arrangements" for and which would be "important to the family."

In the documentary *Marilyn: The Last Word*, Anthony Summers stated: "Robert Kennedy is demanding for her to give him something. He keeps demanding, 'Where is it? Where is it, Marilyn? You've got to tell me where it is! We'll come to some arrangement but the family must have it.' Perhaps he was asking about the diary."

This was confirmed by Marilyn herself, who wrote in that diary, "Bobby was really mad. Acted crazy and searched all my stuff. Told him it's mine. I'll never let him have it."[5]

Norman Jefferies, Marilyn's handyman who also happened to be Eunice Murray's son-in-law, gave a chilling account of that last afternoon to biographer Donald Wolfe. Murray and Jefferies both recalled that Marilyn, not dressed when Bobby and Peter arrived, was still wearing her white terry-cloth robe. "Mr. Lawford made it very clear that he wanted Eunice and I [sic] out of there" Jefferies stated. "When we came back— maybe it was an hour later—their car was gone . . . Marilyn was hysteri- cal and looked awful . . . She was scared and at the same time she was terribly angry."

It was in light of Joe DiMaggio recently asking her to remarry him that Marilyn wanted to bitterly remind Bobby Kennedy about his pledge to marry her. By now, Marilyn had come to terms with the fact that Bobby was not going to divorce his wife Ethel. However, infuriated by his desire to still sleep with Marilyn, she wanted to nail him about his broken promise and total disregard for toying with her emotions. Indeed, the only thing he cared about—and the only reason for him showing up—was for her red diary. Otherwise, he wouldn't have bothered.

"Marilyn had done a turnabout," noted one of private eye Fred Otash's employees. "Lawford said Marilyn had called the White House, trying to reach the President, saying, 'Get your brother away from me—he's just using me.' "

John Miner, the Los Angeles County deputy district attorney who was an investigator into Marilyn's death, claimed to have heard something similar on one of the free-association tapes she recorded for Dr. Greenson: "I want someone else to tell him it's over. I tried to get the President to do it, but I couldn't reach him."

That afternoon, she felt very upset, used, and betrayed after Bobby had been the one to tell *her*, "It's over." Marilyn shot back, "But you promised to divorce Ethel and marry me." According to Fred Otash's rec- ollection of what he heard on the covert recording set up by wiretapper Bernie Spindel, Marilyn said, "I feel passed around—like a piece of meat. You've lied to me. Get out of here. I'm tired. Leave me alone."

Later, when Bobby tried to persuade Marilyn to visit Peter Lawford's house, she told him over the phone, "Stop bothering me. Stay away from me."

"She was convinced that not Jack but Bobby would leave Ethel and all their kids," remarked Michael Selsman from the Arthur P. Jacobs public relations firm when asked by Jay Margolis whether one of the brothers had promised to marry Marilyn. "And they were heavily Catholic. She was under the impression that Bobby would marry her."

Marilyn phoned hairstylist and trusted friend, Sydney Guilaroff, twice on that final Saturday. The first call was immediately after Bobby

Kennedy's departure. Guilaroff told Wolfe, "She was in tears, and I had difficulty understanding her." In his own book, Guilaroff detailed their exchange as follows:

> GUILAROFF: What's the matter, dear?
>
> MARILYN: Robert Kennedy was here, threatening me, yelling at me.
>
> GUILAROFF: Why was Bobby Kennedy at your house?
>
> MARILYN: I'm having an affair with him.
>
> GUILAROFF: Marilyn.
>
> MARILYN: I never told you. I never told anyone. But I had an affair with JFK as well.
>
> GUILAROFF: Both of them?
>
> MARILYN: Both . . . I warned him [Bobby] that I could go public.

Marilyn relayed to Guilaroff that Bobby had then responded, "If you threaten me, Marilyn, there's more than one way to keep you quiet."

Asking if Bobby was still there, Marilyn told Guilaroff, "He left—with Peter Lawford." Guilaroff recommended that Marilyn get some rest and they would discuss this further in a few hours. As Peter Lawford's friend, producer George "Bullets" Durgom, told Fred Otash in 1985, "Bobby was very worried about Monroe getting spaced out and shooting her mouth off."

According to Anthony Summers (who didn't know about that first phone conversation), Marilyn's last call to Guilaroff was at 9:30 p.m. Guilaroff told Wolfe this final call was between "eight and eight-thirty" and that "she was feeling much better and had met with her psychiatrist, Dr. Greenson." Guilaroff informed Wolfe that they ended the call with the following exchange:

> MARILYN: You know, Sydney, I know a lot of secrets about the Kennedys.
>
> GUILAROFF: What kind of secrets?
>
> MARILYN: Dangerous ones.

After that, Marilyn hung up. According to Morris Engelberg, Joe DiMaggio told his son Joe Jr., "The Kennedys killed her." In his book, *DiMaggio: Setting the Record Straight*, Engelberg recalled Joltin' Joe telling him he'd given his son a manilla envelope containing a statement regarding Marilyn's death, to be opened after the Yankee Clipper's own death. "Something the world should know about is in there," the elder DiMaggio had announced. Engelberg subsequently wrote:

> After his father's funeral, I asked him about that envelope. He had given me an opening by volunteering that he had talked with Marilyn the night she died—he said "murdered." He claimed he hadn't opened the envelope because he already knew the message his father had left behind. . . [6]

A SURPRISE EVENING VISIT FROM BOBBY KENNEDY AND GANGSTER SQUAD LAPD PARTNERS ARCHIE CASE AND JAMES AHERN

Norman Jefferies, who witnessed Bobby Kennedy and Peter Lawford earlier in the afternoon, said he watched television with his mother-in-law Eunice Murray later that night. Jefferies was surprised when, "between 9:30 and 10:00 p.m.," the Attorney General and two men dressed in suits ordered him and Mrs. Murray out of the house. In the documentary *Say Goodbye to the President*, Mrs. Murray revealed more than she had previously claimed to have known about that tragic night, when she eerily recalled, "It became so sticky that the protectors of Robert Kennedy, you know, had to step in there and protect *him*. Doesn't that sound logical?"

The men with Bobby Kennedy were identified as veteran LAPD partners Archie Case and James Ahern, members of Chief William Parker's notorious Gangster Squad. The Squad performed illegal activities for the LAPD, strictly off the books. Other Gangster Squad members included its leader Lieutenant William Burns, Sgt. Conwell Keller, Sgt. John O'Mara, Officer Donald Ward, Officer Loren K. Waggoner, and Detective J. Jones.

Fred Otash: "I worked undercover in Hollywood. I worked Vice. I first met Peter Lawford when I was on the LAPD in 1949 when I worked the Gangster Squad."

Former Police Chief Daryl Gates added, "I think Bobby always had an affection for LAPD because of the help we gave him."

Jefferies corroborated Mrs. Murray's recollection to Donald Wolfe: "They made it clear we were to be gone . . . I had no idea what was going on. I mean, this was the Attorney General of the United States. I didn't know who the two men were with him . . . We waited at the neighbor's house for them to leave." This was at 12304 Fifth Helena Drive, the home of Mrs. Mary W. Goodykoontz Barnes.

What's more, within days of Marilyn's death, it was Mrs. Barnes who spoke to Sgt. Jack Clemmons about her first sighting of Bobby Kennedy with Case or Ahern in the afternoon. She also mentioned a second sighting of Kennedy in the evening but this time with *both* Archie Case and James Ahern. After interviewing Sgt. Clemmons in 1993 and 1997, Donald Wolfe wrote, "Three men [Kennedy with Case and Ahern] walked down Fifth Helena Drive. One [Case or Ahern] was carrying a small black satchel similar to a medical bag."

Mary W. Goodykoontz Barnes relayed to Sgt. Jack Clemmons, "I've seen Bobby Kennedy go into that house a dozen times. That definitely was him. I don't know who the other two men were." This was the same house Mrs. Murray and her son-in-law Norman Jefferies stayed in while they waited for Kennedy, Case, and Ahern to leave.

A confidential source revealed to Jay Margolis, "Two of my brothers were FBI agents . . . I had heard that my brother John Anderson had seen Robert Kennedy and two men enter Marilyn Monroe's home. Hours later it was reported that Marilyn Monroe had died."

Anthony Summers asserted that, after 9:30 p.m., Marilyn happily chatted with her friend and sometimes lover José Bolaños, on the private line in her main bedroom. She may well have been reading from her red diary when, according to Bolaños, Marilyn told him "something that will one day shock the whole world."

Then there was a crash. Informing Bolaños she would be right back, Marilyn went to investigate a noise she heard coming from the guest cottage. Summers: "Marilyn ended the conversation by simply laying down the phone—she did not hang up while he was on the line." After arriving at the guest cottage, she found Bobby Kennedy with long-time personal LAPD bodyguards, Archie Case and James Ahern, rifling through one of her two filing cabinets in the guest cottage that they'd forcibly opened in search of the hallowed red diary. This was now in her main bedroom, but

Marilyn's privacy had been violated and she therefore screamed at the trio of would-be thieves to get out of her house.

Later, frightened for his life when in possession of the secret audiotapes capturing these events, Fred Otash provided biographer Ted Schwarz with a sanitized transcript that convinced Schwarz Marilyn committed suicide. Nevertheless, Jayne Mansfield's press secretary, Raymond Strait, was certain that the eleven hours of tapes he actually listened to prove that Marilyn Monroe was murdered.

"[Pathologist Thomas] Noguchi never believed it was suicide, but they shut him up real quick," Strait told Jay Margolis. "I knew Tom Noguchi. He said he never believed for a minute that she committed suicide. He wanted to blow the whole thing on Marilyn Monroe but [his superiors] weren't having it . . . I had all those tapes in my garage in a sealed-up box for ten years . . . I never opened them. Fred called me one night in Palm Springs and he says, 'You still have that box?' 'Well, of course!' 'You bring it down to the Springs. I want to show you something.'"

Interviewed by Peter Harry Brown and Patte Barham, Strait said, "Fred was afraid of the tapes. And he was so afraid that he planned to release a far less graphic version in his upcoming autobiography." Strait also asserted that Marilyn had been murdered: "It was obvious that she was subdued—probably with a pillow—while the drugs were administered."

In his personal notes, Fred Otash himself wrote, "I listened to Marilyn Monroe die," while adding that he taped an angry confrontation between Marilyn and Bobby Kennedy in the hours before her death. "She said she was passed around like a piece of meat," Otash recalled. "It was a violent argument about their relationship and the commitment and promises he made to her. She was really screaming and they were trying to quiet her down. She's in the [guest] bedroom and Bobby gets the pillow and he muffles her on the bed to keep the neighbors from hearing. She finally quieted down and then he was looking to get out of there."

Therefore, after Marilyn entered the guest cottage to see what was going on, Case and Ahern threw her on the bed. Then, per wiretapper Bernie Spindel and Fred Otash, Robert Kennedy covered her face with a pillow to keep her from screaming before ordering Archie Case and James Ahern to give Marilyn Monroe injections of Nembutal in an attempt to relax her hysterical state. Deputy Coroner's Aide Lionel Grandison wrote in his memoirs what he learned from a wiretap conversation that night: Bobby Kennedy had instructed Archie Case and James Ahern to "Give her something to calm her down."

In 1986, Fred Otash had allowed Raymond Strait to hear eleven hours of tapes that were rolling before, during, and after Marilyn Monroe's murder. On the January 7, 1993, episode of Joan Rivers' Fox TV talk show, Raymond Strait informed the host and her viewers, "It was horrible. You could hear the two men [Case and Ahern] talking to each other, saying, 'Give her another one. Don't give it to her too quickly,' and awful smothering sounds." A confidential source states regarding the Nembutal injections, "I don't know if she was injected merely to subdue her or if it was meant to kill her."

Lionel Grandison wrote in his memoirs, "Miner and Noguchi were looking at some bruises on her leg. I could clearly see a bruise just below the knee. Dr. Noguchi was explaining that this was common because many people fall or the body is bruised when being handled after death."

Actually, dead bodies don't bruise. Grandison continued, "My first thought was needle mark, but obviously Dr. Noguchi didn't concur . . . When the final physical diagram and autopsy report were completed, no mention of these details, or the bruise marks on her body, were reported."

Corroborating Grandison's claims, a confidential source told Jay Margolis about a bizarre turn of events just days after Marilyn died: "My friend Marty George was a Los Angeles photographer. He had a job where, once a year, he would go down to the Coroner's Office and take pictures of everybody. I guess they had some sort of shindig where they had to have all their pictures taken for this. And Marty was the kind of guy who was very innocuous. If he was the only person in the room, you could sometimes ignore him and miss him. He really blended in better than anyone I've ever known.

"He was in the file room taking pictures of somebody and that somebody got called out of the room. So, Marty George said, 'Okay, fine.' He was a big fan of Marilyn's and he decided to see if he could find the coroner's report. So, he went over to the files and he opened them up because they were papers in this day. And there it was but it was sealed. He decided that sealed coroner's reports are not legal so he just broke the seal and opened it and read it. He did not take a picture of it because he was so stunned. So, he called me up when he got home and he said,

'What does this mean? No contents in the stomach.' I told him, 'It means she could not have died by barbiturates from the mouth.'

"In the coroner's report, he saw there were needle marks behind her knees, the jugular vein in her neck, and bruises on her arms and her back. He said as far as he was concerned, that doesn't seem very much like suicide. I said, 'It doesn't to me either, and certainly not by barbiturate overdose by mouth with pills, because that leaves some residue in the stomach.' There was nothing because she hadn't eaten or consumed anything for hours before she died. Marty George also said there is an actual reel somewhere unlike coroner's reports, and that there's apparently been cover-up ones made since. I wish he would've taken a picture of it but he didn't think to do that because he was in shock. He very carefully put it back together and put the seal back and put it in the file, but it exists. It's *somewhere*."

In October 1997, Schaefer Ambulance attendant James Hall relayed to biographer Michelle Morgan, "On the autopsy report, Noguchi wrote, 'No needle mark.' A question that has never come up is, did Dr. Noguchi always write, 'No needle mark' on all of the previous autopsy reports or was this a 'special' case?"

As it turned out, the Nembutal injections weren't enough to subdue Marilyn. So, using one of the enema bags already in the guest cottage bathroom, the two LAPD Gangster Squad partners held her down, stripped her clothes off, and gave her an enema filled with broken-down pills containing anywhere from thirteen to nineteen Nembutals and seventeen chloral hydrates. Rendering her unconscious, this criminal act against Marilyn's will accounted for the purplish discoloration of her colon as noted in the official autopsy report. In fact, Lawford's third wife Deborah Gould told Anthony Summers how Lawford stated, "Marilyn took her last big enema."

Funeral director Allan Abbott said to Jay Margolis, "The pathologist never signs the death certificate. He comes out of the lab, and he goes up to the front desk where the deputies work and I knew all of them very well. He tells them the cause of death. And then they fill out the death certificate and put on the cause of death. There was a black guy working at the Coroner's Office named Lionel Grandison. They went to him and said, 'You've got to sign Marilyn Monroe's death certificate' and the Coroner had put on there 'suicide.' Grandison said,

'I read Dr. Noguchi's report about the inflammation of the colon. I don't think we really know what she died of. I'm not going to sign it as "suicide." ' They threatened him with his job. He still wouldn't sign it 'suicide.' So they said, 'Okay, how about "probable suicide?" ' and he said, 'Okay, I'll put that on it.' "

Negating oral ingestion of the pills, a drug-laced enema is the only way that such high levels of chloral hydrate could have been detected in her blood along with the high levels of Nembutal. Incidentally, chloral hydrate injections are not medically practiced. Per the 1982 District Attorney's Report, "The results of the blood and liver toxicological examination show that there were 8 mg. percent chloral hydrate [seventeen 500-mg pills] and 4.5 mg. percent of barbiturates in the blood [forty-fifty 100-mg Nembutals] and 13.0 mg. percent pentobarbital in the liver."

Donald Spoto's Marilyn Monroe biography noted that Marilyn had many receipts for enema paraphernalia (most likely located in more than one of her bathrooms). When the police officially discovered her body, only ten of fifty 500-mg chloral hydrate pills were still in the prescription bottle. According to Gary Vitacco-Robles, "The guest bedroom near the pool shares a bath (at left) with the third bedroom. The middle door accesses a closet. The door to the far right leads to a hallway and a linen

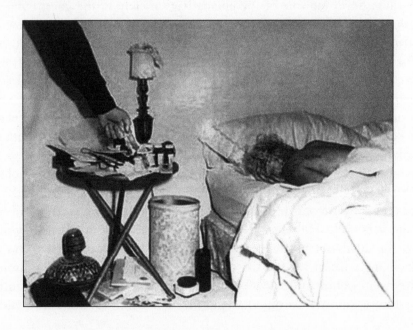

closet." Therefore, the water for the enema had been easily accessible and so were the linens later used to dry Marilyn's body once the enema had been expelled. During the struggle, Marilyn received an injury on her upper back—a bruise not documented in Thomas Noguchi's official autopsy report, but one that is clearly visible in a police photo that captures Marilyn face-down on the bed.

Because the drug-laced enema only rendered her unconscious, Marilyn was still alive when Schaefer Ambulance attendant James Hall arrived with his driver, Murray Liebowitz. Had Marilyn been injected instead with massive amounts of Nembutal and chloral hydrate in one injection, she would have died before Hall and Liebowitz came on the scene.

Less than a minute after they gave Marilyn a drug-laced enema, Kennedy, Case, and Ahern were once again preoccupied with a frantic search for the red diary. At the same time, Marilyn grabbed the only phone, the public line from the guest cottage, to call her masseur friend Ralph Roberts, yet she only reached his answering service. It was 10:00 p.m. The woman at the other end noted that Marilyn asked for Ralph in a "slurred voice," only to be told he was out for the evening. Then she hung up, en route to losing consciousness as a result of the sleep-inducing chloral hydrate coursing through her body; a body that would be leaning on the phone when discovered a short while later by Norman Jefferies and Eunice Murray.

Why would Bobby Kennedy risk destroying his skyrocketing career by becoming directly involved in such a dark turn of events? The fact that he was in Los Angeles from at least 11:00 that morning—when he was spotted on Stage 18 of the Fox lot by studio publicist Frank Neill—until after midnight proves he was willing to take that risk.

Jefferies noted that Kennedy, Case, and Ahern departed Marilyn's home at 10:30 p.m. Thereafter, it was due to the incessant barking of her dog Maf—so named because the white maltese terrier (not French poodle) was a gift from mob-connected Frank Sinatra—that Marilyn was discovered in the guest cottage by Jefferies and Mrs. Murray who stated, "I saw that the telephone was under her. She was lying on it." Jefferies told Donald Wolfe, "I thought she was dead. She was facedown, her hand kind of holding the phone. It didn't look to me like she was breathing, and her color was awful—like she was dead."

Nobody expected what the housekeeper would do next. Jefferies continued to Wolfe, "Eunice took the phone and called an ambulance. Then she put through an emergency call to Dr. Greenson, who was someplace nearby and said he would be right over. He told Eunice to call Dr. Engelberg."

Schaefer Ambulance attendant James Hall, Mrs. Murray, and Norman Jefferies all stated that Marilyn Monroe was still alive when Dr. Ralph Greenson arrived at the scene.

Mrs. Murray told Anthony Summers, "Why, at my age, do I still have to cover this thing up? . . . When he [Dr. Greenson] arrived, she was not dead because I was there then in the living room." Summers asked, "Marilyn was not dead when the first doctor arrived, is that what you're saying?" Mrs. Murray replied, "That's what I'm saying."

Jefferies relayed to Wolfe, "I went to the gates to wait for the ambulance, but before the ambulance got there Peter Lawford and Pat Newcomb arrived. Pat became hysterical and started screaming at Eunice. I had to take Eunice into the house. She [Pat] was a basket case. I think the ambulance arrived before Dr. Greenson."

Norman Jefferies took Mrs. Murray away from the guest cottage, into the living room. Detective Sgt. Robert Byron, who wrote the official police report, informed Anthony Summers: "Engelberg told me he'd had a call from the housekeeper who said Marilyn was either dead or unconscious. He came over and found Marilyn dead."

Matthew Smith interviewed Tom Reddin, who was William Parker's deputy chief. Smith concluded that Chief Parker most likely protected Robert Kennedy from being implicated in any controversy surrounding Marilyn's death simply by association. In other words, being present at the scene. Parker's wife Helen told Anthony Summers that her husband relayed to her days later, "This thing has to be straightened out in more ways than one."

Parker saw to it that Kennedy was shielded from anything that would damage his career. After all, the LAPD chief had his own agenda. For *The Marilyn Files* documentary, Sgt. Jack Clemmons relayed that Parker "was a very ambitious man and he wanted to be head of the FBI . . . He went to the point of trying to plant false stories about J. Edgar Hoover." In the same documentary, former Mayor Sam Yorty concurred: "I know that he would have liked to take the head of the FBI and he certainly would've been good at that. And of course to get that job you have to have Bobby Kennedy."

This seemed within reach considering Kennedy and Parker were close friends since first fighting organized crime together in 1956, alongside Captain James Hamilton. Although Parker could have overheard events via his own bug in Marilyn's home during the time she died, he evidently didn't know all the details. Summers wrote, "Weeks later, when his wife asked how the Monroe case was going, Parker was uncharacteristically vague. 'It seemed to be a big question mark,' Helen Parker recalls. 'I remember him just doing this'—and she draws a big question mark in the air."

Marilyn's first husband Jim Dougherty, himself an LAPD detective, wrote in his second book about her: "Did someone know she was in trouble? Robert Kennedy? Peter Lawford? . . . And were they so terrified about losing their careers, their reputations that they did nothing? If this is true, then they are accountable."

Biographer Ted Schwarz believed Marilyn committed suicide. However, he told fellow biographers Brown and Barham what he heard from Fred Otash: "Otash thought Bobby and Lawford knew what was happening and let her die . . . Otash viewed the death as a 'case of negligent homicide' and confided that 'the Kennedy brothers had already murdered her emotionally.'"

During the autopsy, Dr. Thomas Noguchi became distracted by the findings of the Suicide Prevention Team. He stated in a February 1976 article for *Oui* magazine: "Our physical examination was coupled with what we call a psychological autopsy. In the case of Miss Monroe, there had been previous suicide attempts. In fact, her whole lifestyle, as we reconstructed it, pointed toward suicide rather than an accident."

Funeral director Allan Abbott told Jay Margolis, "They had this first-time autopsy called the 'psychological autopsy' and they called in all these people that knew her, what kind of mood she was in, and so forth. That became a first but they knew it was such a big case that they had to do something over and above procedure to try and convince people of what happened.

"I'm sure Noguchi was under a lot of pressure to consider 'suicide' over 'murder,' which would take the lid off the case. They knew who wanted her out of the way. Therefore, what makes the case so important is who wants the case to go away. If she had taken all the drugs orally, she would've died well before the time she did . . .

"Noguchi seemed to be very cooperative with everyone involved and seemed to come to different decisions at different times, changing his mind about what he claimed were the circumstances. The best way for them to ever convince him to not talk would be to offer him the job as permanent coroner. He was certainly qualified to do the job, but I think he thought he would be the best coroner they ever had. He tried to stay as neutral as possible when he made statements on Marilyn Monroe, but I think he knew an awful lot more than he talked about."

As it turned out, Noguchi curiously replaced Theodore Curphey as LA's chief medical examiner in 1967, an impressive promotion for a man who had been a deputy coroner just five years earlier.

The Suicide Prevention Team investigating Marilyn's "suicide" was comprised of Robert Elkon Litman, M.D., Norman Donald Tabachnick, M.D., and Norman Louis Farberow, Ph.D. Since Marilyn's psychoanalyst Dr. Ralph Greenson was at the death scene when the police were called, they each consulted with Greenson over what happened to Marilyn. Spoto interviewed Dr. Litman, who had been a former student of Greenson's. Litman told Spoto that the Team "didn't consider the murder hypothesis" yet "Greenson wasn't at all sure if she committed suicide. Greenson felt very much undecided in his own mind . . . All I heard from Greenson was that she was involved with men at the very highest level of government. The name Kennedy was not mentioned specifically . . ." Oddly, Litman next said to Spoto that, in 1962, at the time of the Marilyn Monroe investigation, "I didn't see any record of no drugs in the stomach."

In addition, Litman said Curphey told the Team it was suicide and that their function was to determine Marilyn's state of mind: did she or did she not intend to kill herself? Curphey instructed them not to determine *how* she died but only to determine whether she accidentally or intentionally killed herself according to her past history of suicide attempts. Anthony Summers noted, "The head of the Team, Dr. Norman Farberow, said neither Kennedy brother was questioned. He added, 'I'm sure discretion entered into it.'" Farberow attempted to interview Marilyn's last publicist and long-time Kennedy confidant Pat Newcomb, but "she stone-walled me, was uncommunicative."

Dr. Farberow told Jay Margolis that Marilyn's housekeeper Mrs. Murray was also interviewed and that she believed Marilyn accidentally took her life. Farberow relayed, "She said she didn't realize how many pills she had taken." Regarding Marilyn, he explained, "The general pattern that we had found common among women of her age was that she was unhappy and it [suicide] was not a very difficult possibility," yet he conceded, "I have no idea now, at this time, what her intention was in taking so many."

In his own book, *Coroner to the Stars*, Noguchi wrote that, back in 1962, he had asked Dr. Robert Litman, a member of the Suicide Prevention Team who'd participated in the psychological autopsy, "Any chance of murder?" Litman's reply: "The door to the bedroom was locked from the inside. They had to break a window to enter the room. And Mrs. Murray was in her room all evening only a little way down the hall from Monroe's." Noguchi remained skeptical. Yet, with no further evidence at his disposal, he eventually agreed with Dr. Curphey's official conclusion: "probable suicide."

In the early 1980s, Noguchi had more details, including John Miner's memorandum that emphatically discredited the suicide theory. Noguchi would write that, regarding Marilyn's alleged ingestion of 64 pills, "An accidental overdose of that magnitude was extremely unlikely. From my forensic experience with suicide victims, I believe that the sheer number of pills Monroe ingested was too many to swallow 'accidentally.' Thus, if Miner's evaluation in 1962 was correct, the only conceivable cause of Monroe's death was murder." Thomas Noguchi further noted, "I found absolutely no visual evidence of pills in the stomach or the small intestine. No residue. No refractile crystals. And yet the evidence of the pill bottles showed that Monroe had swallowed forty to fifty Nembutals and a large number of chloral hydrate pills."[7]

SCHAEFER AMBULANCE ATTENDANT JAMES EDWIN HALL TOLD THE TRUTH

In his 1983 book, Dr. Thomas Noguchi wrote, "The most prevalent of [the theories] called Monroe's death murder, done to silence her and prevent her from destroying Robert Kennedy's political career. I called her death suicide—both twenty years ago and today—but I admit there are many disturbing questions that have remained unanswered . . ."

As Noguchi himself noted, the assorted murder theories had one thing in common: they all asserted that Marilyn had died from a lethal injection, not by oral overdose of sleeping pills. When, in 1982, he was driving near her home and heard a news announcer on the car radio state that ambulance attendant James Hall was claiming to have witnessed her murder at the hands of a doctor who'd injected a mysterious fluid directly into her heart, the pathologist almost expected to hear that he had been the culprit. He subsequently relaxed when learning that, in a *Globe* newspaper report, Hall had described the killer doctor as having had "a mustache, longish sideburns, and a pockmarked face. Not me."

Based on rigor mortis, Westwood Village Mortuary employee Guy Hockett estimated Marilyn's death to have occurred somewhere between 9:30 and 11:30 p.m. on August 4, 1962. Sgt. Jack Clemmons and Dr. J. DeWitt Fox agreed the two drugs that killed Marilyn hadn't been taken orally. As Deputy Medical Examiner Dr. Thomas Noguchi noted in his official autopsy report on Marilyn Monroe, "The stomach is almost completely empty. The contents is [sic] brownish mucoid fluid. The volume is estimated to be no more than 20 cc. No residue of the pills is noted. A smear made from gastric contents and examined under the polarized microscope shows no refractile crystals . . . The contents of the duodenum is [sic] also examined under polarized microscope and shows no refractile crystals . . . The colon shows marked congestion and purplish discoloration."

In the documentary *Marilyn Monroe: A Case for Murder*, former New York coroner Dr. Sidney Weinberg discussed discrepancies in the autopsy report that bothered him:

> WEINBERG: Let me tell you about the doubts that were raised in my mind. The most pressing thing in the whole report was the lack of finding of barbiturates in the stomach.
>
> INTERVIEWER: As an expert, what does it tell you that there was no residue in her stomach?
>
> WEINBERG: It tells me that the barbiturates that were analyzed in the liver and blood had entered her body in some other manner. Now what other manner could they possibly have entered? One would be by injection.

Another would be via enema. In October 1985, on ABC's *Eyewitness News*, Noguchi said the possibility of foul play shouldn't be ruled out:

> NOGUCHI: She had a bruise on her back or near the hip that has never been fully explained. There is no explanation for it, and it is a sign of violence.
>
> INTERVIEWER: Murder?
>
> NOGUCHI: Could be.

Lawford's close friend Milt Ebbins may have known more about Marilyn's last night than he ever told when he relayed to Donald Spoto, "When there's an overdose of drugs, the first thing the doctor would give her was a shot of adrenaline."

This brings us to the story of Schaefer Ambulance attendant James Edwin Hall who, concerned that his testimony might make him a target, first phoned the LA District Attorney's office on August 11, 1982, under the name "Rick Stone." Refusing to divulge his own phone number, Hall/ Stone said *he* would be the one to always call the District Attorney's office. There, he first talked to Deputy District Attorney Ronald "Mike" Carroll:

CARROLL: One of the things I'm concerned about. You mentioned the man in the business suit used a needle in the heart.

HALL: That's correct.

CARROLL: That must have left a mark, right?

HALL: I'm sure it left a mark in the flesh.

CARROLL: Because as I look over the autopsy report, I don't see a needle mark.

HALL: Yeah, well, he put a needle in her heart. I guarantee it. I was looking right at it . . . He was wearing a business suit and a tie.

CARROLL: And you were there how many minutes approximately?

HALL: Oh, maybe fifteen . . . I know this woman [Pat Newcomb] was hysterical when I got there. She was standing outside screaming, "She's dead! She's dead! I think she's dead!" In my opinion, she was either a heck of an actress or it was quite a shock to her.

CARROLL: How was Monroe dressed?

HALL: She was nude.

CARROLL: Was there any phone around her?

HALL: There was a telephone on a nightstand or a little table alongside the bed. The phone was *on* the hook. It was not off.

CARROLL: When did you next hear about the case?

HALL: I heard it on the radio and the TV and they said pills were scattered all over the floor and the phone was off the hook like she was trying to call somebody. That's not how that room was. Those pills were all in the bottles. All lined up perfectly on the nightstand and the phone was on the hook.

CARROLL: What was the time to the best of your twenty-year memory?

HALL: I'm gonna say between four and six in the morning but that's a long time ago. I know I'd seen the pictures when they carted the body out. It was daylight. When they took her out, it was the morning. I might be wrong on the time. I don't know.

CARROLL: Is there any way you'd be willing to come forward and talk to one of our investigators?

HALL: I'm gonna be very candid with you. I'm very afraid because of people getting shot. I'm not doing this as a good Samaritan. Quite frankly, on a financial basis, it would require expense money.

CARROLL: What kind of expense money?

HALL: I don't know, pal. I'm starving to death and my family is, too. That's the only reason we've been doing this.

CARROLL: Is there anybody working for the ambulance company that would remember you?

HALL: Absolutely. Let me give you a few names. There was a man by the name of Joe Tarnowski and a guy named Tom Fears.

CARROLL: Was that bought out by some other company?

HALL: Well, California Ambulance Service was at that time owned by Walt Schaefer.

When interviewed by Donald Wolfe, James Hall said that, back in 1962, he worked a twenty-four-hour shift, which is why he probably couldn't remember the time of his arrival at the Monroe home. Hall's childhood best friend Mike Carlson explained, "Jim was working nearly twenty-four hours a day. They had a lot of people and a lot of drivers . . . People come. People go. You have multiple ambulances. It was like a firehouse."

What's more, the principals at the scene had waited more than four-and-a-half hours to call the police. When Anthony Summers interviewed the two Schaefer employees mentioned by Hall to Mike Carroll—Joe Tarnowski and Tom Fears—they both confirmed that an ambulance from their company had been dispatched to the Monroe residence that night. Now, when Hall called the District Attorney's Office a second time, Carroll put him in touch with his investigator Alan B. Tomich. Hall subsequently told Tomich what he had witnessed following his arrival at the Monroe residence:

HALL: You go in and you turn to the left and the bed was facing longways as you're looking at it. To the left of the bed was the table that had all the pills on it. She was laying across the bed with her head hanging over the edge of the bed. I threw her on the floor and proceeded to give close-chest heart massage.

TOMICH: She's on her back or on her stomach?

HALL: When she was laying on the bed, she was laying on her back.

TOMICH: Who else was present at the time you arrived?

HALL: A woman [Pat Newcomb].

TOMICH: Then someone else arrived sometime after that?

HALL: The person with me [Murray Liebowitz] went out to get the resuscitation equipment and walked back in the door. Right behind him in walked the gentleman in the brown business suit [Ralph Greenson].

TOMICH: And what did he do?

HALL: He said he was her doctor. He said, "Give her positive pressure," which we did. Then he proceeded to open up his little bag and pulled out a loaded hypodermic syringe and injected the fluid into her heart.

TOMICH: And then what did he do?

HALL: He gave more closed-chest heart massage then said, "I'm releasing you. She's dead."

As James Hall explained to Tomich, in exchange for his testimony there would be "no financial transaction until I take your polygraph to prove what I'm saying is true. At that time, you would pay right there on the spot when it's proved to be true . . . That thing happened twenty years ago. It's a long time. Now I gave you information on the phone that nobody has that you can check out and prove. I'm not just doing it because I'm Joe Goodguy. I'm doing it because of the economy and what's happened financially." When Tomich told Hall he wouldn't pay him beyond the initial expenses, Hall said that was fine. He would simply go to the tabloids, allowing them to give him their own polygraph tests. Tomich chuckled, "Well, then, we'd be getting our information for free, wouldn't we?"

On November 23, 1982, just weeks before the District Attorney's Office concluded its renewed investigation into Marilyn Monroe's death, John Blackburn, Chuck Orman, and Dan McDonald of the *Globe* newspaper publicly released James Hall's account for the first time. *Globe* had paid Hall $40,000 after hypnosis by a professional experienced in police investigations had enabled the former ambulance attendant to recall more details about Marilyn Monroe's murder at the hands of Dr. Ralph Greenson.

In the *Globe* article, Blackburn wrote, "Private investigator John Harrison . . . had been conducting polygraph examinations for 40 years." Harrison told the *Globe*, "When I was first brought into this, I thought the whole thing was a fairy tale, but now I'm thoroughly convinced Hall is telling a true story. He was given a total of six polygraph tests, including control tests, and there was no evidence of any deception."

Blackburn continued, "Hall was interviewed while under hypnosis by Henry Koder, a professional forensic hypnotist with more than 20 years of law-enforcement experience and veteran of hundreds of major crime investigations." Koder told the *Globe*, "Hall was a good subject. I was able to take him back to the night of Marilyn Monroe's death under hypnosis and listened to his step-by-step description of his involvement. He was able to vividly recall that night and pointed out details to me that he hadn't even remembered in earlier questioning. When wakened, Hall was able to give us a very thorough description of the injection doctor for our Identikit composite. Also, I implanted a post-hypnotic suggestion that Hall must be truthful. It would have been impossible for him to lie during the next polygraph without the machine showing a reaction."

The doctor Hall identified in his Identikit composite looked like Marilyn's psychiatrist and Greenson did have a mustache. Hall said the man referred to himself as "her doctor." Engelberg, Marilyn's other doctor, certainly didn't have a mustache.

In addition, Donald Wolfe interviewed polygraph examiner Donald E. Fraser, who subjected James Hall to further tests on August 10, 1992. "There's no question that James Hall is telling the truth," Fraser concluded. "His story regarding the scene and circumstances of Miss Monroe's death is absolutely true. He passed every question in several exhaustive polygraph examinations."

The October 1993 issue of fan newspaper *Runnin' Wild: All About Marilyn* featured a Donald Wolfe article titled "The Ambulance Chase." Fraser told Wolfe that one of the questions posed to Hall was, "Did you witness a man who claimed to be Marilyn Monroe's doctor give her an injection into the left side of her chest?" Wolfe wrote, "Lack of line movement indicates Hall was being truthful." In fact, the fan newspaper reproduced the actual polygraph test given to James Hall by Don Fraser in 1992. "His story and the conversation produced during the polygraph examination would hold up in court," Fraser asserted.

Dr. Greenson's son Danny relayed to James Spada, "I hate all this speculation and especially that guy who says he saw my father plunge a needle into Marilyn's heart. That's ridiculous and I've got to say that it hurts me." Greenson's wife Hildi told Cathy Griffin, "I sometimes have a feeling that this ambulance driver went on a call that night somewhere else and kind of managed to get these things into a different order."

In August, September, and October 1997, James Hall told biographer Michelle Morgan in detail his account of what took place at the Monroe home while he was there. She asked, "The day after Marilyn's death, did you tell anyone what you had seen? If so, what was their reaction?" Hall replied, "I told everyone I knew and everyone who showed even a casual curiosity. Their reaction was mostly one of shock and they all asked, 'What happened?'" Importantly, Hall was asked, "At this point, did you believe that you had seen Marilyn being murdered or did you think that the doctor had tried to help her?" Hall said, "At that time, I believed that Dr. Greenson was trying to help her with an injection of adrenaline."

"Was it definitely Dr. Greenson at Marilyn's house that night? Could it have possibly been someone else?"

"It was definitely Dr. Greenson at Marilyn's house."

In 1986, James Hall stated, "I thought that a doctor had futilely given her adrenaline, a standard procedure, and that she simply expired. So until 1982 I believed that Marilyn Monroe had OD'd . . . The hysterical woman [Pat Newcomb] said it was a possible overdose. A guy [Ralph Greenson] injected her in the heart; I figured it was adrenaline."

On December 19, 2011, and February 3, 2012, Jay Margolis interviewed Mike Carlson who had been James Hall's best friend since he was twelve years old. Asked when Hall had told him about Dr. Greenson and the heart needle, Carlson replied, "Days or weeks right after it happened. Jim always talked about the injustice of it all . . . He had no reason to tell me a story. As time went on, he'd say, 'Nobody'll listen to me.' Then the whole attitude changed. They said pills were laying everywhere. He said there were no pills scattered anywhere when he was there. Jim was in a different room [the guest cottage].

"Another thing he said was that his father Dr. George Hall would go around to the home of celebrities but he would never ever, ever carry a needle with a syringe attached to it ever. That's just not practiced. But this doctor [Ralph Greenson] pulled his syringe out of his caché case with a needle attached and plunged it into her. You just don't do that unless you have some preconceived notion. Jim talked to his father about it. They went back and forth about it and his father said there's no way that anyone would ever, ever do that. It's against protocol."

When queried whether Hall had informed him the solution in Greenson's syringe had been brown, Carlson said, "That's what he told me. Jim could tell you in volumes about it . . . His father was a very famous surgeon—Dr. George Hall practiced in the Los Angeles area. He was a very talented surgeon and he had a prominent position. He at one time worked for County General Hospital and had a private practice as well. . . .

"Dr. Hall said to me on one occasion, 'I'm a surgeon. People come up to me and say, "I've got a headache." I say, "Where does it hurt?" "Right there." So I took a grease marker and marked where it hurt him. I say, "If you want me to find out where the problem is, I'll do it." ' And the way Dr. Hall does it is he fires up a little electric wheel and runs it up against your scalp. He says, 'I'm not a shrink. I don't make any money for counseling. You come to me, we cut . . .'

"Dr. Hall and Walt Schaefer were very good friends. Schaefer Ambulance wanted to have a doctor on staff and Walt Schaefer knew Dr. Hall. Schaefer wanted to go into business with him and Dr. Hall declined. Years later, Jim's father kicked himself and had wished he'd gone with Schaefer because Schaefer had done so well. Schaefer Ambulance had become the predominant ambulance company in Los Angeles."[8]

HALL, LIEBOWITZ, LAWFORD, NEWCOMB, AND IANNONE WITNESSED A MURDER NOT AN ADRENALINE SHOT

There were five witnesses to Marilyn Monroe's murder. Three of the five state that Ralph Greenson was responsible. Two of those witnesses, Kennedy loyalists Pat Newcomb and Sgt. Marvin Iannone have consistently refused to go into accurate detail about that night's events. Before Dr. Greenson interrupted Hall and Liebowitz's attempts to revive Marilyn, James Hall observed, "She was naked. She had no sheet, no blanket . . . There was no water glass. No alcohol . . . We ascertained that her breathing was very shallow, her pulse was very weak and rapid and she was unconscious at that time."

When James Hall arrived in the guest cottage, he saw the same bedside table that was delivered just hours earlier in the morning. Mrs. Murray wrote in her book, "Sometime during the earlier part of the day, the bedside table [for the guest cottage] was delivered and Marilyn wrote a check for it."

Intriguingly, when Hall looked at Marilyn's stomach when he arrived on the scene, he said, "I remember noticing she had a fairly fresh scar there." In fact, on June 29, 1961, Marilyn had her gall bladder removed and the scar that remained was clearly captured in photographs by Bert Stern the last year of her life.

James Hall relayed to Michelle Morgan in September 1997, "No one ever said that Marilyn was in the guest bedroom except myself until now. Just recently, Murray Liebowitz in an interview with the author [Donald Wolfe] of a forthcoming book [*The Last Days of Marilyn Monroe*] admitted that he was with me at Marilyn's house that night and that everything I had said was the truth as to what happened.

"I believe Marilyn was moved [from the guest cottage to her main bedroom] as to fit their story of suicide. Also, she was found facedown on her bed. After death the blood in the body goes to the lowest point by gravity. In this position, the pooling of the blood would cover up any marks (needle or otherwise) on the front of the body . . . As some of my credentials, I would like to offer the following. I have had 14 polygraphs done by the best in the world to include six charts—two sessions—by John Harrison. He said that he had administered at least 200,000 tests up to that time. All of the various polygraph experts say the same thing, that I am telling the truth.

"When I was interviewed by Anthony Summers, author of *Goddess*, I told him that I entered Marilyn's house and turned left into a small bedroom. He said, 'No, you turned right.' I said, 'I know that I turned left.' He asked, 'Did you see the pool?' I answered, 'No.' If you go into the house by way of the front door, you must turn right to access Marilyn's bedroom and, if coming in from the pool, you must turn left to access Marilyn's bedroom. Tony thought the house was the same as it was in 1962. The new owners of the house, after Marilyn, remodeled it. They added a door from the guest house into the kitchen and gutted the guest bedroom and made it a photographic studio." James Hall continued to Michelle Morgan:

> I am a big fan of Marilyn. I have been a fan since I was a young man—just after I first saw her in the film *The Seven Year Itch*. I was an ambulance driver for Schaefer's Ambulance Service stationed in Santa Monica, California. This office serviced the West Los Angeles, Beverly Hills, Westwood, Brentwood, and Santa Monica areas primarily. But we covered all of the Los Angeles basin as needed.
>
> We were just coming in from a run when we got the call. My partner that night was Murray Liebowitz. "Car 82, 12305 5th Helena. Possible overdose. Private emergency. Handle your call, Code Three," the radio blurted out. The address took us to Brentwood. When we got the call, we were close and able to respond in under two minutes.

Just in the short drive I could see a woman running around a little patch of grass before a bungalow. She wore a white nightgown with some kind of robe over it. Her arms flailed the air with frantic signals as she spotted my lights. "She's dead! She's dead!" she started screaming. That woman was Pat Newcomb, Marilyn's publicist and friend.

We went into the house. Through the foyer was an open door with light spilling out into the hall. "In there! She's dead! She's dead!" she said. I don't think she even knew she was screaming.

Countering Hall's recollection, a remarkably defensive Pat Newcomb told biographer Donald Spoto, "Whoever the writer was who said I leaned over the body screaming, 'She's dead! She's dead!' I never saw the body. So what is he talking about, this ambulance driver? . . . How can he say he saw me? I never saw an ambulance."

If so, then what about Norman Jefferies' statements earlier in this book, asserting Mrs. Murray called for an ambulance shortly before Newcomb arrived at the scene? From the time she first opened up to biographer Fred Lawrence Guiles in 1969, Newcomb consistently claimed she didn't learn of Marilyn's death until 4:00 a.m. the next morning, courtesy of a phone call from the actress's attorney Mickey Rudin. Later, we will learn about Newcomb's rather weak alibi. For now, however, let's return to James Hall's 1997 recollection to Michelle Morgan and Hall's first sighting of the person at the center of the unfolding drama . . .

"Oh my God, it's Marilyn Monroe," I said. She lay unconscious, her head hanging off the edge of the bed at an unnatural angle. Her color looked bad and I could see as I got closer that she was barely breathing. She was totally naked and her beautiful body made the scene surreal.

We had to get her off of the bed and onto a hard surface so we could work on her. "Let's get her on the floor," I said as I grabbed her by the arms and pulled her onto the floor. I know I bruised her, but seconds counted when you were saving a life; not bruises. I scanned the room for immediate signs of what happened. A small lamp burned on a bedside table. There was also a bunch of pill bottles grouped neatly around the base of the lamp. They were all capped. There was no sign of a water glass or any alcohol. "Someone is sure over-prescribing here," I said. My father was the kind of physician who doled out drugs with exaggerated caution, so I really noticed all the pill bottles.

"Let's take her out into the foyer so we can work on her," I said. "There's no room in here." We dragged Marilyn into the hallway. As I bent over her, it hit me—there was no vomit, unusual with an overdose which is what the woman managed to tell us that she thought was wrong. When I bent over Marilyn, there was no odor of drugs from her mouth. Another classic symptom.

I began external heart massage. "I've got to get her breathing. Get me an airway!" I yelled at Liebowitz. An airway is a clear plastic tube, curved slightly and about six inches long. I worked the airway down her throat. This would clear anything that might be blocking her throat. Liebowitz ran to the ambulance for the resuscitator, a small apparatus which would pump oxygen into her lungs. I attached it to the airway and it started working. It was pumping the oxygen in and sucking it back out perfectly.

Liebowitz turned as he said, "I'll get the stretcher," then froze. A man had suddenly appeared in the doorway.

"I'm her doctor," he said, moving quickly toward her. "Give her positive pressure." I was astonished. "Where did you come from?" I thought, "How did you get here so fast?" I stared at him. He was wearing a suit. A somewhat big man with darkish hair and a rough complexion. He was clearly agitated and this time he shouted, "I said, 'Give her positive pressure!'" "Jesus Christ," I thought, "What's wrong with you? I've got a machine here that's doing a great job of that. Why take her off it?"

I removed the resuscitator and attached another short length of tube to the airway. The doctor knelt down and began to push on Marilyn's abdomen. I started blowing into the airway. But the doctor was pushing in the wrong place. He was too low on her stomach. I was pinching her nose tight so the air would go into the lungs and not back out through her nostrils.

Every time he pushed, a black line of bile from the stomach rose up the clear tube. I thought, "I'm going to eat it." When he would push, I would stick the end of my tongue over the opening of the tube to stop the stuff from going into my mouth. When he would let up, I would blow again.

"Hey, Doc," I finally said, "you blow and I'll push." I know some doctors aren't used to emergencies but this guy was all thumbs. That's when he muttered, "I've got to make a show of this." I never forgot that remark. "Christ, let's move," I said. "You can work on her in the back of the ambulance." Time was running out and I wanted to save her.

The doctor opened his bag and took out a hypodermic syringe with a heart needle already on it. That needle looked about a foot long. He drew up a liquid from a bottle with a rubber seal and filled the syringe. He mumbled under his breath like he was reading from a medical book, "Insert between the 'blank' and 'blank' rib." I don't remember the numbers. He felt his way down her ribs like an amateur. Then he thrust the needle into her chest. But it didn't go in right. It hung up on the bone, on one of her ribs.

Instead of trying again, he just leaned into it, his cheeks quivered with the effort. He pushed hard and he drove it all the way through the rib, making a loud snap as the bone broke. I know he scarred that rib bone. I had watched a lot of medical procedures and this guy was downright brutal.

As for Peter Lawford and Sgt. Marvin Iannone, James Hall relayed to James Spada, "They walked in at the time he [Ralph Greenson] was injecting her." In 1992, to Beverly Hills Detective Lynn Franklin, Hall identified the police officer with Lawford as Sgt. Marvin Iannone, and in 1993, Hall identified him to Donald Wolfe. Hall continued to Michelle Morgan:

At that time, two men who I assumed were Los Angeles Police officers came in. One wore a Los Angeles Police blue suit and the other wore a jumpsuit. I have identified the man in the jumpsuit from a photo lineup as Peter Lawford who was married to Pat. Pat Lawford was Bobby Kennedy's sister. I have also identified the blue suit. I will only say at this time he is presently the Chief of Police of a major affluent California city [Sgt. Marvin D. Iannone of Beverly Hills].

Dr. Greenson finally removed the needle and put a stethoscope to her heart. "She's dead," he said. "I'm pronouncing her dead." He stood up. It took me a minute to be sure I had heard him right. We could have saved her. I felt sick.

"You can go now," he said. It was obvious we were in the way. I have identified that doctor as Ralph Greenson, Marilyn's psychiatrist. Mrs. Murray was not present in the guest house area. She must have been in the other part of the home.

Outside the house, also pulled down Fifth Helena, was the first call car from the mortuary. "What the hell are they doing here already?" I asked Liebowitz. You don't send for a first call car until you have a dead body. Marilyn had been pronounced dead only minutes before.

In the 1982 *Globe* article, James Hall described Dr. Greenson injecting his patient with a "brownish fluid" out of a pharmaceutical bottle. Said fluid therefore wasn't colorless adrenaline, which only becomes pale red and, eventually, brown on exposure to air and light. Instead, the brown liquid James Hall saw had to be Nembutal, which was the only other drug found in Marilyn's body besides chloral hydrate. This does not mean, however, that the high level of Nembutal came from Greenson's shot, but from the afternoon Nembutal injection, more evening Nembutal injections, and the drug-laced enema containing both chloral hydrate and Nembutal.

There are, indeed, two types of Nembutal: a clear, thin liquid and a dark brown, syrupy elixir. Furthermore, Nembutal must be diluted with water before being administered, yet James Hall was certain that Dr. Greenson didn't dilute the brown solution he injected into Marilyn's heart. Accordingly, it traveled up the brain stem and paralyzed her respiratory center. The doctor would surely have been aware of this, and so, just as surely, he was guilty of murder.

In his May 1986 interview with *Hustler* magazine, Hall remarked that Dr. Thomas Noguchi possibly didn't notice the puncture caused by the needle because the hole was in the crease of one of Marilyn's breasts.

"He said he looked over the whole body with a magnifying glass and didn't find any needle marks, including under the tongue," Hall noted. "But that sounds like a junkie shooting up, not like a reason to look at her heart. You wouldn't put a needle into your own heart, would you?"

Meanwhile, Dr. Thomas Noguchi told biographers Brown and Barham about bruises not documented in the official autopsy report: "I did find evidence which indicated violence. There were bruises on her lower back area—a very fresh bruise—and bruises on the arms."

In 1982, investigator Al Tomich from the District Attorney's Office asked Dr. Hyman Engelberg, "Would you have noticed any fresh needle marks on her at that time if there were any in the chest area?"

"I would have noticed any gross things," came the reply. "I didn't notice any such thing."

Donald Wolfe confirmed that Marilyn's body displayed indicators of cyanosis, consistent with a needle injection. An actual witness to the cyanosis was *Life* magazine photojournalist Leigh Wiener, who said he saw strange blue markings all over her when he photographed Marilyn Monroe hours after her death. "They'll look like a frozen cube of ice," Leigh Wiener explained in a 1987 documentary. "You'll see little streaks of blue running through the body . . . That's how Monroe looked to me when I saw her."

Wiener may have unwittingly held the key to the more than fifty-year-old mystery. This was thanks to his bribing county morgue staff with a bottle of whiskey shortly before midnight on August 5 and capturing frontal images of Marilyn just hours after her death that might reveal a needle mark in the chest area.

"I took a picture of her toe with a tag on it, covered by a sheet," Wiener recalled in the same documentary. "Then they took the sheet off and I took more pictures but it was at eye-level. I couldn't see the face. The pictures were obviously never used. I have them and I've been interrogated by the District Attorney in Los Angeles about them."

Wiener's son Devik told Jay Margolis, "In 1982, a couple of deputy D.A.s knocked on the door during one of the numerous times they reopened the investigation into her death. They wanted to see any photographs and Dad basically said, 'Look, they were black-and-white images, so you could tell nothing about flesh-tones from them. Good day. Good bye.' They were interested in color images. Dad said she was so disfigured that it would have done a disservice to her and a service to no one. He basically died with the mystery of where those images were.

"My dad claimed to have put those negatives in some safety-deposit box. I truly think he might have destroyed the negatives. From the bungalow to the mortuary, there were a total of a hundred and thirty-three images combined. And at the funeral he shot about a hundred and eighty images. Dad only pressed five hundred copies of the *Marilyn: A Hollywood Farewell* book. With all the celebrities he photographed, he left behind such an incredible body of work. It's almost half-a-million images."

Devik Wiener told Margolis that his father never believed Marilyn Monroe committed suicide: "There was so much surrounding her death with the Kennedys, the odds of her overdosing on her own—and I think he would say the same thing—were very slim."

Marilyn's friend, Hollywood reporter James Bacon, remembered, "I stayed there long enough to get a good view of the body before the real coroner's staff arrived—then I made a quick exit . . . She was lying face-down on the bed, face slightly turned to the left on a pillow. Her legs were straight . . . I noticed that her fingernails were dingy and unkempt." The fact is, her nails had changed color because of the cyanosis.

In the documentary *Marilyn Monroe: A Case for Murder*, John Miner recalled Thomas Noguchi's autopsy: "Her body was examined minutely by both of us under magnification to see if we could find any needle mark of any kind anywhere on her body. And her body was observed and there were no needle marks."

Following actor John Belushi's drug-related death, Noguchi conceded in his book that he almost missed a needle mark on Belushi's left arm. "The very fact that the fresh punctures had been so difficult to discover worried me," the pathologist wrote. "Apparently a tiny medically clean needle had been used, and the injection had been made right into the vein, so that only drops of blood revealed them."

In Marilyn's case, according to pathologist J. DeWitt Fox, "The blue post-mortem lividity occurred over the front part of the body. This might have masked or covered up any injection which she might have had in her chest." In Fox's expert opinion, had Marilyn been moved, in this case facedown on the bed, then "the bruise-like discolorations of post-mortem lividity" would conceal an injection mark on her chest caused by the needle Hall saw Greenson putting into her heart.

To quote the 1982 District Attorney's Report on the re-investigation of Marilyn Monroe's death, "Lividity, as described to our investigators, is a process by which blood drains to the lowest point in a deceased person after death due to the joint effect of the pull of gravity and the cessation of the blood pumping mechanism of the body . . . In addition to the rigor mortis observed in Miss Monroe's body, Noguchi and others observed a pattern of lividity on her face and chest."

Sgt. Jack Clemmons, the first policeman officially at the scene, agreed with Dr. Fox's explanation of postmortem lividity and believed James Hall's account. "It was obvious to me, apparent to me, I should say, that Marilyn had been placed in that position," Clemmons remarked. "I felt at the time that the position of the body had to do with post-mortem lividity. When a person dies, their heart stops beating; the gravity will pull the blood to the lowest part of the body. Marilyn being facedown, all the blood came forward. As a matter of fact, the coroner's report particularly noted lividity, reddishness around the face and the chest area. I felt at the time that she was placed in that position to disguise needle marks."

For his part, John Miner conceded to biographers Brown and Barham, "A cursory examination of Monroe's kidneys found them to be clear of drugs. This should have indicated that the stomach may have been bypassed. And the only way that could have happened was by injection."

The 1982 District Attorney's Report attempted to discredit James Hall's testimony by stating: "According to Hall, the doctor ultimately plunged a giant syringe filled with a brownish fluid into her heart, after which she quickly died while on her back on the floor . . . Minor streaks of lividity were . . . found on her back. These minor traces disappeared upon touch. This finding is consistent with the normal practice of transporting bodies from the death scene to the mortuary or Coroner's Office . . . If the mysterious 'doctor' had given Miss Monroe a fatal shot of pentobarbital, leading to her rapid death as described by Hall, the level in her liver would not have been as high as it in fact was because her body would not have had time to metabolize the 'hot shot.'"

Marilyn Monroe died shortly before midnight and Thomas Noguchi began the autopsy after 9:00 a.m., leaving plenty of time for postmortem lividity to hide the needle mark. Still, this doesn't mean Noguchi discovered no needle marks. Testimonies for this book by the likes of Raymond Strait, Allan Abbott, and a confidential source lead to the conclusion that Noguchi inexplicably disregarded his own findings when he wrote the statement: "No needle mark." An admirer of Attorney General Robert Kennedy, as expressed in his 1983 book and in magazine articles, Noguchi did initially note needle marks on other areas of Marilyn Monroe's body before omitting this one on the official autopsy report. Could it be because he knew a needle mark in the heart might implicate Kennedy? In fact, Anthony Summers reported that Noguchi "said he could not be positive the actress was not murdered by injection."

Marilyn died on her back. Regarding the drugs found in her body, the district attorney's report did not consider the possibility that the high Nembutal concentration in the liver was due to several factors: some oral intake throughout the day, the pentobarbital shot in the afternoon, evening pentobarbital injections, and an enema containing thirteen to nineteen Nembutals (as well as seventeen chloral hydrates). This combination would in a matter of hours travel from the blood to the liver to detoxify the substance. Over this period of time, the liver was allowed to reach that very high Nembutal concentration. It could only reach higher levels while she was still alive. John Miner explained the 13 mg. percent of Nembutal in the liver is a "high concentration" and said, "It indicates that however the drugs were administered, hours and not minutes were involved before she died."

Suicide Team member Dr. Robert Litman agreed and explained, "High content in the liver just means she died slowly, the chance to be absorbed." In contrast to the 13 mg. percent of Nembutal, the chloral hydrate in the liver was not tested since it would reveal a much smaller amount, incongruent with a suicide.

John Miner told Donald Spoto, "Dr. Curphey in one of his more exuberant moments said, 'Oh, she gobbled 40 pills all at one time.' That's not possible . . . Why in the hell under these circumstances would the housekeeper be doing laundry at midnight makes zero sense unless the bed clothing had become soiled as a result of the administration of these drugs? . . . Contact with a noxious substance such as the barbiturates, which is an organic acid would account for the discoloration in the large intestine we saw at the autopsy."

Indeed, it took several hours for the liver to absorb a lethal amount of pentobarbital whereas Dr. Greenson's undiluted Nembutal shot to the heart would have killed Marilyn Monroe regardless of the amount injected. "That's murder," Elias Amador, M.D., told Jay Margolis regarding the undiluted heart injection. "That is point-blank murder. That's never done for any reason except to kill."

Sgt. Clemmons said that, when he arrived on the scene at 4:45 a.m. and saw Marilyn's lifeless body in the master bedroom (to where it had been moved following the departure of ambulance attendants Hall and Liebowitz), Greenson was "cocky, almost challenging me to accuse him of something." Clemmons' suspicions were on target as Greenson's guilt was immediately apparent.

Peter Lawford explained how Robert Kennedy had instructed Greenson, "Marilyn has got to be silenced." Lawford relayed, "Greenson had thus been set up by Bobby to 'take care' of Marilyn." The psychiatrist achieved this by an undiluted Nembutal injection to the heart. After all, what better way for any witnesses to assume it couldn't have been anything but an adrenaline shot? This was a common method used to save patients from an overdose.

While one may question whether Peter Lawford's account was second-hand therefore hearsay, James Hall insists Lawford himself saw the heart injection by Greenson. Because Lawford was Kennedy's brother-in-law, that makes Lawford a primary witness. Hall's partner Murray Liebowitz also assured Donald Wolfe that Hall's account of Greenson and the heart needle was accurate.

Thus, there have been three eyewitness accounts detailing Marilyn Monroe's death as a murder at the hands of her own psychiatrist. Not surprisingly, the other two eyewitnesses Pat Newcomb and Sgt. Marvin Iannone have refused to discuss their observations to protect the Kennedy family. In fact, in 1986, James Hall stated regarding Ralph Greenson's shot to the heart: "I say, 'Yes, I saw her get that injection.' So did Pat Newcomb. She was there too. Will she come forward?"

In the documentary *Say Goodbye to the President*, photographer William Woodfield shared his recorded 1964 telephone conversation with Ralph Greenson in which the doctor discussed only what he said he could about Marilyn's last night. Oddly, two years after her death, he was still deferring all inquires to the Attorney General: "I can't explain myself or defend myself without revealing things that I don't want to reveal. I feel I—I can't, you know—you can't draw a line and say well I'll tell you this but I won't tell you that. It's a terrible position to be in to have to say I can't talk about it because I can't tell the whole story . . . Listen, you know, talk to Bobby Kennedy."

According to James Hall, while watching Greenson administer the shot to the heart it was immediately obvious to him that the psychiatrist had never done this before. His line of work hardly necessitated him to carry a medical bag containing a large syringe with a heart needle already attached. Bobby Kennedy provided the syringe courtesy of one of his two long-time personal bodyguards James Ahern or Archie Case, who had accompanied him and Peter Lawford to Marilyn's home earlier that afternoon and later that night.

Dr. Sidney Weinberg concluded, "Knowing the results of the toxicology examination and the negative findings in the stomach, one must seriously consider the possibility of an injection. If I had handled the case, I would have been remiss in my duties if I did not refer it to the district attorney for investigation."

Donald Wolfe wrote that, later in the evening, with Bobby Kennedy present, Marilyn "was injected with enough barbiturate to kill fifteen people." Wolfe, however, is wrong. As John Miner stated, "The amount of drugs found in Marilyn's body was so large that, had it been administered by one injection [containing high dosages of Nembutal and chloral hydrate], the star would have died almost immediately. The body would have only had minutes in which to begin absorbing all those drugs."

Rather, in front of Bobby Kennedy, LAPD partners Archie Case and James Ahern subdued Marilyn by throwing her onto the guest cottage bed. According to private detective Fred Otash and wiretapper Bernie Spindel, Kennedy then placed a pillow over her mouth to keep her from yelling while instructing Case and Ahern to give her Nembutal injections by stating, "Give her something to calm her down."

When that didn't work, the men then forcibly administered an enema containing broken-down Nembutal and chloral hydrate pills. Even though this didn't kill Marilyn within minutes, as a lethal injection containing the same drugs would have done, it at least rendered her unconscious.

The last thing the president's brother wanted was the most famous woman in the world fighting him to get out of her house and away from her two filing cabinets in the guest cottage. Bobby had been obsessively looking for Marilyn's little red diary. So, later on, after the three men left, as James Hall attempted to revive her, in walked Ralph Greenson with a black medical bag from which he "pulled out a syringe with a long heart needle . . . filled it with a brownish fluid and injected it into Miss Monroe's heart."[9]

THE SOUNDMAN

Jay Margolis is so far the only biographer to have interviewed the soundman who accompanied Fred Otash the night Marilyn Monroe died. In this case, a soundman is defined as a person who installs or removes surveillance equipment. On August 4, 1962, said soundman arrived on the scene with Otash *after* Bobby Kennedy had left 12305 Fifth Helena Drive with Case and Ahern and *before* Dr. Ralph Greenson injected Marilyn in the heart with the undiluted pentobarbital injection.

The soundman asked Margolis, "Do you really believe that Bobby Kennedy, who at that time was the Attorney General of the United States of America, would be there, putting a pillow over her face and involved in murdering Marilyn Monroe with all these people around? With Eunice there? Didn't she have a nephew [son-in-law] or somebody there? Otash there? Security people there? Ambulance attendants there? You really think that Bobby Kennedy would stay there? You think he was *that* stupid?

"Bobby Kennedy was stupid because he was horny and so was his brother. They couldn't resist the temptation of attractive women. Many guys in history, their weakness is sex. We all know that and they will do indiscreet and dumb things. The President did. Bobby did. But to be involved in *murder*? I don't personally think that Bobby Kennedy was *that* stupid . . .

"There will never be closure to this. Marilyn was such a famous person admired by millions all over the planet . . . Do you know the connection between Greenson, the housekeeper, and Mickey Rudin? They're all tied to the Kennedys. All the people surrounding Marilyn were all tied to the Kennedys. Their allegiance was all to the Kennedys, not to Marilyn. It was pathetic. Regardless of who did what the night of August 4, 1962, none of those people were on the scene on behalf of Marilyn. They weren't working for Marilyn. They weren't concerned with Marilyn. The Kennedys, her psychiatrist, her doctor, her lawyer, her housekeeper, Peter

Lawford, his wife who was a Kennedy, they were all concerned with the political aspects of it."

Jayne Mansfield's former press secretary Raymond Strait assured Margolis that the soundman knew more than he was telling about Marilyn's last night. "The soundman listened to the tapes and heard the whole damn thing," Strait asserted. "So, he knows what was going on back there. But Fred [Otash] never wanted to mention his name out loud. He would just use his initials. After Marilyn's death, the sound-man went to work for the CIA in Washington for years. And that's why I knew he would never talk about it. He doesn't want anything to do with it. If he were to ever write a book, it would be an immediate bestseller but he wouldn't do that because he'd feel his family would be in danger . . .

"I knew Otash better than anybody that's living. Of course, the sound-man knew him pretty well but not completely because he left him to go work in Washington. He doesn't want his part to come to life because there would just be too many people that would be attracted to him that he wouldn't want to be attracted to him, including certain members of a very prominent family. And he doesn't wanna have his name come up in court.

"He was the soundman and he helped Fred take the bugs out. But Fred had all the files. The soundman didn't have any of those, although he did listen to the tapes because he was the soundman on the damn thing, and for him to deny that he ever did any of that is another way of not being involved. He had nothing to do with anything to do with [moving] Marilyn's body, only to do with the bugs. He listened to those tapes, so he knows what happened . . .

"I knew Peter [Lawford] was there because Fred told me . . . Peter was drunk and hysterical. Fred slapped the shit out of him because of the way he was so hysterical at Marilyn's house. He was just like a hys-terical woman, crying and carrying on. Fred didn't have much patience with that . . .

"Fred was there in the house as she was dying . . . He told me in great detail everything that happened that day . . . Fred's job was to clean the mess up . . . Peter got scared and hysterical so he called Fred . . . Fred says, 'You meet me at Marilyn's house.' And Fred showed up with his sound man and Peter met him there and the sergeant I interviewed told me that Fred was leaving the house when he arrived on the scene."[10]

WALT SCHAEFER'S INVOLVEMENT

As far as James Hall was concerned, his employer, Walter Schaefer, was involved in the cover-up, and he cited Schaefer's denial of ever having employed him as indicative of this.

"In 1985, I was contacted by the Flynt Distributing Co.," Hall said with regard to the noted men's magazine publisher. "They wanted to do an article on my story but they were not able to confirm my employment at Schaefer's. Walter Schaefer told them that he had never heard of James E. Hall. I sent Flynt a copy of my Social Security Administration Statement of Earnings for the year 1962. They went back to Schaefer, showed it to him and he said, 'I have never heard of James E. Hall.' The earnings statement shows one employer for the year—Schaefer's Ambulance.

"I then told Flynt that I was at a court hearing and Schaefer testified, 'I am Walter Schaefer, owner of Schaefer's Ambulance Service, and James E. Hall works for me.' When they showed him the trial transcript he again said, 'I do not know James E. Hall.'

"When Schaefer first started his ambulance service, it was a requirement of the state that a doctor of medicine ride in the back. Schaefer went to his family doctor and offered half of the business if he would be the doctor for the ambulance. Schaefer's personal physician refused the offer. That physician was George E. Hall, M.D., my father! Dad went on to become the Retired Chief of Staff of the City of Los Angeles Receiving (emergency) Hospital System. Schaefer again said, 'I have never heard of James E. Hall or this Dr. Hall.' [Larry] Flynt then told Schaefer, 'Up yours, you lying asshole,' and printed my story."

"It's been a long time, but Hall wasn't simply another set of hands at the wheel," Larry Flynt himself wrote in the May 1986 issue of *Hustler* magazine. "Hall's father had been the doctor Schaefer first asked to ride with him when he began his ambulance business . . . In a court case, Schafer testified that Hall drove an ambulance for him, and Hall was photographed in uniform by a newspaper, hauling a body from a crime scene [on October 4, 1962]." Refer to fan newspaper *Runnin' Wild: All About Marilyn* in the October 1993 issue, Number 12, to see this picture of James Hall.

In 1992, on *The Marilyn Files* live TV special, James Hall explained why Murray Liebowitz was paired with him on the call to Marilyn's house: "Back in 1962, I rented an apartment, my wife and I, and my regular partner Rick [Charles Greider] and his wife rented the apartment next door to us. The apartment house manager was Murray Liebowitz and we all worked together at Schaefer's Ambulance. Rick wanted that night off and had Murray fill in for him."[11]

WHO THE HELL IS
KEN HUNTER?

In December 1982, weeks after James Hall's story appeared in the *Globe*, a man by the name of Ken Hunter claimed to the District Attorney's Office that *he*, not James Hall, had accompanied *his* partner Murray Liebowitz to Marilyn Monroe's home during "the early morning hours of August 5, 1962." This is odd since Marilyn died *before* midnight. Nevertheless, Hunter claimed to the District Attorney's Office they were in and out within minutes after observing that Marilyn appeared to be dead before they arrived on the scene.

Anthony Summers wrote, "In 1985, I talked on several occasions to the late Walter Schaefer, who was then still running the ambulance company he founded. He confirmed, with utter certainty, that a Schaefer ambulance was called to Marilyn's home. Asked whether Murray Liebowitz was one of the crew, he said, 'I know he was.'" On December 14, 1982, the District Attorney's Office conducted the following tape-recorded interview with an unconvincing Ken Hunter:

TOMICH: What happened?

HUNTER: What do you mean?

TOMICH: Well, I mean, what occurred?

HUNTER: Well, I don't know. Nothing really occurred. She was dead and they wouldn't let us take her.

TOMICH: Well—

HUNTER: The coroner came and took her.

TOMICH: Did you go into the house?

HUNTER: Yeah, I believe so.

TOMICH: Did you see Monroe's body?

HUNTER: Yeah.

TOMICH: Where was it at the time?

HUNTER: She was on the bed, hanging off the bed or something.

TOMICH: Do you recall whether she was on her back or her stomach?

HUNTER: Side.

TOMICH: She was on her side?

HUNTER: Yeah, I believe she was on her side. Let's see, yeah, it seems to me she was on her side.

TOMICH: Did either one of you touch her body?

HUNTER: No, I didn't. I don't know if he did.

TOMICH: Did you know if your partner did?

HUNTER: Seems to me he did.

TOMICH: Do you know what he did?

HUNTER: Checked her just to see if—dead or what not. I think she was. I think she was pretty cold at that time. Well, she was blue, the throat, you know, like she had settled, like she had been laying there a while. You know what I mean?

TOMICH: She was blue in any particular portion of her body?

HUNTER: I think—I don't really remember if it was her neck or her side that she was laying on or what. It was—But it seemed to me like—Well, let's put it this way. I could stand across the room and tell that she was dead.

TOMICH: Let me relate a story to you that we've received information from a person that an ambulance attendant was summoned to the residence. That when the ambulance attendant [James Hall] and his partner [Murray Liebowitz] arrived the only person there was a female [Pat Newcomb] standing outside screaming. And that the attendant [Hall] went in and found Marilyn Monroe on the bed, removed her from the bed and began CPR or closed-chest massage. And that in the process of doing this that she started to come around, you know, to regain consciousness and the doctor [Ralph Greenson] came in and plunged a needle into the area of her heart and thereafter pronounced her dead. Does that sound familiar at all?

HUNTER: That's bullshit.

As recorded on page 16 of the district attorney's report, Ken Hunter stated that, upon arriving at Marilyn's home, he and Murray Liebowitz noticed she was already dead and left a few minutes later. This scenario, if it were to be believed, makes it nearly impossible for Marilyn's next-door neighbors to the west, Abe Charles Landau and his wife Ruby Landau, to claim to have seen an ambulance when they arrived home around midnight. After all, they would have had to see it within the few minutes Hunter said he was on the scene, which is highly unlikely. That gives the Landaus approximately five minutes to spot the ambulance before it's gone.

As for Ken Hunter's December 14, 1982, interview, during an early part of the recording, Hunter volunteered to Tomich, "I know that Hall wasn't there. Period." When Tomich asked Hunter if he could remember the name of his partner, Hunter told him, "I'm almost positive it was Liebowitz." As for Hall's story, Hunter was adamant: "The doctor wasn't even in the room!" he asserted before concluding, "It just looked like an accidental suicide." Talking with Tomich about the extent of his employment with Schaefer Ambulance, Hunter's recollection was, at best vague and sketchy:

TOMICH: When did you start with Walt Schaefer?

HUNTER: I don't know. I don't remember.

TOMICH: How long would you say you've been on this job before Monroe's death?

HUNTER: Not long.

TOMICH: Months.

HUNTER: Months. Maybe two months.

TOMICH: Have you been with an ambulance service prior to that time?

HUNTER: I was in Long Beach.

TOMICH: And how long did you work there?

HUNTER: Four or five months.

From the evidence presented, we can safely conclude that James Hall and Murray Liebowitz were the Schaefer Ambulance attendants who went to Marilyn's home, *not* Ken Hunter.

On September 11, 1993, Donald Wolfe interviewed former Schaefer Vice President Carl Bellonzi. He stated that Ken Hunter only started working for Schaefer in the mid-1970s. Bellonzi also assured Wolfe and Margolis that Ken Hunter couldn't have gone to Marilyn's house the night she died because Hunter didn't work for Schaefer Ambulance until the mid-1970s, years *after* Marilyn's died and, even then, never in the Los Angeles area but in Orange County.

"Hunter wore glasses and he was kind of heavyset," Bellonzi recalled to Jay Margolis. "He wasn't really fat. He was just big and heavy. Hunter used to tell a lot of tall stories, lies about things that are not possible. Like an old-time Seder telling stories. Things he says he's done but nobody ever did believe him."

James Hall's Social Security number and his January–December 1962 employment records, shown clearly in *The Marilyn Files* documentary, confirm that he did, in fact, work for Schaefer in August 1962. What's more, Donald Wolfe tracked down a *Santa Monica Evening Outlook* photo of James Hall in his Schaefer Ambulance uniform dated October 4, 1962, and the *Runnin' Wild: All About Marilyn* fan newspaper displayed the same photograph. See Donald Wolfe's article in the October 1993 issue, Number 12, entitled, "The Ambulance Chase." So, who was Ken Hunter, a man who took it upon himself to lie to the D.A.'s Office? Quite simply, the Kennedys hired Hunter to discredit James Hall's account.[12]

FAMOUS CLIENTS
WERE COMMONPLACE AT
SCHAEFER AMBULANCE

Walt Schaefer was the president of Schaefer Ambulance Service. In Culver City and Santa Monica, it was called California Ambulance Service. Funeral Director Allan Abbott informed Jay Margolis, "I knew Schaefer. We both bought our cars from the same place. The same company that built hearses also built ambulances, at least in those days." Born Schaeffer (German), he later changed his name to Schaefer (Jewish). Schaefer Ambulance treated innumerable famous clients throughout the years. In fact, according to former ambulance attendant Edgardo Villalobos, Schaefer even had a famous cousin who was none other than Mae West.

Villalobos explained to Jay Margolis, "Mr. Schaefer was involved with all these people, including celebrities. He had a lot of connections. I used to be a fighter so I acted as a bodyguard for Mr. Schaefer. He always took me places with him. He went to all these big events. I got to meet Governor Jerry Brown. The President at the time once gave him an award, which said: 'The most successful businessman in the country.' Mr. Schaefer hung it up in his office.

"Schaefer is dead but the plate is still there. He used to take me and my wife on a couple of trips to have fun. One time when we were flying to Mexico, Bob Neuman was the pilot and Mr. Schaefer took over the control and he made jokes like 'Let the plane go down' with my first wife acting worried. I was just a regular ambulance driver but he took to me and I got close to him. I liked Schaefer a lot. We had drinks with our families and it never stopped. I worked for Mr. Schaefer for forty years."

Former Schaefer Vice President Carl Bellonzi informed Jay Margolis, "Villalobos was one I trained. I was there at Schaefer for forty-five years." If his memory is correct, Bellonzi said he became vice president in 1985. Bellonzi stated, "I remember there was a Hall." Bellonzi says he also remembers Murray Liebowitz and Villalobos's regular partner the late Larry Telling.

Carl Bellonzi said even he transported celebrities. "I picked up Marie McDonald," Bellonzi recalled to Jay Margolis. "She was having trouble with her back. Marie was called 'The Body' because she had some body. She was a real beauty." Schaefer Ambulance attendant Edgardo Villalobos relayed to Margolis, "In Santa Monica, everybody used to get all the celebrities. We did too [at the main station on Beverly and Western] but not as much as they did. I transported a lot of movie stars. Mr. Schaefer made a beautiful stretch limo for the VIPs. I was wearing a very elegant suit. We used to take celebrities and ambassadors in the VIP car which we called 'The Diplomat.'

"I took George Burns's wife [Gracie Allen] when she was having a fatal heart attack [on August 27, 1964] and she was struggling for her life. I was the attendant and George Burns was sitting right there in front. I'm watching her, facing her, giving her oxygen, and she was struggling. We took her to Cedars of Lebanon where she died the same night.

"I also transported Ward Bond. He and John Wayne were very good friends. Ward was a big guy and in *3 Godfathers* (1948) and all those westerns. He had a ranch in Texas. Before Ward died, me and my partner Larry Telling picked him up from his house over in Coldwater Canyon and he was there on a bridge. He had a heart attack. He saw us and he was a big guy so he said, 'No, no, boys. I don't want you to hurt your back.' He said to walk him to the ambulance and then he'll get in the stretcher. So he walked to the ambulance and we said, 'Now we have to put you in the stretcher.' When we finally got the stretcher ready for him, he says to us, 'It's a big load of shit that you're picking up!' We took him to Saint John's Hospital. Two or three days later, the news said he died in his ranch in [Dallas] Texas [on November 5, 1960].

"I used to pick up Betty White's husband [Allen Ludden] all the time. She wouldn't allow anybody else but me. She said, 'Where's Edgardo? I'm not going if you don't send Edgardo out! My husband will not want to go to the hospital!' I used to be there ready for her in the air ambulance to take him to the hospital. They were very nice good-hearted people and they loved me and I loved them. She was very pretty and young so it had to be a long time ago.

"I picked up Lou Costello [on March 3, 1959] when he was having a heart attack. He was still talking and laughing. I thought maybe he was living in a big mansion but actually he lived in a little common apartment in the Valley and he died at the hospital. I met his daughter and she looks just like him!

"I transported the singer Betty Hutton two or three times to the hospital in an ambulance to Cedars of Lebanon in 1962 . . . Barbara Hutton, I used to transport a lot. She was married to a prince [Pierre Raymond Doan Vinh na Champassak from 1964 to 1966]. I used to pick her up at the Beverly Wilshire Hotel, nobody else, only me and another guy. She had bodyguards and a lot of princes from the Middle East with her there. I always picked up Barbara at the Beverly Wilshire Hotel at the penthouse with her prince because she was married to a guy that was a prince so she became a princess.

"Barbara was a very generous person. She was always giving everybody money and presents. Every time we transported her from the penthouse at the Beverly Wilshire, we take her to the airport and she flew to the Middle East. She was an angel of a person and she loved everybody. I transported her a great number of times. They said something to do with her bones. She could not walk. Before we would take her, they would have us wait outside, and then we would go inside with the stretcher. Every time, Hutton wanted to request me. She always gave me and my partner a $500 tip. The guys I worked with kept saying, 'You're going to get Barbie!' "

Murray Leib's widow Sylvia told Jay Margolis, "Murray knew an awful lot of movie people like Peter Graves. While he did not know any of the Kennedys, he did know the one who was married to one of the Kennedy girls who lived in Malibu. He was very well-known and acted as mediator for them. Peter Lawford. Murray knew him well. He had been in his house to either pick up patients or to take care of a patient. . . .

"Murray knew Howard Hughes because every time Howard Hughes had a party, somebody got hurt and Murray did all of those calls because he did keep his mouth shut. You never could get anything out of him. In fact, Howard Hughes wanted him to quit Schaefer and come work with him but it was like Schaefer pointed out to Murray, 'You'll become a slave if you do that' and Murray said, 'That is true.' So he knew Howard Hughes because he had been called to that house so often. And he knew a lot of them mostly because he had made calls to their house . . . And that's how he knew these people but Murray said he never knew Marilyn until he was on that call . . .

"One time, there was one truck in front of the house and one truck right around the corner, and I think a couple of cars behind that. This woman, the one that rang the bell, she introduced herself as a reporter for *20/20* and she had this huge bag over her shoulder like an oversized purse, and she just said that they were doing something about Marilyn Monroe.

"She said she wanted to interview Murray, and that was about the twentieth anniversary of her death. Murray said, 'I don't have anything to say to you and I want you to take your equipment and get off of my property, and if you don't, I'm going to call the police.' Murray never took a dime from them or from anybody else for any story.

"That was not his thing. He absolutely totally refused them. They offered Murray all the money in the world if he would be interviewed, but he refused them. That's not what he did. No matter what they asked him about Marilyn, Murray said, 'If you wanna know what I know, just read the police report. That's all I know.'

"That's why he did all the celebrity calls that came to Schaefer, if they could get a hold of Murray, unless he was away or something. Because this all happened before I met him. Those were always Murray's calls because he would never ever tell anybody anything. He never spoke about them because he felt the job he had was very confidential.

"Murray was also an attendant to Clara Bow. He also knew Elizabeth Taylor's husband Nicky Hilton. Schaefer ran that place and he used Murray for celebrities because he knew that nobody was going to get anything out of Murray and that he wasn't going to take any money for anything. Murray said [regarding Marilyn Monroe], 'Everybody made money on this story except me.' He never believed that he should take anything or that he should betray any of these people that trusted him. He was like that . . .

"Murray was very well known in the industry because they all trusted him because they knew that their secrets were safe with him. You could never get anything out of him. He was very proud of his reputation with the celebrities. Marilyn has so much publicity and so many people were there and saw all of this, you couldn't keep that a secret . . .

"It was not until a few years before he died that he told me about Marilyn but he always said that she was dead when they got there. She was gone . . . Murray said, 'Nobody murdered her. Nobody killed her. It was just an overdose. There was an empty bottle and the place reeked of alcohol. I don't know how much she drank.' It was just a matter of routine what to do with her because she was a celebrity and he knew they had to tread carefully. The Kennedys were involved in it, too. She was in the middle of a real trauma then because the Kennedys had kicked her out that day. That particular coroner [Noguchi], you could get him to say anything. I remember him well.

"Murray said it was around midnight, I do know that. Eleven o'clock to them. You know, well, if you're working, you don't know if it's eleven or twelve o'clock. He wasn't a clock-watcher. I have an idea she was murdered because this girl had everything to live for but she had the Kennedys in her pocket and those people thought nothing of doing something like that. You know that by their history. But nobody should have influence enough to take over the press and take over the hospitals and doctors but to my knowledge, I never met this attendant [James Hall]."

Over the years, James Hall told of his run-ins with celebrities or those related to celebrities as an attendant for Schaefer Ambulance while he was working in the Santa Monica office. These included actor-comedian Ernie Kovacs, MGM's costume designer Irene Gibbons, Sammy Davis, Jr.'s mother Elvera Sanchez, and even Barbara Burns, the daughter of comedian Bob Burns.

"Dr. George E. Hall, was a Beverly Hills surgeon and former chief of staff of Los Angeles receiving hospitals, the city's emergency system," Hall relayed. "My mother was a surgical nurse. A prominent member of my family was my uncle John Nance Garner, Vice President for two terms under Franklin D. Roosevelt." Hall's impressive family background is augmented by the fact that Dr. George E. Hall and Walt Schaefer were very good friends despite Schaefer later unconvincingly claiming in the 1980s that he knew neither James Hall nor his father.

"When Jim was fourteen-years-old, he was swinging on rings doing doubles and triples, you know, gymnastics, and he fell and broke his neck," recalled Hall's childhood best friend Mike Carlson. "Right from the back of his head right where your neck is all the way to the center of his back. They attached all these wires to his back and all. After that, he was walking kind of stiff. He was in the hospital for three years so he was very familiar with the practices associated with his family like his dad and what the process was. I would say he was very into his job."

"In 1961 I started with Walt Schaefer's California Ambulance Service," James Hall explained. "Dad called Schaefer and got me the job. My dad would show and tell us a lot of little moves . . . like when you're delivering a baby . . . how to push and all that type of stuff. It helped a lot."

In fact, Dr. Hall's advice would prove very useful the following year when Hall took the ambulance call for a famous actress-singer. "I picked up Betty Hutton," Hall remembered. "When we entered her house, we were facing the couch, and her bedroom was down the hallway to the right. We took her from her home, and at that time she had a real long Italian name like a producer or something."

James Hall is absolutely correct even down to the Italian last name. Hall said, "We took her to Cedars of Lebanon Hospital, to the Pavilion. The only cases that went to the Pavilion were obstetrics or babies. They thought she was miscarrying, but she wasn't. From what I understand, she later had a baby."

On June 20, 1962, in the *El Paso Herald*, a story ran in Hollywood through the *United Press International* called "Betty Hutton Has Baby Girl." It read: "Singer Betty Hutton yesterday gave birth to a seven-pound girl at Cedars of Lebanon Hospital. Attendants said both mother and daughter were 'doing fine.' It was the first child for Miss Hutton by her marriage to Musician Pete Candoli." Indeed, Carolyn Candoli was born on June 19, 1962, less than two months before James Edwin Hall witnessed the murder of Marilyn Monroe by Dr. Ralph Greenson.[13]

THE MEN AT BEVERLY
AND WESTERN

Schaefer's main office is still located at 4627 Beverly Boulevard in Los Angeles. This is where Schaefer Ambulance attendant Edgardo Villalobos and his driver Larry Telling received the first call to Marilyn Monroe's home. Anthony Summers, author of *Goddess: The Secret Lives of Marilyn Monroe*, interviewed seven Schaefer attendants who remembered the ambulance call from Marilyn's house on the night of August 4, 1962: Joe Zielinski (not Zilinski), Carl Bellonzi (later a company vice president), Thomas "Tom" Jesse Fears, Hugh "Lucky" Patrick O'Bligh (not Sean, and company vice president before Bellonzi), Joe Tarnowski (later Tarno but his widow goes by Tarnowski), Edgardo Villalobos, and Murray Liebowitz (later Leib). Other attendants who remember the ambulance call to Marilyn's home are Ruth Tarnowski (who worked as a Schaefer attendant especially when it was necessary to pick up female psych patients and as a Schaefer nurse all the rest of the time), the late Richard "Dick" Williams, Donald Altrock, Rick Staffer, James Hall's regular partner Rick Charles Greider (a.k.a. Rick Summers), and Villalobos' partner Larry Telling.

In August 1962, during the time that James Hall responded to the ambulance call to Marilyn Monroe's home, Edgardo Villalobos relayed, "Hugh Patrick O'Bligh was the Vice President of Schaefer. They called him Lucky. He was much older than me. He was working for the studios in Burbank the last time I saw him. We loved the guy. Carl Bellonzi stepped in after Lucky but Carl didn't have the knowledge that Lucky had. Lucky was there way before Carl and was a good man but unfortunately Lucky was a very heavy drinker . . . Mr. Schaefer called him Irish. He never called him Lucky . . . Because Carl was like a son to Mr. Schaefer, they made him the Vice President."

Out of these thirteen attendants/drivers (not including James Hall) who remember the ambulance call to Marilyn Monroe's home, only three are still alive: Carl Bellonzi, Ruth Tarnowski, and Edgardo Villalobos. The latter clearly remembers what happened at the Schaefer Ambulance main office on Beverly and Western on that fateful evening. He has never been quoted regarding Marilyn Monroe until now.

"The other guy was Larry Telling, my partner," Villalobos told Jay Margolis. "We got the call first, but there was an ambulance closer in the area, so they canceled us and Hall got the call from Santa Monica. I didn't get to go because I didn't respond to the call. I was at Beverly Boulevard and Western, the main station. The dispatcher wrote three slips: one they threw in the trash, another they kept for so many years, and the other they gave to us. But they kept our slip there and that's why reporters kept bothering me. The dispatcher never wrote a new slip. On the old slip, it had the driver, attendant, and call number. If I had transported Marilyn, I would have told it exactly how it was, but I didn't transport her.

"One day, I pulled into the driveway coming in after a call and the media was there. They questioned me. They questioned Mr. Schaefer, too. They were always bugging me, asking, 'Did you transport Marilyn Monroe?' They kept insisting, and it was because of the slip. They never changed the slip after I got the first call. The dispatcher, when he canceled us, he forgot to write the other guy's slip!

"If you call a private ambulance to any city in the LA area to pick up a patient, it should be a very, very short time, normally three minutes, four minutes, five minutes . . . Hall is the one who got the call. He was in that area. I didn't respond to the call, but later on, when there was all this investigation, they kept coming to me because according to them I got the call . . . I do remember exactly everything that went on. Reporters came up to me and said I took her and I said, 'I didn't take her.' They told me, 'We know you did. We know you're lying.' But we did get the call. They canceled me and then they continued to give him the call. So Hall got the call. His partner's name was Murray. A real nice guy. I knew the guy very well . . . Murray was a very nice person. I really liked him."

Villalobos heard Hall's account of Greenson administering the needle to Marilyn's heart. "The psychiatrist is not supposed to inject," he confirmed. "He has no business doing that . . . We are qualified to know the difference if they're still alive or not breathing. If they're alive we transport, but if they're not alive we don't pick up the patient. You're not allowed to pronounce them dead. The city comes in . . . The only time you stick a long needle into people's hearts is after you give them mouth-to-mouth resuscitation and, if that doesn't work, the doctor has to be there with the long needle and he shoves it into the heart, but *not* a psychiatrist! There was a murder there because he was not the doctor. He might be her psychiatrist, but not her medical doctor, so he can't go sticking no needle into her heart . . .

"Many times, we witness [an adrenaline shot] when the doctor comes in and we have a patient, and they get the needle and the doctor shoves it right here [in the heart]. That's how they do it, but not brown liquid. A lot of people in Los Angeles, they all say Marilyn Monroe got murdered. Right after Marilyn died, there were all kinds of people asking me questions. I couldn't convince them that I did not transport Marilyn Monroe.

"At Schaefer, they used to change me around. One time [about a year after Marilyn's death], I was in an ambulance in one of the intensive care units and there was a strange nurse who I've never seen before. We know most of our nurses because we have a nurse riding in the critical care units. This nurse was a very nice and pretty girl. All of a sudden she started asking me questions so I suspected she was hired to try to find out information from me . . . Sometimes, a police officer would be in the back of the ambulance as a new attendant because private ambulances have a little problem sometimes because attendants would steal so they had somebody undercover. So that's why I got suspicious of the nurse who I thought was undercover trying to get information about me on Marilyn Monroe. I could've been wrong but I don't think I was wrong . . . That girl was sizing me up a lot. She said, 'Tell me, how about Marilyn Monroe?' I said, 'What about Marilyn Monroe?' 'Tell me how it was.' 'I know already what you're trying to find out. I did not transport Marilyn Monroe.'

"She *was* a nurse, but somebody—probably a writer or reporter—sent her to see if she could get information from me. There were so many people who tried to get information because they all knew it was murder. I'm not one of those guys who believes things that don't exist. My belief was if I was the one who transported Marilyn Monroe in those days, in the beginning of all that investigation, I wouldn't be here because they could not afford to have me running around when I know everything. I bet you they would have bumped me off."

Oddly enough, Edgardo Villalobos said Murray Liebowitz's regular partner disappeared shortly after Marilyn's death. Villalobos told Margolis, "Look what happened to Murray's partner Ryan. He was Murray's permanent attendant. And they were always together. After Marilyn died, nobody heard from him. He completely disappeared out of the sky. Very weird. Very mysterious. We all knew Ryan was an attendant, but nobody found Ryan. We never saw him anymore. His last name I don't know. They would've made *me* disappear somehow because they wouldn't want me to give out the information. The big people cannot afford to be exposed, so they would try to take care of that guy somehow. I said to the people asking me questions, 'You guys are going to get me killed.'"

After learning that Hall had yielded to the man in the business suit identifying himself as Monroe's doctor, Villalobos explained, "You have to listen to a doctor. The doctor calls the shots. We cannot intervene . . . I knew there was something going on because reporters were really hard after me. I kept telling them I knew nothing because, as I told you, they just canceled us, but my name and my partner's name remained there on the slip. It was a Code Three. During all the excitement, the dispatcher didn't write a new slip for them. That's why they were bothering me a lot, because they put on it our name and location and everything else."

Edgardo Villalobos was interviewed before Former Schaefer Vice President Carl Bellonzi. Villalobos told Jay Margolis which Schaefer employee dispatched the ambulance call on the night of August 4, 1962, "Joe Tarnowski was a driver but then he became a dispatcher. By the way, he was the dispatcher! . . . Joe Tarnowski was the dispatcher."

Without being prompted, Bellonzi said to Margolis that Joe Tarnowski was indeed the dispatcher for the call coming from Marilyn Monroe's home: "I know who the dispatcher was at that time, and that was Tarnowski. Joe Tarnowski. He was the dispatcher at that time. I remember that call and I remember him being the dispatcher on that call."

Villalobos told Margolis, "Ruth Tarnowski was a nurse for Schaefer in the Santa Monica area and used to ride with the ambulances because they needed female attendants. She also worked at Culver City Memorial and then worked in a lot of convalescents."

Schaefer nurse and sometimes-attendant Ruth Tarnowski, confirmed that her late husband Joe was the dispatcher on August 4, 1962, "At the time Marilyn died, Joe and I were married and living in West LA. I worked 11 to 7 as a nurse at Schaefer's and when I got home at 7, he had already left for work. Later, I called him and he told me he dispatched the call to Marilyn Monroe's house. When he came home, he said it was really weird because everybody [at Schaefer Ambulance] was talking about it and that Robert Kennedy was one of the last ones to see her alive. It was funny the way they found her. It wasn't like she OD'd. Joe thought Marilyn was mixed up with the Kennedys. It was murder and that was covered up by the FBI."

Mrs. Tarnowski added, "Marilyn went to University High when I was going there. She was a nice girl. Later on, they made her up from head to toe. I almost didn't recognize her. When she was at Uni, she was Norma Jeane."

Villalobos relayed to Margolis, "I used to fight. Amateur boxing. There were five of us and the car dealer in Oxnard used to sponsor us. And they took us to the Hollywood Legion Stadium to fight there where all the movie stars used to go. Marilyn Monroe was at the fight. She came into the ring to give us all a kiss. We lined up and three guys were ahead of me. Something happened while we were standing there but I almost got a kiss from her. Three more guys and I would've gotten a kiss."[14]

THE SANTA MONICA
HOSPITAL "STORY"

"We took Marilyn Monroe in on an overdose and of course she succumbed at the hospital," Walt Schaefer stated in a 1985 interview. "She
was alive when she was picked up, yes."

Schaefer told a similar story to another reporter: "I came in the
next morning and found on the log sheet we had transported Marilyn
Monroe. I understood that she had overdosed. She was under the influence of barbiturates. They took her on a Code Three, an emergency, into
Santa Monica Hospital, where she terminated."

Asked how Marilyn could possibly have been brought back to her home
in Brentwood, Schaefer replied, "Anything can happen in Hollywood."

Years later, Hall's partner Murray Liebowitz would change his last
name to Leib. When Jay Margolis interviewed Murray Leib's now ninety-
six-year-old widow, Sylvia, she stated that, throughout the years, her
husband told her Marilyn Monroe was taken to the hospital and then
returned home after she was dead.

Since Murray Leib finally admitted to biographer Donald Wolfe that
James Hall's account was accurate, and because Mrs. Leib stated in a
previous chapter of this book that Murray only told her about Marilyn
Monroe during the last few years of their forty-year marriage, it is our
conclusion that Murray was simply protecting his wife Sylvia by continuing to echo Walt Schaefer's original testimony:

> MARGOLIS: Were Murray Leib along with James Hall the
> ambulance drivers the night that Marilyn died?
>
> LEIB: Murray was the ambulance driver. He was
> always the driver when he worked for Schaefer.
> Generally, when there were celebrity problems,

they always called on him . . . She was dead when he got there but they still had to take her to the hospital. That's the law. They can't do anything until an M.D. pronounces them dead. I think they took her to St. John's Hospital. Murray was always of the opinion that she took the pills herself. They took her to the hospital. When they got there, the doctor came out and said she was gone. Murray says to him, "Well, what do you want me to do with her?" because the hospital won't take a body . . . Then they took her back.

MARGOLIS: It was James Hall who was his partner?

LEIB: When we saw it on television, Murray did approve that he was there. That he was with him.

MARGOLIS: That James Hall was with him?

LEIB: Yes. He was with him but he wasn't the driver.

MARGOLIS: James Hall was given grueling polygraph tests in which he was proven to not be lying about the guest cottage.

LEIB: Murray always referred to her as "at home" so I can't say whether "at home" was a guest cottage.

MARGOLIS: The autopsy report said that there were no pills in Marilyn's stomach, which means she did not swallow the 64 pills they said she swallowed.

LEIB: That the table next to her was loaded with pills.

MARGOLIS: That is correct, but they were all "neatly-capped," just like James Hall said. This was not someone who was "hellbent to overdose," to put it in his own words.

LEIB: What are they trying to do now, to prove that she was murdered?

MARGOLIS: She made her last call at 10:00 p.m. and died before midnight. Why are there no pills in her stomach? James Hall's account correlates with the fact that she was killed.

LEIB: I don't think the Mafia was involved with this . . . There was a lot going on. She was involved with the Kennedys. They passed her down from one brother to the next. I do believe they had to get rid of her and she was really in the way . . . If she was really murdered, somebody needs to pay for that.

A 1992 *Hard Copy* documentary featuring Anthony Summers surprisingly endorsed Walt Schaefer's and Murray Leib's original testimony via a key player the night she died. American writer John Sherlock relayed what his friend Dr. Greenson had told him. "She died in the ambulance going to St. John's or St. Joseph's or wherever in Santa Monica," Sherlock stated. "And they turned around and took her back."

In its October 1993 issue, *Runnin' Wild: All About Marilyn* printed Walt Schaefer's retraction of his original hospital statement. It had been soon before his death that Schaefer explained why he lied about Marilyn Monroe being taken to the hospital: "Eighty percent of my business came from the County and government agencies."

In his 1992 book *The Marilyn Files*, author Robert Slatzer wrote: "Schaefer admitted he'd lied to [LAPD Sgt. Jack] Clemmons the first time and confirmed his story to me . . . The Kennedys were involved and he knew his business would be ruined if he talked."

Sylvia Leib volunteered to Margolis, "Murray didn't like the owner who owned the ambulance. Schaefer lied. Later on, he admitted he lied, didn't he? They asked him why he lied and he said, well, most of his business was the movie industry and they trusted him. But Murray wouldn't have said anything that wasn't true."

Taking Schaefer's retraction into consideration, we can conclude that Marilyn Monroe was never at any time transported to Santa Monica Hospital. Sylvia Leib, the late Walt Schaefer, and the District Attorney's Office all agree that Murray Leib went to Marilyn's house that night under the name Murray Liebowitz. "I don't want to be involved in this," a frantic Murray Leib told Anthony Summers over the phone in 1985. "I wasn't on duty that night. I heard about it when I came to work next morning . . . I'm not worried about anything, there's nothing to worry about. Don't bother to call me anymore."

Publicly, for over thirty years, Murray Leib never rocked the boat but simply followed Walt Schaefer's initial story: Hall was not there that night, Marilyn was taken to the hospital, she died there, and was then transported back to her home in Brentwood. The important point to note here is how Sylvia Leib remembered her husband Murray admitting that James Hall *was* his partner when they both saw Hall on television. Mrs. Leib could not have mistaken Hall for Ken Hunter because Hunter was never on television and his photograph was never circulated in the media.[15]

MURRAY LEIB AND THE
MYSTERIOUS CAR WASHES

Edgardo Villalobos volunteered to Jay Margolis, "Murray bought himself a car wash on Pico Boulevard." Meanwhile, Leib's widow Sylvia denied the stories about the Kennedys bribing Murray with enough money to buy car washes following Marilyn's death. Importantly, Mrs. Leib has assumed all these years that the genesis of the bribery allegations involving car washes began and ended with one man: James Hall.

Hall said in 1992 that Murray Liebowitz has "been interviewed by numerous people and he won't talk. On a radio talk show, an attendant who later rode with Liebowitz called in and said that everyday Liebowitz would stop at six different car washes."

According to Hall, Murray Liebowitz volunteered to his fellow Schaefer Ambulance attendant, "Well, you remember I told you I'd tell you what happened to Marilyn that night? Well, I'm not going to tell you that, but I will tell you this . . ."

Liebowitz then admitted that the Kennedys did in fact bribe him, "After her funeral, I came into a very large sum of what you would call hush money and I bought these car washes. I own them. And the only reason that I'm still working at Schaefer's is to keep up appearances."

"When we were watching that television program, Murray was laughing," Mrs. Leib told Jay Margolis. "He was hysterical at what this man [James Hall] was saying. He thought it was funny. It was just a regular routine ambulance call . . . He [James Hall] *was* there. He was with Murray when they took her to St. John's. When he got there, Murray said, 'She was dead' and I believe him because he wasn't one to lie about it. He had to take her and have her declared dead. The ambulance driver is not allowed to declare her dead. As many years as he was on the ambulance, he certainly knew a dead person when he met one. When he got there, apparently someone had called the hospital because they knew he was bringing Marilyn in and they would not let him bring her into the hospital.

"The only doctor Murray spoke to was the doctor at St. John's who came out to declare her dead. A doctor came out and examined her and signed the death certificate. And Murray said to the doctor, 'Well, what am I supposed to do with her if I can't leave her here?' They would not let him leave her there. The doctor said, 'Just take her back to her house,' and that's what they did. By the time he got her back home, the cops were there and the place was surrounded with police and he never pretended to know anymore."

Mrs. Leib repeatedly told Jay Margolis over the course of three comprehensive interviews that, even though she disputes Hall's account, her husband did relay how Hall was in fact Murray's partner on the night of August 4, 1962. Murray and Sylvia Leib had watched James Hall on television. In fact, Mrs. Leib still refers to James Hall as "the man on television."

"He did nothing but tell lies," she asserts. "I saw him on television once interviewed. He told them whatever it was they paid him for. One of the questions they asked him on television was 'What did Murray do with all this money?' and he said, 'Well, he bought a car wash.'

"My husband Harry Siegel and I built that car wash on Venice and Sepulveda . . . He died after about seven years. Then I was alone with it for about three-and-a-half years before I met Murray. I owned that car wash for about ten years before I met him . . . That's how I met Murray; he was a customer at my car wash for a lot of years. There were three managers and we worked hard. Our car wash was between three studios and all of those people were our customers, so we had our share of celebrities . . . The car wash is still there and fully in business. All the years we owned it, it was called Double Wash Car Wash because every car was washed twice."

Mrs. Leib said she first met Murray in 1967, five years after Marilyn died. At this time, Mrs. Leib claims that she retained total and complete ownership of the car wash and that Murray never had any interest in the property. "HLW Corporation is not owned by Sylvia Siegel and HLW Corporation wasn't listed as the owner of the car wash," asserted HLW Corporation Vice President John Watkins. "It was listed as the owner of the land . . . Today, it would require a huge investment about four million dollars or so to buy a car wash.

"Back then you might have been able to get into something like that for fifty-thousand or a hundred thousand dollars . . . Now HLW owns the car wash also but they didn't back in 1967; they just owned the land . . . There was another name Sylvia Leib . . . She had leased it from 1957. The lease officiated in 1957. She constructed the improvements and they were marginal . . . If they really had money from hush-up money, they would have been able to buy the land too and put up something much more significant than a car wash that was operating on marginal improvements. They were just leasing the land."

In fact, Mr. Watkins is correct. A court document stated: "HLW Corporation has owned the property at 11166 Venice Boulevard, in Culver City (the subject site) since July 6, 1955 . . . HLW Corporation has leased the subject site to various tenants for use as an automobile washrack and gasoline sales station since February 22, 1957." Sylvia Leib told Jay Margolis that she owned the car wash with her first husband Harry Siegel from 1957 until his death seven years later then she became the sole owner. Mrs. Leib stated, "Harry was born in 1913 and died at fifty-one years old on July 19, 1964." After her first husband passed away, Murray became an employee of Mrs. Leib, befriending her. "No one else ever owned it," continued Sylvia Leib. "But Murray did work there. He was an employee, a sort of helper but as far as owning it, no. Never . . .

"Murray was in the service and was in two wars. He was in World War II and in Korea. He was 89 when he died on January 24, 2009. He was born November 14, 1919. We were married exactly 40 years. We were not married when Marilyn died, but very shortly after. He was briefly married before and locally. His ex-wife, I think, was a customer, too, a couple of years before I met him. I remember that woman. She was a beautiful woman with long black hair. Beautiful, beautiful woman. I don't even remember what her name was. They weren't married very long because she was an alcoholic. I think she went somewhere on a trip or something, came back sick, and died . . . I married Murray on October 5, 1968. We were married in a Jewish Temple but in Las Vegas by a rabbi not in the court or anything. At that age, I definitely didn't want a wedding . . . I sold the car wash I would say in 1975 or 1976. I moved into this house in 1980 . . .

"I had full ownership of that car wash," Mrs. Leib asserted. "After Harry died, I'm the only one that owned it. No one else ever owned it . . . You can go down to City Hall to see who owned the car wash. Not only did we own it, we built it. Murray never owned it . . . That driver [James Hall] that he had with him the night Marilyn died, well, he somehow got the idea that Murray bought that car wash with money that the Kennedys gave him but that's not true. I owned that car wash for at least ten years before I even met him."

To his knowledge, Edgardo Villalobos said Murray bought two car washes, one within a year of Marilyn's death located on 3131 West Pico Boulevard in Los Angeles, today called Pico Car Wash. The second car wash was allegedly purchased by Murray in 1967 on 11166 Venice Boulevard in Culver City, presently Shine & Brite Hand Car Wash.

Villalobos relayed, "Murray bought car washes, two of them that I know. The one I found out about first was the one on Manhattan and Pico, and years later, the one in West LA . . . Dick Williams was an ambulance driver and he told me about the one on Pico. He knew Murray and he's the one that said, 'That's Murray's car wash.' He told me it was his. I keep hearing that Murray got some money from somebody, and there's a scandal there, and he bought hot car washes. Somebody gave him money because that's the next thing that happened. He took a lot of money. The reporters kept bugging me, saying I transported her, and I said, 'No, I didn't transport her.' That's when I start hearing that Murray took the money but it was quite a while after Marilyn's death. Not immediately . . . I don't believe she committed suicide. I have a feeling somebody took care of business there . . .

"The one in West LA they said was Murray's, too. Sepulveda and Venice was probably right because I heard Murray had a car wash near the Culver City station, which was in that area. I knew Murray really well. He didn't have anything. He didn't own it before. He was poor. He was no wealthy person. Where did he get the money to buy the car washes? It's a very expensive thing.

"The guys were out of hand in Santa Monica and not doing their job, so Mr. Schaefer said, 'I want you to go work over there and manage the place,' and that was seven or eight years after Marilyn died. So, I left the main house [on Beverly] to work at the Santa Monica station as a manager. That's when I learned about the other car wash in West LA, over lunch. When I was working there in the Santa Monica station, the guys would get around, and that's when I found out Murray wasn't even working there anymore. I remember clearly, he stopped working on an ambulance. He completely left the ambulance service. It makes sense because of the car washes. I stayed there in Santa Monica for two years then came back to the main station."

Mrs. Leib curiously added, "All the people that worked on the ambulance with Murray came to the car wash [on Sepulveda and Venice]. Murray spoke to them and I know he knew them."

Although Mrs. Leib denies that her late husband Murray received bribes from the Kennedys, she nonetheless believes the Kennedys were directly responsible for Marilyn Monroe's death. "The only thing that upsets me about the whole thing is that the Kennedys would get away with this," Mrs. Leib said to Jay Margolis. "I don't care about anything else. Somebody sat down and figured out how they were going to get away with this. I can't see why the Kennedys shouldn't be held more accountable than if I had done this. I think it's terrible for one family to have this kind of influence. I do. The idea of passing her around like that from the President to Bobby Kennedy with a wife and kids and respectability is terrible. It's awful. They used her like a dirty dishrag and she certainly was no match for the Kennedys. She knew a lot of things that they didn't want her to know but that's why she's dead. If one of them did do it, I'd like to see them held responsible."[16]

DETECTIVE LYNN FRANKLIN PULLS OVER A VERY DRUNK PETER LAWFORD

In the *Say Goodbye to the President* BBC TV documentary, former LA Mayor Sam Yorty recalled, "Chief Parker told me confidentially that Bobby Kennedy was supposed to be north of Los Angeles. Some say he was making a speech. But that actually, he said he was seen at the Beverly Hilton Hotel in Los Angeles . . . on the very night that she died." Detective Thad Brown's brother Finis, also a detective, relayed to Anthony Summers, "I talked to contacts who had seen Kennedy and Lawford at the Beverly Hilton Hotel the day she took the overdose."

At 12:10 a.m. on August 5, 1962, a very drunk Peter Lawford, driving a Lincoln Continental sedan, was heading east along Olympic Boulevard. His speed was estimated to be 70–80 mph. Franklin flashed on his red light. After reaching the intersection at Robertson, the Lincoln soon came to a stop. Based upon Franklin's own book and his interview with biographers Brown and Barham, the following was the exchange:

> FRANKLIN: Pete, what the hell do you think you're doing? . . . Your headlights are off and you were traveling seventy-five miles an hour.
>
> LAWFORD: I'm sorry. I have to get somebody to the airport.
>
> FRANKLIN: You're heading in the wrong direction. You should be headed west not east.
>
> LAWFORD: But first I have to check my friend out of the Beverly Hilton Hotel.
>
> FRANKLIN: You're still headed wrong. The Hilton is two miles in the other direction.

Franklin glanced at Dr. Greenson in the front passenger seat.

LAWFORD: He's a doctor. He's just riding along with us to the airport.

Aiming his flashlight at the back seat, Franklin was surprised to see Bobby Kennedy.

FRANKLIN: Evening, sir.

Kennedy nodded.

LAWFORD: We've got to get the Attorney General checked out of the Hilton, and there's only a few minutes before his plane leaves.

FRANKLIN: Well, you wouldn't have gotten there at all the way you were heading. The Hilton and the airport are both miles in the opposite direction.

Kennedy became mad at Lawford.

KENNEDY: I told you, stupid!

Kennedy then turned to Detective Franklin.

KENNEDY: Can we go now?

FRANKLIN: Sure. Just don't take it at seventy-five miles an hour.

Lawford turned the car around and drove away.

In the hours before Marilyn's death was announced, Franklin did not make the connection between Marilyn and Bobby Kennedy who, he told biographers Brown and Barham, "was wearing chinos and a tattered dress shirt."

If we look back at Heymann's interview with Peter Lawford, the British actor mentioned himself along with Bobby Kennedy and Greenson as co-conspirators responsible for Marilyn's death. These were the same three men pulled over by Detective Franklin who, in his book, noted:

"The significant thing that might be related to the hit attack on me was that I . . . could testify . . . Robert Kennedy had been in Los Angeles . . . in the company of a doctor [Ralph Greenson] who had treated Monroe that same night and who . . . may have been responsible for her death."

In fact, Lynn Franklin met Schaefer Ambulance attendant James Hall in 1992 during the filming of *The Marilyn Files* documentary and took special interest in what Hall had to say about Dr. Greenson. Franklin subsequently deduced, "I'm not trying to cover the case here, but for my money, she was murdered and Robert Kennedy at least knew about it, maybe ordered the killing, and certainly tried to cover it up." On September 26, 2010, retired OCID detective Mike Rothmiller responded to a phone call from Jay Margolis:

MARGOLIS:	Do you know what happened to Marilyn's diary?
ROTHMILLER:	No.
MARGOLIS:	Did Donald Wolfe quote you correctly regarding what you saw in the diary?
ROTHMILLER:	Yes.
MARGOLIS:	Do you think Lynn Franklin's for real?
ROTHMILLER:	I think he's for real.
MARGOLIS:	Do the police believe she was murdered?
ROTHMILLER:	Many do.
MARGOLIS:	Do you think she was murdered?
ROTHMILLER:	That's what it appears to be.

Lawford's best friend Joe Naar told biographer James Spada, "Peter wouldn't dare go over there. He made sure it was me who was going to go over there." Confirming what he'd told biographer Donald Spoto, Naar assured Margolis he answered a call from Peter Lawford at 11:30 p.m., about forty minutes before Lawford was pulled over by Detective Franklin.

When informed about Lynn Franklin's recollection, Naar exclaimed, "He is so full of shit. That is the most insane thing I have ever heard. I've *never* heard that one. Bobby was in the back seat? Peter was driving? I was on the phone with Peter most of that night. How in the world could he be in the car driving and drinking? He hadn't had a drink. That's one-on-one with me at 11:30 at night. Now who's telling the truth?

"What asshole would believe that jerk-off cop who's trying to get his name in the papers? Don't even repeat that story. You say it once and it gets out there and somebody repeats it and ten times later someone thinks it's the truth. If they had any idea of the truth it's not even one thousand percent close. It's somebody's imagination. What are they, writers or something? I mean that's the most insane thing I've ever heard. You're giving them too much respect. You're interviewing the wrong people. They know shit about it. Why would you talk to these assholes?"

After Margolis pointed out that Lynn Franklin was a well-decorated officer who had received the prestigious CHA Award, Joe Naar remarked, "If you're the highest decorated officer, you don't need that kind of publicity. He wouldn't talk like that. And of course, they're gonna put medals after his name . . .

"People like Warren Beatty think I know exactly what happened. That I'm covering it up because I'm a friend of the [Kennedy] family, and that what really happened is that Bobby came down and killed her. It's such bullshit. Warren heard all sorts of things. In those days, everybody was talking about how Bobby killed her. 'Bobby had her killed.'"

Refuting Joe Naar's insistence that Peter Lawford wasn't drunk on the night of August 4, Officer Lynn Franklin stated to Brown and Barham that the British actor "appeared drunk, terrified, and coming apart at the seams." Furthermore, Fred Otash confirmed that Lawford "looked like hell, trembling in the manner of a junkie going through cold turkey withdrawal. He was drunk, stoned, and an emotional basket case."

Lawford's close friend Milt Ebbins recalled, "I spoke to Peter at his house at one-thirty that night. Bullets Durgom told me he was there until one-thirty. At three o'clock I called Peter and there was no answer. He always disconnected the phone when he went to bed. He was very drunk when I spoke to him at one-thirty, and he couldn't have driven in that condition. I'm sure he passed out and that was that . . . Peter was getting drunker by the minute . . . He'd be coughing then be silent."

So, while Naar recalled spending most of the night talking with Lawford, Ebbins was adamant that Lawford had his phone disconnected. Never mind that a police officer (Franklin), a former police officer (Otash), and a best friend (Ebbins) all attested that Lawford was inebriated that night.[17]

DETECTIVE FRANKLIN CONNECTS THE DOTS

In the documentary *Marilyn Monroe: A Case for Murder*, Marilyn's next-door neighbors to the west, Abe Charles Landau and his wife Ruby Landau, placed the sighting of an ambulance close to midnight:

> LANDAU: We had been out to a party. We came home and the place was like Grand Central Station. The cars were all the way up the alley . . . Some limousine was here. I don't know who it was. And, of course, police cars and the ambulance.
>
> REPORTER: After you went inside your house, what happened?
>
> LANDAU: Someone knocked on the door and wanted to know what we knew about Marilyn Monroe, and we told them nothing.
>
> REPORTER: Did the visitor describe himself as a reporter? Did he identify himself as a police officer?
>
> LANDAU: He didn't identify himself at all.

In 1992, during and after the filming of *The Marilyn Files* TV special, Detective Lynn Franklin talked to James Hall and Fred Otash. The two men reported remarkably similar observations. They each independently placed Sgt. Marvin Iannone at the scene with Peter Lawford. After speaking with Otash, Franklin noted in his book how "at about 11:45 p.m. on the night of her death, the place had been bustling with activity. An ambulance was at the scene."

Franklin wrote that, in addition to Fred Otash, he "got another witness to verify Iannone's presence at the Monroe residence, well before he was officially dispatched. James Hall . . . an attendant with Schaefer Ambulances that night, told me that Sgt. Iannone and Peter Lawford had been present in the home when Dr. Greenson injected Marilyn with the fatal heart needle."

Detective Lynn Franklin placed the pieces together, pointing toward Kennedy involvement in Marilyn's death. "Fred Otash . . . told me that he had bugged the homes of Peter Lawford and Marilyn Monroe," Franklin wrote. " 'I've got something you must hear, Lynn,' he told me. 'Iannone is dirty as hell . . .' His wire-taps had recorded a conversation between Peter Lawford and Marvin Iannone at five to midnight on August 4, 1962." Franklin also relayed how Otash recorded and made note of a failed attempt by Peter Lawford to phone Sgt. Marvin Iannone at LAPD's Purdue station at 1:45 a.m. on August 5, 1962.

Sgt. Marvin Iannone's presence at the house around 11:45 p.m. suggests he was stationed at the Monroe residence on orders from the Attorney General. As Greenson injected the heart needle into Marilyn's chest, James Hall saw Lawford and Iannone enter the guest cottage. Iannone had done this kind of detail for the Kennedys several times before. As biographer Donald Wolfe noted, "Iannone was known to work for Hamilton in Intelligence, and whenever the President or the Attorney General visited the Lawfords, Iannone received the special duty assignment from Hamilton to work the Lawford beach house."[18]

GREENSON'S MOTIVES
FOR KILLING HIS PATIENT

As a March 2, 1961, letter to Ralph Greenson proved, Marilyn Monroe was simultaneously carrying on trysts with Frank Sinatra and her former co-star Yves Montand, a French actor, although according to Marilyn, Montand eventually begged off.

Hildi Greenson addressed the rumors that her late husband had bedded his star patient, "It's just ludicrous. It's so dumb." But Peter Lawford said Greenson *was* sleeping with her. This is something Lawford claimed he didn't know until after Marilyn's death when he heard Mafia-Teamster tapes and listened to "sounds of their lovemaking." Since her home was bugged, one of the places where Marilyn and Greenson slept together was on 12305 Fifth Helena Drive. Ralph Greenson himself relayed, "I always had a weak spot in my heart to rescue damsels in distress. But I learned from that. Don't trust it, boy, don't trust it."

But this damsel in particular was the quintessential sexy woman. Greenson's daughter Joan remembered how everything Marilyn did unconsciously radiated sex like a force in her body.

"Why was it that no matter what she did she was striking?" Joan Greenson asked. "Why was it that she could just sit still on a bench, or in a chair, and you would end up staring? . . . There have been many sexy ladies in Hollywood but nothing like Marilyn. I was fascinated to see the way she sat. She would cross her legs at the knees, and lean forward; her left elbow was on top of her knee; her right elbow in the palm of her hand; her chin resting on her right palm.

"This seemed like a very natural and easy pose for her. She often would listen in that position. I had a chance to watch someone move around who was totally at home with their body. And I never tired of watching . . . Marilyn wore nothing under her clothes. She didn't wear underpants or stockings or bra for the most part. I must admit when I first realized this, I found it shocking. Marilyn really hated to have anything that restricted any of her natural movements . . . She could also be extremely exhibitionistic."

Mansfield's former press secretary Raymond Strait told Jay Margolis, "Women like that who are very lonesome and feel like they've been abandoned are always trying to find some man that will love them and they think that sex is the way they do it. Nine times out of ten, they're looking for a father image. Jayne Mansfield, same way. She was three years old when her father died of a heart attack. The difference between Jayne and Marilyn is Marilyn was used by men while Jayne used men. Just a reverse."

Greenson once told a candidate in training, "There is the problem of a change in motivation that happens when, for example, the patient develops an acute sexual transference. Instead of coming for treatment because they want to get rid of symptoms or neurosis, they come out of love for you . . . This happens almost routinely with women patients."

Some of Greenson's colleagues bitterly called him on what seemed like reckless actions on the psychiatrist's part. Dr. Leo Rangell, a rival of Greenson's said, "This was seductive behavior, not therapeutic behavior . . . We all have very needy, traumatized patients. Very few of them end up in our families . . . She did because she was Marilyn Monroe! Even 'family therapy' doesn't mean therapy in the analyst's family . . . His earlier writings would never condone what he did."

Dr. Melvin Mandel relayed, "If it was true that she came from a tremendously deprived background, you couldn't go on with her in a strictly analytic way. It wouldn't work . . . If an analyst . . . has an unconscious wish to be on stage (and Greenson *was* a superb performer), he may . . . identify himself with prominent people."[19]

Peter Lawford mentioned to Heymann that Marilyn's free-association tapes referenced the affair with her psychiatrist and how Mafia-Teamster tapes recorded "sounds of their lovemaking" at 12305 Fifth Helena Drive. In fact, Marilyn Monroe's aggressively seductive behavior is documented in full bloom in a paper Greenson wrote on January 12, 1964, entitled, "Drugs in the Psychotherapeutic Situation." It is safe to assume Ralph Greenson was writing about his star patient in this work because the descriptive characteristics fit her perfectly.

He wrote, "Sometimes all that is necessary is time; just waiting without interfering will give the patient the opportunity to recover his reasonable ego. Sometimes it may be necessary to interfere quite drastically, psychologically or even by introducing drugs . . . For example, an hysterical-depressive-impulsive woman patient became furious with me when she felt I was rejecting her sexual wishes and stormed out of the office. She was an intelligent woman . . . with a history of promiscuous behavior prior to her unhappy marriage to an austere academician [Arthur Miller].

"The above incident occurred during the fourth month of her analysis with me . . . She was impulsive and there was a history of some acting out in her adolescent spitefulness and defiance. Her motivation for treatment had been strong, since she had depressive moods, was sexually frigid, and was unable to work effectively in her job . . . She did return the following day . . . She still felt angry about my supposed cruel rejection of her, but by the middle of the hour I was able to work on this material to try to find past events in her life when she felt similarly rejected . . .

"About one year later, a similar constellation of events occurred, and again she fell into a rage. She refused to work on this but vented her fury on me by silence, nail biting, and leaving the hour early . . . That evening her husband had to leave her alone to attend a meeting, and she reacted to this unforeseen event as if it were another *maternal rejection* . . . The pre-oedipal hatred for the mother, which had been stirred up, plus being deserted by her husband unleashed primitive anger, spite, oral sensual desires, and a powerful need to be punished, which she could not contain."

Besides the need to conceal sexual indiscretions that could destroy his highly successful psychoanalytic career, Dr. Ralph Greenson had an alternative motive for silencing his star patient. The fact is, Greenson was at his wits end treating Marilyn Monroe. A little more than two weeks after her death, he would complain to his friend and colleague Dr. Marianne Kris that he was becoming a victim of countertransference, which, he explained "is an inappropriate reaction of the therapist to his patient."

According to Greenson, analysts' "difficulty with empathy disrupts their timing and dosage of interpretation so that their interventions feel tactless and inaccurate . . . Anger, sexual feelings, boredom, sleepiness, restlessness and uncontrollable laughter" on the part of the analyst "are all indications of the possibility of countertransference."

Greenson pointed out that all people experience transferences. However, during an analytic session, a transference is a patient's "experiencing of feelings, drives, attitudes, fantasies, and defenses toward a person in the present" such as the analyst "which do not befit that person but are a repetition of reactions originating in regard to significant persons of early childhood, unconsciously displaced onto figures in the present."

Ralph Greenson wrote about the maddening frustrations he experienced while treating Marilyn: "If I behaved in a way which hurt her she reacted as though it was the end of the world and could not rest until peace had been re-established, but peace could be reconciliation and death. As a consequence I became aware that any negative transference required instant handling, with the result that she would call me at all hours of day and night, whenever any negative transference cropped up. I saw her seven days a week because she was terribly lonely, the more so as she began to get rid of a lot of people around her who only took advantage of her."

Curiously, Greenson helped his patient decide who was taking advantage of her and told Marilyn she should try to make friends outside the people she worked with at the studio. After he saw little improvement in Marilyn's psychological state, Greenson actually questioned the methods he'd been employing with her, "I have some misgivings about how correct was I in my form of treatment and how much was I being led by countertransference feelings," which are, "inappropriate reaction[s] of the therapist to his patient."

It was, perhaps, Greenson's ego as well as monetary considerations that prevented him from acting ethically by withdrawing from the case. Indeed, after Marilyn's death, he continued to take on new patients and "treat" them despite being aware of his own countertransference feelings.

There is strong evidence that Dr. Greenson grew increasingly tired of playing "surrogate father" to Marilyn Monroe. "There was a real washing out of the usual doctor boundaries," remarked Dr. Robert Litman of the Suicide Prevention Team. "I would never suggest that there was anything wrong in the relationship. He virtually adopted a person. There's a danger when someone gets that involved."

The idea of adding Marilyn to his household was too much for Greenson to handle, especially in light of how she contacted him at all hours, several days a week. Still, as Professor Douglas Kirsner ominously noted, "Greenson told his colleagues that he decided to offer his family as a substitute for the family Monroe never had because she would have killed herself sooner if he had committed her to a mental hospital."

On August 15, 1962, Greenson penned a letter to Marilyn's poet friend Norman Rosten. "I should have played it safe and put her in a sanitarium," he admitted, "but that would only have been safe for me and deadly for her."

Greenson's son Danny agreed that, following Marilyn's hospitalization at the Payne Whitney Psychiatric Clinic in early 1961, his father "felt that therapy as he knew it wasn't working. He couldn't hospitalize her, because everyone came to stare and gawp at her, which was awful, and medication wasn't helping in her case."

Milt Ebbins, meanwhile, recalled the good doctor making "a statement that Marilyn was doomed and eventually she would've done it anyway."

Greenson was convinced that, during the last month of Marilyn's life, she couldn't go one day without a crisis, and his brother-in-law Mickey Rudin agreed. Rudin, who was the attorney for Frank Sinatra as well as Marilyn Monroe, told Donald Spoto that Greenson's relationship with Marilyn "helped kill him . . . 'Don't get yourself all emotionally involved' . . . should have been a rule for a psychoanalyst . . . He involved her *totally* beyond what he should have with the family . . . He totally involved her where he was worried about her all the time."

Rudin pointed to the great difficulty Greenson had experienced months earlier, before departing on May 10, 1962, for a much-needed five-week vacation: "When he went to Europe, I was delighted. He needed a week. Some time. Just needed it. There wasn't a crisis just with the picture [*Something's Got to Give*]. There was a crisis every day."

Apparently, this had been the case as early as June 29, 1961, when Marilyn was recovering from the removal of her gall bladder. "At that time she was recovering from gall bladder surgery," Greenson recalled. "She was taking very little medication, but she was terribly, terribly lonely . . . I saw her at that time seven days a week, mainly because she was lonely and had no one to see her, nothing to do if I didn't see her."

Mickey Rudin told J. Randy Taraborrelli, author of *Sinatra: Behind the Legend*, "She could have a crisis over what she was having for lunch, she was that emotional and high-strung. She could have had an imagined crisis."

When Donald Spoto took a look at Marilyn's phone records, he saw that she'd consistently call her lawyer Mickey Rudin anywhere up to eight times a day. "I wasn't impatient with her," Rudin told Spoto. "It was time-consuming as hell. It was a pain in the ass."

It was also Rudin, described by Frank Sinatra's former valet George Jacobs as a "combination bag man, hit man, and Hollywood hustler," who explained why Greenson had been so insistent on taking that five-week European vacation during the spring of '62: "His wife was Swiss. This was an annual pilgrimage to her family. He'd probably beat his head if he didn't. How much exhaustion can a man who had a coronary condition take? . . . The problem faced with Marilyn having to do the picture [*Something's Got to Give*] is that . . . she didn't have any money."

Marilyn's long-time friend Gloria Romanoff reflected to Margolis, "She never had any real money. The house she died in was the first home she ever owned. It was a very simple house but it was everything to her. Marilyn was just very genuine. She had so little money and now it pains me that these people who are in charge of her estate are making fortunes, money she could have used."[20]

From March 1962 until her death, Marilyn was living on 12305 Fifth Helena but would occasionally drop by her old apartment on 882 North Doheny Drive. Hildi remembered one time after an analytic session at the Greensons', her husband later learned she had taken in a taxi cab driver, who had driven her home. Greenson said he took action against this self-destructive behavior by allowing Marilyn to become one with the family.

She would often join in, politely offering to clean the dishes after supper with the Greensons. Hildi reflected, "My husband said, when he wanted to bring her into the house, 'This is just not a case that one can analyze. She has to work through a great deal more before she can be analyzed.' She needed to become a whole person again." Greenson once told his patient-friend actress Celeste Holm, "Celeste, this woman has no concept of family life. She was with Marianne Kris for years, but not one thing has touched her. So I'm trying to give her a model. I'm trying to give her some concept of the way it ought to be."[21]

Soon, Marilyn became a member of Greenson's family and at one point, wearing dark glasses, a wig and scarf, joined his son Danny to help him find an apartment. She was even showing up to Greenson's lectures in this disguise as well. Joan wrote, "Father liked to give lectures, and he was an excellent public speaker. He would wait for the last few stragglers and latecomers to settle into their seats. At this moment I looked around, and I saw one of the stragglers was Marilyn in disguise. She looked incredible. She had on a brown, dowdy wig, with a scarf over it, tied under her chin. She had on her sporty mink coat, under which she had this terrible, brown Pucci dress—the color was drab and dead. On her feet, without socks, thank God, were loafers.

"Marilyn sat in the seats just behind Mother and myself. When most of the auditorium was emptying, I watched as Marilyn got up and started to walk out. I watched the faces turn around and follow her with their eyes as she slowly made her way up the aisle. I knew no one recognized her, and only a few close friends of the family knew who that person was. But just her movement up the aisle made people stop and take notice and watch her as she exited. I told her that I thought her disguise was great, and we both thought it was pretty funny."

Hildi recalled, "When we'd have chamber music, my husband would invite her to come and listen. She'd sit in a corner and she'd turn away from the people and the musicians—just listening very intently, all huddled up." Greenson's patient actress Janice Rule became jealous when she learned that Marilyn had been invited to his living room recitals. Janice snidely remarked, "You knew I love music. How come you never invited me?" "You were never that ill." Greenson participated in these recitals albeit as a lousy violinist.

"She would sit in the living room in the big wing-backed chair," Joan reflected. "As Mozart, Schubert, or Vivaldi would start to be played, Marilyn would get totally lost and absorbed in the music. Slowly, she would start to move with the music, her arms and her torso. Her eyes would remain closed. Her movements were so beautifully sensual, and so seemingly private and personal." During the spring of 1962, an excited Marilyn invited her poet friend Norman Rosten and his wife Hedda to the Greensons' on several occasions.

Greenson detailed in his 1964 paper what happened when he announced to his star patient that he would have to depart for his European vacation on May 10, 1962. He wrote, "When I left for a five week summer vacation I felt it was indicated to leave her some medication which she might take when she felt depressed and agitated, i.e. rejected and tempted to act out. I prescribed a drug which is a quick acting antidepressant in combination with a sedative, Dexamyl®. I also hoped she would be benefited by having something from me to depend on . . .

"When I returned she told me that she carried a supply of the tablets with her at all times in a silver pill box, which she had bought especially to hold them. She never became severely depressed during my absence and felt that the possession of the pills had been a safeguard, a magical protection for her in my absence.

"A dream in which the silver pill box turned green just like the pills (that is, *everything turned into Greenson*) seemed to explain the unconscious meaning . . . *I felt it was indicated to prescribe drugs for her.* I can condense the situation by saying that, at the time of my vacation, I felt she would be unable to bear the depressive anxieties of being alone. The administering of the pill was an attempt to give her something of me to swallow, to take in, so that she could overcome the sense of terrible emptiness that would depress and infuriate her . . . *Drugs may aid in the interval between visits.*"[22]

Greenson's friend and colleague Milton Wexler conceded that not all meaningful treatments of psychoanalysis are successful, especially the unorthodox ones. "Greenson began to write more and more about the importance of the real relationship between the analyst and the patient," Milton Wexler relayed yet disagreed with this unconventional method and stated, "Once the symptoms were imbedded in that characteristic way of responding to the world, no amount of interpretation, enlightenment or bringing the unconscious into consciousness would do any good."

In Greenson's 1964 paper, he made it clear that Marilyn Monroe tried to come onto him during their first four months of analysis. When he rejected her sexual wishes, she saw it as another rejection and became very angry with him. A year later, she tried to come onto him again and he claimed he rejected her again. The psychiatrist wrote that she "fell into a rage." Peter Lawford said, to his great surprise no less, that Greenson finally succumbed to the seduction of the world's ultimate sex goddess.

Lawford told Heymann he heard Mafia-Teamster tapes of Marilyn and Greenson making love. Greenson himself admitted in his writings that she was very seductive and that because of her, he had fallen victim to countertransference. Greenson wrote, "One of the most frequent signals of countertransference reaction is . . . reacting sexually . . . to the transference manifestations" of the analysand. In other words, when a therapist has sex with his patient.[23]

In a 1974 paper titled "On Transitional Objects and Transference," which was compiled along with others in his 1978 book *Explorations in Psychoanalysis*, Ralph Greenson discussed the frustrations that he felt while treating Marilyn Monroe during the last months of her life and how he broached the subject of his European vacation. "I told an emotionally immature young woman patient, who had developed a very dependent transference to me, that I was going to attend an International Congress in Europe some three months hence," Greenson wrote. "We worked intensively on the multiple determinants of her clinging dependence, but made only insignificant progress."

The psychiatrist explained how he was trying to not make Marilyn so dependent on him. "The situation changed dramatically when one day she announced . . . she had discovered something that would tide her over my absence," Greenson wrote. "It was not some insight, not a new personal relationship, it was a chess piece. The young woman had recently been given a gift of a carved ivory chess set."

Still making little progress as time went on, Ralph Greenson continued to note Marilyn's growing attachment to him in the months leading up to her singing "Happy Birthday" for Jack Kennedy. This took place at Madison Square Garden on May 19, 1962. One piece from Marilyn's new chess set occupied the center of the discussion between the psychiatrist and his star patient. Greenson relayed, "The evening before her announcement, as she looked at the set, through the sparkling light of a glass of champagne, it suddenly struck her that I looked like the white knight . . . The realization immediately evoked in her a feeling of comfort, even triumph. The white knight was her protector."

Marilyn considered the white knight a temporary substitute for the psychiatrist while he left the country. "The patient's major concern about . . . my absence was a public performance of great importance to her professionally," explained Ralph Greenson. "She now felt confident of success because she could conceal her white knight in her handkerchief or scarf; she was certain that he would protect her from nervousness, anxiety or bad luck."

On May 10, 1962, Greenson dashed to Europe for a little rest and relaxation before his scheduled lectures. Joan explained, "Father was to give a lecture in Israel for the International Psychoanalytic Society, and from there they planned to visit my mother's family in Switzerland."

Greenson wrote, "I was relieved and delighted to learn . . . that her performance had indeed been a smashing success . . . However, I received several panicky transatlantic telephone calls from her. The patient had lost the white knight and was beside herself with terror and gloom, like a child who has lost her security blanket."

Eunice Murray remembered, "Marilyn took a handsome chess piece from the set she had bought in Mexico—one knight to wrap in her handkerchief while she sang. A friend [Dr. Greenson] had suggested she take it and pretend he was right there with her to lend her courage. Marilyn . . . lost it somewhere in New York."

"That vacation we had, it was constant telephone calls," Greenson's wife Hildi recalled. "We were in Israel and we got phone calls from Marilyn and from the studio. Finally, when we got to Switzerland, my husband said, 'I promised them I'd come back and we'll save the picture.' That was the idea."

Greenson wrote more than two weeks after his patient's death, "I left Marilyn in the hands of a colleague [Milton Wexler] whom she knew and I told her that I would return if it was necessary. As you know, after three weeks my colleague called me, and finally she called me, and I returned to Los Angeles [late on the night of June 6]. She was depressed, but within 24 hours of my return she had bounced up again and I reported to the movie studio that she would return to work within 48 hours. They, however, in their fury at Elizabeth Taylor, decided to fire Marilyn, which they did [on June 8]."

According to Greenson's daughter Joan, she and her brother Danny received a call from Marilyn on June 2, the day after Marilyn's thirty-sixth birthday, and the actress "sounded really druggy. Her thick-tongued-ness usually was a sign that she had taken lots of sleeping medication but still couldn't sleep . . . Danny and I went to her house. Her room was dark. The black-out drapes were pulled shut, and not a drop of light was let in. Marilyn was in bed with just a sheet pulled up around her. Her bed looked like she had had a bad night. It was totally disheveled. She asked Danny to come sit next to her bed and talk to her . . .

"What a sad picture, to have Marilyn in that darkened cave of a room so terribly unhappy. And there seemed that there was little, if anything, anyone could do to help her. What a terrible feeling of helplessness and hopelessness. My father didn't seem to be able to help her. I knew she had been talking to him on the telephone. Nothing seemed to be able to help . . . She seemed like such a contrast. In a sense she was so child-like herself yet she was so streetwise and suspicious of things and could see the ulterior motives. She'd had such a rotten childhood, and now she had made it and it felt like if there was any fairness in the world, Marilyn should have it easy and good now."

Hildi added, "She was bright and lovely and interesting, but there was something really very schizzy about her."

"Marilyn didn't want to interrupt the psychiatrist's trip with her problems," Mrs. Murray reported. "His son had made a point of requesting that Marilyn let him get through the speaking engagement in Switzerland and a side trip to Tel Aviv without calling him home."

Dr. Milton Wexler was to be phoned during an emergency while Ralph Greenson was out of the country. "A Dr. Wexler was on call for Dr. Greenson's patients," Mrs. Murray remembered. "When he came out to visit Marilyn, he took one look at the formidable array of sedatives on her bedside table and swept them all into his black bag. To him, they must have seemed a dangerous arsenal."

"It was clear that there was really no way Marilyn was going to make it through that picture without my father here or without some massive help," Joan Greenson recalled. "Father flew from Switzerland to New York, New York to LA. He took a cab home. I remember greeting him at about 10 p.m. at the front door. He looked really tired. I took his suitcase into the house, and he found his car keys and went straight to the garage. He said he would just stop by and see Marilyn and would be back shortly."

Dr. Greenson took up the story in his 1974 paper: "A colleague of mine [Milton Wexler] who saw her in that interval said that all his interventions were to no avail and he reluctantly suggested that I cut short my trip and return. I hated to interrupt my vacation and I doubted whether my return would be beneficial."

It turned out to be very beneficial. In fact, the moment Marilyn saw Ralph Greenson after his early return to the United States, as the psychiatrist explained, "Her anxiety and depression lifted. It then became possible to work . . . on how she had used me as a good luck charm rather than an analyst. The talisman, the chess piece, served her as a magical means of averting bad luck or evil. It protected her against losing something precious."[24]

Nevertheless, by June 22, 1962, Greenson was telling colleagues and friends that he was fed up with Marilyn Monroe. In letters to his friend Lucille Ostrow and fellow psychoanalyst Anna Freud, he complained about Marilyn having ruined his vacation and how, in light of her firing from *Something's Got to Give*, his early return home had been a complete waste of time. Greenson wrote to Anna Freud, "This was a most frustrating experience, since now I was back home and she was feeling fine, but she no longer had to work and therefore I was free to return to Europe, which was impossible."

On July 2, 1962, Freud replied, "I have tried to follow your fate in the newspapers and I saw that your patient was acting up. But I did not realize that this would interrupt your holiday and I do feel sorry for this. I wonder what will happen to her and with her." Marilyn Monroe was now the subject of gossip among leading psychoanalysts.

Freud family maid Paula Fichtl relayed how she heard from Anna that Ralph Greenson was "the last person to phone [Marilyn] the night of her death. Later it is even claimed that he had killed Marilyn Monroe. In 1985, the Swiss newspaper *Blick*, which reprinted this allegation was sentenced to a fine—of which 10.000 Swiss francs went to the Anna Freud Centre in London."

"That felt very good, winning my suit," Hildi Greenson told private investigator Cathy Griffin.

"That was the story that she was shot in the heart?"

"Yeah, and they had to pay and I sent it to the Anna Freud Clinic in London. They had to give $20,000 . . . They had to pay me for my lawyers in Switzerland and the lawyer here, and I think I came out with the travel fare for going to Switzerland."

Indeed, contrary to what Donald Spoto claimed in his Monroe biography, the assertions that she was murdered didn't commence with the writings of authors Frank Capell (*The Strange Death of Marilyn Monroe*, 1964), Norman Mailer (*Marilyn: A Biography*, 1973), and Robert Slatzer (*The Life and Curious Death of Marilyn Monroe*, 1974). On January 5, 1964, the *Oakland Tribune* noted, "Following her death, Dr. Greenson was flooded with mail from haters who denounced him as a 'criminal so-and-so . . . a Communist quack . . . a Hollywood murderer.' There were so many threats to his life that Dr. Greenson was compelled to turn them over to his lawyer."

Just over two weeks after Marilyn died, Dr. Greenson wrote to Dr. Kris: "And on top of it all, the notoriety, the press all over the world writing about it and constantly linking my name with this tragic event, and often so wrongly . . . I was besieged by phone calls from all over the world. I received many terrible letters from people, accusing me of being a murderer or going after her money." Frank Capell's controversial red pamphlet indeed was released two years *after* the threats to Greenson's life. According to Greenson himself, these threats began within days of Marilyn's death.[25]

DOES GREENSON'S OFFICIAL STORY CHECK OUT?

In late 1973, Ralph Greenson publicly stated that, on August 4, 1962, after leaving Marilyn's house, he and his wife had dinner at the residence of a Mr. and Mrs. Arnold Alberts. However, a confidential source revealed to Jay Margolis that Greenson actually went to the home of actor Eddie Albert and his wife Margo. Albert would star in the 1963 movie *Captain Newman, M.D.*, based on Greenson's own World War II experiences.

According to Greenson, he didn't return home until "around midnight" and was tempted to call Marilyn but "didn't want to wake her." For years, his family has maintained that he did not receive a call from the Monroe home until at least 2:00 a.m. on August 5. The police report stated that Greenson arrived there shortly after 3:30. Dr. Hyman Engelberg then pronounced Marilyn dead at 3:35 or at 3:50 a.m., depending on whether the first or follow-up reports are to be believed.

Interestingly, Mrs. Murray blurted out to Sgt. Jack Clemmons, the first policeman officially on the scene, that Marilyn's lifeless body was discovered around midnight, and Clemmons stated that neither Greenson nor Engelberg disagreed with this recollection. However, in 1982, when investigator Al Tomich of the District Attorney's Office asked Engelberg about his arriving at midnight and then waiting several hours to call the police, the physician dismissed this as "Nonsense. Absolute, utter nonsense."

Later, Clemmons noted how the three principals told Detective Sgt. Robert Byron a different story from the one he'd first heard: Mrs. Murray had called Dr. Greenson at 3:30 a.m. Living less than two miles away, Greenson told her he would be right over and instructed the housekeeper to call Dr. Engelberg. Greenson then arrived before Engelberg and, using a fireplace poker, broke the only unbarred window to Marilyn's bedroom because, he claimed, her door was locked.

"The door was locked to the bedroom," Hyman Engelberg said to Al Tomich. "Mrs. Murray first looked in through the window and saw her, and the way they got in was, I guess, through the window. Either they smashed a pane or turned a lock or were able to push it open. I don't recall which."

A photograph still exists of a man's hand pointing at the broken window, proving someone could not reach in to undo the latch without cutting his or her fingers on the glass. According to the official police report, Engelberg stated that, within five minutes of receiving the 3:30 a.m. call from Mrs. Murray, he got dressed and drove to Marilyn's home before then pronouncing her dead another five minutes later. However, this would have been impossible if one is to believe what the same physician claimed twenty years later.

"I was parked in the basement of the parking area of a small apartment house and somebody parked in back of me," Engelberg recalled in a statement he made to the District Attorney's Office. "That must have delayed me about ten or fifteen minutes . . . I was living in an apartment on Beverly Boulevard, just west of Doheny."[26]

Contrary to the official police report, Joan Greenson wrote in her unpublished manuscript that the call to the Greenson home, alerting her parents that Marilyn was in trouble, was made "in the middle of the night," *not* at 3:30 a.m.

"I went to bed around 8:00," Joan recalled. "I fell asleep fairly quickly and didn't hear my parents come home . . . I was awakened sometime in the middle of the night by the phone ringing. Then I heard my father . . . head down the stairs . . . Mother followed, and I heard the car drive away."

"I was very worried, and my daughter was here and we immediately stayed up," Hildi Greenson added. "We just went downstairs and sat around until my husband called me and said that Marilyn was dead."

This contradicted what Joan wrote in her manuscript: "I must have been in my bed for maybe five minutes when I heard the phone ring, and I got out of bed and went back to my mother's bedroom, and I knew it was Father on the phone. Mother turned to me and said, 'It's all over.'"[27]

Greenson, Engelberg, and Mrs. Murray subsequently told the police that Marilyn's door had been locked. Hildi said the same thing to private investigator Cathy Griffin: "Her room was locked and with a bolt lock. It wasn't a lock that you could go through with a credit card and open it or undo it. It was locked and my husband had to break the window to get in." When asked by Griffin if Marilyn usually locked the door when she went to bed, Mrs. Greenson replied, "I don't think so, but it was locked that night."

As it happens, with the exception of those leading outside, none of the doors in the Monroe home had locks that operated. This was confirmed by secretary Cherie Redmond who wrote to Marilyn's close friend Hedda Rosten, "There isn't one door in the place that locks." And David Marshall also noted, "Linda Nuñez . . . explained . . . that no one in her family ever had a key to any of the locks on any of the interior doors . . . The locks were old-fashioned skeleton key deadbolts . . . No one in her family ever locked any doors other than the front and back for that reason."

If biographers Peter Harry Brown and Patte Barham were accurate in their assertion that Mrs. Murray had a skeleton key attached to her own keychain, then why would Dr. Greenson need to break the window to gain entrance to Marilyn's bedroom? Besides, after her terrible experience at the Payne Whitney Psychiatric Clinic, Marilyn wasn't eager to go behind any more locked doors. Accordingly, when Marilyn's genealogist Roy Turner asked his friend Eunice Murray if Marilyn's door was locked on the night of August 4, 1962, she replied, "No."

Turner told Jay Margolis, "I never felt Marilyn killed herself . . . When I met Mrs. Murray, it was either '82 or '83. I think that was about the only time we ever sat down face-to-face. We had talked on the phone and written letters. I told her about what I was doing and how I was coming out to California and that I would like to interview her. And she was okay with that, so I picked her up and we went to a café down in Venice.

"At that time, she was living with her twin daughters in Santa Monica. She showed me a few things of Marilyn's that Joe DiMaggio had given her. At that point, she was very lucid. I had sent her a questionnaire with some questions on it. She got answers down for some of the questions and she didn't answer some of the questions. Next to 'Was Marilyn's bedroom door locked?' she answered, 'No.'

"The BBC show aired in 1985. It was called *Say Goodbye to the President* and Mrs. Murray was being interviewed . . . As soon as it was over, I called her on the phone and taped the conversation. I told her I just watched her on the BBC and said, 'You made this statement and it just blew my mind because you say Robert Kennedy was there that day. And out of all of our conversations, you never once mentioned that he was there the day of Marilyn's death.' She said, 'Yes, he was definitely there the day she died.' That was the most important statement on that tape.

"When I was in eighth grade, I wrote Dr. Greenson because I was doing a school project. We had to do a biography on a famous person and I chose Marilyn. I told him what I was doing and he basically answered that there wasn't a whole lot he could tell me. But Dr. Greenson did say he did not believe Marilyn committed suicide and that was not her intent at that particular time in her life."[28]

On her last night, Joe DiMaggio, Jr., phoned Marilyn at 7:00 p.m. and the call lasted until 7:15. Donald Spoto noted, "In his . . . police interview, he said . . . Marilyn picked up the phone while he was watching on television the seventh inning of a baseball game: the Baltimore Orioles against the Anaheim Angels . . . The game began . . . after seven-thirty Eastern Daylight Time, which would have put the seventh inning at about ten o'clock," or 7:00 p.m. California time. Joe DiMaggio, Sr., said, "They spoke for about fifteen minutes and Marilyn seemed quite normal and in good spirits."

"When I left at 7:15, she seemed somewhat depressed," Dr. Greenson wrote to Dr. Marianne Kris in a highly defensive letter. "A half hour later she phoned me at home to tell me she had gotten some good news and she seemed quite pleasant and more cheerful . . . She sounded pleasant on the phone, although somewhat depressed, but by no means acutely so."

Ralph Greenson and Eunice Murray claim Marilyn called him at home to inform the psychiatrist of Joe DiMaggio, Jr.'s phone call and how happy she was to hear her stepson break off his engagement to Pamela Reis. As for what happened next, Greenson relayed, "About an hour later, someone [Mickey Rudin] called the housekeeper and said that Marilyn had sounded funny on the phone, but the housekeeper said that Dr. Greenson had just been there and she did not want to disturb Marilyn."

Seemingly protecting himself at every corner, the good doctor produced an answer to every possible question regarding the timeline of Marilyn's last night. "At midnight, the housekeeper awakened and saw that there was a light on in Marilyn's room, which was most unusual," Greenson wrote. "The housekeeper was afraid to awaken Marilyn who would have become enraged, and so she fell asleep again."

Contradicting the psychiatrist's recollection about "the light on in Marilyn's room," Mrs. Murray conceded, "I knew that the new white wool carpet filled the space under the door. The surface wool had piled up as a result of contact with the swinging door. This I remembered later . . . Such are the pitfalls of demands under pressure when accurate reporting is desired." Now that Mrs. Murray retracted her own account about seeing the light under the door, Greenson's version is highly suspect.

This added twist about Mrs. Murray falling "asleep again" resolves the discrepancy of the "midnight" discovery of the body as told to Sgt. Jack Clemmons. Hildi Greenson countered, "People say that there were four hours before it was reported, and I think Eunice did that out of a kind of unconscious guilt. She wished she had awakened at midnight and called, but she didn't."

The psychiatrist's wife claimed Mrs. Murray got up at midnight and was alarmed about Marilyn but inadvertently fell asleep. Consequently, Greenson's wife says, Mrs. Murray waited until the early morning hours of August 5 to reach her husband for help. Hildi Greenson stated, "Eunice Murray awakened at midnight and saw . . . the light under the door, and wondered about it, but fell asleep while wondering. She didn't get up. She saw the door . . . and said, 'I wonder why she has the light on,' because she usually didn't go to sleep with the light on."

The psychiatrist's wife concluded her story by stating: "The 'if' then was, *if* [Mrs. Murray] hadn't fallen asleep at midnight, [Marilyn] probably still could have been saved. By the time [Mrs. Murray] called, which was somewhere between two and three, it was too late . . . [Ralph] said, 'Eunice called and Marilyn's door is locked and she can't get in.'"

Joan Greenson recalled what her father said happened after he took the call from Mrs. Murray and went over to Marilyn's home: "Her bedroom door was locked, there was a light, and a telephone cord under the door. He knew Marilyn never liked to sleep that way . . . He took a poker from the fireplace, went to the side window of her bedroom, broke the glass, and reached in to let himself in."

By lying to his family about Marilyn Monroe's time of death, Greenson attempted to purge himself of his own involvement in her murder. "He could see that she had been dead for some time," Joan Greenson relayed. "He said she felt cold, but she was clutching the telephone in her hand, and he had trouble getting it out of her hand to hang it up . . . Father never believed for a moment that she meant to kill herself. He felt sure it was an accident."

For a man who admitted to not having a great memory that night, Dr. Hyman Engelberg told a remarkably similar story to the District Attorney's Office: "That particular line about being called at midnight, I remember Mrs. Murray telling us clearly that she went to sleep around midnight and she saw the light on under Miss Monroe's door. She woke up a few hours later and felt a little uneasy and the light was still on."

In his letter to Dr. Marianne Kris, Greenson continued: "At 3:30 the housekeeper awakened and saw the light and phoned me. I was there in five minutes, broke the window in the bedroom, found Marilyn lying dead, clutching the phone in her hand so strongly that I could not remove it." With these words, Ralph Greenson suggests that Marilyn was deceased many hours before he arrived on the scene, which was not true.

In fact, Greenson next accurately pinpoints the time of death. "It seems she had died around midnight," the psychiatrist wrote. "I do not think she consciously wanted to die at this moment but expected to be rescued; this time, however, it failed."

In an October 1992 interview, contradicting Dr. Greenson's account to the police while unwittingly corroborating the recollection of Schaefer Ambulance attendant James Hall, Greenson's brother-in-law and best friend Mickey Rudin conceded to Donald Spoto that the psychiatrist was at Marilyn's home *before* midnight:

> RUDIN: I got home. I got a call from Romi. He was over there. Marilyn had been found dead.
>
> SPOTO: And that was certainly before midnight.
>
> RUDIN: It wasn't a particularly late dinner party [at Mildred Allenberg's] . . . The call came in . . . as I got home because I remember now taking the call from the breakfast room.

According to Mickey Rudin, he rushed to the Monroe home immediately after Greenson called him.[29]

Per the police report, Mickey Rudin's phone call to Mrs. Murray was 9:00 p.m. allegedly to check on her employer. At this time, Marilyn was fine and not dying. Intriguingly, Anthony Summers noted: "Dr. Greenson confirmed privately, years later, that Robert Kennedy was present that night and that an ambulance was called."

The accounts of Detective Franklin, Eunice Murray, Norman Jefferies, and Mickey Rudin fly in the face of Greenson's official version to the police. His story about a fireplace poker is clearly a fabrication. In fact, Mrs. Murray's claimed that, before calling Greenson, she went around to the side of the house and used a poker to "part the draperies," but Pat Newcomb told Donald Spoto, "Those were heavy curtains that had no middle-divider."[30]

DID CHIEF PARKER
COVER UP BOBBY
KENNEDY'S TRACKS IN
LOS ANGELES?

Anthony Summers learned that, about forty-five minutes after Detective Sgt. Robert Byron was awakened at 5:00 a.m. on August 5, he arrived at Marilyn's home where he and Lieutenant Grover Armstrong, Chief of Detectives in West LA, interviewed Milton Rudin, Dr. Hyman Engelberg, and Eunice Murray. Dr. Greenson was no longer around, yet the two veteran cops subsequently noted inconsistencies in the recollections provided by the lawyer, the internist, and the housekeeper who, they reported, was "possibly evasive."

More than two decades later, Byron told Summers he had the distinct impression that Mrs. Murray had been coached on what to say, and that Engelberg and Rudin were withholding material information. "I got some wild answers," Byron recalled. "There was a lot more they could have told us . . . I didn't feel they were telling the correct time or situation, but we did not do what we'd normally do and drag them into the station." This, apparently, was due to the "fact" that there had been no signs of violence at the scene and that, as later confirmed by the autopsy report, Marilyn had died of self-inflicted barbiturate poisoning. Still, Byron also noted that police sources back then did inform him of her having been visited by Attorney General Robert Kennedy the day of her death.

Byron was correct that Greenson couldn't have been at the house by the time newspaper and TV reporters showed up. After all, it would have been nearly impossible for the psychiatrist to escape their prying camera lenses. Consequently, there are no known photographs of Ralph Greenson on the scene.

Chief William Parker liked Bobby Kennedy, especially his stance on organized crime. However, as Parker's wife Helen told Anthony Summers, her husband "wanted special attention paid to this particular case by the investigators, and he tried to send the best men out there, including detectives from the downtown office, because there was so much talk that she was close to John or Robert Kennedy."

According to Mrs. Parker, the police chief's Catholic faith and concern about the Kennedys being fried by their political opponents convinced him the whole matter had to be "straightened out" immediately.

However, as biographers Brown and Barham explained, "With the stroke of a pen, Chief Parker began the cover-up by refusing to assign a full-time detective team to the Monroe case."

Sgt. Byron's conviction that Mrs. Murray had been speedily coached to provide the police with false information was just one of several investigation-worthy factors that were now summarily ignored. Furthermore, when celebrity columnist May Mann reported on what she considered to be an inept probe into Marilyn Monroe's untimely death, she instantly received a call from Chief Parker. Mann relayed, "He said it would be bad for my health if I kept writing stories like that." What basically took place was a cover-up, not an investigation, and the case was allowed to turn cold.

In the late summer of 1992, former OCID (Organized Crime Intelligence Division) detective Mike Rothmiller released his book *LA Secret Police: Inside the LAPD Elite Spy Network*, exposing the corruption he witnessed firsthand within the police department. Brown and Barham wrote, "It was this unit [the OCID] which had undertaken the clandestine probe of Monroe's death. Organized by the dictatorial Chief Parker in 1959, the fifty-seven man unit apparently rampaged beyond the bounds of legality."

Rothmiller said the unit would "accumulate dirt on the movers and shakers of LA's political and entertainment establishment. The intelligence chiefs were ruthless and corrupt . . . And they had the power to ruin lives and reputations—or to safeguard. This is precisely what they did with the Monroe investigation . . . they protected the name of the Kennedy dynasty." Brown and Barham concluded, "It was this circle of handpicked detectives who investigated Monroe's death three times (in 1962, 1975, and 1982). Every scrap of paper about the death wound up in the hands of these investigative power brokers."

Thirty years after having arrived at Marilyn's home around 6:30 in the morning of August 5, 1962, Detective Daniel K. Stewart told a reporter on TV news show *Hard Copy*, "I saw Marilyn's body and I noted at the time that the Coroner was just getting ready to move her body out."

In June 1968, Stewart was assigned to the investigation into Robert Kennedy's assassination. "When I got down to the hospital, the officers in charge were intelligence division officers," he recalled, "and they said, 'This is really weird,' because they had been watching Robert and Jack at Marilyn's place."

When the *Hard Copy* interviewer questioned him about Marilyn's last night, Stewart confirmed that Robert Kennedy was under surveillance by the OCID: "They picked him up, I think, at Santa Monica Airport, followed him, took him up to Marilyn's, took him *back* to the airport [actually LAX] later that night. He then went and left town. I've worked with these people long enough as an officer that their integrity is 100%."

Mansfield's press secretary Raymond Strait who listened to eleven hours of Otash's tapes concurred, "Bobby skipped out of town and said he was never there but everybody knew he was there. You cover your tail as best you can. He took a quick hop up to San Francisco and acted like he was 400 or 500 miles away . . . I know that he went straight to Santa Monica and went up north to the Bay area to his friends."

In 1970, biographer Patte Barham interviewed Peter Lawford's mother Lady May Lawford, who relayed, "I already knew that a dark helicopter, like the one the Kennedy boys used, had been parked on the beach. And I knew that neighbors saw Bobby dashing in and out on Saturday." Lawford's next-door neighbor Ward Wood, who was married to Lynn Sherman, recalled, "It was Bobby all right. He was in khakis and a white shirt open at the neck."

Reporter Joe Hyams unsuccessfully tried to obtain the helicopter logs from Conners Helicopter Service in Santa Monica. Then his friend William Woodfield went back and talked to the pilot claiming he was doing a story on celebrities who had recently used their service including Frank Sinatra. The pilot agreed on the basis of positive publicity for their company. Woodfield related to Anthony Summers that one log in particular displayed an entry for August 5.

"The time in the log was sometime after midnight," Woodfield remembered. "I think between midnight and two in the morning. It showed clearly that a helicopter had picked up Robert Kennedy at the Santa Monica Beach." James Zonlick worked for Hal Conners's helicopter service as one of his main pilots.

Zonlick recalled, "Hal had picked Robert Kennedy up at the beach house and left him at Los Angeles International Airport . . . He was a little pleased that we'd handled that V.I.P. sort of person." Connor's daughter Patricia said her father Hal arrived later than usual on the night of Marilyn's death. She relayed, "Next morning, I remember saying, 'Did you hear Marilyn Monroe died?' and he didn't really answer at all."

Four days after Marilyn's death, Hyams and Woodfield called the Attorney General's Office to "put the story to rest." A Kennedy aide replied, "The Attorney General would appreciate it if you would not do the story."

Jay Margolis spoke with Daniel Stewart, but on that occasion the former detective was more evasive than his recollections from *Hard Copy*.

> MARGOLIS: So, you don't believe that Bobby Kennedy was in Los Angeles that last day?
>
> STEWART: I'm not going to tell you what my belief is.
>
> MARGOLIS: Did they establish a crime scene at the Monroe residence?
>
> STEWART: I'm not going to tell you that because you've got the wrong guy. If you want to talk to someone who's got it, talk to Marv Iannone. He was the Sergeant-in-Charge of all the detectives. He calls everyone else around. He left LAPD and until about fifteen months ago, he was Chief of Police of Beverly Hills. He was Chief there for about fifteen years and he just retired. His father was on the job as a Deputy Chief.
>
> MARGOLIS: And you effectively believe it was suicide, right?
>
> STEWART: Not a suicide. She just forgot how many pills she took. An accidental.

Stewart's perception echoed that of most police officers who, after entering Marilyn's home on August 5, saw no evidence of foul play and simply assumed she took her own life, either intentionally or accidentally. Murder was neither discussed nor encouraged and, because nobody considered it a crime scene, standard procedures were never conducted.

Former intelligence captain Neil Spotts, who investigated the Monroe case when it was reopened in 1975, told Brown and Barham: "It was such an obvious case. Because she had most certainly killed herself . . . They found Mrs. Murray, learned of the discovery, found the empty pill bottles, and saw her hand grasping the telephone. There was absolutely nothing suspicious at the scene. Marilyn died by her own hand."

"Nobody cared," Sgt. Jack Clemmons complained to the same biographers.

" 'Should we call the lab boys?' a young patrolman asked the ranking lieutenant standing next to him. 'What for?' the uniformed officer shot back. 'It's just another Hollywood broad who killed herself.' "

Marilyn's friend reporter George Carpozi, Jr., related to Joanne Green-Levine, "They never conducted a criminal investigation. What they did was they had a psychiatric study of a bunch of doctors who concluded that she killed herself either accidentally or deliberately."

Odd things began to happen even after Marilyn's body was removed from her home. Deputy Coroner's Aide Lionel Grandison wrote in his memoirs that Deputy Cronkright relayed to him how Twentieth Century-Fox "signed a release" of her body but this was strange to Grandison who knew permission was needed first by the Coroner's Office. Grandison learned how Greenson and Engelberg were "sure it was a common drug overdose" and requested a release of her body to Westwood Mortuary.

"As the Deputy in charge, it was my call," Grandison wrote. "Although it was common practice to deputize a mortuary to act on behalf of the coroner, the circumstances must completely rule out the need for a complete autopsy with organ examination or the possibility of death at the hands of another . . ."

Grandison therefore decided to phone Marilyn's residence. Sgt. R.E. Byron received his call and after some questioning, Byron surprisingly stated, "Ms. Monroe's remains were authorized for release by

Peter Lawford, her friend, and Twentieth Century-Fox, her employer . . ." Lionel Grandison subsequently relayed, "Fox Studios and LAPD were already issuing press releases and holding press conferences describing her death as a suicide . . ."

At the time of Marilyn's death, Robert Dambacher was a deputy coroner. His partner's name was Cletus Pace. "Cleet and I were dispatched at eight in the morning to go out to Westwood Village Mortuary to pick up her remains," Dambacher told Jay Margolis. "Westwood had gone to the residence. We brought her body back to the Coroner's Office in Downtown Los Angeles. In retrospect, she should have come in to the Coroner's Office right in the beginning, right from the residence to the Coroner's Office, but she didn't . . . I think she took a deliberate overdose of drugs. She had enough drugs in her to kill about three of us. You can't accidentally take that many pills."

In a photo now licensed by Keystone/Getty Images, a young Bob Dambacher stands in front of the older, bespectacled Cleet Pace as they remove Marilyn Monroe from the Westwood Village Mortuary, a building with window blinds to the left and right. Many people have mistakenly assumed the men were taking the body away from Marilyn's home, but as Dambacher confirmed, "I never did go to the residence."

Meanwhile, those reporting on Marilyn's death back in 1962 quickly grew suspicious of the secrecy surrounding it. The *New York Herald Tribune*'s Joe Hyams later recalled, "I had a source at the telephone company. My source came back and said the Secret Service has already been here and taken our records. Kind of weird . . . That's the first time in my memory as a reporter that they ever, ever stepped in that fast to start a hush."

Hyams told Anthony Summers he contacted the telephone company "the morning after her death." On August 8, 1962, columnist Florabel Muir wrote in the *New York Daily News* how sources asserted, "Strange 'pressures' are being put on Los Angeles police investigating the death of Marilyn Monroe." Muir wrote:

> The police have impounded the phone company's taped record of outgoing calls . . . The purported pressures are mysterious. They apparently are coming from persons who had been closely in touch with Marilyn the last few weeks.

Los Angeles Times reporter Jack Tobin, in whom Chief Parker's colleague Captain James Hamilton had often confided, informed Anthony Summers, "Hamilton told me he had the telephone history of the last day or two of Marilyn Monroe's life. When I expressed interest, he said, 'I will tell you nothing more.'"

In fact, the 1982 District Attorney's Report surprisingly deduced, "Confidential LAPD records supplied to our office support the published media reports that toll records were seized by the Los Angeles Police Department. Toll records from General Telephone Company covering the period from June 1, 1962 to August 18, 1962 were secured by the Police Department."

For their part, the Kennedys also had to exercise damage control over an absolutely hysterical Pat Newcomb. "I believe that the Kennedys were concerned that Pat, being a close friend of Marilyn's, would become very emotional and might at some point mention something to somebody about the extent of the relationship between the Kennedys and Marilyn," Newcomb's fellow press agent Michael Selsman explained. And Joe Hyams noted that, while both Eunice Murray and Pat Newcomb conveniently disappeared for a time following Marilyn's death, the latter "reappeared very hastily, working for the Kennedys in Washington. It just began to look like a vast cover-up."

Marilyn's last professional photographer, George Barris, relayed to Jay Margolis: "I'll tell you about Pat Newcomb. When Marilyn died, they couldn't reach Pat. All the press, the newspapers, the radio, television, they couldn't find her. When my story came out in the *Daily News*, I get a phone call. I was at the *Daily News* office. She called me there. I said, 'Where are you? Everybody's looking for you.'"

"I don't want to talk to anyone," Newcomb informed Barris, "but I'd like to see you."

"Where are you?" Barris asked.

"I'm at the Sherry-Netherland," Newcomb replied, referencing the large hotel situated close to Central Park in New York. "Can you come over?"

"Sure."

"I'll give you a name to call me."

Newcomb had adopted an alias to avoid other press reporters. So, after arriving at the Sherry-Netherland, George Barris asked to see the person who had checked in there under a false name and, on being directed to her room, he immediately enquired what had been going on.

"George, I was invited to stay with Bobby Kennedy," Newcomb explained before announcing, "I'm going to Paris."

"I think the Kennedys paid for that trip," Barris told Margolis. "Where was she going to get the money? She wanted to get away from everything, same as I didn't want the press bothering me. 'Do you know anybody in Paris?' 'No.' So, I gave her the name of a friend and I said, 'Look, if you're lonely and you want to see Paris, call this person I can trust and he won't tell the press you're there or anything. And he'll take you to dinner and show you Paris.' Then I gave her the name and phone number of a friend so she could have somebody to meet.

"She thanked me and I left. But she called me one day and said, 'George, I'm working in Washington. I know you took a lot of these wonderful pictures of Marilyn.' I knew she wanted some. It was as a memento, something to remember Marilyn. At my own expense, I flew down. I met her at the office near Bobby Kennedy. She had a job working for motion pictures. We chatted a while. She had tears in her eyes. I then flew back to New York. So, she had a collection of photos of Marilyn for her own personal use. She doesn't want to talk about Marilyn because she was so close to her."[31]

BEHIND THE SCENES AT MARILYN MONROE'S FUNERAL

On August 8, 1962, at the Pierce Brothers Westwood Village Memorial Park Cemetery, funeral director Allan Abbott helped with Marilyn's service and acted as one of the pallbearers. "We had provided limousine service for JFK in Los Angeles for the Democratic Convention before he was elected President," Abbott told Jay Margolis. "The Secret Service came in and searched all of our cars and looked for microphones and bugs. They wanted backgrounds on all the drivers that were being used so they were very careful about it . . .

"I drove the limo on Clark Gable's service and the service for Ernie Kovacs where I was a hearse driver on that. There's no question what killed Ernie Kovacs. That's why they stopped building that rear-engine car because it would go out of control. The interesting part about working that service is that Kim Novak showed up and she was just gorgeous then. Frank Sinatra and Jack Lemmon were two of the six pallbearers carrying the casket. Kim and Ernie made a movie together called *Bell, Book, and Candle* (1958) . . .

"Clarence Pierce, who was the younger of the two brothers, originally put out the call to tell me to get out to the cemetery to help get things all situated for Marilyn's funeral. He told me Marilyn would come in to the cemetery when she was like twenty years old. She would have a book and a sack lunch. She would sit there and read and eat her lunch. It's nice that she ended up in a place where she felt so much solace and felt so at ease there because she was always under a lot of pressure to perform and she took everything so seriously . . .

"I actually stood at the door of the chapel and checked everybody's invitation. Nobody got in there without an invitation, including Frank Sinatra. Joe DiMaggio didn't like Hollywood people at all. There were four active pallbearers. If you look at the picture in Leigh Wiener's book, you'll see four people walking from the chapel behind the hearse. The guy in the front-left is Sydney Guilaroff and he has a handkerchief up to his eyes. He was crying. The guy directly opposite him was Marilyn's makeup man Whitey Snyder. Behind the two of them are me and my partner Ron Hast. Our company was called Abbott & Hast."

Abbott's partner Ron Hast relayed, "Founded in 1957 by my business partner Allan Abbott, and myself, our company provided essential services commonly utilized by funeral homes on a regular or at-need basis, such as twenty-four-hour first-call services, hearses, limousines, floral transportation, long-distant statewide transportation, death certificate services, with experienced personnel. We had also developed the Casket Airtray (1960), and production of formal station wagon conversions for death care.

"On a monthly rotation of regional funeral homes, the Coroner's Office assigned Ms. Monroe to the Westwood Village Mortuary and Cemetery; a very small, low-volume firm in West Los Angeles. It was owned by James and Clarence Pierce, and operated as a satellite from their primary location in Los Angeles. Apparently, by the time the coroner's investigation was completed, Mr. Joe DiMaggio engaged the quaint cemetery mortuary to follow through with arrangements, private funeral, and entombment in its outdoor mausoleum crypt.

"We received a call from Clarence Pierce one Sunday morning, asking to pick up one of our new station wagon formal conversions to transport Marilyn Monroe from the Coroner's Office to Westwood. They were aware that the press was anticipated in large numbers, and the event would be newsworthy. Clarence Pierce made the call—well documented in the news. We were later informed the transfer was the first death event telecast over Telstar, the first satellite to broadcast news worldwide.

"We were soon contacted again to arrange for one of our three new hearses: a 1962 Eureka Landau Cadillac Side Service. This led to a request for Allan and I to arrive at the mortuary for a planning conference. It was soon determined that there were many loose ends and unknowns to address. Allan inquired about security, explaining potential liability concerns with privacy assurance and other matters. He gave examples of photographs and other problems that surfaced in the past. He was then assigned to follow through, and ordered six armed and uniformed guards that soon arrived and were rotated through the entire event.

"In the course of constant issues, I was asked by a well-dressed woman for a moment of privacy. She then offered me $10,000 to be privately alone with Marilyn Monroe's body for ten minutes. I explained the trust for privacy and security that was placed with us, the importance of that commitment, and respectfully declined her request. I admit to recognizing the value of her suggested gift, having then recently paid $12,250 each for three new hearses.

"As a deputy Los Angeles registrar, I signed and received Marilyn's death certificate and burial permit. The certificate, at that time, only indicated 'pending investigation and autopsy.' The original certificate was later replaced with a 'final certificate,' indicating the cause of death, with new and permanent signatures.

"In the course of all details, we were involved in the preparation room, at the door of the chapel during services (less than fifty people were invited), and asked to be pallbearers during the transfer from chapel to hearse to outdoor crypt following chapel formalities. Ms. Monroe's hairdresser and makeup artist [Sydney Guilaroff and Whitey Snyder] were the other two pallbearers.

"Over the past 50 years, we have received numerous inquiries regarding Marilyn Monroe and her final event. There is no question that her sudden, unexpected and mysterious death—as well as her image frozen in time—fuels curiosity about every detail of her life and death."

On August 7, according to biographer Donald Spoto, Joe DiMaggio maintained a nighttime vigil over Marilyn's body until her makeup man, Whitey Snyder, arrived the next morning to apply the final touches. However, Allan Abbott told Jay Margolis this wasn't true: "Joe DiMaggio left at eleven o'clock at night. Out of all the celebrity funerals I worked on, the only one my wife ever had any interest in going to and seeing was Marilyn's. So, we arrived at Westwood Cemetery Mortuary at eight-forty-five—because the visitation was going to conclude at nine o'clock—and figured we would talk to Pat Spinelli for about twenty minutes. Pat was the night girl who answered the phone.

"Come ten o'clock, Joe's still going from the chapel to the cemetery. He would go out there and cry. Then he'd come back in and walk up to the casket, stay there for a while, then turn and walk out to the cemetery again. He did this five or six times. Pat said, 'I'm not going to tell Joe DiMaggio he's got to leave.' We just sat there and kept talking and she

told me how, the night before that night, she slept on a rollaway bed. And she rolled it in and slept next to Marilyn to make sure nobody got in secretly and got around her and got a picture of her. She slept there every night. Pat told me that absolutely nobody else stayed . . .

"We stayed there until almost eleven. Finally, I told my wife, 'I'm really sorry but I've got to work this service tomorrow. We have to leave.' We moved our car only twenty or thirty feet and I see Joe and his entourage leaving. So, I backed the car up and we went back inside. I said, 'Boy, that was perfect timing.' Just a minute or two later and I would've been gone. Pat took us into the visitation room and, as we stood there, immediately my wife started crying. We were very, very intensely looking at her. I had seen the horrible, horrible Coroner's picture where Marilyn was just totally unrecognizable. My wife says to me, 'Look at how big her eyes are!' I've never heard anybody make that observation, but she was absolutely right . . .

"In Leigh Wiener's book, it says we're employees of Westwood. I guess we were there working that day for Westwood so I guess you could say loosely we were employees of Westwood. We had over a hundred funeral homes in Los Angeles that used our services and these two mortuaries, the mortuary cemetery in Westwood and Pierce-Hamrock in Downtown did not own a hearse, did not own a limousine and that really was not unusual. A lot of people find that very surprising. Every single service they had was by our staff and our cars. So I could just go into our dispatch office any afternoon, see what was on the sheet for the next day, and assign myself on whatever I wanted to go on."

As for the man who performed the autopsy on Marilyn Monroe, Allan Abbott told Jay Margolis, "I never met [pathologist Thomas] Noguchi until after Marilyn's funeral. They were talking about him all the time and they called him 'The Knife . . .' Noguchi was a working fool. He would do six or eight or ten embalmings in a day if he had to. Charles Maxwell embalmed Marilyn Monroe. Whitey Snyder was taking credit for dressing her and he kind of intimated that he moved her breasts around a little bit to make them more pointy. That was not true. Mrs. Mary Hamrock was the one who got credit for doing that. She and the two brothers Clarence and James Pierce opened a business on Venice Boulevard together . . . As Abbott & Hast, we provide funeral cars, hearses, and limousines to provide the service of a funeral home. The downtown location was called Pierce-Hamrock . . .

"Obviously, when people found out that Westwood had been called to take care of Marilyn, everybody wants to get in on the act and see whatever there is to see . . . I get to the cemetery and there's about a hundred or so people there. I recognized most of them, like [gossip columnist] Hedda Hopper, a lot of photographers, and there were a lot of members of the public there, too.

"I heard that within ten minutes of my arrival, photographers were offering $30,000 for a picture of Marilyn dead. I could actually see guys going over and trying the doors. At that time, Westwood had their embalming room, which was a separate Spanish-style building that wasn't really connected to the main building at all. Somehow they found out that that's where the embalming room was and they were checking the doors and trying the windows and everything.

"I went inside and the manager's wife was there and I said, 'Where's Guy Hockett?' and she says, 'He's down at the Coroner's Office picking up the paperwork on Marilyn.' 'Why? You got a really huge problem developing out there at the cemetery. You've got to get some security here!' 'Well, I'm not authorized to do that!' So, she calls downtown, gets Clarence, and he says to her, 'Whatever Allan needs, get it.' I said, 'You got a Yellow Pages?' She handed it to me. Then I decided on Pinkerton Security Services with guards.

"I called them up and said, 'I need six uniformed guards here at Westwood Village Cemetery as quickly as you can possibly get them here.' 'Do you want them wearing side-arms?' 'Absolutely.' The embalmer and the Pinkerton guards arrived at almost the same time. We went into the embalming room and took the sheet off of Marilyn and I absolutely could not believe that was her. She was such a mess. She had purple blotches all over her face, which is from a condition called lividity. Whenever a person dies, the gravity pulls the blood to the area of your body that's the lowest.

"The other thing that was readily apparent was that her neck was very swollen. So, the embalmer said, 'I've got to get this swelling out of her neck.' He had me roll her up on her side . . . Marilyn's neck was bloated because I think Noguchi was in there, looking around and probing. In your neck, you have something called a hyaline bone and it's not a very strong bone. Most people that are strangled, it breaks their hyaline bone and you can see what the actual cause of death is, such as manual strangulation or ligature, anything that's used in place of hands such as a belt or hose or even a piece of nylon . . .

"Of course, she was already embalmed at the Coroner's Office, so she was as stiff as a brick. He made this marquee diamond incision on the back of her neck, removed about three square inches of skin and then made this baseball stitch and just pulled all the skin as tight as he could, which really did the trick as far as getting all that swelling out. It made her neck the normal size. Before he made the incision, he cut some hair off the back of her head just to get it out of the way so he could do that.

"I got a call from the front office. Mrs. Hockett says, 'The executor just dropped off the clothing and everything,' and by that time we were just about ready to start dressing her. I said, 'Alright, I'll be right up to get it.' I go to the office, which was in a separate building, and I start looking through the stuff. I said, 'There's no panties.' 'She never wore them and they couldn't find any, so they just didn't bring any.' But they brought a bra, some tiny falsies, and a green Pucci gown that had a Florence, Italy label in it . . .

"We had just finished dressing Marilyn. Charles Maxwell, the embalmer, I only knew as Frenchie because he spoke with a very heavy French accent. Frenchie said, 'Look, they brought in falsies, but they're way too small to do any good, so I guess we'll stick them in the bra.' Then we were cleaning up to get ready for her hairdresser and makeup man when Mrs. Hamrock came walking into the embalming room and just stood there for a long, silent time, looking at her. She said, 'That doesn't look like Marilyn. She's flatter than a pancake!'

"Not only do they make a Y-incision at the autopsy, they cut each of the ribs so they can get to all the internal organs. The whole chest caves in. When Mrs. Hamrock heard about this thing about the falsies, she just walked over to the embalming table and grabbed the neck of this Pucci dress, pulled on it, reached in there and grabbed the falsies, took them out of there, and threw them in a waste basket. Then she went over and stuffed the bra completely with cotton. She kind of moved things around a little bit, then took a step back, looked at it, and said, 'Now *that* looks like Marilyn Monroe.' Then she walked out the door . . .

"I kept thinking about those falsies in the trash can. Gosh, I knew how much my wife would love those. I was in my early twenties and kind of embarrassed, wanting to retrieve these falsies. So, the embalmer walked over to wash his hands. I didn't take my eyes off of him. I just kept watching him to make sure he didn't see me. I was standing next to the trash can and I reached in, felt the falsies, squeezed them into my fist, and put them into my pocket without even looking . . .

"If Mrs. Hamrock hadn't come in, I would have never ended up with the falsies. It wasn't until Whitey and Sydney showed up that I was able to find out the purpose of the falsies. I don't think Sydney had any particular idea about it, but Whitey said, 'Oh, yeah, she'd been using those for a few years now. She puts on a bra and a sweater, then she stuffs these up inside there so that, when you look at her in the sweater, you see the outline of her nipples.' She wanted people to think she was not wearing a bra. She liked to be provocative. I would have never known why they were used because to me, they should have been about four inches in diameter, which is all the ones I've ever seen. But the whole purpose of these was not to make her breasts seem larger, because she was well-endowed. It was to just make more definition in her sweater . . .

"Then, when I got outside, I pulled them out of my pocket and some of the hair that was cut off of her was between the two falsies. They could get DNA from hair. Her hair was actually fairly short and it hadn't been bleached for probably a month because it was growing out almost half an inch. It was dishwater blonde . . ."

On April 20, 2006, *48 Hours Mystery* correspondent Peter Van Sant interviewed Dr. Steven Karch on the possibility of using DNA to determine more information regarding the drugs found in Marilyn's body. Such DNA tests could prove with scientific evidence that Marilyn Monroe did not take her own life. Van Sant reported what he learned and relayed, "Dr. Steven Karch is one of the nation's top forensic pathologists . . . All it would take are a few strands of that famously blonde hair . . . Dr. Karch says tests could be run to look for poisons or paralyzing drugs, not done back then." Dr. Steven Karch himself stated, "Somebody would have to open the crypt and take some hair and fingernails and analyze it."[32]

DR. GREENSON CALLS THE POLICE TO SAY MARILYN MONROE COMMITTED SUICIDE

Contrary to what is stated on the official police report of Marilyn Monroe's death, it was Ralph Greenson who phoned in the "suicide" of the most famous woman in the world. Over the years, LAPD Sgt. Jack Clemmons consistently confirmed this to documentarians and biographers. As for the August 5 phone call at 4:25 a.m. from 12305 Fifth Helena Drive, biographers Brown and Barham noted, "At first the man on the phone was so agitated that Clemmons couldn't understand him. He was talking very fast and seemed to have a European accent." Greenson had a soft Brooklyn/Viennese accent.

The caller said, "Marilyn Monroe is dead. She just committed suicide." Deputy District Attorney John Miner reacted rather strongly to this information: "That's right. Clemmons says Greenson said he was calling with respect to Monroe, that she had committed suicide. I don't think that ever happened. It's contrary to the kind of man Greenson was. I think Clemmons said that to cover himself for not having followed department regulations."

In an article published on August 5, 1973, Greenson stated that he told Dr. Hyman Engelberg and housekeeper Eunice Murray, "Okay, I'll call the police." Speaking to Sgt. Clemmons, Greenson purportedly said, "I want to report the death of a person, a sudden and unexplained death." Clemmons came right over. When he arrived, he found three people: a sarcastic Greenson, a frightened Mrs. Murray, and a sullen

Engelberg. Greenson pointed to the empty bottle of Nembutal, implying that it spoke for itself. The psychiatrist did not cry over the death of his patient. Clemmons told Brown and Barham, "I strongly disliked Greenson's attitude. He was cocky, almost challenging me to accuse him of something."[33]

THE GREENSON AND ENGELBERG AGREEMENT

Ralph "Romi" Greenson, M.D., and her physician Hyman "Hy" Engelberg, M.D., long-standing friends, allegedly failed to let each other know what they were prescribing for Marilyn days before she died. Anthony Summers wrote, "Dr. Greenson would later say he had brought in Dr. Engelberg to try to wean Marilyn away from sleeping pills. The two doctors agreed to keep in touch concerning the drugs they prescribed for her, but the system may have broken down."

Peter Lawford agreed with Hyman Engelberg's diagnosis for Marilyn: she was bipolar. Lawford relayed to Heymann, "Marilyn had a death wish of sorts but didn't actually want to die, at least not in her more sane moments. In my opinion, she had manic-depressive tendencies and should have been on a different type of medication."

In 1982, Engelberg told the District Attorney's Office, "I saw her Friday evening [August 3, 1962]. It was to give her an injection of liver and vitamins . . . usually in the buttocks, sometimes possibly in the upper arms where you usually give intramuscular injections . . . Probably in the buttocks because that's the usual place I would put it." Ralph Greenson explained to Dr. Marianne Kris how all drugs were prescribed by Engelberg and not Greenson himself, "I had an internist who would prescribe medication for her and to give her vitamin injections and liver injections, so that I had nothing to do with the actual handling of medication. I only talked about it with her and he kept me informed."

Greenson said he didn't know anything about Engelberg's August 3 Nembutal prescription, while Engelberg claimed he knew nothing about any chloral hydrate prescriptions. If what both these doctors asserted is true, then they negligently placed Marilyn Monroe in a highly perilous situation. Chloral hydrate decreases the metabolic rate of Nembutal, making the Nembutal less likely to be absorbed quickly into the liver and, therefore, more likely to be lethal. Both doctors would have known the effect of chloral hydrate on Nembutal. Yet, their claims of ignorance took precedence over everything else.

Engelberg emphatically stated that Marilyn could only have obtained chloral hydrate in Tijuana because, he believed, no American doctor would write the prescription. However, Engelberg *did* write one such chloral hydrate prescription on June 7, 1962, one day before Marilyn was fired from *Something's Got to Give*. As noted by Detective Sgt. Robert E. Byron and his team, a prescription bottle was recovered from Marilyn's bedroom, dated July 25, for fifty 500-milligram chloral hydrates, and it was refilled on July 31. Toxicologist Raymond Abernathy also noted the same dates for the original and refilled chloral hydrate prescriptions, as detailed in the coroner's report.

In total, fifteen pill bottles were found on Marilyn's bedside table, according to Westwood Memorial Mortuary employee Guy Hockett and his son Don, yet Abernathy only inventoried eight (an unidentified bottle was later added to the original seven). The statements Greenson made to biographer Maurice Zolotow, *Something's Got to Give* set photographer William Read Woodfield, and even Marilyn's housekeeper Mrs. Eunice Murray confirm that the psychiatrist suggested chloral hydrate for his star patient. Mrs. Murray wrote in her book, "Under Dr. Greenson's guidance, she was taking only chloral hydrate pills for sleep." After interviewing Greenson, Zolotow wrote in a September 14, 1973, article, "Her psychiatrist, Dr. Ralph Greenson, was attempting to cut down her dependence on Nembutal by switching her to chloral hydrate as a sleep-inducer."

When Woodfield telephoned Greenson and asked him why he allowed such heavy doses of chloral hydrate for Marilyn, Greenson snidely replied, "Well, I've made a number of mistakes in my time." Engelberg stated it wasn't unusual to prescribe Nembutal for Marilyn. In fact, Engelberg told the District Attorney's Office in 1982 that Nembutal was the only sleeping medication he ever prescribed for Marilyn. In the same interview, Engelberg relayed, "I don't know of anything Dr. Greenson gave her. Maybe he did. I cannot answer for him . . . As far as I know, I was the only one writing prescriptions, but I couldn't swear to that."

Greenson's wife Hildi told private investigator Cathy Griffin, "The idea was that she was never to be said no to when she wanted a prescription, because the only thing that would happen was she would go somewhere else . . . So, whenever she asked for a drug, she would get it."

Greenson's daughter Joan explained, "All she had to do was call her doctor and he would prescribe it to her. Then the physician was to call later and tell him . . . If Father felt that it was an excessive amount or too dangerous, he would usually pour some out when he was at Marilyn's house."

Greenson wrote in a 1964 paper, "The administering of a drug is a responsibility since it may cause physical side effects, it may be emotionally upsetting to the patient, misused by the patient, and it may lead to addiction and death." If it's true that Greenson and Engelberg had a plan to "wean" Marilyn off barbiturates, as communicated by Greenson to the Suicide Prevention Team, it seems more than curious why Engelberg would consistently lie on the record by stating he never prescribed chloral hydrate for Marilyn when he clearly did.

Greenson wrote in a letter to his friend and colleague Dr. Marianne Kris on August 20, 1962, "I later found out that on Friday night she had told the internist [Engelberg] that I had said it was all right for her to take some Nembutal, and he had given it to her without checking with me, because he had been upset himself for his own personal reasons."

Engelberg had just split from his wife after some twenty-seven years of marriage. Meanwhile, biographer Donald Spoto made a chilling point about how Greenson knew Marilyn well enough to know which medication had caused her to be "somewhat drugged."

The accounts of biographer Fred Lawrence Guiles and Engelberg himself directly contradict Greenson's story about Marilyn "tricking" Engelberg into giving her some Nembutal on August 3. According to Guiles, Marilyn asked for the Nembutal prescription because she regarded chloral hydrate as a mild sedative that didn't always do its job. She wanted something that actually worked because, apparently, she had developed a tolerance to the other drug. In 1982, Engelberg told the District Attorney's Office that, since it was standard operating procedure to prescribe Nembutal for Marilyn, he didn't consider it an unusual request.

Hildi Greenson disclosed what, she claimed, her husband did during the weeks leading up to Marilyn's death: "In trying to help Marilyn get off the barbiturates she was on, he was giving her a different kind of medication [chloral hydrate] that is not quite as addictive and he was able to turn the tide, as it were. She was getting less and less dependent on the drugs."

In her book, Mrs. Murray discussed the ineffectiveness of chloral hydrate as it related to her employer. Marilyn had said to her, "You know they used to give these to the soldiers in the war for sleeping. They're really very mild." Mrs. Murray stated on an April 1992 edition of *Hard Copy*, "She was taking something she said was very mild. She called it chloral hydrate. And she would take it with a glass of milk or something of the sort." Why would chloral hydrate be found in Marilyn's system the night she died when she specifically requested the stronger drug from her physician?

Greenson attempted to resolve this discrepancy in his letter to Dr. Kris, claiming his alleged final 7:30–7:40 p.m. phone call with Marilyn ended in the following manner: "At the end of the conversation she asked me whether I had taken away her Nembutal bottle . . . I said to Marilyn I had not taken her Nembutal, and I didn't know she was taking Nembutal, and she quickly dropped the subject. I thought perhaps she was just confused."

Would other doctors have dismissed Marilyn's Nembutal remark as casually as Greenson did? His daughter Joan later said, "Ironically, one of these doctors, Dr. Hyman Engelberg, gave her a prescription for Nembutal the Friday before she died, but he didn't inform my father because he separated from his wife that day. He was moving out of the house that day."

Joan explained what she claimed her father did when he arrived at Marilyn's home: "That Saturday he had checked her medication. No new pills were there. He had not received a call that she had gotten new medication. It was a small oversight."

Hildi Greenson agreed: "It happened on a bad day. A divorce either became final or [Engelberg] was moving out of his house. The internist forgot to call. My husband didn't know that she had the Nembutals or Seconals, or whatever they were."

In the police report #62-509 463, Hyman Engelberg stated that, by the time Marilyn refilled his original prescription for twenty-five pills, there should have been a total of fifty Nembutals. He was right. In Anthony Summers' updated version of *Goddess* (2000), following page 432, there is a photograph of a Monroe prescription on which Engelberg's name and the date July 25, 1962, are visible. This was the original 100-milligram Nembutal prescription for twenty-five pills, which was then refilled on August 3. The 1982 District Attorney's Report read: "The refilled prescription recovered at the scene dated August 3, 1962, was attributed to a refill Dr. Engelberg had given Miss Monroe on that date."

Not only did Engelberg "forget" to tell Greenson about the August 3 refill, but he also "forgot" to tell him about the original prescription on July 25. Pat Newcomb told Donald Spoto, "She asked for some Nembutals. Engelberg was having problems with his wife . . . Greenson didn't know she was in this state of wanting these pills. The fact that Engelberg forgot to tell Greenson was malpractice. It was fifty pills and she already had chloral hydrate."

If Greenson and Engelberg were telling the truth regarding their ignorance of one another's prescriptions, we would have to assume Marilyn took only three Nembutals before swallowing the remaining forty-seven on that final evening. To do this, Marilyn would have had to hoard Engelberg's pills from the original prescription (July 25) *and* the refill on August 3. Given her regular use of those drugs, could she really have waited almost a week-and-a-half before finally deciding to take most of the pills in one go on August 4?

The two doctors knew this didn't make any kind of sense, so Greenson and Engelberg concocted a cockamamie story about how Marilyn went behind both their backs to get *another* Nembutal prescription and *another* refill. The problem is, they weren't very creative. Referring to Twentieth Century-Fox employee Dr. Lee Siegel, the 1982 District Attorney's Report read in part: "The Suicide Team found that Dr. Siegel had prescribed an unknown quantity to Miss Monroe on July 25, 1962, and also noted that she had received a refill of pills on August 3, 1962, and attributed that prescription to Dr. Siegel."

The dates of Siegel's alleged prescriptions are the same dates for both of Engelberg's prescriptions. To put it simply, Greenson and Engelberg said Marilyn went doctor shopping in order to make it appear as if she had access to fifty Nembutal pills the day she died. The fact that she didn't have enough Nembutals on hand to match the amount later found in her bloodstream means Marilyn was *not* responsible for her own death.

Dr. Robert Litman was a member of the Suicide Prevention Team. He told Donald Spoto, "I am stuck with the information that she went out and got pills from Siegel and Engelberg." Lee Siegel vehemently denied that he ever saw Marilyn again after the studio fired her on June 8. His alleged Nembutal prescription and refill aren't mentioned in any of the police reports, and when the case was reopened again in 1982 the district attorney's report conceded: "The prescriptions attributed to Dr. Siegel were not recovered by the Coroner's representatives." So, there is no proof that they ever existed.[34]

Peter Lawford had a significant role in the death of Marilyn Monroe. On August 8, the day of her funeral, Lawford told a reporter that he was the last person to speak to the actress when on the phone with her four nights earlier. He would later report that this took place at around 7:30 p.m. on August 4. Meanwhile, Joe DiMaggio "held Bobby Kennedy responsible for her death," according to good friend Harry Hall. Displaying plenty of animosity toward the President and Attorney General, DiMaggio told the funeral director, "Be sure that none of those damned Kennedys come to the funeral." Joltin' Joe's close friend Morris Engelberg asserted, "No woman in the world will ever be loved the way he loved her. He loved her in life and in death."

Peter Lawford and his wife Pat Kennedy were quite upset when DiMaggio barred them from the service. "It seems to be a concerted effort to keep some of Marilyn's old friends from attending," Lawford remarked. DiMaggio, on the other hand, privately growled, "If it wasn't for her so-called friends, Marilyn would still be alive today."

After they were denied entrance to Marilyn's funeral, the Lawfords boarded a plane and headed for the Kennedy compound in Hyannis Port, Massachusetts. Pat Newcomb joined them there soon afterward and, as documented by a photograph of them aboard the *Manitou* dated August 12, 1962, they then went on a Maine cruise together. Newcomb, Lawford, and JFK are all smiling in the photo, taken four days after Marilyn's funeral. Meanwhile, according to biographer C. David Heymann, Bobby Kennedy "left San Francisco on a camping trip to Oregon with his children," three days after his erstwhile mistress's demise. "Ironically," Heymann continued, "they were joined there by his early travel companion, Supreme Court Justice William O. Douglas."

The official police report #62-509 463 filed by Detective Sgt. Robert Byron on August 8, 1962, read in part: "An attempt was made to contact Mr. Lawford, but officers were informed by his secretary that

Mr. Lawford had taken an airplane at 1:00 p.m. His secretary stated that she did expect to hear from him and that she would request that he contact this Department at his earliest convenience."

Lawford would continue to ignore the police department's interview requests for the next thirteen years, which was, to say the least, both strange and suspicious when the issue at hand was an alleged suicide.

Coroner Curphey gave Dr. Litman and the Suicide Prevention Team their conclusion to the case *before* they even began the official investigation. Declaring it a suicide, Curphey told them to work backward and, as Litman later informed biographer Donald Spoto, the Team eventually decided it was a case of "probable suicide" based on the "physical evidence" and the "past history of having made overdoses."

Deputy District Attorney John Miner disagreed. In 1962, while serving under District Attorney William McKesson, Miner was also the liaison to the coroner. In this capacity, he oversaw the autopsy performed on Marilyn Monroe by Dr. Thomas Noguchi. "It takes time to swallow thirty or forty capsules," Miner later stated. "And if she had swallowed them, she would have been dead before they all dissolved. There would be residue in her tummy."

Something unheard of then happened next. Miner remembered, "I was called on a Sunday, and the techs wouldn't even have gotten to the specimens until the following day . . . Somebody took those specimens and flushed them down the toilet . . . Somebody wanted the diagnosis of suicide to stick and didn't want any interference by analysis of the scientific evidence."

Noguchi himself told Anthony Summers, "For some reason, I felt uncomfortable and shortly after the case was formally closed I called Toxicology and requested the check . . . Abernathy told me the organ specimens had been destroyed."

Years later, talking about Coroner Curphey, Thomas Noguchi recalled, "He certified the manner of death to be 'probable suicide.' When you weigh all the factors, it tends to indicate a more likely suicide. But the office could not find necessary factors to state it as suicide."

Oddly, Dr. Greenson told Dr. Litman he wasn't sure if Marilyn had committed suicide. And Greenson went a step further during the late afternoon of August 8, the day of her funeral, after Coroner Curphey had dispatched John Miner to interview the psychiatrist in his Beverly Hills office on 436 Roxbury Drive. Sitting there with Miner, who happened to be a colleague of his from the Psychoanalytic Institute, Greenson said he was certain his star patient had *not* committed suicide.

Miner would remain adamant about this throughout many years. "What we really have is a coroner chief medical examiner who had a pre-conceived notion of what happened and labeled it accordingly and was *completely wrong*," he'd remark. "Curphey chose to adopt it and in a way it was the easiest political solution."

Miner ruled out suicide by oral ingestion as, in this particular case, it wouldn't have been medically possible. "With that massive amount of intake, there would have been undissolved capsules," he reasoned. "She would have died before all of those capsules had been absorbed. So, the notion of oral intake of the barbiturates simply does not scientifically stand up. It just didn't happen that way."[35]

On October 13, 1973, biographer Maurice Zolotow publicly released portions of an interview he had conducted with Dr. Greenson, discussing the last day of Marilyn Monroe's life. The Greenson family has sealed the full Greenson-Zolotow interview in Special Collections at UCLA, ensuring it will remain unseen by members of the public until January 1, 2039, along with most of Greenson's other writings alluding to his legendary patient. Greenson chillingly told Zolotow:

> I will always believe it was an accidental suicide, because her hand was on the receiver, her finger still in the dial. I'm convinced she was trying to phone me. If only she had reached me . . . Her room was locked and bolted—doors and windows. How could a murderer have entered?

That same year, author Norman Mailer noted in his Marilyn Monroe book that, "Dr. Thomas Noguchi stated for *Time* magazine that 'no stomach pump was used on Marilyn.'"

On October 23, 1973, ten days after Maurice Zolotow released portions of his interview with Dr. Greenson, the latter used an article titled, "Psychiatrist Breaks Silence in Defense of Marilyn Monroe" yet again attempting to dispel murder theories as well as rumors of sexual liaisons with men in high office. The article categorically stated that Greenson "has denied that the actress may have been murdered. He also denied that

Photographed on the set of *The Asphalt Jungle* in 1950. (Getty Images)

Photographed by David Conover in 1947. (Getty Images)

Photographed by Ed Clark in 1950. (Getty Images)

Photographed by Don Ornitz in 1951. (Getty Images)

Photographed by Phil Burchman in 1951.
(Getty Images)

Photographed by Earl Theisen in
1951. (Getty Images)

Photographed by Nickolas
Muray in 1952.
(Getty Images)

Photographed by Frank Powolny in 1952.
(Getty Images)

Photographed by Frank Powolny in 1953.
(Getty Images)

January 14, 1954—MM
marries Joe DiMaggio.
(Popperfoto/Getty Images)

April 24, 1954—Peter Lawford marries Pat Kennedy. (United Photo Press)

Photographed by Milton Greene in 1955. (Getty Images)

December 1956—Portrait of American psychiatrist and psychoanalyst Dr. Ralph Greenson (a.k.a. Romeo Samuel Greenschpoon, 1911–1979). (Photo by J. R. Eyerman/Time & Life Pictures/Getty Images)

March 1, 1957—Fred Meade (L), LA distributor of *Confidential* magazine, talks with private investigator Fred Otash who, the previous day, testified before a State Senate committee about the operational methods of investigators working for the magazine.
(United Photo Press)

January 11, 1961—President-elect John F. Kennedy with brother-in-law Peter Lawford, after flying to West Palm Beach, Florida, from Washington, DC. Nine days later, JFK would deliver his inaugural address.
(Associated Press)

May 19, 1962—Cecil Stoughton captures (L-R) Robert Kennedy, Marilyn Monroe, John F. Kennedy, and Arthur Schlesinger, Jr. at the birthday party thrown for the President at Arthur Krim's New York apartment.
(Time & Life Pictures/Getty Images)

August 5, 1962—Police photo of MM's bedroom following her death. (Associated Press)

August 5, 1962—Police photo captures a smudge on the wall of MM's bedroom (possibly blood) that was subsequently airbrushed out of the version released to the general public.
(Confidential source)

August 5, 1962—Reverse side of the same, un-retouched police photo, bearing the pencil inscription: "3 COL W/MARILYN break, P2A."
(Confidential source)

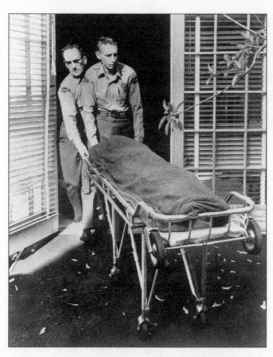

August 5, 1962—Deputy Coroners Cletus Pace and Robert Dambacher remove MM's body from the Westwood Village Mortuary in order to transport her back to the Coroner's Office. (Keystone-France/Gamma-Keystone/Getty Images)

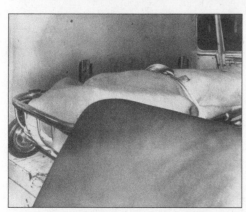

August 5, 1962—MM lies on a stretcher inside a hearse following the removal of her body from 12305 Fifth Helena Drive. (Associated Press)

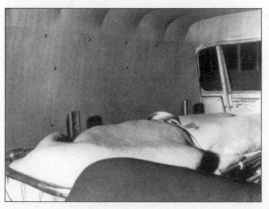

August 5, 1962—MM's body arrives at the Westwood Village Mortuary. (United Press International)

August 5, 1962—MM's housekeeper, Eunice Murray, is helped into the driver's seat of her green Dodge by son-in-law Norman Jefferies, MM's handyman, as she leaves the Monroe home following the movie star's death. (Associated Press)

August 5, 1962—A police officer points to an assortment of medicine bottles on MM's bedside table. Police said a sleeping pill bottle was empty. (Associated Press)

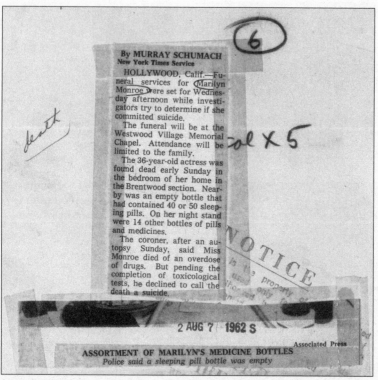

By MURRAY SCHUMACH
New York Times Service

HOLLYWOOD, Calif.—Funeral services for Marilyn Monroe were set for Wednesday afternoon while investigators try to determine if she committed suicide.

The funeral will be at the Westwood Village Memorial Chapel. Attendance will be limited to the family.

The 36-year-old actress was found dead early Sunday in the bedroom of her home in the Brentwood section. Nearby was an empty bottle that had contained 40 or 50 sleeping pills. On her night stand were 14 other bottles of pills and medicines.

The coroner, after an autopsy Sunday, said Miss Monroe died of an overdose of drugs. But pending the completion of toxicological tests, he declined to call the death a suicide.

2 AUG 7 1962 S

Associated Press

ASSORTMENT OF MARILYN'S MEDICINE BOTTLES
Police said a sleeping pill bottle was empty

(Associated Press)

August 5, 1962—Gene Anthony photographed his wife outside MM's house. A couple of dog toys belonging to Maltese terrier Maf—a gift from Frank Sinatra—can be seen near the edge of the swimming pool at right. (Associated Press)

August 5, 1962—MM publicist Pat Newcomb is intercepted by a reporter as she departs 12305 Fifth Helena Drive in Mrs. Murray's green Dodge following the movie star's death. (United Press International)

On August 7, 1962, it was announced that MM's funeral service would take place at Westwood Village Memorial Chapel the following day and that, due to limited space, no celebrities were to be invited. The exception was MM's second husband Joe DiMaggio, who'd attend alongside relatives and close friends. (United Press International)

August 7, 1962—
The mausoleum at
LA's Westwood Village
Memorial Park where
MM's body would
be interred on the
following afternoon.
(Associated Press)

August 8, 1962—
Curious members
of the public take a
look at MM's crypt.
(Associated Press)

August 8, 1962—MM's former business
manager, Inez Melson, arrives at the
funeral service. (Associated Press)

August 8, 1962—Four pallbearers hold MM's casket (L-R): hairstylist Sydney Guilaroff, makeup man Allan "Whitey" Snyder, funeral director Allan Abbott, and Abbott's business partner Ron Hast. (Keystone-France/Gamma-Keystone/Getty Images)

August 1, 1963—People pay their respects to MM as the first anniversary of her death approaches. Twice a week fresh red roses would be placed beside her crypt as a perpetual remembrance from Joe DiMaggio.
(United Press International)

September 9, 1964—Peter Lawford "representing the family" at the opening of the John F. Kennedy library exhibit in Miami, Florida. (*Miami Herald* staff photographer Albert Coya)

October 5, 1964—Peter Lawford arrives for work at Paramount Studios after taking an eight-minute helicopter flight from his LA home. Pilot Hal Conners, seated inside, used this same helicopter to transport Robert Kennedy from Lawford's beach house to Los Angeles International Airport during the early morning hours of August 5, 1962. (Associated Press)

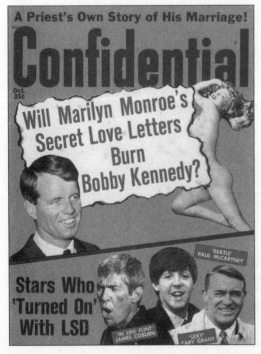

Confidential magazine, October 1967. (Steven Williams and George Ramos)

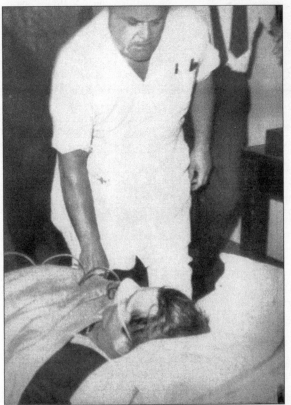

June 5, 1968—Sen. Robert F. Kennedy arrives at Central Receiving Hospital shortly after being shot three times at the Ambassador Hotel while talking to campaign workers. He was taken immediately to surgery, where a team of neurosurgeons began efforts to remove the bullet from his brain. (Associated Press)

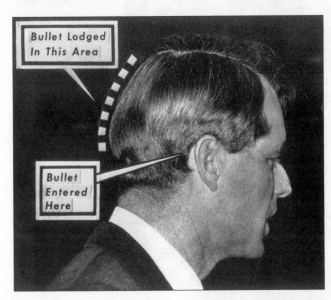

June 5, 1968—Photo diagram locates the spot behind Sen. Robert Kennedy's ear where the fatal bullet of the third shooter entered the Senator's head, as well as the approximate area of the head where a large part of the bullet was lodged after fragmenting. (Associated Press)

June 5, 1968—Sen. Robert F. Kennedy was shot at the near end of the steel counter being inspected by police officers in a kitchen corridor of the Ambassador Hotel in Los Angeles. He staggered backwards and fell at a spot where an "X" is chalked on the floor. Ceiling tiles were removed by LAPD to inspect for bullet holes. (Associated Press)

1970s—Schaefer Ambulance driver Edgardo Villalobos with attendant Gilbert Venagas standing in front of a Schaefer Ambulance VIP car known as "The Diplomat." (Edgardo Villalobos)

1970s—"The Diplomat." (Edgardo Villalobos)

SCHAEFER
AMBULANCE
SERVICE

Paramedic and CCT
Air Ambulance

(213) 468-1600

(From the
collection
of Edgardo
Villalobos)

1970s—Edgardo Villalobos
inside his Schaefer
Ambulance vehicle.
(Edgardo Villalobos)

1970s—
Schaefer
Ambulance
vehicle.
(Edgardo
Villalobos)

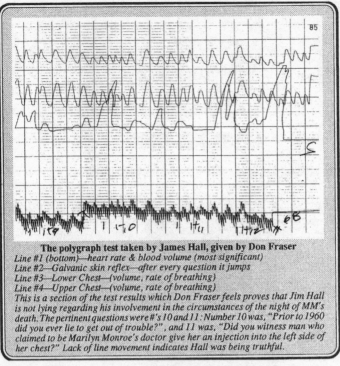

85

The polygraph test taken by James Hall, given by Don Fraser
Line #1 (bottom)—heart rate & blood volume (most significant)
Line #2—Galvanic skin reflex—after every question it jumps
Line #3—Lower Chest—(volume, rate of breathing)
Line #4—Upper Chest—(volume, rate of breathing)
This is a section of the test results which Don Fraser feels proves that Jim Hall is not lying regarding his involvement in the circumstances of the night of MM's death. The pertinent questions were #'s 10 and 11: Number 10 was, "Prior to 1960 did you ever lie to get out of trouble?", and 11 was, "Did you witness man who claimed to be Marilyn Monroe's doctor give her an injection into the left side of her chest?" Lack of line movement indicates Hall was being truthful.

Schaefer Ambulance attendant James Edwin Hall's 1992 polygraph results, conducted by Donald E. Fraser, a state-licensed polygraphist and graduate of the University of Southern California. (© 2014 Michelle Justice. Reprinted with permission from fan newspaper *Runnin' Wild: All About Marilyn*, October 1993.)

October 19, 2000: Letter from comedian Bob Hope to Schaefer Ambulance driver Edgardo Villalobos. (From the collection of Edgardo Villalobos)

BOB HOPE

October 19, 2000

Dear Edgardo,

I'm glad to know that you and your buddies got a chance to see my show in Korea.

Some of my fondest memories are of the men and women I entertained during the wars. And, knowing what sacrifices you and the others were making to protect our way of life, made anything I went through to get there seem like a walk in the park.

My thanks to you.

Bob Hope

she had been having an affair with the late President John F. Kennedy or his brother."

"I've decided that all I can do I've tried to do," Greenson said, "and somewhere it is written that this woman is not a bad woman and was not involved with all the political figures. Somewhere, if you will read long enough, you will find it."

Nevertheless, just days after Marilyn died, Greenson had told the Suicide Prevention Team a completely different story: the actress had been in a "close relationship with extremely important men in government." It was "sexual" and the men were "at the highest level."[36]

At around the same time, Mrs. Murray recounted an accidental death story to Mr. and Mrs. Landau, the movie star's next-door neighbors to the west. Abe Charles Landau subsequently recalled: "Mrs. Murray told us that Marilyn had taken an overdose of sleeping pills. She said Marilyn would take pills. Then she would wake up, forget that she had taken some, and take some more. And that's what Mrs. Murray said happened."

Still, more than a decade later, in the July 16, 1973, issue of *Time* magazine, a Marilyn Monroe–related feature again flipped this on its head: "It was not a case, says Noguchi, of 'automatism'—that gray area in which a person used to taking pills becomes groggy, takes a few too many, and slips over the edge of death." Under close scrutiny, Ralph Greenson's account of what took place on that fateful night comes apart at the seams.[37]

THE KENNEDY VERSION

WAS LAWFORD'S CALL TO EBBINS A CRY FOR HELP OR JUST A REALLY GOOD ALIBI?

Milt Ebbins, Peter Lawford's best friend and vice president of his production company Chrislaw, claimed he received a frantic telephone call from the actor at around 7:15, 7:40, or close to 8:00 on the evening of August 4, 1962, depending on which version of his account one chooses. Ebbins recalled Lawford being concerned that something was wrong with Marilyn; that maybe she took too many sleeping pills. As we've already seen, there was absolutely nothing wrong with Marilyn at 7:15 or 8:00 or even 9:30 p.m.

Biographers Peter Harry Brown and Patte Barham noted that, according to "master publicist" Rupert Allan, "Lawford's story sounded as though it had been written for him by a public relations expert. It seemed more like an alibi than an actual event."

Ebbins refuted any notion of Lawford driving to the Monroe residence on the night she died. "I was a confidant of Peter's," Ebbins informed Donald Spoto. "Believe me, I was a confidant of this man. He would've dropped it to me in a minute . . . Others told him, '[Comedian] Mort Sahl will go with you . . .'"

Ebbins further claimed that *he* phoned Marilyn's house: "I called and got a busy signal. The operator said it was out of order. It's off the hook!"

Now that we know Marilyn was not in trouble anytime before 9:30 p.m., it's easy to see right through Ebbins' fabrication. Nevertheless, it's also interesting that he told Spoto, "Peter Lawford wanted to go badly. I said, 'Peter, don't do it. Please let me at least call Mickey Rudin and alert him and *then*, if we do that, you can go . . .'"

Milt Ebbins claims he phoned Mickey Rudin who at that time was at Mildred Allenberg's house. Rudin supposedly said to Ebbins, "Let me check it out and I'll get back to you." A few minutes later, Rudin called Ebbins and relayed, "I talked to Mrs. Murray. She looked through the crack in the window. She said, 'She's fine. She does this every night. Every night she does this.'" Rudin allegedly concluded to Ebbins, "You don't have to go over there. Please don't go over there. You're just gonna cause problems . . ."

When Milt Ebbins reiterated this to Peter Lawford, the actor still insisted on paying Marilyn a visit and demanded to talk with her lawyer and manager Mickey Rudin. Rudin then contacted Lawford and persuaded him to change his mind, but Lawford, "getting drunker by the minute," persisted in calling Ebbins and repeating his desire to drive over to 12305 Fifth Helena Drive. "Go!" Ebbins recalled finally snapping. "You don't need me," prompting Lawford to purportedly back down and say, "I'm not going. I'm not going."

Accordingly, addressing the possibility that Peter Lawford *did* subsequently visit Marilyn and then meet with private investigator Fred Otash, Milt Ebbins told biographer James Spada, "I know the way this story may go and I'm prepared for it. I can't dispute you because you're liable to have proof that it was true. All I can say is that I think my version is the true one."

Spoto told Ebbins that, at eleven thirty on the night of August 4, Lawford called his best friend Joe Naar and urged him, "Go over to Marilyn's house." Spoto then recounted how Naar puts his trousers on and got ready to leave when he received another call from Lawford, saying, 'I just had a call from the doctors. They're there. Everything's fine.'"

Ebbins countered, "That's a lot of crap . . . Number one, Peter never talked to Rudin that night because Rudin told me to tell him [about Marilyn's death] . . . I called Peter immediately and the phone was dead. And [his maid] Erma Lee says, 'We don't answer the phone when Peter goes to bed. Nobody picks up the phones downstairs. Upstairs, he pulls it out of the wall . . .'"

According to Milt Ebbins, Erma Lee was Peter Lawford's mistress as well as his maid, and she insisted he never left his house that night. Furthermore, Ebbins claimed he received a call from Mickey Rudin at around four in the morning, saying, "We've got some problems." When

Ebbins asked, "How's Marilyn?" Rudin replied, "Not good," before revealing that was something of an understatement. "What's the matter with her?" Ebbins enquired, prompting Rudin to say, "Well, I'm here with Dr. Engelberg and Dr. Greenson, and they just pronounced her dead and we just notified the police. And you're the first one that knows about it . . . You better tell Peter."

As for accusations that Bobby Kennedy had Marilyn Monroe killed, Ebbins told Spoto, "Come on! Bobby Kennedy had more ways. He could've gotten rid of Marilyn Monroe with a phone call to Peter Lawford . . . Of course, we noted she had a mental problem for years. Marilyn thought she was going to wind up like her mother. She was scared to death of that."

Milt Ebbins told James Spada, "Marilyn was destined to die. She'd tried suicide four times. Peter felt guilty about not going over to save her, but Dr. Greenson told him, 'Don't feel responsible—it was bound to happen. She would have done it again if it hadn't worked that time . . .' Greenson told Peter that Marilyn had tried to commit suicide four or five times and he said, 'Peter, she was doomed. It was only a matter of time,' that unless she was confined for a lengthy period, she was going to die . . . The only thing I could think of was to get her lawyer, manager, and doctor involved, and it was done in minutes . . . I was on the phone to Peter all night the night Marilyn died. Until one-thirty at least. After that, he wouldn't answer the phone."

Director Bill Asher remembered, "I heard from Peter at eight or nine . . . Then he called later, maybe midnight, probably one o'clock to go over with him."

Lawford's good friend producer George "Bullets" Durgom was a guest at his Saturday evening party on August 4 where, Durgom claimed, the host expressed his concern about visiting Marilyn's home. In the *Say Goodbye to the President* documentary, Durgom recalled how Lawford "mentions maybe I ought to go up there and see if she's okay. I said, 'Well, I don't know, Peter, if you should do that at this time. I mean, I'm sure everything's all right. If we go up there and there is anything going on, who knows what kind of story this will wind up being?'"

Milt Ebbins told Spoto, "There were two numbers. Peter didn't have the other number . . . Rudin asked me to let him check it out—to see if there was any trouble." Rudin agreed to this account and said, "I did not call [Greenson]. He had had enough quite frankly. He had spent the day with her. But I did call the housekeeper."

On August 9, 1962, Ebbins told a reporter about Lawford calling him on that Saturday night: "He said Miss Monroe told him she would like to come but that she was tired and was going to bed early. He said he noticed nothing unusual, except that she did sound tired."[38]

This is odd: on August 9, 1962, Ebbins recalled there being "nothing unusual," yet thirty years later he informed Donald Spoto about a tremendous panic and how "Peter Lawford wanted to go badly."

Peter Lawford's mother Lady May Lawford, who once described her son as "such a big mistake," relayed what she recalled happening on August 4: "The night that Marilyn died, I called Peter out at the Santa Monica beach house . . . In the background I thought I heard that awful Boston accent of Bobby Kennedy . . . Then [Peter] hung up." Lawford's mother was absolutely certain Marilyn Monroe shared a bed with both Kennedy brothers. "I knew that Marilyn was seeing Jack Kennedy," Mrs. Lawford asserted. "I also knew that Marilyn was seeing Bobby Kennedy. They often used Pat and Peter's beach house . . . If Jack or Bobby asked him to, he would have done anything . . . So it is with Marilyn's death—Peter had a part in the cover-up."[39]

On October 7, 1985, Milt Ebbins told his "story," which was riddled with inaccuracies. All the things he said didn't happen on Marilyn's last night actually *did* happen. "I talked to Peter on the telephone several times that night," Ebbins recalled. "He never left his beach house in Santa Monica. Bobby definitely was not in Southern California that night and neither man went to Marilyn's house. Forget about the ambulance. It just couldn't have happened. Peter called in the afternoon and asked me to dinner with Bullets Durgom and Joe Naar and his wife—and Marilyn. I declined. He called again to say Marilyn couldn't come and that she was anxiety-ridden. He was upset and wanted to go to Marilyn's house in Brentwood. I told him not to. We all knew Marilyn took too many pills and was drinking heavily."

Unembalmed blood sent out for testing later showed no alcohol was consumed that last day. Ebbins continued: "I suggested we call Mickey Rudin, Marilyn's attorney, and her psychiatrist, Dr. Ralph Greenson, Mickey's brother-in-law, and ask them to go to her house. I got Mickey and told him about Peter's apprehension.

"Mickey called me about 7:30 to say he had talked to Mrs. Murray, a psychiatric nurse hired by Greenson, who said she looked in on Marilyn. Murray told Mickey, 'She does this every night. She takes the pills, calls somebody and falls asleep. She's fine.' Mickey said Mrs. Murray had looked through the drapery of an outside window and saw Marilyn lying on the bed asleep. The lights were on and the radio was going. I told Peter this and he insisted on talking to Mickey. Mickey called Peter and convinced him all was well but Peter was still apprehensive and wanted to go to Marilyn's. I told him Mrs. Murray would tell him the same thing she told Rudin.

"This was no conspiracy to kill Marilyn, you know, involving Mickey and Mrs. Murray, for God's sake. Peter called me twice more when he was getting a little drunk, expressing his fear that Marilyn was very ill. Peter called me once after midnight and he was bombed. By this time Mort Sahl had stopped by to talk to me. Mort was there when, about five minutes to 4:00 a.m., Mickey called. And I asked him, 'How's Marilyn?' He said, 'Not good. I'm here with Dr. Greenson and Dr. Engelberg. We broke into her bedroom. They pronounced her dead. We just called the police.' I was stunned and told Mort. We were the first to know, except for Mickey and the two doctors. I tried to call Peter but he had pulled the phone jack from the wall—which he did every night—and I couldn't reach him. So I went to bed and later when I did reach Peter, he had already been told.

"Peter was guilt-ridden because he hadn't gone to Marilyn's house. I told him that Marilyn was doomed. She had tried to commit suicide five or six times previously. This time she made it. I never heard Bobby's name mentioned, much less about him arriving at Peter's house in a helicopter that night. Peter was my closest friend. He would have told me if Bobby had been here or if Marilyn had been taken away in an ambulance.

"That is the unadulterated story of the night Marilyn died. The rest of that stuff is pure fantasy. How could Bobby be in town that night? He was in Northern California with his wife and children. And he and Peter were never close friends. If Peter had bailed Bobby out of a jam, don't you think they would have been friends for life? But when Pat and Peter divorced, Peter became persona non grata with the Kennedys. Bobby never called Peter when he came to town, neither did Teddy or any other family member. The authorities are satisfied Marilyn committed suicide and died alone. The stories going around are circulated by people who want their names in the papers."

Ebbins clearly did not have a firm grasp regarding the time element that night. He said, "Mickey called me about 7:30 to say he had talked to Mrs. Murray." Rudin told the police he called the housekeeper at 9:00 p.m. In 1975, Lawford informed the police that 7:30 was when Marilyn was going under. Fifteen minutes earlier, at 7:15, Marilyn had happily finished her phone call with Joe DiMaggio, Jr. Also, Ebbins' account contradicts many of the things we know. Without a doubt, an ambulance arrived at Marilyn's home. And after midnight a helicopter did, in fact, transport Robert Kennedy from the Lawford beach house in Santa Monica to Los Angeles International Airport. He subsequently took a private plane back to San Francisco.

Ebbins' story is further called into question because he appeared to have an answer for everything. Either he was covering up what he knew or, more likely, he didn't know anything about what happened that night and simply agreed to go along with a pre-packaged story he rehearsed many times. Why would the principals involved tell him about what really went on? And if, as Ebbins himself admitted, he remained in his own home all evening, how can he be regarded as a reliable witness?

Although Ebbins said Lawford was "persona non grata with the Kennedys," a *People* magazine article dated January 14, 1985, called Ebbins' statement into question. Malcolm Boyes wrote that Peter Lawford remained "on good terms with the Kennedys. In fact, presidential candidate Robert Kennedy, after winning the California primary in 1968, was headed for a Lawford-hosted party when he, too, was killed by an assassin's bullets." James Spada questioned Dolores Naar about this:

SPADA: Peter mentions that he campaigned for Bobby and in fact there was going to be a party at his house after the California primaries. Now, would Pat have been there?

DOLORES NAAR: We were all to go to that. Pat would have been there. There was a bit of a rapprochement between Pat and Peter at that time, mostly for Bobby's sake. Whatever worked for that family—there was a bond there.

Gloria Romanoff concurred with Ebbins that Bobby Kennedy was never Peter's good friend, "I don't think there was a lot of affection between Bobby Kennedy and Peter Lawford. I think Bobby Kennedy tolerated him because he was Pat's husband. I don't think he was terribly fond of Peter and Peter knew that." Of course, Detective Lynn Franklin noted how, after getting the correct directions to the Beverly Hilton Hotel, Bobby Kennedy had chided Peter Lawford, exclaiming, "I told you, stupid!" Nonetheless, Bobby Kennedy and Peter Lawford continued to see one another even though, as many people attest, there was no love lost between the two men.[40]

BILL ASHER ALSO
CLAIMS LAWFORD
PHONED HIM IN A PANIC

In 1992, according to Milt Ebbins and director Bill Asher, the latter's production company optioned the book *Double Cross* for a movie. This was the book that accused Chicago Mob boss Sam Giancana of sanctioning Marilyn Monroe's murder. To Donald Spoto, Asher largely echoed Ebbins's account of Marilyn's last night, but he also added a new twist: the possibility of seeking the advice of a very important man.

Accustomed to Marilyn not turning up for her appointments, Asher claimed to have told his friend Peter Lawford that he wasn't prepared to sit around and wait for her to appear at his dinner party. So, he returned home and received a call from Lawford at "about eight or nine," saying he couldn't reach Marilyn on the phone. Apparently, Lawford had talked with Marilyn earlier in the evening and, allegedly having consumed some wine, she had fallen asleep during their phone conversation.

"She's wasn't stressed at all," Asher recalled being told. "She was a little slurry. She had a couple of drinks but it wasn't anything that anyone would have been concerned about. There were times she would get incapacitated and you'd be worried about her."

Later, according to Asher, at around midnight, he received another call from Lawford, suggesting they pay Marilyn a visit. "It's the only thing I always felt badly about because we didn't go," Asher remarked. "I said, 'Your brother-in-law's the President of the United States! It might not be an appropriate thing for you to go over there' . . . I know he called Milt . . . I told him to call the old man, Joe [Kennedy] . . ."

Donald Spoto's research assistant Charlie relayed to Bill Asher how Joe Naar recalled getting a call from Peter Lawford, asking him to go to Marilyn's house before then getting another call between 11:30 and midnight saying "Forget it. Everything's fine." Asher confirmed the timeline sounded correct, although he never heard anything about Marilyn doing fine.

If Asher and Naar told the truth about receiving those calls from Peter Lawford, there's a hole in Lawford's story that is bigger than the Grand Canyon. After all, why would he call Joe Naar at 11:30 at night, telling him to go by himself to check on Marilyn who lived just four blocks away, before then calling Joe back minutes later telling him not to bother? Furthermore, why would Lawford then call Bill Asher between midnight and 1:00 a.m., requesting that he accompany him to Marilyn's place, if he had already told Naar not to go? Quite simply, the story doesn't check out.[41]

DOLORES NAAR CLAIMS
DR. GREENSON GAVE
MARILYN SEDATIVES

Talking with Jay Margolis, Dolores Naar claimed that, en route to the Lawfords' dinner party, she and Joe were supposed to give Marilyn a ride there. However, there was a change of plans before they set out: "Peter called our house and said, 'Don't pick up Marilyn. She's not coming.'"

The Naars told biographer James Spada that they received the call from Lawford at about 7:30 p.m. "I read in one of the books that Bobby was upstairs," said Dolores. "They were hiding him. I don't believe any of it. There was no way Bobby Kennedy was there."

According to Joe in his interviews with both Spoto and Margolis, Lawford called again at 11:30 p.m., this time to ask him to check on Marilyn. In Spoto's interview with him, Joe quoted Lawford as saying the following: "I just talked to Marilyn and I'm scared. I don't like the way she sounds. I think she's taken some pills. Will you go check up on her?"

As we know, Joe agreed before a second call, a couple of minutes later, informed him there was no need to go. Dolores explained to James Spada that to her husband Joe over the phone, Lawford "said that he'd spoken to Marilyn's doctor and [Dr. Greenson] had said that he had given her sedatives because she had been disturbed earlier and she was probably asleep, so don't bother going. [Lawford] said, 'You'll just wake her up.'"

MARGOLIS: How were you apprised of the conversation between Joe and Peter? Did Joe tell you that Marilyn had received sedatives from her doctor?

DOLORES NAAR: Well, I was there.

MARGOLIS: So, you were listening in on the phone with Joe while Peter was calling?

DOLORES NAAR: I was in the room.

In a subsequent interview, Margolis returned to the same subject.

MARGOLIS: As far as that last call from Peter goes, telling you and Joe not to go around 11:30 p.m., Joe said to me in an interview that Peter told him Dr. Greenson had said, "She does this all the time. Don't go."

DOLORES NAAR: That's right. He said Dr. Greenson had given her something to sleep and she's fine. That's what Peter told Joe. "So you don't need to go."

Perhaps Peter Lawford was alluding to Ralph Greenson's undiluted Nembutal injection, which would not only put Marilyn to sleep but ensure that she'd never wake up. Even though she believed Marilyn died an accidental death, Dolores Naar still considered Lawford's actions to be more than a little suspicious. She told James Spada, "Peter probably called Jack or Bobby and was told to take care of things—do whatever he had to do. And *do it yourself*—don't involve anybody else under any circumstances."

Spada made some chilling points: "These were an odd pair of telephone calls in an evening replete with oddities. Why did Peter, who had been worried about Marilyn since 7:30, wait until the Naars had returned home to indicate any concern to them over Marilyn? And why did he first ask Joe to go over to Marilyn's (after being told by Mickey Rudin that she was okay) and then, just a few minutes later, tell him *not* to go?" Remember, the Naars only lived four blocks away from Marilyn. Dolores told Spada she believed Lawford's two calls were "calculated to mislead us. Joe and I wondered, 'Why did he call us the second time and tell us not to go?' Maybe because by then he knew that Marilyn was dead."[42]

CONCLUSION

Peter Lawford fed Joe and Dolores Naar a "story," confusing many Marilyn Monroe biographers in the process. After the Naars left the party, Pat Newcomb arrived at the Lawford beach house at 9:30 p.m., according to George "Bullets" Durgom. Then, before Bobby Kennedy departed Marilyn's house with LAPD partners Archie Case and James Ahern, someone called Lawford, telling him to get over there and hire a cleanup crew.

In turn, Lawford contacted private detective Fred Otash and they agreed to meet at 12305 Fifth Helena Drive. Otash brought along his soundman (who was interviewed by Jay Margolis). Next, Lawford drove Pat Newcomb from the Lawford beach house to Marilyn's residence, arriving at around 10:30 p.m., soon after Bobby left with Case and Ahern. If Schaefer Ambulance attendant James Hall and his driver Murray Liebowitz had been allowed to transport Marilyn to the hospital, she would most likely be alive today.

She wasn't yet dead when Hall arrived in the guest cottage and she was responding positively to resuscitation efforts by Hall and Liebowitz who had a resuscitator on Marilyn until Ralph Greenson suspiciously ordered its removal before injecting her in the heart with an undiluted Nembutal injection. Thus, there was a premeditated plan to murder her on the part of Robert Kennedy, Ralph Greenson, and Peter Lawford—a plan that, according to the British actor, had originated with the Attorney General.

None of the principals involved counted on Mrs. Murray calling an ambulance. After Marilyn died, Lawford would express deep guilt over what really happened to her. Marilyn Monroe had been murdered and he was involved. Lawford informed his friends that Marilyn had accidentally overdosed on sleeping pills. Joe Naar said to biographer Laurence Leamer, "I blame the changes in Peter and his final decline into the bottle on Marilyn's death. Peter kept saying, 'I should have let you go. I killed her.'"

163

Peter Lawford's strange actions in front of his friends could be amply explained if he was trying to come up with an alibi. His best friend Joe Naar told Jay Margolis, "You're trying to sort out the truth and put a puzzle together, but at this late date it's going to be extremely difficult. So, how in the world are you *ever* going to find out the truth? I don't know how you, in all good conscience, can do this. It's so hard to put it all together. My own wife Dolores said it was not Sunday night, it was Saturday night. So, if we can differ on what night it was, then you can imagine what you're up against. I mean, how is that possible, we don't even know which night it was?"

Former FBI agent Bill Roemer believed neither Bobby Kennedy nor the Mafia had anything to do with Marilyn's death. However, he answered in the affirmative to support the convening of a grand jury, "I would, yeah. I think there have been so many questions now and there's so much conjecturing. It would be nice to put it all out in the open once and for all so there'd be no question to what exactly happened."

Celebrated Italian psychologist Luciano Mecacci deduced, "Marilyn's death was in the end a relief for everyone: for the Kennedys, who had been freed from the nightmare of a scandal; for the CIA and the FBI, who were reassured about a possible leak of secret material; and for Greenson, who had been released from a personal and professional commitment that was becoming too demanding."

Fred Otash said the FBI and the CIA had bugged Marilyn's house. Concerned about her "tell all" press conference, they wouldn't miss Marilyn if she suddenly died. Certainly, J. Edgar Hoover was not a stupid man. FBI agent John Anderson reported back to him that Bobby Kennedy went inside Marilyn's house alongside Case and Ahern shortly after 9:30 p.m. Before ten o'clock, Marilyn became embroiled in a physical struggle and that struggle was recorded via wiretap. It was then noted that Kennedy, Case, and Ahern left at 10:30. Through cause and effect, Hoover knew that the Kennedys were involved. What's more, Bobby was fully aware that Hoover had knowledge about his participation in the murder of a movie star.

In the years to come, the FBI director would play games with Bobby Kennedy, always sticking it to him about Marilyn Monroe. On July 8, 1964, Hoover wrote to Bobby regarding Frank Capell's soon-to-be-released *The Strange Death of Marilyn Monroe*: "His book will make reference to your alleged friendship with the late Miss Marilyn Monroe. Mr. Capell stated that he will indicate in his book that you and Miss Monroe were intimate, and that you were in Miss Monroe's home at the time of her death."

"He said she was murdered," Hoover's teenage neighbor Anthony Calomaris told Anthony Summers decades later, "that it wasn't a suicide, that the Kennedys were involved." However, Hoover would never think of having Bobby arrested. It was not in his character. Instead, he blackmailed the Attorney General to secure his current position as head of the FBI, reminding Bobby who was really running the country. Besides, exposing the Kennedys in this scandal could destroy the belief the nation had in its own government during the pre-Watergate era. It would be inconceivable that Hoover would make such a move.

When Bobby Kennedy saw Marilyn Monroe on February 1, 1962, not knowing that the Lawford home was bugged by the FBI director, Marilyn told Bobby she knew Hoover was following her and she wondered when Bobby was going to fire him. Bobby said he wasn't in a position to do so at the moment. Anthony Summers wrote, "For Edgar, reading the transcript in Washington, Kennedy's words must have held some comfort. He now knew, for sure, from the mouth of one of the brothers, that the Kennedys were afraid to dismiss him—for the time being. That gave him all the more reason to go on watching to keep on piling up compromising information."

In 1961, after disagreeing with J. Edgar Hoover at a function for the Justice Department, Ethel Kennedy "put an anonymous note in the FBI's 'suggestions' box proposing that the Director be replaced by the Los Angeles Police Chief William Parker, whom Hoover loathed." The potential for blackmail resolved the discrepancy of why Bobby Kennedy publicly expressed his gratitude toward Hoover, a man he was known to hate. On August 7, 1962, at the Seattle World's Fair, Kennedy uncharacteristically supported J. Edgar Hoover in public and said something that must have made Parker cringe, "I hope Hoover will continue to serve the country for many, many years to come."

On September 18, 1965, Bobby Kennedy attended a ceremonial lineup for Mickey Mantle at Yankee Stadium. Gay Talese of *Esquire* magazine wrote: "Mantle stepped forward. He stood with his wife and children, posed for the photographers kneeling in front. Then he thanked the crowd in a short speech and, turning, shook hands with the dignitaries standing nearby. Among them now was Senator Kennedy . . ."

Interestingly, Joe DiMaggio was also at the event attended by Robert Kennedy. "Kennedy posed with Mantle for a photographer, then shook hands with the Mantle children, and with Toots Shor and James Farley," wrote Gay Talese. "DiMaggio saw him [Robert Kennedy] coming down the line and at the last second he backs away, casually . . . and Kennedy seemed not to notice it . . . just swept past shaking more hands . . ."

Not even a year later on July 16, 1966, Kennedy's old friend Police Chief William Parker died of a heart attack while in attendance at a military dinner where he was a guest speaker.

According to Peter Lawford, Bobby Kennedy had "convinced" Ralph Greenson that Marilyn Monroe would also publicly reveal *his* affair with her. This was not true and therefore Bobby had successfully manipulated the psychiatrist for his own ends. Once Greenson realized this, it was too late and he had experienced firsthand what it was like to be used by one of the Kennedy brothers. This is why Lawford concluded that Greenson had been "set up" by Bobby to murder his star patient.

In fact, according to biographer C. David Heymann, Peter Lawford told him, "MM's affair with Greenson took on a far greater meaning at the time of her death. Marilyn, as everyone later discovered, had threatened Bobby with the prospect of holding a press conference at which she planned to announce her assignations with both the President and the Attorney General.

"Such an admission would no doubt have resulted in a major scandal. Bobby, on hearing of Marilyn's plans—and somehow knowing of her concomitant relationship with Greenson—called the good doctor and convinced him that his star patient also intended to disclose her romantic dealings with the psychiatrist."

Robert Kennedy told Greenson, "Marilyn has got to be silenced." Therefore, Lawford deduced, "Greenson had thus been set up by Bobby to 'take care' of Marilyn."

Greenson had indeed been tricked into murdering Marilyn Monroe, and therefore his recorded reference to the Attorney General ("Talk to Bobby Kennedy") was a bitter and illuminating remark. In fact, the psychiatrist wrote, "The ending at this particular time seemed so unfair and in a way unnecessary, and I feel that I have hurt my whole family with this since they all got to know her and cared about her . . . She was a Cinderella girl who did not live happily ever after." Ralph Greenson conceded, "She was a poor creature, whom I tried to help and ending up hurting."

As for the movie star's last publicist, Pat Newcomb, Lawford told Heymann: "After Marilyn's death, the Kennedys gave Pat a job in Washington and soon sent her off to Europe so the American press couldn't get hold of her."

Everyone deserves the right to due process of law and that right was not afforded to Marilyn Monroe in 1962. Now, more than a half-century has passed since her death and most of those involved are now deceased. So, the only justice that can be afforded Marilyn is to name her murderers: Robert Kennedy, Peter Lawford, and the man who finally ended her life, Dr. Ralph Greenson.

"I had become a prisoner now of a form of treatment which I thought was correct for her but almost impossible for me," Ralph Greenson chillingly wrote to Dr. Marianne Kris more than two weeks after he murdered Marilyn Monroe. "I was her therapist, the good father who would not disappoint her and who would bring her insights, and if not insights, just kindness."

Greenson felt an overwhelming responsibility by continuing to treat his star patient. He claimed he wanted to help her but that all his efforts were futile. The psychiatrist relayed, "She was making progress, but at times I felt I couldn't go on with this, particularly since so often it became 6 or 7 days a week."

In the months leading to her death, Marilyn Monroe became a source of incessant aggravation to Ralph Greenson and his massive ego. "I had become the most important person in her life and there was nothing I could do except hope that as she improved still more she would become more independent," the doctor explained. "I also felt guilty that I put a burden on my own family."

The most famous woman in the world had many plans for the future. She didn't like being typecast into the same role. "I'm tired of playing sex kittens," said Marilyn Monroe. "I want roles that I can get my teeth into—roles that enable me to show a side of myself which appeals to an intelligent public . . . But sex is not enough . . . If I stick with the sex bit who will be paying to see me when I'm fifty?"

In her second-to-last interview with *Life* magazine, in July 1962, Marilyn Monroe told Richard Meryman: "I never quite understood it—this sex symbol—I always thought symbols were those things you clash together! That's the trouble, a sex symbol becomes a thing. I just hate to be a thing. But if I'm going to be a symbol of something I'd rather have it sex than some other things they've got symbols of!" Not only was she "the symbol of the eternal feminine," as acting coach Lee Strasberg eulogized about Marilyn at her funeral, she was a human being. May she finally rest in peace.[43]

POSTSCRIPT
CASE CONFIRMED: THE SECOND AND THIRD SHOOTERS IN THE ROBERT KENNEDY ASSASSINATION

On June 5, 1968, Robert Kennedy was shot twice by a second shooter and fatally wounded by a third shooter, all within five and a half seconds (12:15:59–12:16:04). Talking with investigative reporter Dan Moldea, Dr. Thomas Noguchi, who performed the autopsy on the Senator, mentioned the order of the shots fired at Robert Kennedy, all of which were from back-to-front: "The [rear of the right] shoulder pad shot as he was raising his arm [which didn't actually hit Kennedy], the two shots to his right armpit, in which one of the bullets lodged in the back of his neck, and, lastly, the shot to the mastoid [where a large part of the bullet fragmented and lodged in his brain]. This was the shot that was fatal. In other words, the [two] nonfatal wounds first and then the fatal wound."

Eyewitness Don Schulman, a KNXT-TV employee, stated he was in the crowd behind RFK at the time of the shooting and said he saw someone dressed as an Ace Security guard "standing directly to the side and back of Kennedy," Schulman told investigative reporter Ted Charach in 1971. "He was standing on the right-hand side."

In fact, immediately after the shooting, Schulman first relayed his account of what he saw to Jeff Brent of the Continental News Service who broadcasted his account over the radio. Minutes after that, KNXT news anchor Jerry Dunphy reported on television while Sirhan Sirhan was *still* at the Ambassador Hotel that "Don Schulman of KNXT tells us that Kennedy was shot three times . . ."

As noted in the FBI files on the RFK assassination, Schulman is adamant that he saw "Kennedy being shot three times. The guard definitely pulled out his gun and fired." To Ted Charach, Schulman said Sirhan Sirhan was "from three to six feet" from Kennedy during the shooting and facing the Senator, not behind him.

"That bullet which killed Kennedy, it was an inch away from his head," stated Karl Uecker, the hotel assistant maître d' who grabbed Sirhan's gun arm after Sirhan's second shot. "This bullet [an inch away] didn't come from Sirhan. Did not come from Sirhan because he never got that close."

"One was Sirhan Sirhan and the other one was the security guard," Don Schulman told Jay Margolis asserting that he witnessed two shooters nearly sixteen minutes after midnight, while at the same time confirming that Kennedy had been shot three times. "I was standing by the doorway. The cameramen had been standing there for quite some time, holding the camera, and they wanted me to signal them when the crowd was moving. They heard Kennedy was going to stop by the kitchen and thank some people. As he left, after his speech, I got shoved in with a lot of other people. All of a sudden, Sirhan was the man who jumped out and yelled obscenities at Kennedy and shot at him while the guard next to Kennedy pulled his gun and fired. I went out and the first person I saw was reporter Jeff Brent who interviewed me for Continental Radio about ten to twelve minutes after the shooting . . . I was interviewed by a lot of people. I saw what I saw. The security guard shot Kennedy. He disappeared for quite some time."

Schulman was absolutely correct that Kennedy was indeed shot three times as autopsy surgeon Dr. Thomas Noguchi later confirmed early the next morning after the Senator was pronounced dead.

Twenty-eight-year old Irene Gizzi, a Youth for Kennedy chairman in Panorama City, was there at the Ambassador Hotel. According to Ms. Gizzi, Jay Margolis is the first person to interview her since a police lieutenant arrived at her home on June 6, 1968. During the shooting, she said she was in the lower ballroom known as the Ambassador Room, not in the pantry and not in the upper ballroom, which is the Embassy Room [both upstairs]. "First, Robert was speaking in the upper ballroom," asserted Irene Gizzi to Jay Margolis. "Then he was going to come down into the lower ballroom and speak." However investigative reporter Shane O'Sullivan importantly noted a last minute change: "After the speech [in the Embassy Room] . . . Kennedy didn't go downstairs to the Ambassador Room . . . He was ushered through the back of the platform by [Karl] Uecker and led . . . into the backstage hallway . . . He was led to his right . . . into the pantry, en route to an impromptu press conference in the Colonial Room."

On March 12, 2014, Jay Margolis presented a photo line-up to Ms. Gizzi of three possible suspects for the now-infamous polka-dot dress girl and three possible suspects for her male companion who Irene Gizzi calls the guy with the medallion. From the six photos, Ms. Gizzi identified to Margolis the girl in the polka-dot dress as Kathryn "Kathy" Ainsworth (born Kathryn Madlyn Capomacchia on July 31, 1941) and her companion as Thomas "Tommy" Albert Tarrants III (born December 20, 1946), pictured below in 1967, months before the RFK assassination.

Irene Gizzi therefore became the first person at the Ambassador Hotel on June 5, 1968, to actually identify via photographs these two individuals out of all the books written on the assassination of Robert Kennedy. Even Tarrants himself fixes his own proximity to the RFK assassination *and* the MLK assassination two months before when he wrote in his first book, "In early spring [1968], I had been in California conferring with

the West Coast coordinator of the Minutemen, a paramilitary underground organization."

As for late 1967, Tarrants revealed, "I decided to take a trip to Los Angeles to deepen my ties with Dr. Wesley Swift, a leader in radical-Right circles." "Tarrants would later testify he bought a rifle from Swift with plans to use it to shoot Dr. Martin Luther King, Jr.," wrote Pulitzer Prize-winning reporter Jack Nelson who was once Bureau Chief of the *Los Angeles Times*. Nelson quoted Thomas Tarrants who said, "That was my ambition, to shoot Dr. King. I hated Dr. King."

On April 4, 1968, using Thomas Tarrants's own car, Ainsworth and Tarrants had disrupted police radios very shortly after Martin Luther King, Jr. was assassinated. Nevertheless, in late December 2007, talking with Jerry Mitchell of the *Clarion-Ledger* newspaper, Tarrants denied any involvement in the MLK assassination even though he admittedly hated Dr. King at that time. As for the charge that he helped disrupt police radios, Tarrants claimed, "I don't know they had people with the technical expertise to do that."

"The police interviewed me afterwards," Irene Gizzi recalled to Jay Margolis regarding the RFK assassination. "I gave what information I could then about the girl in the polka-dot dress and the guy with the medallion because those were the two that stood out from a group of five.

"The three men with them were wearing white [dress] shirts [with ties] and khaki pants. They were shorter than he [Tarrants] was because he was the tallest in the group . . ."

Of these three men, on March 25, 2014, Irene Gizzi identified to Jay Margolis two CIA agents, George Joannides (1922–1990) and David Sanchez Morales (1925–1978), who, according to Gizzi, were *together* in the same group of five along with Tommy Tarrants, Kathy Ainsworth, and a person we shall call Unidentified Man in Profile because Ms. Gizzi told Margolis she only saw this individual in profile.

The five were waiting in the Ambassador Room downstairs shortly before the shooting upstairs in the pantry. Per existing footage taken at the Ambassador Hotel on June 4 and 5, 1968, Joannides, Morales, and Unidentified Man in Profile were all wearing suits with ties and coats. However, during different times, Morales can be seen with and without his suit coat where he's just wearing a white dress shirt with a tie.

At the time of the RFK assassination, the CIA Director was Richard Helms. "Joannides was born in Athens in 1922," wrote Shane O'Sullivan. "Joannides joined the CIA in 1951 and spent eleven years in Greece and Libya before posting to JMWAVE in Miami as deputy to the chief of psychological warfare operations, David Atlee Phillips . . . On July 31, 1963, Joannides was promoted to chief of psychological warfare operations at JMWAVE . . . He died on March 9, 1990, at the age of sixty-seven."

As for Unidentified Man in Profile, O'Sullivan wrote on page 446 of his book how the bottom photograph on page 452 "showed a third man . . . with blonde hair and horn-rimmed glasses." This blonde man may or may not be James Hardesty Critchfield (January 30, 1917–April 22, 2003), who was the CIA's chief in the Middle East on June 5, 1968. Tom Polgar, Joannide's former station chief in Saigon, at first identified both Joannides and Critchfield to O'Sullivan's colleagues David Talbot, *New York Times* bestselling author of *Brothers: The Hidden History of the Kennedy Years,* and *Washington Post* reporter Jefferson Morley.

Two weeks after identifying both men to Talbot and Morley, Polgar took back the certainty of the two identifications but curiously added that the

Ambassador photographs were, in Polgar's words, "not incompatible" with Joannides and identified the blonde man with the horn-rimmed glasses as, in Polgar's words, "not incompatible with James Critchfield." Ms. Gizzi told Margolis this man with blonde hair and horn-rimmed glasses could *possibly* be the man she saw with Tarrants, Ainsworth, Morales, and Joannides, but she is not certain.

"You saw George Joannides and David Morales," Jay Margolis verified to Ms. Gizzi on March 25, 2014. Margolis had shown her photographs of these two individuals from Shane O'Sullivan's book on pages 452 and

474. On page 474, Ms. Gizzi identified David Morales on the far left only, ignoring the other two pictures on the right purporting to also be Morales.

Margolis queried, "The unidentified third man [with blonde hair and horn-rimmed glasses] on page 452 on the bottom you say looks like the third man."

"Looks like the third man—" replied Ms. Gizzi.

"—with Joannides and Morales along with Ainsworth and Tarrants," confirmed Margolis. "So we have four of the five individuals [from the five-person group Ms. Gizzi witnessed] identified."

The second photograph of Unidentified Man in Profile looking upwards was taken from Shane O'Sullivan's 2007 documentary *RFK Must Die: The Assassination of Bobby Kennedy*.

Jay Margolis gave Ms. Gizzi a red felt-tip pen to draw a crude stick-figure diagram with the sole purpose of showing the exact position of the five-person group including George Joannides, Thomas Albert Tarrants III (Medallion), Kathy Ainsworth (Polka-Dot Dress Girl), David Sanchez Morales, and Unidentified Man in Profile (who may or may not be the blonde man with horn-rimmed glasses).

"When I saw them [Tarrants, Ainsworth, Joannides, Morales, and Unidentified Man in Profile]," Ms. Gizzi continued, "they were to the right of the entrance to the lower ballroom [the Ambassador Room]. They were against the right-hand wall, kind of in the shadows, their back almost leaning on the wall with the medallion guy [Tarrants] who was kind of casual.

"This other guy George Joannides had an arm like behind him [a hand gesture which, as Ms. Gizzi confirmed, is clearly shown in the two photographs on page 452 of O'Sullivan's book]. The arm was with the elbow crooked out. That made him look familiar. That made it strike a familiarity. The girl was dancing around with her arms up and she was the one wearing the polka-dot dress.

"Another guy David Morales was just standing casually facing sideways talking to Unidentified [Man in Profile] who had his hands kind of down and he wasn't doing anything. There was nobody else here [in the group of five] and for one thing none of the group were wearing Kennedy hats or buttons . . .

"I do not recall a bald man with the group [of five]. All hair on all of them . . . At the time I saw them, she [the polka-dot dress girl Kathy Ainsworth] was talking to him [the man with the medallion Tommy Tarrants]. The medallion guy wasn't even looking at her, but I've seen a lot of guys do that with girls but he was staring across at the staircase. He wasn't looking at her at all and she was nervous, dancing around. It seemed like she was trying to get his attention.

"They were all fairly close together but they weren't cheek-by-jaw. These three [Joannides, Ainsworth, and Tarrants] were closer together than these two [David Morales and Unidentified Man in Profile] but these two [Morales and Unidentified in Profile], you could see they were with that group [of five].

"First off, the polka-dot dress girl stuck out and secondly, the medallion guy stuck out, and thirdly, the whole group [of five including Morales, Joannides, and Unidentified Man in Profile] stuck out with no paraphernalia on. I said to Kathy Lentine, 'I wonder what they're doing here because it seems like she [Ainsworth] is awfully nervous.' But we just figured they were from one of the opposing camps and they had taken off their paraphernalia and didn't want to be outted . . . The police were trying to say that I saw Sirhan with this group. No, I didn't. I never saw Sirhan. They showed me pictures and all the pictures resembled Sirhan. 'Did you see this guy there?' and I said 'No.' Another thing the police kept asking was if they [the group of five] were Middle Eastern."

"I was in Dallas when we got that motherfucker," CIA agent David Morales chillingly bragged to his attorney Robert Walton, "and I was in Los Angeles when we got the little bastard [Robert Kennedy]." Walton explained to Shane O'Sullivan "how [Morales] had worked on the Bay of

Pigs and how he had to watch all the men he had recruited and trained get wiped out because of Kennedy."

Both George Joannides and David Morales worked for the CIA at the covert Miami, Florida base known as JMWAVE. "I transferred to South Florida, to JMWAVE," Bradley Ayers told O'Sullivan. "I arrived in April 1963. I worked under a fellow by the name of David Morales, who was the chief of operations. The concept was to conduct covert paramilitary operations involving infiltration and commando raids in an effort to destabilize Castro's Cuba. We also embarked on efforts to assassinate Fidel Castro."

"Acquaintances in the Birchers told me of a mysterious figure involved in anti-Castro guerrilla activities," wrote Thomas Albert Tarrants III. "A staunch anticommunist, he [David Morales] had actually been on raids to Cuba himself. He was active in securing support and supplies for such groups in Florida. Our relationship... provided me with my first exposure to the shadowy and exciting world of clandestine activities and international intrigue. Because it was sanctioned and covertly supported by the Central Intelligence Agency and because it was anticommunist, I saw it as a patriotic effort to fight communist aggression."

By the conclusion of his book, Shane O'Sullivan was not certain whether three CIA agents David Morales, George Joannides, and Gordon Campbell [November 20, 1918–December 22, 2002] were actually present at the Ambassador Hotel on June 5, 1968. Now that Irene Gizzi has identified both Morales and Joannides in attendance together, we must focus on the Embassy Room footage of Joannides speaking to a man claiming to be Michael D. Roman, which is in fact a cover name for Gordon Campbell. "When I showed Bradley Ayers this footage [of a man purporting to be Michael D. Roman], it reinforced his identification of Campbell," wrote O'Sullivan. "The stance, bearing, behavior, and facial expressions all called to mind the man he knew at JMWAVE."

Morales, Joannides, and Campbell worked at JMWAVE in high positions of power and all three knew each other well. "I met the assistant chief of station, a fellow by the name of Gordon Campbell, who later became my case officer," Bradley Ayers explained. As mentioned above, Ayers also worked under David Morales. In addition to Campbell, Ayers had identified David Morales to O'Sullivan from the same photograph shown to Irene Gizzi by Jay Margolis.

"The Roman family recognized the figure of Joannides in the photographs," Shane O'Sullivan intriguingly reported but under a different name. Michael Roman's son told O'Sullivan, "Both my sister and mother confirm the darker-haired man is Frank Owens [sic]. He died a number of years ago [on March 9, 1990] and his wife may also have passed away or is at a care facility."

"Owens [actually George Joannides] was a regional sales manager for Michael Roman [who was in fact Gordon Campbell]," O'Sullivan noted, "and seems to match a 'Frank S. Owen' from New York interviewed by the FBI on October 21 [1968]. Owen registered at the Ambassador on June 4, listened to Kennedy's speech in the Embassy Room, and remained there during the shooting."

Therefore, David Morales, George Joannides (using Frank S. Owen as a cover identity), and Gordon Campbell (using Michael D. Roman as a cover identity) were three CIA agents present together at the Ambassador Hotel when RFK was gunned down. The Roman family agreed that the man they knew as Michael D. Roman was inside before, during, and after the assassination. He attended a sales conference for the Bulova Watch Company at the Ambassador Hotel, just not under the name Gordon Campbell. "Forty percent of Bulova's revenue came from the defense industry," O'Sullivan reported, "and sources told me it was a well-known CIA cover. Roman had been appointed Vice President by [General Omar M.] Bradley in 1964." It was highly effective for both Joannides and Campbell—until now.

"I still don't understand why the police kept trying to say that it was only Sirhan Sirhan," Irene Gizzi continued to Jay Margolis. "There were just too many suspicious things that had gone on that evening. The group was the most suspicious, including the taller gentleman with the medallion, and the young pretty girl wearing a polka-dot dress. She's the only one I saw that evening wearing a polka-dot dress. . . .

"I remember that he was tall. He was good-looking and was wearing a medallion. That stuck out. It was very flashy. He was talking with the girl in the polka-dot dress who was kind of dancing around a little bit seeming nervous and excitable, and there were three other men [Morales,

Joannides, and Unidentified Man in Profile] with them . . . I was in my twenties. We had worked for Jack and now we were working for Bobby.

"When we came into the lower ballroom [the Ambassador Room], they were in a group on the right-hand side of the entrance, directly across from the staircase on the left. They were conspicuous because they weren't wearing any Kennedy paraphernalia. They weren't carrying anything that had anything to do with the nominating campaign or any political campaign so that's why they stood out.

"They were kind of in the shadows trying to stay back on the right-hand side, no more than five feet from the doors, against the wall, which also wouldn't make sense if you wanna get up near the stage to be where you can hear the speaker.

"That was the only thing that stood out at that time. When the shots rang out, and when we all figured out it wasn't firecrackers, when we turned around, they had disappeared right after the gunshots. All of the group were gone. Most of us weren't because we didn't know exactly where to go or what to do . . .

"When you enter the lower ballroom [the Ambassador Room], the staircase was on the left, and the guy with the medallion, his group, including [Joannides, Morales, Unidentified Man in Profile, and] the girl with the polka-dot dress, were on the right. He [Tarrants] could have very easily gone up those stairs while Bobby was speaking [in the Embassy Room] or entered the pantry [also upstairs] because people were coming up and down those stairs all during that time. He was wearing the medallion, which was very flashy, which is like a gold chain with a large sunburst or eagle on it. I think it was an eagle with flares behind it so it would appear almost round but it wasn't really round . . .

"The police didn't shut the main doors until after Rosey Grier threw three reporters down the stairs. The police then shut the doors and locked everybody in. There were a lot of people screaming to get out. We were there until two-fifteen in the morning. From there we went to Good Samaritan because we were praying. I don't think any of us got home until eight or nine in the morning . . . Unless the cops got all the footage, there's a bunch of people that have footage because there were television crews there. I know there were radio people there too but they didn't have cameras."

The late Professor Philip H. Melanson, PhD notated in his first book, "Three drawn guns were reported by witnesses: Sirhan's, uniformed security guard Thane Cesar's and that of an unidentified man wearing a suit." Don Schulman told Special Counsel Thomas F. Kranz, "I had thought I saw three guns [but only witnessed Sirhan's and Cesar's actually being fired]."

Professor Melanson interviewed a lady requesting confidentiality he has named "Martha Raines." He relayed, "Martha Raines asserts that a gun besides Sirhan's or Cesar's was fired . . . Martha Raines told the author of seeing a man fire a gun in the pantry."

"According to [Martha] Raines, the man fired a handgun of some kind," Melanson wrote. "She recalled that the gunman 'was not composed.' He didn't shoot 'more than once or twice' before running out of the pantry."

"And, as I recall, one of them [the shots] was high and should have gone into the ceiling," Mrs. Raines concluded to Professor Melanson. "I don't know what these people found when they did their ballistics tests . . . but it appeared to me there should have been a gunshot in the ceiling." What role did the five-person group seen by Irene Gizzi play? They certainly were not at the Ambassador to celebrate Kennedy's victory. All were avowed Kennedy haters. The CIA men hated the Kennedy brothers for the Bay of Pigs and the supposed failure to resist the communist threat. Thomas Tarrants admitted to a "great fondness for firearms and marksmanship." He and Kathy Ainsworth were violent KKK terrorists and despised the Kennedys for pushing racial integration in the South. Tarrants expressed in his first book "a dislike for John Kennedy and his policies on race and federal intervention . . . My defiance of authority began when authority placed itself on the side of federal intervention to integrate—the policy of an ideology I viewed as un-American . . . As I saw it, America was being undermined by the communist-Jewish conspiracy."

Security guard Thane Eugene Cesar demonstrated a remarkably similar motive for RFK's murder to Ted Charach when interviewed in 1969. "I definitely wouldn't have voted for Bobby Kennedy because he had the same ideas as John did," Cesar stated, "and I think John sold the country down the road. He gave it to the Commies . . . He literally gave it to the minority... The black man now for the last four to eight years has been cramming this integrated idea down our throat and so you learn to hate him."

After interviewing Mr. and Mrs. Bernstein, LAPD Sgt. Paul Sharaga relayed, "The woman stated that she and her husband were just outside the Embassy Room when a young couple, in their late teens or early twenties, came running by in a state of glee, very excited, very happy, shouting, 'We shot him! We shot him! We killed him!' And the woman says, 'Who? Who did you kill?' And the young lady said, 'Kennedy! We shot him! We killed him!'

"I immediately put out a broadcast with a description of the suspects: male and female Caucasian, the female Caucasian wearing a polka-dot dress . . ."

In fact, Kennedy was shot at 12:15 a.m. and the LAPD logger tape recording for Sgt. Paul Sharaga was as follows: "12:28:53 '2L30, description of the suspect; at 3400 Wilshire Boulevard; male Caucasian, 20 to 22, 6 ft. to 6 ft. 2, very thin . . . wearing a brown—brown pants and a light brown shirt; direction taken unknown at this time.'" At the time of the shooting, Tarrants was twenty-one, 6 ft. 3 (according to Jack Nelson's book), very thin, and Ainsworth was twenty-six but had a youthful appearance.

After running into Mr. and Mrs. Bernstein just outside the Embassy Room, Tommy Tarrants and Kathy Ainsworth next ran into twenty-year old Sandra Serrano, a Youth for Kennedy co-chairman in Pasadena-Altadena, who, according to Shane O'Sullivan, was "sitting on the fire escape below the southwest corner of the Embassy Room." Serrano first relayed her account an hour-and-a-half after the shooting to Sander "Sandy" Vanocur from NBC. Sandra Serrano stated, "This girl came running down the stairs in the back and said, 'We've shot him! We've shot him!' and I said, 'Who did you shoot?' and she says, 'We shot Senator Kennedy!' A boy came down with her. He was about twenty-three years old . . . She had on a white dress with polka-dots. She was light-skinned, dark hair, and she had a funny nose."

In fact, Kathy Ainsworth was bragging to the Bernsteins and to Sandra Serrano that "we" had just shot the Senator. After analyzing footage in the Embassy Room shortly after the shooting in the pantry, it appears that CIA agent Gordon Campbell is holding onto the medallion guy's weapon (hidden underneath Campbell's dress shirt so it doesn't show) using his right hand to firmly press it against his chest as a Latin man with a mustache is curiously guiding Campbell to an exit.

But the CIA connection didn't stop there. LAPD Lieutenant Manuel Pena and LAPD Sgt. Enrique "Hank" Hernandez, chosen to investigate the RFK assassination, were also CIA agents, and they controlled the flow of information. "The way they've written it, it sounds like I was brought back [out of retirement] and put into the [RFK] case as a plant by the CIA," Pena relayed to attorney Marilyn Barrett on a 1992 recording, "so that I could steer something around and . . . guide the investigation to a point where no one would ever discover a conspiracy or something." FBI agent Roger LaJeunesse, who investigated the RFK case with the LAPD, confirmed that Pena worked for the CIA for at least ten years.

Since there were three shooters, it is important to focus our attention on the powder burns found on the Senator. "It is scientifically highly unlikely," Noguchi explained to investigative reporter Ted Charach regarding the possibility that Sirhan Sirhan's gun, being at least three feet from the Senator, would have produced the powder burns Noguchi later found on Kennedy's body. "In this case, there was an abundance of powder burn embedded deep in the tissue . . . Because of the soot in the hair, I believed that the muzzle distance of the fatal shot had been from one to three inches away . . ."

Given the undeniable scientific evidence presented before him, Noguchi concluded, "I now knew the precise location of the murder weapon at the moment it was fired: one inch from the edge of his right ear, only three inches behind the head . . . Thus I have never said that Sirhan Sirhan killed Robert Kennedy . . ."

Thane Eugene Cesar told Ted Charach he did indeed draw his gun but claims he did not fire. Cesar himself conceded he was positioned behind the Senator holding his right elbow with his left hand, guiding him through the crowd when suddenly Cesar got powder burns in his eyes. "I got powder in my eyes," Cesar stated to Ted Charach. "I was a little behind Bobby so I would say I was about three feet from the flash [of Sirhan's gun] . . . and as I said I got a little bit of powder in my eyes." Cesar could only have received blowback from his own gun if he pulled the trigger at the Senator's head but he did not. The powder burns came from the gun of the third shooter who fired the fatal shot.

Professor Melanson intriguingly noted a third witness to the third gun in the pantry, besides Martha Raines and Don Schulman, and wrote, "In addition to Sirhan's gun and that of security guard Cesar, Lisa Urso saw another one . . . She sighted the gun immediately after the shooting, just as Sirhan's gun was wrestled from him . . . Schulman is no longer the only second-gun witness [or third-gun witness]. And there may be more such witnesses like Urso and Raines whose sightings of second or third guns have not yet been recorded." Lisa Urso stated she saw a man "by Kennedy" with a suit holding a gun after the shooting stopped.

In court, testifying at Sirhan Sirhan's trial, Ambassador Hotel busboy Juan Romero asserted that the shooter was *not* in the room. Harry F. Rosenthal from the Associated Press wrote on February 16, 1969, "Shortly after midnight Romero saw someone coming toward Kennedy."

Romero relayed, "I thought it was a person who couldn't wait to shake his hand. I seen the guy put a hand at the Senator's head. And then I saw a gun. Then I saw Sen. Kennedy stretched out in front of me. I leaned down and picked up his head."

"Romero was asked if the man who did the shooting was in the room," Rosenthal continued. "He shook his head. Sirhan was asked to stand." Romero replied, "I don't believe that's him."

Therefore, Juan Romero is one of two known eyewitnesses to the third gunman firing his weapon, the other being Martha Raines. Romero was close enough to Kennedy and the third gunman that Romero got powder burns on his ear, not from Cesar's two non-lethal right armpit shots, but from the third shooter's fatal shot to RFK's head. Since the shooting happened within five and a half seconds, there wouldn't have been enough time for Cesar to raise his weapon from Kennedy's right armpit all the way to the back of the Senator's head to make that last fatal shot. In fact, Cesar also got powder burns like Romero, not on his ear, but in his eyes. Both of these powder burns came from the third gunman to the back of Kennedy's head.

"I've known Juan Romero for more than twenty years," Rigo Chacon told Jay Margolis. "Juan has told me several times that he felt the heat of the bullet by his ear. If somebody fires from your side or behind you, and the bullet is only a short distance, a couple inches or more from your ear, you are gonna feel the heat . . . If Juan was standing behind Kennedy, and somebody fired from behind him, then that's the bullet from which he felt the heat . . . What Juan told me and what he has told me repeatedly is that he did say that Bobby told him, 'Is anybody hurt? Is everybody okay? . . . ' Up until this day, Juan is traumatized. When I took him to see Kennedy he felt compelled to talk to Bobby at his grave and apologize and tell him he was sorry [for distracting him by shaking his hand]. Later, he told me he felt better that he finally got that done because the spiritual part of him, he was sincere in believing that he was talking to Bobby Kennedy and apologizing. He's a very, very humble man."

In his official autopsy report, Noguchi confirmed Don Schulman's unwavering assertion that three shots did indeed hit Kennedy. What's more, Noguchi relayed how "the all-important bullet that had caused Kennedy's death" came from behind RFK's head. Noguchi conceded: "The bullet had entered the skull an inch to the left of Kennedy's right ear . . . and shattered . . . But such small metallic bits could not be matched definitively to Sirhan's gun. That meant that other evidence would be needed to establish that Sirhan Sirhan was in fact the assassin."

In the yet-to-be-published *An Open & Shut Case* by Robert J. Joling, J.D., and Philip Van Praag, the authors provided an airtight case that none of Sirhan's bullets hit Kennedy. On the other hand, they assumed that Cesar was the only other shooter besides Sirhan and they attributed the fatal blow to Cesar.

However, Joling is wrong that Cesar killed Kennedy. Presumably without a photo identification of the third shooter until now, thanks to Irene Gizzi, no one, including Joling, pursued Martha Raines's description of the medallion guy as "approximately 6-feet 2-inches tall, Caucasian, with dark, wavy hair and wearing a suit (not a uniform)." In fact, at Sirhan Sirhan's trial, Juan Romero's eyewitness testimony of seeing the third shooter was completely ignored and dismissed.

Romero testified that he had seen a gunman deliver the fatal wound to the Senator's head and clearly affirmed this person was *not* Sirhan Sirhan. The third shooter could not have been Cesar because he was already the second shooter. The security guard does not fit the description of a person running towards the Senator, who appeared like he "couldn't wait to shake his hand," as Juan Romero explained. "I seen the guy put a hand at the Senator's head. And then I saw a gun." Positioned directly behind the Senator, Cesar had by this time finished shooting his gun, hitting Kennedy twice to the right armpit. In fact, the third shooter's fatal shot to RFK's head was to come next.

As a former attorney and judge, Robert Joling told Jay Margolis he had been studying the RFK assassination since it occurred. Joling revealed to Margolis how he interviewed Don Schulman and found him completely credible. In 2007, Joling's co-author Philip Van Praag provided strong support to Schulman's account by analyzing audio evidence from free-lance reporter Stanislaw Pruszynski who inadvertently left his recorder on and discovered later that he had recorded the shooting. Van Praag established how at least thirteen shots were fired that day, more than Sirhan had in his own eight-shot .22 caliber Iver Johnson Cadet 55SA revolver. Joling and Van Praag noted in their book: "Shouldn't there be some bullets on the scene that identify with Sirhan's gun? . . . Or was the LAPD Property gun (H18602) . . . the gun destroyed in July, 1968— used to produce the test-fired bullets?"

In fact, not including Kennedy himself, it can never be determined whether any of the remaining bullets from the five other victims came from Sirhan's gun simply because H18602 was the gun used to test-fire the bullets and this gun belonged to Jake Williams, *not* Sirhan Sirhan. Sirhan's gun was actually labeled H53725 but this was *not* the gun used to perform the ballistics tests. The man who performed the test-firing, LAPD criminologist DeWayne Wolfer, widely-considered by many of his colleagues to be unqualified for his position, later explained it away by a "clerical error."

However, this cannot be a simple "clerical error" when Jake Williams's gun was the weapon actually being test fired as if it were Sirhan's own gun, which it was not. Therefore, Wolfer lied when he testified under oath that the "Sirhan death weapon and no other gun in the world fired the fatal shot that killed Senator Kennedy." The other shooting victims on June 5, 1968, not including Kennedy, had each been shot one time. They were as follows: Paul Schrade, who was grazed on the forehead, Elizabeth Evans, also grazed on the forehead while searching for her shoe, Ira Goldstein, who was wounded in his left hip, Irwin

Stroll, hit in his left shin, and William Weisel who took a shot to the left abdomen.

Intriguingly, both Thane Eugene Cesar and Sirhan Sirhan were carrying a .22 on the day of RFK's assassination despite Cesar lying to police that he brought a Rohm .38. In fact, Cesar was never asked to actually produce his weapon to authorities to see if it really was a .38 he was carrying or if it was a .22. They merely took Cesar at his word that it was a .38. Cesar owned a nine-shot .22 caliber Harrington & Richardson revolver also known as an H&R 922.

An AP Wire Photo dated June 5, 1968, released to the news services only hours after the shooting, correctly showed how Kennedy was shot in the back of the head near his right ear. Inexplicably against Sirhan's right to due process, the autopsy report itself was not accessible to Sirhan's defense team until after the beginning of Sirhan's trial on January 7, 1969, more than seven months following the RFK assassination.

The autopsy report and the June 5 Associated Press photo both show how Kennedy was shot from behind but every credible witness places Sirhan facing Kennedy the entire time. This discrepancy appears to be purposefully hidden from Sirhan's defense team so no one would think to point out that it wasn't physically possible for Sirhan to be RFK's true assassin. The Associated Press, by visiting RFK at Central Receiving Hospital and later Good Samaritan Hospital, knew from nurses and doctors on June 5 the exact location of the fatal bullet that killed Kennedy before Dr. Thomas Noguchi performed the autopsy on the Senator at 3:30 a.m. on June 6.

Unfortunately, four important eyewitnesses were either never asked the right questions or were simply ignored: Don Schulman's comments about the Senator being shot from the rear by Thane Cesar, Juan Romero's sighting of a third gun behind Kennedy's head, Martha Raines who, in addition to Romero, also saw a third shooter fire his weapon, and Irene Gizzi who miraculously identified four out of five dangerous persons in the Ambassador Room.

The four individuals identified by Ms. Gizzi included two Ku Klux Klan terrorists (Tarrants and Ainsworth) and two powerful CIA agents (Morales and Joannides). Irene Gizzi also made it clear how all four were working side-by-side shortly before the shooting in a five-person group, along with Unidentified Man in Profile who, according to Ms. Gizzi, may or may not be the "unidentified third man" with "blonde hair and horn-rimmed glasses" on page 452 of Shane O'Sullivan's book. As for Sirhan Sirhan, he was blamed for killing Kennedy even though none of his bullets were proven to hit the Senator.

"We got the call there at the Ambassador Hotel," Schaefer Ambulance driver Edgardo Villalobos told Jay Margolis. "The guy with me was Darryl Stump. I guarantee he's not around because I looked like his son then. We were way over at Beverly Boulevard. Joe Tarnowski radioed us for the call. There were a lot of people in that crowd during all the confusion. We responded but we didn't get to transport him because the city was there.

"They were different from us. They wore police uniforms, not paramedics, just regular technicians, the g-unit they called it and they were ambulance guys. When you see them, they had a badge and you think you're looking at LAPD. But that was their uniform back in those days. The police was there with them and they all worked together.

"So the technicians from the city [Robert Hulsman and Max Behrman] grabbed our stretcher, took over, put Bobby in it and away they went. They didn't give us a chance to do anything, which is a very rude thing to do because we were there responding to the call however the city can take over. They put our stretcher in their ambulance so we went along after and followed them to pick up our stretcher. The city got the first call and Schaefer got the second call. In certain areas, anything the city cannot handle, we get.

"When the pictures came out in the media the next day, they showed how they covered Bobby with a big brown blanket on top of the stretcher and it had a big red circle that said S.A.A.S. (Schaefer's Air Ambulance Service), which was like an advertisement. When they took our stretcher, it was made with our equipment, including the blanket on top of the stretcher . . . They first took him to Central Receiving Hospital. Then everything went bad. They were not prepared. Kennedy needed blood desperately and they didn't have blood. So they transferred him to Good Samaritan where he died the next day."

Twenty-five days after the RFK assassination, on June 30, 1968, at the Meridian, Mississippi, home of Jewish leader Meyer Davidson, the FBI ambushed Tommy Tarrants and Kathy Ainsworth, who were trying to plant a bomb on the front doorstep of Davidson's house. The couple were caught in gunfire similar to the film *Bonnie and Clyde* (1967) and surprisingly the bomb Tarrants was carrying didn't explode when he dropped it. Kathy Ainsworth, an elementary school teacher, who at the time was pregnant with her first child, died at the scene while her then-lover Thomas Tarrants had been shot *nineteen* times and survived. Following his astonishing recovery thanks to orthopedic surgeon Dr. Leslie Rush of Rush Memorial Hospital, Tarrants was initially put on death row yet was later inexplicably removed. He reasoned how "there were too many for the extra cells on death row."

Consequently Tarrants only served eight years in prison at Parchman State Penitentiary before officially being released on December 13, 1976, at 8:30 a.m. Authorities were convinced he had transformed into a born-again Christian and no longer considered him a threat to society. Tarrants later became President of the C.S. Lewis Institute from 1998 to 2010 and is now Vice President of Ministry. He had previously been a co-pastor. An ordained minister, he currently possesses a Doctor of Ministry Degree in Christian Spirituality and a Master of Divinity Degree. "Nonetheless, some wouldn't be convinced," Thomas Tarrants wrote in his first book. "They no doubt still view my conversion as a gimmick for freedom." After all, Tarrants himself conceded he was once regarded as "the most dangerous man in Mississippi."

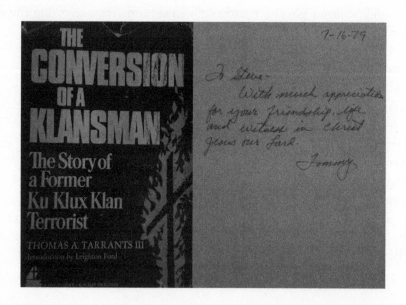

TIMELINE

Note: Estimated times are indicated with a ~ symbol.

AUGUST 4, 1962:

8:00 a.m.
Mrs. Eunice Murray arrives for work.

9:00 a.m.
Isidore Miller calls from New York. Mrs. Murray assures Miller that Marilyn will return his call after she finishes dressing. Mrs. Murray never communicates the message to Marilyn.

Miller is Marilyn's ex-father-in-law, one of her closest friends, and the kindest father figure she ever knew. To Marilyn, he is known as "Dad."

9:00–10:15 a.m.
Marilyn's best friend Ralph Roberts massages her back in her bedroom using his portable massage table. He notes she is "in wonderful shape and not tense."

~ 10:20 a.m.
Ralph lets himself out the front door while Marilyn enters the kitchen and says good morning to Mrs. Murray. Per Mrs. Murray, Marilyn pours herself a glass of grapefruit juice. She does not eat or drink alcohol for the rest of the day. Tests of her unembalmed blood later reveal she hadn't had a drop of alcohol that day.

~ 10:30–11:00 a.m.
Mrs. Murray noted, "Sometime during the earlier part of the day, the bedside table was delivered and Marilyn wrote a check for it. The citrus trees were also delivered that day and were placed in the rear yard."

Presumably the deliverers placed the bedside table where it belonged: in the guest cottage. There was already a bedside table in Marilyn's main bedroom.

11:00 a.m.

Per Frank Neill, Twentieth Century-Fox studio publicist, he saw Bobby Kennedy arrive on the Fox lot, Stage 18, via helicopter. Bobby jumps out and quickly enters a car waiting for him with Peter Lawford inside.

Peter's neighbor Ward Wood would later spot Bobby in the afternoon noting, "It was Bobby all right. He was in khakis and a white shirt open at the neck."

12:00 p.m.

Pat Newcomb, who stayed overnight at Marilyn's, awakens and per Pat and Mrs. Murray and later Greenson, Marilyn gets angry with her because Marilyn had no sleep the night before. In 1985, Mrs. Murray would concede that Bobby Kennedy was the real reason Marilyn was upset that day, not her alleged lack of sleep.

2:00 p.m.

Per the police report, Joe DiMaggio, Jr., 20, who was in the Marines, calls from Camp Pendleton in San Diego. Joe, Jr., said he could hear Mrs. Murray telling the operator that Marilyn was not home. Mrs. Murray never communicates the message to Marilyn.

~ 2:00 p.m.

Bobby and Peter arrive at Marilyn's. Peter slips into her home to tell Mrs. Murray and Marilyn's handyman Norman Jefferies (also Murray's son-in-law) to get lost for an hour. Per Jefferies, Peter gives them money for Cokes and they leave in Jefferies' pick-up. Per Peter, Marilyn offers Bobby some food she ordered from Briggs Delicatessen the day before: mushrooms, meatballs, and a magnum of champagne. Uninterested, Bobby says he's here for one reason: to tell her she can't contact him or his brother Jack Kennedy again.

Bobby and Marilyn argue for several minutes before per Peter, Marilyn threatens a press conference to announce her affairs with both Kennedy brothers. Later per Sydney Guilaroff, he learned from Marilyn that

Bobby had responded, "If you threaten me, Marilyn, there's more than one way to keep you quiet." Per Peter, Marilyn then impulsively takes a kitchen knife lying next to the tray of food and lunges at Bobby. Peter joins in to help. Bobby eventually knocks her down to the ground and kicks the knife away from her.

During their typical Saturday afternoon bridge party, Marilyn's next-door neighbor to the east at 12304 Fifth Helena Drive, Mary W. Goodykoontz Barnes, her guest Elizabeth Pollard, and two other ladies witness Bobby leave Marilyn's. They see him run back to a white Lincoln convertible (which Kennedy borrowed from FBI agent William Simon whenever he visited Marilyn). Bobby Kennedy then retrieved one of his two long-time personal bodyguards Archie Case or James Ahern. From an upstairs window, they see Kennedy with Case or Ahern return through Marilyn's courtyard back to Marilyn and Peter. The neighbors notice the man in the suit is carrying a little black case.

Regarding Bobby, one of the card-playing ladies shouted to the others, "Look, girls, there he is *again!*" Then, while Peter and Bobby restrain her, Case or Ahern subsequently sedates Marilyn with a heavy intramuscular pentobarbital injection under her left armpit.

While she's temporarily stunned and immobile on the ground from the drugs, Bobby and Peter enter Marilyn's home with the sole purpose of looking for her red diary, a potential basis for blackmail, where she documented highly sensitive political information.

Bobby keeps looking while screaming, "Where the fuck is it?" but can't find "it." Peter meanwhile flips through Marilyn's address book and calls Ralph Greenson to come over and tend to his patient. The psychiatrist agrees to be there within the hour. At this time, Marilyn musters enough energy to enter her house and furious that her privacy is being violated, screams and chases the men from her home. They leave without the diary.

～ 2:30–2:45 p.m.

Marilyn calls her friend Sydney Guilaroff and relays to him much of what had happened. Per Sydney, she's hysterical and tells him she's having an affair with both Kennedy brothers and that Bobby had threatened her. She said Bobby left with Peter Lawford. Sydney tries to calm Marilyn down and promises her they will talk later in the evening.

3:00 p.m.
When Greenson comes out by the pool, per Pat Newcomb, the psychiatrist dismisses her so he can be alone with Marilyn.

4:30 p.m.
Per the police report, Joe DiMaggio, Jr., calls and again Joe, Jr., can hear Mrs. Murray tell the operator that Marilyn is not home. Mrs. Murray never communicates the message to Marilyn.

5:00 p.m.
Peter claimed he called Marilyn inviting her to his regular Saturday evening dinner party. She tentatively agrees.

6:00 p.m.
Ralph Roberts calls Marilyn to confirm their dinner engagement at her house that night. Greenson answers the public phone. Asking if he can talk to her, Greenson replies: "She's not here" before rudely hanging up.

7:00 p.m.
Peter claimed he called Marilyn and that this time she begged off saying she was tired.

7:00–7:15 p.m.
Per the police report, Joe DiMaggio, Jr., phones for the third time. Mrs. Murray answers again but this time summons Marilyn from her bedroom to take the call. Mrs. Murray overhears how ecstatic and joyful Marilyn is at this time. Joe, Jr., tells Marilyn he broke off his engagement to Pamela Reis, a girl Marilyn didn't like. She says to Joe, Jr., that he's too young to get married anyway. Per Joe DiMaggio, Sr., Marilyn and his son "spoke for about fifteen minutes and Marilyn seemed quite normal and in good spirits."

7:15 p.m.
Greenson leaves Marilyn's. He goes home to prepare for dinner at the residence of actor Eddie Albert and his wife Margo.

~ 7:30 p.m.
Peter calls Marilyn to see if he can still get her to come to his party. Those at the Lawfords' a half-hour later: Joe and Dolores Naar, producer "Bullets" Durgom, and Lawford maid Erma Lee Riley.

Instead of "Say goodbye to Jack . . ." private eye Fred Otash said he heard Marilyn say over wiretaps, "No, I'm tired. There is nothing more for me to respond to. Just do me a favor. Tell the President I tried to get him. Tell him goodbye for me. I think my purpose has been served."

~ 7:30 p.m.
Per Dolores Naar, Peter calls the Naars and tells them not to bother picking up Marilyn because "she's not coming."

~ 7:30–7:40 p.m.
Per Greenson and Mrs. Murray, Marilyn calls Greenson while he is shaving. He notes she is in high spirits because Joe DiMaggio, Jr., broke off his engagement.

~ 7:40–8:00 p.m.
Milt Ebbins alleges Peter phones him in a panic, worrying that Marilyn may have taken too many pills and that they should go over there. Ebbins says he warned him against it because he's the President's brother-in-law. Before going over there, Ebbins asks Peter to wait until he calls Mickey Rudin first. Ebbins later reaches Rudin at Mildred Allenberg's party.

~ 8:00–9:00 p.m.
Sydney Guilaroff got a call from Marilyn who sounds better. She told him she had just met with her psychiatrist. Before ending the call, Marilyn relayed to Sydney she knows a lot of secrets in Washington, a reference to her red diary.

~ 8:00–9:00 p.m.
Dress manufacturer and long-time friend Henry Rosenfeld calls Marilyn and he reports she sounded normal.

~ 8:00–9:00 p.m.
Peter's friend Bill Asher claims Peter called him to see if he would go along with him to Marilyn's house to find out if she's okay. Asher advised against it because Peter is the president's brother-in-law and that maybe they should call "old man Joe" Kennedy to seek his advice.

9:00 p.m.
Per the police report, Mickey Rudin called Mrs. Murray who informed him that Marilyn was fine, which she was.

9:30 p.m.
Per George "Bullets" Durgom, Pat Newcomb arrives at Peter's party. She wears what appear to be pajamas and a dark coat over it.

~ 9:30–9:45 p.m.
Per Mrs. Murray, her son-in-law Norman Jefferies, Marilyn's next-door neighbor to the east Mary W. Goodykoontz Barnes at 12304 Fifth Helena Drive, and FBI agent John Anderson, Bobby Kennedy goes into Marilyn's house alongside LAPD veteran partners Archie Case and James Ahern, members of Chief William Parker's off-the-books Gangster Squad. They happen to also be Bobby Kennedy's personal bodyguards in Los Angeles ever since Jack Kennedy was a senator. They instruct Jefferies and Mrs. Murray to leave. Bobby, Case, and Ahern then proceed to the guest cottage with the sole purpose of looking for Marilyn's red diary. They break into one of the two large filing cabinets and make a loud ruckus.

~ 9:45 p.m.
At this time, Marilyn is busy in her main bedroom chatting happily on her private line with her friend and sometimes lover José Bolaños. Marilyn tells Bolaños to hold on a moment while she goes to investigate the noise. According to Bolaños, she doesn't hang up but never comes back on the line.

~ 9:50 p.m.
Marilyn storms into her guest cottage and she screams at Bobby. Case and Ahern throw her onto the bed, and per Bernie Spindel and Fred Otash, Bobby then shoves a pillow over her face to keep her from making noise.

Per Deputy Coroner's Aide Lionel Grandison, Bobby Kennedy ordered Case and Ahern, "Give her something to calm her down." Raymond Strait, who heard eleven hours of Otash's bugging tapes, relayed to Joan Rivers, "It was horrible. You could hear the two men [Case and Ahern] talking to each other, saying, 'Give her another one. Don't give it to her too quickly' and awful smothering sounds. After hearing those tapes, there's no doubt in my mind that Marilyn was murdered." A confidential source relayed to Jay Margolis, "There were needle marks behind her knees, the jugular vein in her neck, and bruises on her arms and back."

Bobby had instructed Case and Ahern to give Marilyn injections of Nembutal to "calm her down." After that didn't effectively subdue

Marilyn, Case and Ahern, stripped her of her clothes and using water and enema paraphernalia already available in the guest cottage bathroom along with Marilyn's own Nembutal and chloral hydrate prescriptions, they forcibly administer to Marilyn a drug enema containing seventeen chloral hydrates and between thirteen to nineteen Nembutals to knock her out. Marilyn often took enemas daily and Bobby knew this.

10:00 p.m.

From the guest cottage, right after the enema had been given to her, Marilyn grabs the phone, the public line, and makes her last call to best friend Ralph Roberts. She reaches his answering service. When told he's out for the evening, she hangs up before lapsing into unconsciousness from the drugs.

⁓ 10:20–10:25 p.m.

Someone calls Peter and tells him to get to Marilyn's house, ordering him to hire a professional to remove any link with the Kennedys and the famous movie star.

10:30 p.m.

Per Jefferies, Bobby leaves with Case and Ahern. After his second search for Marilyn's red diary that day, Bobby is thoroughly frustrated that he, Case, and Ahern couldn't find it despite more than a half-hour search.

⁓ 10:30–10:35 p.m.

Jefferies and Mrs. Murray return. They hear Maf barking in the guest cottage and walk over. Per Jefferies and Mrs. Murray, they by their own independent accounts find Marilyn facedown leaning on the phone.

⁓ 10:35–10:50 p.m.

Per Jefferies, a frightened Mrs. Murray takes the phone from Marilyn and calls an ambulance then calls Greenson who tells her to call Engelberg. Engelberg claimed to the District Attorney's Office in 1982 that he went to the house "immediately" upon receiving the call; however, he was double-parked so he had to move his car first. Engelberg would later tell investigative reporter Sylvia Chase that when he was called, it "must have been around eleven or twelve" and that an ambulance is "pure imagination."

However, one-time Schaefer Vice President Carl Bellonzi, Schaefer Ambulance attendant Edgardo Villalobos, and Schaefer nurse and sometimes-attendant Ruth Tarnowski all confirmed to Jay Margolis that not only was an ambulance called to Marilyn Monroe's house but Schaefer Ambulance driver Joe Tarnowski was the dispatcher on that call.

Villalobos stated that he and his late driver Larry Telling first received the call at Beverly and Western, the main station, before the call was transferred to James Hall and Murray Liebowitz in Santa Monica, who were more realistically able to respond to the call as they were closer.

After Mrs. Murray phoned for the ambulance and the two doctors, then per Jefferies, Peter Lawford and Pat Newcomb arrive together. Peter drove since Pat left her car at the Lawfords'.

Per Jefferies, Pat screams at Mrs. Murray. Jefferies says he then escorts Mrs. Murray into the main house. At that point, Mrs. Murray responsibly takes possession of Marilyn's red diary (in the main bedroom) and one of Marilyn's address books. She places them into her purse or basket of things. Then per Mrs. Murray and Jefferies, they wait in the living room and stay there until Marilyn is eventually declared dead in the guest cottage.

Per Strait, before arriving at Marilyn's, a worried and hysterical Peter had called private eye to the stars Fred Otash to meet him at Marilyn's house. Strait said, "Fred's job was to clean the mess up . . . Fred was there as she was dying."

Right after Mrs. Murray and Jefferies had left the guest cottage, Pat phoned the Hollywood Bowl. With his soundman, Otash arrives and Peter approaches them. Otash immediately assigns the soundman to the main house to remove all bugging equipment. Per twenty-four-year-old Jacobs press agent Michael Selsman and twenty-one-year-old Natalie Trundy, the person who phoned the Hollywood Bowl was Pat Newcomb. Per Natalie, an usher tells her boyfriend-at-the-time Arthur Jacobs, Marilyn's publicist, that Marilyn's "dying or on the point of death."

Otash and Peter hurriedly take an unconscious Marilyn off the guest cottage bed. Per Strait, Peter "was just like a hysterical woman" and "Fred slapped the shit out of him" since they have to act quickly before the ambulance arrives on scene. Otash and Peter hastily remove the soiled sheets off the bed. Mrs. Murray is later told to do the laundry when the ambulance leaves.

After Marilyn is quickly cleaned and dried off from the expelled enema, Peter and Otash place Marilyn faceup back on the bed. The linens used to clean and dry her off were easily accessible from a nearby linen closet down one of the guest bedroom hallways.

Finally, Peter and Otash dash to her main bedroom and grab the rest of Marilyn's pill bottles and neatly stack them onto the bedside table in the guest cottage, which was according to Mrs. Murray, delivered that very morning. When they're done, they slip out of the room and return to the main house.

11:00 p.m.
Arthur Jacobs arrives on the scene but does not go into the guest cottage.

~ 11:00 p.m.
Schaefer Ambulance attendant James Hall and his driver Murray Liebowitz arrive. Per Hall, Pat Newcomb is the first person he and his partner saw. From the outside, still hysterical, she screams at Hall and Liebowitz, "She's dead! She's dead! I think she's dead!" When Hall asked her what's the matter, Newcomb replied, "I think she took some pills." Pat then directs them into the guest cottage where they find a naked Marilyn lying faceup on the bed with her head hanging over the edge, still unconscious with no sheet or blanket underneath her. Hall noted no odor of pear from her mouth so Marilyn definitely did not orally ingest the seventeen chloral hydrates.

~ 11:00–11:30 p.m.
With Liebowitz's help, Hall drags Marilyn away from the guest room and into the hallway where there's a hard surface. Next, Hall said he and Liebowitz dropped Marilyn "on her fanny," taking credit for the bruise on the "left side of [her] lower back," which Noguchi noted in his official autopsy report was "a very fresh bruise." Hall therefore deduced years later, "Dead bodies don't bruise. She was still alive."

Hall tells Liebowitz to get the resuscitator from the van. When Liebowitz returns, Hall puts an airway down Marilyn's throat and per Hall, Marilyn's color is coming back and Hall believes they can safely take her to the hospital. Hall then tells Liebowitz, "Get the gurney."

11:30 p.m.
Peter's best friend Joe Naar and his then-wife Dolores claim Peter called (which could have only been from Marilyn's house), asking Joe, who lived

four blocks from Marilyn, to go over and check on her. Two minutes later, according to the Naars, Peter calls back telling them not to go. Dolores thought the two calls, so close to each other were "calculated to mislead us."

~ 11:30–11:45 p.m.

Before Liebowitz leaves the guest cottage to retrieve the gurney, suddenly Greenson arrives and says he's "her doctor." Greenson tells Hall to remove the resuscitator, which was in fact doing its job. Hall defers to him because he had always been told to never challenge an M.D. Per Hall, Greenson then takes a syringe with a long heart needle already attached to it out of his medical bag and tells Hall, "I've got to make a show of this."

Next, Greenson fills the syringe with a "brownish fluid" (Nembutal) from a pharmaceutical bottle. Hall then notes something peculiar about Greenson: "he had to count down her ribs—like he was still in premed school and had really never done this before."

This makes sense since he's a psychiatrist who doesn't normally deal with needles. As Dr. Greenson injects Marilyn in the heart, James Hall saw Peter Lawford and Sgt. Marvin Iannone enter the guest cottage. Greenson did not dilute the solution first making the shot lethal regardless of what's in the syringe and the amount injected into the body. The five eyewitnesses to Marilyn Monroe's murder by Ralph Greenson were Schaefer Ambulance attendant James Hall, Schaefer Ambulance driver Murray Liebowitz, Peter Lawford, Pat Newcomb, and Sgt. Marvin D. Iannone. Within minutes, Marilyn dies.

In the early 1990s, Hall would identify the hysterical woman as Pat Newcomb and the man who comforted her as Peter Lawford. In 1992, to Detective Franklin, Hall identified the policeman as Sgt. Marvin D. Iannone. In 1993, Hall also identified him to Donald Wolfe.

Per Officer Lynn Franklin, Otash said that at 11:45 p.m. he "observed Sgt. Iannone, in uniform, in conversation with Peter Lawford."

Greenson then tells Hall he can leave because he's going to pronounce her dead. For years, says Hall, he believed the solution was adrenaline in an attempt to save her but now Hall thinks the shot was intended to murder her.

Greenson's brother-in-law and Marilyn's attorney Mickey Rudin would later claim on a recorded interview that he arrived sometime before midnight and that Greenson was the one who called him to say Marilyn was dead.

~ 11:45–11:50 p.m.

Marilyn's next-door neighbor to the west, Abe Charles Landau, arrives home with his wife Ruby Landau and they see several cars parked up the narrow street including a limousine, a police car (per Hall and Otash, Sgt. Marvin Iannone's), and an ambulance (Hall and Liebowitz's).

Per Jefferies, not long after Marilyn's death, plainclothes officers orchestrated the "locked room" story. They broke the window Greenson would later claim to police he had to break in order to enter Marilyn's bedroom yet the movie star's inside doors, not including the front and back doors, had no operable locks many years before she owned the house.

Next, the principals at the scene move the pill bottles and Marilyn's body to the main bedroom, and lay her facedown on the bed to disguise needle marks through the process of postmortem lividity.

AUGUST 5, 1962:

~ 12:00–1:00 a.m.

Peter's friend Bill Asher claims Peter called him, saying they should go over there to check on Marilyn. Asher, admittedly irritated by this call, claims he again advised against it.

12:10 a.m.

Near the intersection of Robertson and Olympic Boulevards, Beverly Hills Detective Lynn Franklin pulls over an inebriated Peter Lawford in his Lincoln Continental sedan with the headlights off going 70–80 MPH with Greenson in the front seat and Bobby Kennedy in the backseat. Not eager to give Peter a ticket with Bobby in the backseat, Detective Franklin gives them proper directions to go to the Beverly Hilton Hotel since Peter, drunk and hysterical, was driving in the opposite direction heading toward downtown Los Angeles. At the time of the stop, Franklin said he did not correlate Bobby Kennedy with Marilyn Monroe as news of her death was still hours away.

~ 12:30–2:00 a.m.

Bobby takes a helicopter from the Lawfords' to Los Angeles International Airport, boards a private plane, and is flown back to San Francisco.

4:25 a.m.

Norman Jefferies, Pat Newcomb, Mickey Rudin, and Hyman Engelberg are all at the scene when Greenson calls the police reaching watch commander Sgt. Jack Clemmons. In Greenson's own words (from a newspaper article on August 5, 1973), he claims to have said he wants to "report the death of a person, a sudden and unexplained death" while Clemmons says Greenson told him his star patient had instead committed suicide, not an accidental death as Greenson allegedly told his family.

4:45 a.m.

When Clemmons arrives, he talks to a sarcastic Greenson, a frightened housekeeper (Mrs. Murray), and a depressed Engelberg. Greenson tells Clemmons that Marilyn committed suicide. Greenson points to the empty bottle of Nembutal, which he implies speaks for itself. According to his initial suspicions, Clemmons believed Marilyn was murdered and that her body had been moved.

He asserts she did not die facedown on the bed in the soldier's position: her arms at her side and her legs perfectly straight. Clemmons would later reflect that Marilyn had been placed that way to disguise needle marks. He also found it strange how Mrs. Murray was running the laundry after Marilyn's death.

During this time, Jefferies, Newcomb, and Mickey Rudin hide in rooms Clemmons later admitted he didn't search, including the guest cottage. Clemmons reflected he should have looked since he had noticed quite a few cars in Marilyn's courtyard.

5:25 a.m.

Per the 1982 District Attorney's Report, Clemmons notifies Detective Sgt. Robert E. Byron of Marilyn's death.

~ 5:30 a.m.

Sgt. Marvin Iannone dismisses Clemmons from the scene.

~ 5:45 a.m.

By the time Detective Sgt. Byron arrives, he notes Greenson is no longer at the house but places Pat Newcomb on the scene. Had Greenson still been there, he surely would have been hounded by reporters and couldn't have conceivably escaped their photographs, none of which have survived.

Westwood Village Mortuary employees Guy Hockett and his son Don arrive. The elder Hockett notes that rigor mortis is advanced and places Marilyn's death roughly between 9:30 to 11:30 p.m. on August 4.

~ 6:00–6:30 a.m.

Per reporter Joe Hyams, the Hocketts strap Marilyn into a gurney then lift the gurney into their Ford Panel truck and drive away.

~ 6:30–7:00 a.m.

Per Jefferies and Mrs. Murray, before the police seal the house, they notice that Pat Newcomb doesn't want to leave. Per Jefferies, he sees Pat "looking through drawers and going into Marilyn's bedroom. She had spent Friday night at the house and perhaps she was looking for something she left there. The police had to control her . . . They had trouble getting her out of the door." That's because she was looking for the red diary that Jefferies a day later said he saw in Mrs. Murray's possession, the same diary that Bobby Kennedy couldn't find the night before.

Note: On Monday, August 6, Jefferies will witness Mrs. Murray give the red diary and one of Marilyn's personal address books to a driver for the Coroner's Office before executrix Inez Melson arrives. After a day at the Coroner's Office, per Deputy Coroner's Aide Lionel Grandison, the red diary was gone.

~ 8:00–8:45 a.m.

Per Deputy Coroner Robert Dambacher, he and his partner Cletus Pace transferred Marilyn Monroe's remains from the Westwood Village Mortuary back to the Coroner's Office in downtown Los Angeles.

~ 9:00 a.m.

Dr. Thomas Noguchi will perform the autopsy overseen by Deputy District Attorney John Miner. Noguchi noted what he later considered strange observations, "The stomach is almost completely empty. The contents is [sic] brownish mucoid fluid. The volume is estimated to be no more than 20 cc. No residue of the pills is noted. A smear made from the gastric contents and examined under the polarized microscope shows no refractile crystals . . . The contents of the duodenum is [sic] also examined under polarized microscope and shows no refractile crystals . . . The colon shows marked congestion and purplish discoloration."

Thomas Noguchi at first notated needle marks on Marilyn's body, but in a later revision of the autopsy report, Noguchi had handwritten "No needle mark," which contradicted his initial findings. A confidential source relayed to Jay Margolis, "There were needle marks behind her knees, the jugular vein in her neck, and bruises on her arms and back." In addition, according to Allan Abbott, Noguchi also found a needle mark under Marilyn's left armpit. Last, there was the needle mark to the heart, which apparently was never included on any of the autopsy reports, especially the "official" one.

9:30 a.m.
Bobby Kennedy attends Mass in Gilroy, California, with his wife Ethel and four of their children at St. Mary Parish.

10:30 a.m.
Noguchi completes the autopsy, signing his report on Marilyn Monroe, reluctantly declaring her death a "probable suicide."

AUTOPSY REPORT

OFFICE OF COUNTY CORONER
File 8 #1128
Date: Aug. 5, 1962
Time: 10:30 a.m.

ACUTE BARBITURATE POISONING
INGESTION OF OVERDOSE
(final 8/27/62)

ANATOMICAL SUMMARY
EXTERNAL EXAMINATION:

Lavidity [sic] of face and chest with slight ecchymosis of the left side of the back and left hip.
Surgical scar, right upper quadrant of the abdomen.
Suprapubic surgical scar.

RESPIRATORY SYSTEM:

Pulmonary congestion and minimal edema.

LIVER AND BILIARY SYSTEM:

Surgical absence of gallbladder.
Acute passive congestion of liver.

UROGENITAL SYSTEM:

Congestion of kidneys.

DIGESTIVE SYSTEM:

Marked congestion of stomach with petechial mucosal hemorrhage.
Absence of appendix.
Congestion and purplish discoloration of the colon.

EXTERNAL EXAMINATION:

The unembalmed body is that of a 36-year-old well-developed, well-nourished Caucasian female weighing 117 pounds and measuring 65½ inches in length. The scalp is covered with bleached blond hair. The eyes are blue. The fixed lividity is noted in the face, neck, chest, upper portions of arms and the right side of the abdomen. The faint lividity which disappears upon pressure is noted in the back and posterior aspect of the arms and legs. A slight ecchymotic area is noted in the left hip and left side of lower back. The breast shows no significant lesion. There is a horizontal 3-inch long surgical scar in the right upper quadrant of the abdomen. A suprapubic surgical scar measuring 5 inches in length is noted.

The conjunctivae are markedly congested; however, no ecchymosis or petechiae are noted. The nose shows no evidence of fracture. The external auditory canals are not remarkable. No evidence of trauma is noted in the scalp, forehead, cheeks, lips or chin. The neck shows no evidence of trauma. Examination of the hands and nails shows no defects. The lower extremities shows no evidence of trauma.

BODY CAVITY:

The usual Y-shaped incision is made to open the thoracic and abdominal cavities. The pleural and abdominal cavities contain no excess of fluid or blood. The mediastinum shows no shifting or widening. The diaphragm is within normal limits. The lower edge of the liver is within the costal margin. The organs are in normal position and relationship.

CARDIOVASCULAR SYSTEM:

The heart weighs 300 grams. The pericardial cavity contains no excess of fluid. The epicardium and pericardium are smooth and glistening. The left ventricular wall measures 1.1 cm. and the right 0.2 cm. The papillary muscles are not hypertrophic. The chordae tendieneae are not thickened or shortened. The valves have the usual number of leaflets which are thin and pliable. The tricuspid valve measures 10 cm., the pulmonary valve 6.5 cm., mitral valve 9.5 cm. and aortic valve 7 cm. in circumference. There is no septal defect. The foramen ovale is closed.

The coronary arteries arise from their usual location and are distributed in normal fashion. Multiple sections of the anterior descending branch of the left coronary artery with a 5 mm. interval demonstrate a patent lumen throughout. The circumflex branch and the right coronary artery also demonstrate a patent lumen. The pulmonary artery contains no thrombus.

The aorta has a bright yellow smooth intima.

RESPIRATORY SYSTEM:

The right lung weighs 465 grams and the left 420 grams. Both lungs are moderately congested with some edema. The surface is dark red with mottling. The posterior portion of the lungs shows severe congestion. The tracheobronchial tree contains no aspirated material or blood. Multiple sections of the lungs show congestion and edematous fluid exuding from the cut surface. No consolidation or suppuration is noted. The mucosa of the larynx is grayish white.

LIVER AND BILIARY SYSTEM:

The liver weighs 1890 grams. The surface is dark brown and smooth. There are marked adhesions through the omentum and abdominal wall in the lower portion of the liver as the gallbladder has been removed. The common duct is widely patent. No calculus or obstructive material is found. Multiple sections of the liver show slight accentuation of the lobular pattern; however, no hemorrhage or tumor is found.

HEMIC AND LYMPHATIC SYSTEM:

The spleen weighs 190 grams. The surface is dark red and smooth. Section shows dark red homogeneous firm cut surface. The malpighian bodies are not clearly identified. There is no evidence of lymphadenopathy. The bone marrow is dark red in color.

ENDOCRINE SYSTEM:

The adrenal glands have the usual architectural cortex and medulla. The thyroid glands are of normal size, color and consistency.

URINARY SYSTEM:

The kidneys together weigh 350 grams. Their capsules can be stripped without difficulty. Dissection shows a moderately congested parenchyma. The cortical surface is smooth. The pelves and ureters are not dilated or stenosed. The urinary bladder contains approximately 150 cc. of clear straw-colored fluid. The mucosa is not altered.

GENITAL SYSTEM:

The external genitalia shows no gross abnormality. Distribution of the pubic hair is of female pattern. The uterus is of the usual size. Multiple sections of the uterus show the usual thickness of the uterine wall without tumor nodules. The endometrium is grayish yellow, measuring up to 0.2 cm in thickness. No polyp or tumor is found. The cervix is clear, showing no nabothian cysts. The tubes are intact. The openings of the fimbria are patent. The right ovary demonstrates recent corpus luteum haemorrhagicum. The left ovary shows corpora lutea and albicantia. A vaginal smear is taken.

DIGESTIVE SYSTEM:

The esophagus has a longitudinal folding mucosa. The stomach is almost completely empty. The contents is brownish mucoid fluid. The volume is estimated to be no more than 20 cc. No residue of the pills is noted. A smear made from the gastric contents and examined under the polarized microscope shows no refractile crystals. The mucosa shows marked congestion and submucosal petechial hemorrhage diffusely. The duodenum shows no ulcer. The contents of the duodenum is also examined under polarized microscope and shows no refractile crystals. The remainder of the small intestine shows no gross abnormality. The appendix is absent. The colon shows marked congestion and purplish discoloration. The fecal contents is light brown and formed. The mucosa shows no discoloration.

The pancreas has a tan lobular architecture. Multiple sections shows a patent duct.

SKELETOMUSCULAR SYSTEM:

The clavicle, ribs, vertebrae and pelvic bones show no refractile lines. All bones of the extremities are examined by palpation showing no evidence of fracture.

HEAD AND CENTRAL NERVOUS SYSTEM:

The brain weighs 1440 grams. Upon reflection of the scalp there is no evidence of contusion or hemorrhage. The temporal muscles are intact. Upon removal of the dura mater the cerebrospinal fluid is clear. The superficial vessels are slightly congested. The convolutions of the brain are not flattened. The contour of the brain is not distorted. No blood is found in the epidural, subdural or subarachnoid spaces. Multiple sections of the brain show the usual symmetrical ventricles and basal ganglia. Examination of the cerebellum and brain stem shows no gross abnormality. Following removal of the dura mater from the base of the skull and calvarium no skull fracture is demonstrated.

Liver temperature taken at 10:30 a.m. registered 89° F.

SPECIMEN:

Unembalmed blood is taken for alcohol and barbiturate examination. Liver, kidney, stomach and contents, urine and intestine are saved for further toxicological study. A vaginal smear is made.

T. NOGUCHI, M.D.
DEPUTY MEDICAL EXAMINER
TN:ag:G
8-13-62

REPORT OF CHEMICAL ANALYSIS
LOS ANGELES COUNTY CORONER

Toxicology Laboratory
Hall of Justice
Los Angeles, California

File No. 81128
Name of Deceased: Marilyn Monroe
Date Submitted: August 6, 1962
Time: 8 a.m.
Autopsy Surgeon: T. Noguchi, M.D.

Material Submitted	Blood X	Liver X	Stomach X
	Brain	Lung	Lavage
	Femur	Spleen	Urine X
	Kidney X	Sterum	Gallbladder
	Drugs X	Chemicals	Intestines X

Test Desired: Ethanol, Barbiturates

Laboratory Findings:

Blood: Ethanol   Absent
Blood: Barbiturates   4.5 mg. percent
Phenobarbital is absent.

Drugs: (1) 27 capsules, #19295, 6-7-62, Librium, 5 mgm. #50
    (2) 17 capsules, #20201, 7-10-62, Librium, 10 mgm. #100
    (3) 26 tablets, # 20569, 7-25-62, Sulfathallidine, #36
    (4) Empty container, #20858, 8-3-62, Nembutal, 1½gr. #25
    (5) 10 green capsules, #20570, 7-31-62, Chloral Hydrate, 0.5 gm. #50 (Refill: 7-25-62—original)
    (6) Empty container, #456099, 11-4-61, Noludar, #50
    (7) 32 pink capsules in a container without label, Phenergan, #20857, 8-3-62, 25 mg. #25

Examined by: Raymond Abernathy Head Toxicologist.
Date: August 6, 1962

REPORT OF CHEMICAL ANALYSIS
LOS ANGELES COUNTY CORONER

Toxicology Laboratory
Hall of Justice
Los Angeles, California

File No. 81128
Name of Deceased: Marilyn Monroe 1st Supplement
Date Submitted: August 6, 1962
Time: 8 a.m.
Autopsy Surgeon: T. Noguchi, M.D.

Material Submitted	Blood X	Liver X	Stomach X
	Brain	Lung	Lavage
	Femur	Spleen	Urine X
	Kidney X	Sterum	Gallbladder
	Drugs X	Chemicals	Intestines X

Test Desired: Chloral Hydrate, Pentobarbital

Laboratory Findings:

Blood: Chloral Hydrate   8 mg. per cent
Liver: Pentobarbital   13.0 mg. per cent

Drugs: Correction—delete #7 on original report of August 6 and add:
(7) 32 peach-colored tablets marked MSD in prescription type vial without label.
(8) 24 white tablets #20857, 8-3-62, Phenergan, 25 mg. #25

(SEE ORIGINAL REPORT)

Examined by: Raymond Abernathy Head Toxicologist.
Date: August 13, 1962

Re: Death Report of Marilyn Monroe—
LA Police Dpt.

Death was pronounced on 8/5/62 at 3:45 a.m., Possible Accidental, having taken place between the times of 8/4 and 8/5/62, 3:35 a.m. at residence located at 12305 Fifth Helena Drive, Brentwood, in Rptg. Dist. 814, Report # 62-509 463.

Marilyn Monroe on August 4, 1962 retired to her bedroom at about eight o'clock in the evening; Mrs. Eunice Murray of 933 Ocean Ave., Santa Monica, Calif., 395-7752, CR 61890, noted a light in Miss Monroe's bedroom. Mrs. Murray was not able to arouse Miss Monroe when she went to the door, and when she tried the door again at 3:30 a.m. when she noted the light still on, she found it to be locked. Thereupon Mrs. Murray observed Miss Monroe through the bedroom window and found her lying on her stomach in the bed and the appearance seemed unnatural. Mrs. Murray then called Miss Monroe's psychiatrist, Dr. Ralph R. Greenson of 436 North Roxbury Drive, Beverly Hills, Calif, CR 14050. Upon entering after breaking the bedroom window, he found Miss Monroe possibly dead. Then he telephoned Dr. Hyman Engelberg of 9730 Wilshire Boulevard, also of Beverly Hills, CR 54366, who came over and then pronounced Miss Monroe dead at 3:35 a.m. Miss Monroe was seen by Dr. Greenson on August 4, 1962 at 5:15 p.m., at her request, because she was not able to sleep. She was being treated by him for about a year. She was nude when Dr. Greenson found her dead with the telephone receiver in one hand and lying on her stomach. The Police Department was called and when they arrived they found Miss Monroe in the condition described above, except for the telephone which was removed by Dr. Greenson. There were found to be 15 bottles of medication on the night table and some were prescription. A bottle marked 1½ grains Nembutal, prescription #20853 and prescribed by Dr. Engelberg, and referring to this particular bottle, Dr. Engelberg made the statement that he prescribed a refill for this about two days ago and he further stated there probably should have been about 50 capsules at the time this was refilled by the pharmacist.

Description of Deceased: Female Caucasian, age 36, height 5.4, weight 115 pounds, blonde hair, blue eyes, and slender, medium build.

Occupation: Actress, Probable cause of death: overdose of Nembutal, body discovered 8/5/62 at 3:25 a.m. Taken to County Morgue—from there to Westwood Mortuary. Report made by Sgt. R.E. Byron, #2730, W. LA Detective Division. Next of kin: Gladys Baker (Mother).

Coroner's Office notified. The body was removed from premises by Westwood Village Mortuary.

(8/5/62 11 a.m. WLA hf—J.R. Brukles 5829)

LOS ANGELES POLICE DEPARTMENT

FOLLOW-UP REPORT
Report # 62-509 463

Type Crime: DEATH REPORT
Date and Time Occurred: 8-4/5-62 8P/3:35A
Date and Time of this Report: 8-6-62 4:15P
Location of Occurrence: 12305 Fifth Helena Drive
Victim's Name: MONROE, Marilyn

Upon re-interviewing both Dr. Ralph R. Greenson (Wit #1) and Dr. Hyman Engelberg (Wit #2) they both agree to the following time sequence of their actions.

Dr. Greenson received a phone call from Mrs. Murray (reporting person) at 3:30A, 8-5-62 stating that she was unable to get into Miss Monroe's bedroom and the light was on. He told her to pound on the door and look in the window and call him back. At 3:35A, Mrs. Murray called back and stated Miss Monroe was laying on the bed with the phone in her hand and looked strange. Dr. Greenson was dressed by this time, left for deceased residence which is about one mile away. He also told Mrs. Murray to call Dr. Engelberg.

Dr. Greenson arrived at deceased house at about 3:40A. He broke the window pane and entered through the window and removed the phone from her hand.

Rigor Mortis had set in. At 3:50A, Dr. Engelberg arrived and pronounced Miss Monroe dead. The two doctors talked for a few moments. They both believe that it was about 4A when Dr. Engelberg called the Police Department.

A check with the Complaint Board and WLA Desk, indicates that the call was received at 4:25 a.m. Miss Monroe's phone, GR 61890 has been checked and no toll calls were made during the hours of this occurrence. Phone number 472-4830 is being checked at the present time.

RE-INTERVIEW OF PERSONS KNOWN
TO MARILYN MONROE

August 6, 1962

G.H. ARMSTRONG, COMMANDER, WEST LA DETECTIVE DIVISION

Date and Time Reported: 8-10-62 8:30A

The following is a resume of the interview conducted in an effort to obtain the times of various phone calls received by Miss Monroe on the evening of her death. All of the below times are estimations of the persons interviewed. None are able to state definite times as none checked the time of these calls.

MILTON RUDIN

Mr. Rudin stated that on the evening of 8-4-62 his exchange received a call at 8:25P and that this call was relayed to him at 8:30P. The call was for him to call Milton Ebbins. At about 8:45P he called Mr. Ebbins who told him that he had received a call from Peter Lawford stating that Mr. Lawford had called Marilyn Monroe at her home and that while Mr. Lawford was talking to her, her voice seemed to "fade out" and when he attempted to call her back, the line was busy. Mr. Ebbins requested that Mr. Rudin call Miss Monroe and determine if everything was alright, or attempt to reach her doctor. At about 9P, Mr. Rudin called Miss Monroe and the phone was answered by Mrs. Murray. He inquired of her as to the physical well being of Miss Monroe and was assured by Mrs. Murray that Miss Monroe was alright. Believing that Miss Monroe was suffering from one of her despondent moments, Mr. Rudin dismissed the possibility of anything further being wrong.

MRS. EUNICE MURRAY

Mrs. Murray stated that she had worked for Marilyn Monroe since November, 1961, that on the evening of 8-4-62 Miss Monroe had received a collect call from a Joe DiMaggio, Jr. at about 7:30P. Mrs. Murray said that at the time of this call coming in, Miss Monroe was in bed and possibly had been asleep. She took the call and after talking to Joe DiMaggio, Jr., she then made a call to Dr. Greenson and Mrs. Murray overheard her say, "Joe Jr. is not getting married, I'm so happy about this." Mrs. Murray states that from the tone of Miss Monroe's voice, she believed her to be in very good spirits. At about 9P, Mrs. Murray received a call from Mr. Rudin who inquired about Miss Monroe. Mr. Rudin did not talk to Miss Monroe. Mrs. Murray states that these are the only phone calls that she recalls receiving on this date.

Note: It is officers opinion that Mrs. Murray was vague and possibly evasive in answering questions pertaining to the activities of Miss Monroe during this time. It is not known whether this is, or is not intentional. During the interrogation of Joe DiMaggio, Jr., he indicated he had made three phone calls to the Monroe home, only one of which Mrs. Murray mentioned.

JOE DIMAGGIO—Miramar Hotel, Room 1035, Santa Monica

Mr. DiMaggio was informed of the rumor which quoted him as saying that he would not invite Mr. Lawford to the funeral services because he could have saved Marilyn's life and didn't. Mr. DiMaggio denied this, stating that he had not talked to any member of the press, nor had he said such a thing to anyone who might have repeated it to the press. He stated that the decision to limit the number of people was a mutual agreement, decided upon in order to keep from hurting the feelings of many of Marilyn's friends who might be accidentally overlooked.

JOE DIMAGGIO, JR.—Miramar Hotel, Room 1035, Santa Monica

Joe DiMaggio, Jr. was in his father's suite and interviewed immediately after the above interview. He stated that he had placed three collect calls to Miss Monroe on 8-4-62 and that the first call was about 2P. He could overhear the operator talk to Mrs. Murray who informed the operator that Miss Monroe was not in. The second call was placed at approximately 4:30P and again was answered by Mrs. Murray, and again he was unable to contact Miss Monroe. The third call was placed at approximately 7P and on this occasion Mrs. Murray stated that she would see if Miss Monroe was available and in a few moments Miss Monroe came on the phone and he held a short conversation with her. During the conversation, he told Miss Monroe that he was not going to get married. The time of the last call is estimated to be 7P, as he states it was during the 6th or 7th innings of the Angels-Orioles baseball game in Baltimore.

JAY MARGOLIS AND RICHARD BUSKIN

PETER LAWFORD

An attempt was made to contact Mr. Lawford, but officers were informed by his secretary that Mr. Lawford had taken an airplane at 1P, 8-8-62. It is unknown at this time the exact destination, however his secretary stated that she did expect to hear from him and that she would request that he contact this Department at his earliest convenience.

R.E. Byron #2730
W.LA Detectives

POLICE REPORTS on MARILYN MONROE DEATH

8-5-62
L. Selby, OIC, Homicide Special Sec., R.H.D.
Date of Report: 8-27-74

At the request of Commander McCauley, an attempt was made to determine the number and type of police reports taken by this Department in connection with Marilyn Monroe's death which occurred in W.LA Div. on August 5, 1962. Commander McCauley also requested we determine if any of these reports were still available at this time.

In this regard, Sgt. Sturgeon, O.I.C., R. & I. Div., was contacted and requested to make a search of R. & I. files in an attempt to locate any reports we may have. He stated he could locate no records pertaining to the 1962 death of Miss Monroe. He further stated that all original crime reports that are controlled by R. & I. Div. are destroyed after a 10-year retention period. All reports, file cards, and DR blotters are included in the destruction.

Note: Attached is a copy of correspondence dated Sept. 4, 1973, to Assistant Chief D.F. Gates from Assistant Chief D.H. Speck pertaining to the "retention and destruction of crime reports."

The files at R.H.D. were checked for any records of the death of Miss Monroe. This division has no such records.

Investigators contacted W.LA Div. and were informed that they had no crime reports in their files pertaining to Miss Monroe's death. It was further determined from present W.LA investigators that the original W.LA detective who handled the case was Sgt. R.E. Byron, now retired.

Mr. Byron was contacted . . . He stated he was called to the scene of Miss Monroe's death. Lieuts. Gregoire and Armstrong also responded. Byron stated he completed a death report and believes that he classified it as "accidental." Byron believes that he subsequently made a follow-up report to the original death report but is not sure how that was classified.

Byron does not have copies of any of these reports nor does he know of any existing copies.

CONFIDENTIAL

Employees Reporting: LA Murray 6692 RHD

BIBLIOGRAPHY

Acacia, John. *Clark Clifford: The Wise Man of Washington*. Kentucky: University Press of Kentucky, 2009.

Alford, Mimi. *Once Upon a Secret: My Affair with President John F. Kennedy and Its Aftermath*. New York: Random House Trade Paperbacks, 2013.

Allen, Maury. *Where Have You Gone, Joe DiMaggio?* New York: Signet, 1976.

Arnold, Eve. *Marilyn Monroe: An Appreciation*. New York: Knopf, 1987.

Badman, Keith. *The Final Years of Marilyn Monroe: The Shocking True Story*. London: J.R. Books, 2010.

Banner, Lois W. *MM—Personal: From the Private Archive of Marilyn Monroe*. New York: Abrams, 2011.

Barnes, Ralph Mosser. *Motion and Time Study: Design and Measurement of Work—Seventh Edition*. New Jersey: John Wiley & Sons, 1980.

Barris, George. *Marilyn: Her Life in Her Own Words*. New York: Birch Lane Press, 1995.

Belmont, Georges. *Marilyn Monroe and the Camera*. London: Schirmer Art Books, 2007.

Berthelsen, Detlef. *Alltag Bei Familie Freud: Die Erinnerungen Der Paula Fichtl. (Life of the Freud Family: The Memoirs of Paula Fichtl)* Hamburg: Hoffman Und Campe, 1987.

Blaine, Gerald, and Lisa McCubbin. *The Kennedy Detail: JFK's Secret Service Agents Break Their Silence*. New York: Gallery Books, 2010.

Braden, Joan. *Just Enough Rope: An Intimate Memoir*. New York: Villard Books, 1989.

111111111

1111111111

Bradlee, Benjamin C. *Conversations with Kennedy*. New York: Norton Paperback, 1984.

Brashler, William. *The Don: The Life and Death of Sam Giancana*. New York: Harper & Row, 1977.

Brodsky, Jack, and Nathan Weiss. *The Cleopatra Papers: A Private Correspondence*. New York: Simon & Schuster, 1963.

Brown, Peter, and Patte Barham. *Marilyn: The Last Take*. New York: Signet, 1993.

Buchthal, Stanley, and Bernard Comment, eds. *Fragments: Poems, Intimate Notes, Letters by Marilyn Monroe*. New York: Farrar, Straus and Giroux, 2010.

Buntin, John. *LA Noir: The Struggle for the Soul of America's Most Seductive City*. New York: Three Rivers Press, 2009.

Burke, Richard E. *The Senator: My Ten Years with Ted Kennedy*. New York: St. Martin's Press, 1992.

Buskin, Richard. *Blonde Heat: The Sizzling Screen Career of Marilyn Monroe*. New York: Billboard Books, 2001.

-----. *The Films of Marilyn Monroe*. Illinois: Publications International, 1992.

Cagin, Seth, and Philip Dray. *We Are Not Afraid: The Story of Goodman, Schwerner, and Chaney, and the Civil Rights Campaign for Mississippi*. New York: Nation Books, 2006.

Capell, Frank A. *The Strange Death of Marilyn Monroe*. New York: The Herald of Freedom, 1964.

Capote, Truman. *Music for Chameleons*. New York: Vintage International, 1994.

Carpozi, George, Jr., *Marilyn Monroe: "Her Own Story."* New York: Belmont, 1961.

Carroll, Ronald H., and Alan B. Tomich. "The Death of Marilyn Monroe—Report to the District Attorney." December 1982, pp. 1-29.

Chekhov, Michael. *To the Actor: On the Technique of Acting*. New York: Harper & Row, Publishers, 1953.

Christie's. *The Personal Property of Marilyn Monroe*. New York: International Flavors & Fragrances, 1999.

Clayton, Marie. *Marilyn Monroe: Unseen Archives*. New York: Barnes & Noble Books, 2004.

Clifford, Clark M., and Richard Holbrooke. *Counsel to the President: A Memoir*. New York: Anchor, 1992.

Cockburn, Alexander, and Jeffrey St. Clair. *Whiteout: The CIA, Drugs and the Press*. New York: Verso, 2001.

Conway, Michael, and Mark Ricci, eds. *The Films of Marilyn Monroe*. New Jersey: The Citadel Press, 1979.

Cramer, Richard Ben. *Joe DiMaggio: The Hero's Life*. New York: Touchstone, 2001.

Crane, Cheryl, and Cliff Jahr. *Detour: A Hollywood Story*. New York: William Morrow, 1988.

Critchfield, James H. *Partners at the Creation: The Men Behind Postwar Germany's Defense and Intelligence Establishments*. Annapolis: Naval Institute Press, 2003.

Dallek, Robert. *An Unfinished Life: John F. Kennedy*. New York: Little, Brown and Company, 2003.

Davis, Sammy, Jr. *Hollywood in a Suitcase*. London: Granada Publishing, 1980.

De Dienes, Andre. *Marilyn: Mon Amour*. London: Bracken Books, 1993.

De La Hoz, Cindy. *Marilyn Monroe: The Personal Archives*. London: Carlton Books, 2010.

Demaris, Ovid. *Captive City: Chicago in Chains*. New York: Lyle Stuart, 1969.

De Toledano, Ralph. *J. Edgar Hoover: The Man in His Time*. New York: Manor Books, 1974.

-----. *R.F.K.: The Man Who Would Be President*. New York: Signet: 1967.

DiEugenio, James, and Lisa Pease, ed. *The Assassinations: Probe Magazine on JFK, MLK, RFK and Malcolm X*. Washington: Feral House, 2003.

Dougherty, Jim. *To Norma Jeane with Love, Jimmie.* Missouri: BeachHouse Books, 2001.

-----. *The Secret Happiness of Marilyn Monroe.* Chicago: Playboy Press, 1976.

Dunne, Dominick. *The Way We Lived Then: Recollections of a Well-Known Name Dropper.* New York: Crown Publishers, 1999.

Editors of *Life. Remembering Marilyn.* New York: Time, Inc., 2009.

Engelberg, Hyman, M.D., and Henry F. Greenberg. *The Doctor's Modern Heart Attack Prevention Program.* New York: Funk & Wagnalls, 1974.

Engelberg, Morris, and Marv Schneider. *DiMaggio: Setting the Record Straight.* Minnesota: MVP Books, 2004.

Evans, Mike. *Marilyn Handbook.* London: MQ Publications Limited, 2004.

Evans, Peter. *Nemesis: Aristotle Onassis, Jackie O, and the Love Triangle That Brought Down the Kennedys.* New York: HarperCollins, 2004.

Exner, Judith, and Ovid Demaris. *My Story.* New York: Grove Press, 1978.

Fanta, J. Julius. *Sailing with President Kennedy: The White House Yachtsman.* New York: Sea Lore Publishing, 1968.

Farber, Stephen, and Marc Green. *Hollywood on the Couch: A Candid Look at the Overheated Love Affair Between Psychiatrists and Moviemakers.* New York: William Morrow & Company, 1993.

Federal Bureau of Investigation. *John Roselli: The FBI Files (Volume One + Two).* Filiquarian Publishing, LLC, 2009.

-----. *Marilyn Monroe: The FBI Files.* Filiquarian Publishing, LLC, 2007.

-----. *Robert F. Kennedy Assassination: The FBI Files.* Filiquarian Publishing, LLC. 2007.

Feingersh, Ed. *Marilyn in New York.* Munich: Schirmer/Mosel, 2008.

Finn, Michelle. *Marilyn's Addresses: A Fan's Guide to the Places She Knew.* London: Smith Gryphon Publishers, 1995.

Fowler, Will. *Reporters: Memoirs of a Young Newspaperman.* Malibu: Roundtable Publishing Company, 1991.

Franklin, Joe, and Laurie Palmer. *The Marilyn Monroe Story.* New York: Rudolph Field Company, 1953.

Franklin, Lynn. *The Beverly Hills Murder File.* Indiana: 1st Books Library, 2002.

Freeman, Lucy. *Why Norma Jeane Killed Marilyn Monroe.* New York: Hastings House, 1993.

Garrow, David. *Bearing the Cross: Martin Luther King, Jr., and the Southern Christian Leadership Conference.* New York: William Morrow, 1986.

Gates, Daryl F. *Chief: My Life in the LAPD.* New York: Bantam Books, 1993.

Gentry, Curt. *J. Edgar Hoover: The Man and the Secrets.* New York: Norton Paperback, 2001.

Giancana, Sam, and Chuck Giancana. *Double Cross: The Explosive Inside Story of the Mobster Who Controlled America.* New York: Skyhorse Publishing, 2010.

Gilmore, John. *Inside Marilyn Monroe.* California: Ferine Books, 2007.

Graham, Sheilah. *Confessions of a Hollywood Columnist.* New York: Bantam Books, 1970.

Grandison, Lionel, Jr., and Samir Muqaddin. *Memoirs of a Deputy Coroner: The Case of Marilyn Monroe.* California BAIT-CAL Publishing, 2012.

Greenson, Joan. *Untitled 90-Page Marilyn Monroe Manuscript.* Greenson Papers, Special Collections, UCLA.

Greenson, Ralph, M.D. *Explorations in Psychoanalysis.* New York: International Universities Press, 1978.

-----. *The Technique and Practice of Psychoanalysis.* Connecticut: International Universities Press, 1967.

-----. "Drugs in the Psychotherapeutic Situation." January 12, 1964. Greenson Papers, Special Collections, UCLA.

Guilaroff, Sydney, and Cathy Griffin. *Crowning Glory: Reflections of Hollywood's Favorite Confidant*. Santa Monica: General Publishing Group, 1996.

Guiles, Fred Lawrence. *Legend: The Life and Death of Marilyn Monroe*. New York: Stein and Day, 1984.

-----. *Norma Jeane: The Life of Marilyn Monroe*. New York: McGraw-Hill 1969.

Guthman, Edwin O., and Jeffrey Shulman, eds. *Robert Kennedy: In His Own Words*. New York: Bantam Books, 1989.

Hancock, Larry. *Someone Would Have Talked*. Texas: JFK Lancer Productions & Publications, 2003.

Haspiel, James. *The Unpublished Marilyn*. Edinburgh: Mainstream Publishing Company, 2000.

-----. *Young Marilyn: Becoming the Legend*. New York: Hyperion, 1994.

-----. *Marilyn: The Ultimate Look at the Legend*. New York: Owl Book, 1993.

Hays, Thomas G., Arthur W. Sjoquist, and the Los Angeles Police Historical Society. *Los Angeles Police Department (Images of America: California)*. South Carolina: Arcadia Publishing, 2005.

Hersh, Seymour M. *The Dark Side of Camelot*. New York: Back Bay Books, 1998.

Hethmon, Robert. *Strasberg at the Actors Studio: Tape-Recorded Sessions*. New York: Theatre Communications Group, 1996.

Heymann, C. David. *Bobby and Jackie: A Love Story*. New York: Atria, 2009.

-----. *RFK: A Candid Biography of Robert F. Kennedy*. New York: A Dutton Book, 1998.

-----. *A Woman Named Jackie*. New York: Lyle Stuart, 1989.

Hodel, Steve. *Black Dahlia Avenger: The True Story*. New York: HarperCollins, 2004.

Houghton, Robert A. *Special Unit Senator: The Investigation of the Assassination of Senator Robert F. Kennedy*. New York: Random House, 1970.

Hudson, James. *The Mysterious Death of Marilyn Monroe*. New York: Volitant, 1968.

Israel, Lee. *Kilgallen*. New York: Delacorte Press, 1979.

Jacobs, George. *Mr. S: My Life with Frank Sinatra*. New York: HarperEntertainment, 2004.

Jaffe, Lee. *The Technique and Practice of Psychoanalysis, Volume III: The Training Seminars of Ralph R. Greenson, M.D.* New York: International Universities Press, 2004.

Johnson, Dorris, and Ellen Leventhal, ed. *The Letters of Nunnally Johnson*. New York: Knopf, 1981.

Joling, Robert J., J.D., and Philip Van Praag. *An Open & Shut Case*. United States of America: JV & Co., LLC, 2008.

Kahn, Roger. *Joe & Marilyn: A Memory of Love*. New York: William Morrow & Company, 1986.

Kaiser, Robert Blair. *"RFK Must Die!:" Chasing the Mystery of the Robert Kennedy Assassination*. New York: The Overlook Press, 2008.

Kappel, Kenneth. *Chappaquiddick Revealed: What Really Happened*. New York: St. Martin's Paperbacks, 1989.

Kazan, Elia. *Elia Kazan: A Life*. New York: Da Capo Press, 1997.

Kelley, Kitty. *His Way: The Unauthorized Biography of Frank Sinatra*. New York: Bantam Books, 1986.

-----. *Jackie Oh!* New York: Ballantine Books, 1979.

Kennedy, Edward M., ed. *The Fruitful Bough*. Halliday Lithograph Corporation. Privately printed, 1965.

Kennedy, Robert. *The Enemy Within*. New York: Popular Library, 1960.

Kessler, Ronald. *The Secrets of the FBI.* Broadway Paperbacks: New York, 2012.

-----. *In the President's Secret Service: Behind the Scenes with Agents in the Line of Fire and the Presidents They Protect.* New York: Three Rivers Press, 2010.

Kirkham, James F., Sheldon Levy, and William J. Grotty. *Assassination and Political Violence: A Staff Report to the National Commission on the Causes and Prevention of Violence.* New York: Praeger, 1970.

Kirkland, Douglas. *An Evening with Marilyn.* New York: Welcome Books, 2005.

Kirsner, Douglas. *Unfree-Associations: Inside Psychoanalytic Institutes.* Maryland: Jason Aronson, 2009.

-----. (2007) " 'DO AS I SAY, NOT AS I DO': Ralph Greenson, Anna Freud, and Superrich Patients." *Psychoanalytic Psychology,* 24: 475–486.

-----. (2005) "Politics masquerading as science: Ralph Greenson, Anna Freud, and the Klein wars." *Psychoanalytic Review,* 92: 907–927.

Klaber, William, and Philip H. Melanson. *Shadow Play: The Murder of Robert F. Kennedy, the Trail of Sirhan Sirhan, and the Failure of American Justice.* New York: St. Martin's Press, 1997.

Kotsilibas-Davis, James, and Joshua Greene. *Milton's Marilyn: The Photographs of Milton H. Greene.* New York: teNeues, 1998.

Lawford, Lady May, and Buddy Galon. *Mother Bitch: Lady Lawford Exposes the Kennedys, the Royal Family & Her Own Son, Peter Lawford.* New York: S.P.I. Books, 1992.

Lawford, Patricia Kennedy, ed. *That Shining Hour.* Halliday Lithograph Corporation. Privately printed, 1969.

Lawford, Patricia Seaton, and Ted Schwarz. *The Peter Lawford Story: Life with the Kennedys, Monroe and the Rat Pack.* New York: Carroll & Graf Publishers, Inc., 1988.

Leamer, Laurence. *The Kennedy Women: The Saga of an American Family.* New York: Ballantine Books, 1996.

Leaming, Barbara. *Marilyn Monroe*. New York: Three Rivers Press, 1998.

Luitjers, Guus. *Marilyn Monroe: In Her Own Words*. London: Omnibus Press, 1991.

-----. *Marilyn Monroe: A Never-Ending Dream*. New York: St. Martin's Press, 1986.

Mailer, Norman. *Marilyn*. New York: Warner Books, 1975.

Margolis, Jay. *Marilyn Monroe: A Case for Murder*. Indiana: iUniverse, 2011.

Marshall, David. *The DD Group: An Online Investigation into the Death of Marilyn Monroe*. Nebraska: iUniverse, 2005.

Martin, Ralph G. *Seeds of Destruction: Joe Kennedy and His Sons*. New York: G.P. Putnam's Sons, 1995.

McCann, Graham. *Marilyn Monroe*. New Jersey: Rutgers University Press, 1988.

Mecacci, Luciano. *Freudian Slips: The Casualties of Psychoanalysis from the Wolf Man to Marilyn Monroe*. Scotland: Vagabond Voices, 2009.

Melanson, Philip H. *The Robert F. Kennedy Assassination: New Revelations on the Conspiracy and Cover-Up*. New York: S.P.I. Books, 1994.

Meyers, Jeffrey. *The Genius and the Goddess: Arthur Miller and Marilyn Monroe*. Chicago: University of Illinois Press, 2010.

Miller, Arthur. *Timebends*. New York: Grove Press, 1987.

-----. *After the Fall*. New York: Bantam Books, 1965.

Miracle, Berniece Baker, and Mona Rae Miracle. *My Sister Marilyn*. North Carolina: Algonquin Books, 1994.

Moldea, Dan E. *The Killing of Robert F. Kennedy: An Investigation of Motive, Means, and Opportunity*. New York: W.W. Norton & Company, 1995.

Monroe, Marilyn [and Ben Hecht]. *My Story*. New York: Stein and Day, 1974.

Moore, Robin, and Gene Schoor. *Marilyn & Joe DiMaggio*. New York: Manor Books, 1977.

Morgan, Michelle. *Marilyn Monroe: Private and Confidential*. New York: Skyhorse, 2012.

-----. *Marilyn Monroe: Private and Undisclosed*. New York: Carroll & Graf, 2007.

Murray, Eunice, and Rose Shade. *Marilyn: The Last Months*. New York: Pyramid Books, 1975.

Nelson, Jack. *Terror in the Night: The Klan's Campaign against the Jews*. New York: Simon & Schuster, 1993.

Nemiroff, Robert A., M.D., Alan Sugarman, Ph.D., and Alvin Robbins, M.D. *On Loving, Hating, and Living Well: The Public Psychoanalytic Lectures of Ralph R. Greenson, M.D.* Connecticut: International Universities Press, 1992.

Newfield, Jack. *Robert Kennedy: A Memoir*. New York: E.P. Dutton & Co., 1969.

Noguchi, Thomas T., M.D., and Joseph DiMona. *Coroner to the Stars*. London: Corgi Books, 1984.

Novotny, Mariella. *King's Road*. New York: Manor Books, 1972.

O'Brien, Michael. *John F. Kennedy: A Biography*. New York: St. Martin's Press, 2005.

O'Sullivan, Shane. *Who Killed Bobby?: The Unsolved Murder of Robert F. Kennedy*. New York: Union Square Press, 2008.

Oppenheimer, Jerry. *The Other Mrs. Kennedy*. New York: St. Martin's Paperbacks, 1995.

Otash, Fred. *Investigation Hollywood!* Chicago: Henry Regnery Company, 1976.

Parker, Robert, and Richard Rashke. *Capitol Hill in Black and White*. New York: Dodd, Mead & Company, 1986.

Peary, Danny, ed. *Close-Ups: The Movie Star Book*. New York: Fireside, 1988.

Quirk, Lawrence J. *The Kennedys in Hollywood*. Texas: Taylor Publishing Company, 1996.

Rappleye, Charles, and Ed Becker. *All American Mafioso: The Johnny Rosselli Story*. New York: Doubleday, 2001.

Reeves, Thomas C. *A Question of Character: A Life of John F. Kennedy*. New York: Forum, 1997.

Reymond, William. *Marilyn, le dernier secret*. Paris: Flammarion, 2008.

Riese, Randall, and Neal Hitchens. *The Unabridged Marilyn: Her Life from A to Z*. New York: Bonanza Books, 1990.

Rollyson, Carl E., Jr. *Marilyn Monroe: A Life of the Actress*. New York: Da Capo Press, 1993.

Rosten, Leo. *Captain Newman, M.D.* New York: Harper & Brothers, 1961.

Rosten, Norman. *Marilyn: An Untold Story*. New York: NAL/ Signet, 1973.

Rothmiller, Mike, and Ivan G. Goldman. *LA Secret Police: Inside the LAPD Elite Spy Network*. New York: Pocket Books, 1992.

Russell, Jane. *Jane Russell, an Autobiography: My Path & My Detours*. New York: Franklin Watts, 1985.

Sakol, Jeannie. *The Birth of Marilyn: The Lost Photographs of Norma Jeane by Joseph Jasgur*. London: Sidgwick & Jackson, 1991.

Schlesinger, Arthur M., Jr. *Robert Kennedy and His Times*. New York: Mariner Books, 2002.

Schwarz, Ted. *Marilyn Revealed: The Ambitious Life of an American Icon*. Maryland: Taylor Trade Publishing, 2009.

Schwarz, Ted, and Mardi Rustam. *Candy Barr: The Small-Town Texas Runaway Who Became a Darling of the Mob and the Queen of Las Vegas Burlesque*. Maryland: Taylor Trade Publishing, 2008.

Selsman, Michael. *All Is Vanity: Memoirs of a Hollywood Operative*. California: New World Digital Entertainment, 2009.

Shaw, Sam, and Norman Rosten. *Marilyn: Among Friends*. Australia: Magna Books, 1992.

Shaw, Sam. *The Joy of Marilyn: In the Camera Eye.* New York: Peebles Press International, 1979.

Shevey, Sandra. *The Marilyn Scandal.* New York: Jove Books, 1990.

Skolsky, Sidney. *Don't Get Me Wrong—I Love Hollywood.* New York: G.P. Putnam's Sons, 1975.

Slatzer, Robert. *The Marilyn Files.* New York: S.P.I. Books, 1992.

-----. *The Life and Curious Death of Marilyn Monroe.* London: W.H. Allen, 1975.

Smith, Matthew. *Marilyn's Last Words: Her Secret Tapes and Mysterious Death.* New York: Carroll & Graf Publishers, 2005.

Smith, Dr. Paul A., and Richard E. May, ed. *Official Report of the Proceedings of the Democratic National Convention and Committee.* Washington, D.C.: National Document Publishers, 1964.

Spada, James. *Peter Lawford: The Man Who Kept the Secrets.* New York: Bantam Books, 1991.

Spada, James, and George Zeno. *Monroe: Her Life in Pictures.* New York: Doubleday, 1982.

Speriglio, Milo. *The Marilyn Conspiracy.* New York: Pocket Books, 1986.

Spindel, Bernard B. *The Ominous Ear.* New York: Awards Book, 1968.

Spoto, Donald. *Marilyn Monroe: The Biography.* New York: HarperCollins, 1993.

Stanislavski, Constantin. *An Actor Prepares.* New York: Theatre Art Books, 1948.

Steinem, Gloria, and George Barris. *Marilyn.* New York: Henry Holt and Company, 1986.

Stern, Bert. *Marilyn Monroe: The Complete Last Sitting.* Munich: Schirmer/Mosel, 1992.

Strait, Raymond. *Bob Hope: A Tribute.* New York: Pinnacle Books, 2003.

-----. *Here They Are Jayne Mansfield.* New York: S.P.I. Books, 1992.

-----. *The Tragic Secret Life of Jayne Mansfield*. London: Robert Hale & Company, 1976.

Strasberg, Susan. *Marilyn and Me: Sisters, Rivals, Friends*. New York: Warner Books, 1992.

-----. *Bittersweet*. New York: Putnam, 1980.

Sugarman, Alan, Robert Nemiroff, and Daniel Greenson. *The Technique and Practice of Psychoanalysis, Volume II: A Memorial Volume to Ralph R. Greenson*. Connecticut: International Universities Press, 2000.

Summers, Anthony, and Robbyn Swan. *Sinatra: The Life*. New York: Vintage Books, 2006.

Summers, Anthony. *Goddess: The Secret Lives of Marilyn Monroe*. London: Phoenix, 2000.

-----. *The Secret Life of J. Edgar Hoover*. New York: Pocket Star Books, 1994.

Taraborrelli, J. Randy. *The Secret Life of Marilyn Monroe*. New York: Grand Central Publishing, 2009.

-----. *Sinatra: Behind the Legend*. New Jersey: Carol Publishing Group, 1997.

Tarrants, Thomas Albert, III, John Perkins, and David Wimbish. *He's My Brother*. Michigan: Chosen Books, 1995.

Tarrants, Thomas Albert, III. *The Conversion of a Klansman: The Story of a Former Ku Klux Klan Terrorist*. New York: Doubleday and Co., 1979.

Thomas, Evan. *Robert Kennedy: His Life*. New York: Simon & Schuster, 2007.

Turner, Dave. *Society of Former Special Agents of the FBI*. Kentucky: Turner Publishing Company, 1996.

Turner, William, and Jonn Christian. *The Assassination of Robert F. Kennedy: The Conspiracy and Coverup*. New York: Carroll & Graf Trade Paperback, 2006.

Van Meter, Jonathan. *The Last Good Time: Skinny D'Amato, the Notorious 500 Club & the Rise and Fall of Atlantic City*. New York: Crown Publishers, 2003.

Victor, Adam. *The Marilyn Encyclopedia*. New York: The Overlook Press, 1999.

Vitacco-Robles, Gary. *Cursum Perficio: Marilyn Monroe's Brentwood Hacienda*. Nebraska: iUniverse, 1999.

Wahl, Charles William. (1974). "Psychoanalysis of the Rich, the Famous and the Influential." *Contemporary Psychoanalysis*, 10: 71–76.

Wallis, Brian, and John Vachon. *Marilyn August 1953: The Lost LOOK Photos*. New York: Calla Editions, 2010.

Warner, Silas L. (1991). "Psychoanalytic Understanding and Treatment of the Very Rich." *Journal of the American Academy of Psychoanalysis*, 19: 578–594.

Weatherby, W.J. *Conversations with Marilyn*. New York: Mason/Charter, 1976.

Wecht, Cyril, M.D., J.D., Mark Curriden, and Angela Powell. *Tales from the Morgue*. New York: Prometheus Books, 2005.

Wertheimer, Molly Meijer, ed. *Inventing a Voice: The Rhetoric of American First Ladies of the Twentieth Century*. Maryland: Rowman & Littlefield Publishers, 2004.

Wexler, Milton. *A Look through the Rearview Mirror*. Illinois: Xlibris Corporation, 2002.

Wexler, Stuart, and Larry Hancock. *The Awful Grace of God: Religious Terrorism, White Supremacy, and the Unsolved Murder of Martin Luther King, Jr*. California: Publishers Group West, 2012.

Wiener, Leigh. *Marilyn: A Hollywood Farewell*. Los Angeles: Publishing Company, 1990.

Wilson, Earl. *Show Business Laid Bare*. New York: G.P. Putnam's Sons, 1974.

-----. *The Show Business Nobody Knows*. Chicago: Bantam, 1973.

Wolfe, Donald H. *The Black Dahlia Files: The Mob, the Mogul, and the Murder That Transfixed Los Angeles*. New York: HarperCollins, 2005.

-----. *The Last Days of Marilyn Monroe*. New York: William Morrow & Company, 1998.

Young-Bruehl, Elisabeth. *Anna Freud: A Biography*. New York: Summit Books, 1988.

Zolotow, Maurice. *Marilyn Monroe: Revised Edition*. New York: Perennial Library, 1990.

-----. *Marilyn Monroe: An Uncensored Biography*. New York: Bantam Books, 1961.

DOCUMENTARIES

"In Search of. . . " *The Death of Marilyn Monroe* History Channel documentary, 1980.

The Death of Marilyn Monroe documentary with Donald Wolfe, Michael Selsman, Joe Hyams, Lynn Franklin, and George Barris, n.d.

History's Mysteries: *The Death of Marilyn Monroe* documentary, A&E Television Networks, 2000.

JFK: A Presidency Revealed History Channel documentary, A&E Television Networks, 2003.

JFK's Women: The Scandals documentary, Quickfire Media, 2006. Director/Producer Harvey Lilley.

KNBC *Hard Copy* 4/20 Edition on Marilyn Monroe, 1992.

The Legend of Marilyn Monroe documentary, 1964. Producer David L. Wolper, narrated by director John Huston.

The Marilyn Files documentary, KVC Entertainment, 1991. Producer Melvin B. Bergman.

The Marilyn Files Live TV Special, 1992. Hosted by Bill Bixby.

Marilyn in Manhattan TV documentary, 1998. Narrated by Cynthia Adler.

Marilyn: The Last Word (A Reenactment of the Events Leading Up to Her Tragic Death) *Hard Copy* documentary, 1993.

Marilyn's Man documentary, Viking Films, 2005. Director Schani Krug.

Marilyn Monroe: The Final Days TV documentary, 2001.

The Reporters Special Edition—*Marilyn Monroe: A Case for Murder* TV documentary, 1988, starring attorney Raphael Abramowitz, Krista Bradford, and Steve Dunleavy.

RFK Must Die: The Assassination of Bobby Kennedy (An Investigative Documentary by Shane O'Sullivan). E2 Films, 2007.

Say Goodbye to the President BBC documentary with Anthony Summers, 1985.

The Second Gun documentary, 1973: Directed by Theodore "Ted" Charach, and co-produced by Theodore Charach and Gérard Alcan.

Something's Got to Give documentary, 1990. Henry Schipper of Fox-Entertainment News.

MAJOR NEWSPAPER ARTICLES

Adams, Tim. "Michael Munn: The Celebrity Biographer Reveals All." The *Guardian*. 25 July 2010.

Barnes, Bart. "Washington Insider Clark Clifford Dies: Reputation of Adviser to Presidents Suffered in Bank Scandal." *Washington Post*. 11 October 1998.

Barris, George, and Theo Wilson. "TWILIGHT OF A STAR: Above All Else, MM Wanted to Act." *Daily News*. 17 August 1962.

-----. "TWILIGHT OF A STAR: Here's MM, Barefoot and Bubbly." *Daily News*. 14 August 1962.

Blackburn, John, Chuck Orman, and Dan McDonald. "I Saw Marilyn Murdered." *Globe*. 23 November 1982, Volume 29, Number 47, pp. 1, 3-5, 7-8.

Buchwald, Art. "Let's Be Firm on Monroe Doctrine." *Washington Post*. 19 November 1960.

Carlson, Michael. "FBI Agent and CIA Fixer Who Became Howard Hughes's Bagman." The *Guardian*. 20 August 2008.

"Did the CIA Kill Bobby Kennedy?" The *Guardian*. 20 November 2006.

Davis, Lisa. "The Right Photographer." *Los Angeles Times*. 27 June 1993.

Galloway, Stephen. "Taping Marilyn Monroe." The *Hollywood Reporter*. 6 June 2013.

Goldberg, Jerry. "Robert F. Kennedy Is Dead." *Valley Times* [San Fernando Valley, CA]. 6 June 1968.

Harrod, Horatia. "50 Things You Didn't Know About Marilyn." *Daily Telegraph*. 31 July 2012.

"How Bobby Kennedy Silenced Marilyn Monroe." *Star*. (USA), 8 September 1998, Volume 25, Number 36, pp. 6-7, 38.

Jackson, Harold. "James Critchfield Obituary: A CIA Agent, He Worked with Hitler's Former Spies in a Disastrous Project to Undermine the Soviet Bloc." The *Guardian*. 25 April 2003.

Judis, John. "Political Affairs: A Biography of Robert F. Kennedy Focuses on His Love Life." *New York Times*. 3 January 1999.

Justice, Michelle, and Roman Hryniszak. *Runnin' Wild: All About Marilyn*. October 1994, Number 16.

-----. *Runnin' Wild: All About Marilyn*. July 1994, Number 15.

-----. *Runnin' Wild: All About Marilyn*. April 1994, Number 14.

-----. *Runnin' Wild: All About Marilyn*. January 1994, Number 13.

-----. *Runnin' Wild: All About Marilyn*. October 1993, Number 12.

-----. *Runnin' Wild: All About Marilyn*. July 1993, Number 11.

-----. *Runnin' Wild: All About Marilyn*. April 1993, Number 10.

-----. *Runnin' Wild: All About Marilyn*. January 1993, Number 9.

-----. *Runnin' Wild: All About Marilyn.* October 1992, Number 8.

-----. *Runnin' Wild: All About Marilyn.* July 1992, Number 7.

-----. *Runnin' Wild: All About Marilyn.* April 1991, Number 6.

-----. *Runnin' Wild: All About Marilyn.* January 1992, Number 5.

-----. *Runnin' Wild: All About Marilyn.* October 1991, Number 4.

-----. *Runnin' Wild: All About Marilyn.* July 1991, Number 3.

-----. *Runnin' Wild: All About Marilyn.* April 1991, Number 2.

-----. *Runnin' Wild: All About Marilyn.* January 1991, Number 1.

Leigh, Wendy. "Jane Russell: My Friend Marilyn Did Not Kill Herself" *Daily Mail.* 3 March 2007.

Luther, Claudia. "Actress [Jane Russell] Redefined Movie Mores: She Turned Sexy Image to Comic Effect." *Los Angeles Times.* 1 March 2011.

McLellan, Dennis. "John Miner, Investigator of Marilyn Monroe's Death, Dies at 92." *Los Angeles Times.* 4 March 2011.

Mitchell, Jerry. "Book Probes MLK Killing: Authors Suggest White Knights of Ku Klux Klan May Have Played Role in Civil-Rights Leader's 1968 Slaying." The *Clarion-Ledger.* 30 December 2007.

Nelson, Valerie J. "Psychiatrist Robert Litman Dies; Co-Founded Suicide Prevention Center." *Washington Post.* 14 March 2010.

Oliver, Myrna. "Fred Otash; Colorful Hollywood Private Eye and Author." *Los Angeles Times.* 8 October 1992.

O'Neill, Ann W. "Ex-Prosecutor Says Monroe Dumped Robert Kennedy." *Los Angeles Times.* 14 December 1997.

Pace, Eric. "Judith Exner Is Dead at 65; Claimed Affair with Kennedy." *New York Times.* 27 September 1999.

Pease, Lisa. "The Other Kennedy Conspiracy: The Assassination of Robert Kennedy Never Received the Scrutiny It Deserves." *Salon.* 21 November 2011.

"Psychiatrist Breaks Silence in Defense of Marilyn Monroe." *Yuma Daily Sun.* 23 October 1973.

Randerson, James. "New Evidence Challenges Official Picture of Kennedy Shooting." The *Guardian*. 22 February 2008.

Rosenthal, Harry F. "Testifies He Told RFK after the Shooting: You Can Make It!" The *Kokomo Tribune* [Kokomo, Indiana]. 16 February 1969, p. 20.

Schickel, Richard. "Jottings from an Earnest Soul." *Los Angeles Times*. 1 November 2010, pp. D1, D4.

Scott, Vernon. "Debunking MM Murder Rumors Latest Hollywood Industry." *European Stars and Stripes*. 7 October 1985.

Shearer, Lloyd. "Marilyn Monroe—Why Won't They Let Her Rest in Peace?" *Parade*. 5 August 1973.

Sherrill, Bob. "Busy Nights in Camelot." *Washington Post*. 11 October 1998.

"Sirhan Trial: State Will Call 7 Eyewitnesses." The *Press-Courier* [Oxnard, California]. 16 February 1969, p. 17.

Stewart, Marilyn. "Former KKK Terrorist Cites C.S. Lewis' Faithful Obedience. *Baptist Press*. 9 August 2006.

Thomas, Evan. "The Woman Who Knew Too Much. A VERY PRIVATE WOMAN: The Life and Unsolved Murder of Presidential Mistress Mary Meyer." *Washington Post*. 11 October 1998.

Trueheart, Charles. "Joan Braden's Book Proposal: Kiss & Sell? Memories of Rocky, RFK & Friends." *Washington Post*. 8 September 1987.

Turner, Christopher. "Marilyn Monroe on the Couch: To Dr. Ralph Greenson, Marilyn Monroe Was More Than Just a Patient. Now, for the First Time, His Family Recall Their Favourite 'Big Sister.'" *Telegraph*. 23 June 2010.

Welkos, Robert W. "New Chapter in the Mystery of Marilyn: Her Own Words?" *Los Angeles Times*. 5 August 2005.

Wilson, Earl. "Marilyn Monroe Will Divorce Arthur Miller." *Los Angeles Mirror*. 11 November 1960.

Yarrow, Andrew L. "Washington Book Proposal Withdrawn." *New York Times*. 10 September 1987.

Zolotow, Maurice. "Monroe's Last Days: Drowsy Death in a Barbiturate Darkness." *Chicago Tribune*. 14 September 1973.

-----. "MM's Psychiatrist a Troubled Man." *San Antonio Light*. 13 October 1973, p. 9-A.

MAJOR MAGAZINE ARTICLES

Allan, Rupert. "Marilyn Monroe. . . . . . A Serious Blonde Who Can Act." *Look.* 23 October 1951, pp. 40–44, 46.

Boyes, Malcolm. "The Passing of Peter Lawford Rekindles Memories of the Joys and Sadness of a Camelot Lost." *People.* 14 January 1985.

Bryan, C.D.B. "Say Goodbye to Camelot: Marilyn Monroe and the Kennedys." *Rolling Stone.* 5 December 1985, Number 462, pp. 36–37, 39, 41, 74–76, 80.

Carpozi, Jr. George. "Was Marilyn Murdered? Shocking New Facts Uncovered About Her Death." *Motion Picture.* November 1975.

Carroll, Donald. "Conversation with Dr. Thomas Noguchi." *Oui.* February 1976, pp. 66–68, 74, 118, 120–122.

DePaulo, Lisa. "The Strange, Still Mysterious Death of Marilyn Monroe." *Playboy.* December 2005, pp. 76, 78, 82, 192, 194–196.

Donaldson, Martha. "One Year Later: Marilyn Monroe's Killer Still at Large!" *Photoplay.* August 1963, pp. 52–53, 74–75.

Elliott, Osborn, ed. "Bobby's Last Longest Day." *Newsweek.* 17 June 1968, pp. 20–43.

Flynt, Larry. "Marilyn Was Murdered: Eyewitness Account by James E. Hall." *Hustler.* May 1986, pp. 36–38, 40, 48, 50, 82, 84, 86.

Gable, Kathleen. "Clark Gable as I Knew Him. . . . . ." *Look.* 29 August 1961, pp. 68–72, 75–76.

Hartford, Bob. "Marilyn Monroe's Bitter Battle Against Sex." *The National Police Gazette.* January 1960.

Hersh, Seymour. "Secrets and Lies." *Vanity Fair.* November 1997, pp. 96, 100, 107–108, 110, 112, 114–115, 119-122.

Miner, John. "Marilyn Uncensored." *Playboy.* December 2005, pp. 80–81, 197–200.

Miracle, Mona Rae. "Marilyn." *Sothebys Auction Catalogue for the Personal Property of Marilyn Monroe: The Berniece and Mona Miracle Collection.* February 8–March 1, 2001.

Moldea, Dan E. "Who Really Killed Bobby Kennedy?" *Regardie's.* June 1987.

Rebello, Stephen. "Somebody Killed Her." *Playboy.* December 2005, pp. 79, 186–188, 190.

Scaduto, Anthony. "Was Marilyn Monroe Murdered? Do the Kennedys Know?" *Oui.* October 1975, pp. 34–36, 42, 110, 112–114, 116, 118.

Scheer, Julian. "Carl Sandburg Talks About Marilyn Monroe." *Cavalier.* January 1963, pp. 12-15.

Schreiber, Flora Rheta. "Remembrance of Marilyn." *Good Housekeeping.* January 1963, pp. 30–32, 135.

Smith, Liz. "The Exner Files." *Vanity Fair.* January 1997, pp. 30, 32, 34, 37–40, 42–43.

Taylor, Gene. "Will Marilyn Monroe's Secret Love Letters Burn Bobby Kennedy?" *Confidential.* October 1967.

"Tribute to Marilyn from a Friend. . . . . Carl Sandburg." *Look.* 11 September 1962, pp. 90–94.

"Two Myths Converge: NM Discovers MM." *Time.* 16 July 1973, pp. 60–64, 69–70.

ENDNOTES

1   (SUMMERS 2000, p. 461: Natalie Trundy explained how Arthur Jacobs had to "fudge the press.")

(BROWN AND BARHAM 1993, pp. 352–353: Rupert Allan said, "It was carefully done and beautifully executed . . .")

(CARPOZI, GEORGE, JR., INTERVIEW WITH DEBORAH CHIEL. 6 NOVEMBER 1992: "Bobby then calls Peter Lawford . . .")

(HEYMANN 1989, pp. 366–367: Peter Lawford said, "Marilyn realized the affair [between her and Jack Kennedy] was over but couldn't accept it . . .")

(MAILER 1975, p. 364: Pat Newcomb giving Norman Mailer permission to borrow a Marilyn Monroe free-association tape, proving that Marilyn Monroe's free-association tapes did in fact exist.)

(LAWFORD, PETER. INTERVIEW WITH C. DAVID HEYMANN. 1983. Transcript located at the State University of New York at Stony Brook: "I suppose the most surprising revelation in Marilyn's own tapes . . .")

(HEYMANN 1998, p. 322: Peter Lawford said, "I also got hold of portions of the [Mafia-Teamster] tapes, and heard what seemed to be sounds of their lovemaking . . .")

(LAWFORD, PETER. INTERVIEW WITH C. DAVID HEYMANN. 1983: Transcript located at the State University of New York at Stony Brook: "Marilyn's house was being bugged by everyone—Jimmy Hoffa, the FBI, the Mafia, even Twentieth Century-Fox . . .")

(HEYMANN 1998, p. 315)

(LAWFORD, PETER. INTERVIEW WITH C. DAVID HEYMANN. 1983: Transcript located at the State University of New York at Stony Brook: "MM's affair with Greenson took on a far greater meaning at the time of her death . . .")

(HEYMANN 1998, p. 322)

(HEYMANN 1998, p. 540: Peter Lawford said, "I certainly think Marilyn would have held a press conference . . .")

(JACOBS 2004, pp. 169, 172–173: "When the cops said it was an overdose . . .")

(NEWCOMB, PATRICIA. INTERVIEW WITH DONALD SPOTO. 3 AUGUST 1992: "There's no way they could've done this. I resent it so much . . .")

(GATES 1993, p. 165: "Frankly, I never bought into the theory that she killed herself because he dumped her . . .")

(ROTHMILLER 1992, pp. 113–114: Former OCID (Organized Crime Intelligence Division) detective Mike Rothmiller said, "Airport detail. LAPD higher-ups wanted to know who was coming in and out of LA, and this little intelligence activity was part of OCID's routine . . .")

(SELSMAN, MICHAEL. INTERVIEW WITH JAY MARGOLIS. 1 JANUARY 2012: "After Marilyn died, I worked at Fox and Paramount . . .")

(SELSMAN, MICHAEL. INTERVIEW WITH JAY MARGOLIS. 1 JANUARY 2012: "I never saw her happy. I never saw her laugh . . .")

(SELSMAN, MICHAEL. INTERVIEW WITH JAY MARGOLIS. 28 MARCH 2011: Arthur Jacobs told Selsman that Bobby Kennedy was at Marilyn's home in the afternoon.)

(MARTIN, JEANNE. INTERVIEW WITH JAY MARGOLIS. 11 NOVEMBER 2010)

2   (LAWFORD, PETER. INTERVIEW WITH C. DAVID HEYMANN. 1983. Transcript located at the State University of New York at Stony Brook: "You could apparently hear [on Mafia-Teamster tapes] the voices of Marilyn and JFK as well as Marilyn and RFK, in addition to MM and Dr. Ralph Greenson . . .")

(HEYMANN 1998, p. 316)

(SUMMERS 2000, p. 317: "Lawford was 'desperately attempting' to obtain compromising sound tapes of 'parties' he had attended in Barr's dressing room.")

(OTASH, FRED. INTERVIEW WITH JAMES SPADA. 15 NOVEMBER 1988: "Something strange happened with Lawford one day . . .")

(STRAIT 1992, p. 155: Raymond Strait said, "I've listened to tapes in which Jayne and the President . . .")

(STRAIT, RAYMOND. INTERVIEW WITH JAY MARGOLIS. 28 JULY 2013: "Otash knew conversations between me and Jayne before . . .")

(NAAR, JOSEPH. INTERVIEW WITH JAY MARGOLIS. 2 SEPTEMBER 2010)

(BADMAN 2010, p. 296: Milt Ebbins on Lawford.)

3   (From the collection of YouTube member SGTG77: In a 1980s documentary, George Barris relayed, "I said, 'Marilyn, this is the last picture I'm going to take of you . . .'")

(From the collection of YouTube member SGTG77: In another 1980s documentary, George Barris remembered, "When I was in New York . . .")

(Harrod, Horatia. "50 Things You Didn't Know About Marilyn." *Daily Telegraph*. 31 July 2012: "On August 1, [three] days before her death, she was rehired by Fox on a $1 million, two-picture deal.")

(Barris, George, and Theo Wilson. "MARILYN SPEAKS: Star's Own Words in Last Weeks." *Daily News*. 14 August 1962: "A touch of Marilyn Monroe's whimsy is apparent in her last foto, taken by writer-photographer George Barris. After a long day's session [on July 13, 1962], Barris asked for one last picture. 'OK, George,' said Marilyn, pursing her lips as though for a kiss, 'and it's just for you.'")

(STEINEM 1986, p. 181: George Barris took the last photograph of Marilyn Monroe on July 13, 1962.)

(BARRIS 1995, pp. 122, 151)

(BARRIS, GEORGE. INTERVIEW WITH JAY MARGOLIS. 21 SEPTEMBER 2012: Barris said he regretted not going back to see Marilyn right away.)

(BARRIS, GEORGE. INTERVIEW WITH JAY MARGOLIS. 14 AUGUST 2012: Barris did not find out about Marilyn holding a press conference until after her death; therefore, he could not possibly have agreed to hold a press conference for her as alleged in a 2012 book.)

(BARRIS 1995, p. 133: George Barris said, "She never seemed happier . . .")

(Barris, George, and Theo Wilson. "TWILIGHT OF A STAR: Here's MM, Barefoot and Bubbly." *Daily News*. 14 August 1962: Marilyn said to Barris, "The happiest time of my life is now . . .")

(BARRIS 1995, p. 138)

(Barris, George, and Theo Wilson. "TWILIGHT OF A STAR: Above All Else, MM Wanted to Act." *Daily News*. 17 August 1962: Marilyn said to Barris, "I like to stay here (in California) but every once in awhile I get that feeling for New York . . .")

(BARRIS, GEORGE. INTERVIEW WITH JAY MARGOLIS. 7 JANUARY 2011: "Why would she take her own life? . . .")

(BARRIS 1995, p. ix: "I had always wanted to work on a book with Marilyn Monroe, from the first time I met her on a freelance photographic assignment back in September 1954. At that time she was in New York City on location for *The Seven Year Itch*.")

(BARRIS, STEPHANIE. INTERVIEW WITH JAY MARGOLIS. 20 NOVEMBER 2012: Margolis asked Mr. Barris's daughter Stephanie to quickly ask her father the title of his favorite Marilyn Monroe film. After speaking to him, Stephanie came back to the phone and stated, "His favorite one is *The Seven Year Itch*.")

(BARRIS 1995, p. ix: "What I particularly liked about Marilyn was that she didn't act like a movie star . . .")

(MORIARTY, EVELYN. INTERVIEW WITH RICHARD BUSKIN. 29 JULY 1993: "Buck Hall was the assistant director . . .")

(BARRIS, GEORGE. INTERVIEW WITH JAY MARGOLIS. 7 JANUARY 2011: "When I arrived, she said, 'What are you doing here?! I heard you were in Rome with Elizabeth Taylor! . . .'")

(BARRIS 1995, p. xv: "So, for the weeks from June 9 until July 18, I was busy working with Marilyn.")

(BARRIS 1995, p. 51: "I don't think anyone was ever more determined, and I never encountered a model who worked as hard as she did.")

(BARRIS 1995, p. xvi: "I will never believe that she took her own life. It will always be my conviction that she was murdered.")

(BARRIS, GEORGE. INTERVIEW WITH JAY MARGOLIS. 29 NOVEMBER 2010: "I'll never forget her because she was kind, and she was honest, and she was loveable...")

(BARRIS, GEORGE. INTERVIEW WITH JAY MARGOLIS. 7 JANUARY 2011: "When I was in the country, I was with my brother-in-law . . .")

(RUSSELL, JANE. INTERVIEW WITH JAY MARGOLIS. 29 NOVEMBER 2010: "I met him one time after his brother had been killed . . .")

(Leigh, Wendy. "Jane Russell: My Friend Marilyn Did Not Kill Herself." *Daily Mail*. 3 March 2007.)

(MORIARTY, EVELYN. INTERVIEW WITH RICHARD BUSKIN. 29 JULY 1993: "There's no way she killed herself . . .")

(ERENGIS, GEORGE. INTERVIEW WITH RICHARD BUSKIN. 8 JUNE 1995: "On the Monday following her death, I went into Marilyn's dressing room . . .")

("Debbie Reynolds: Marilyn Monroe Was at Risk." *Daily Express.* 12 April 2010: "I saw her two days before she died and warned her . . .")

(*Marilyn Monroe: A Case for Murder* documentary, 1988—Debbie Reynolds relayed, "Her life was very sad. And the ending was very sad indeed . . .")

(HALL, MONTE. INTERVIEW WITH JAY MARGOLIS. 24 JANUARY 2014: "I was at the wedding. Marilyn was married by a judge in a San Francisco courthouse . . .")

(Turner, Dave. *Society of Former Special Agents of the FBI.* Kentucky: Turner Publishing Company, 1996, p. 241: "Hall, Monte A. 1951–1976, membership number 002827")

(ENGELBERG 2004, p. 239: Morris Engelberg relayed, "Joe DiMaggio was in love with Marilyn Monroe until the moment he died . . .")

(ENGELBERG 2004, p. 282: "She didn't die of natural causes, and she wasn't going to kill herself . . .")

(RUSSELL, JANE. INTERVIEW WITH JAY MARGOLIS. 29 NOVEMBER 2010: "I think she was going to remarry Joe DiMaggio.")

(RUSSELL, JANE. INTERVIEW WITH JAY MARGOLIS. 1 DECEMBER 2010: Russell explained how she learned of the marriage plans from mutual friends shortly before Marilyn's death.)

(Miracle, Mona Rae. "Marilyn." *Sothebys Auction Catalogue for the Personal Property of Marilyn Monroe: The Berniece and Mona Miracle Collection.* February 8–March 1, 2001: Mona Rae said, "Berniece's heartbreak at handling Marilyn's funeral was ameliorated by the help Joe . . .")

4 (SUMMERS 2000, p. 408: On August 3, "During the day, Marilyn ordered food and liquor worth forty-nine dollars— a major purchase when translated into today's prices—from the Briggs Delicatessen.")

(CAPELL 1964, p. 13: "Don J. Briggs, Incorporated… Creditor's Claim No. P-458935" for August 3, 1962 in the amount of $49.07.)

(HEYMANN 1989, pp. 368–369: "In anticipation of [Bobby Kennedy and Peter Lawford's] visit Marilyn had set out a buffet of Mexican food—guacamole, stuffed mushrooms, spicy meatballs— which she had ordered from a nearby restaurant, and a chilled magnum of champagne.")

(HEYMANN 1998, pp. 321–322: Peter Lawford said, "They argued back and forth for maybe ten minutes.")

(HEYMANN 1989, pp. 368–369)

(SUMMERS 1994, p. 347)

(SUMMERS 2000, p. 470: "Marilyn, says [Lawford's third wife Deborah] Gould, had refused to accept messages from Kennedy passed on through Lawford, and Kennedy now decided to confront her for the last time.")

(SUMMERS 2000, p. 470: Debbie Gould said Bobby Kennedy "came straight to see Marilyn at her home. Marilyn knew then that it was over, that was it, final, and she was very distraught and depressed.")

(NEWCOMB, PATRICIA. INTERVIEW WITH DONALD SPOTO. 3 AUGUST 1992: "I was at her house that afternoon until three and that's when Greenson came and told me to leave…")

(Zolotow, Maurice. "MM's Psychiatrist a Troubled Man." *San Antonio Light.* [San Antonio, TX] 13 October 1973, p. 9-A: Ralph Greenson said, "It was clear she had taken some sleeping pills during the day.")

(MURRAY 1975, p. 124: Mrs. Murray said, "Pat was still asleep, and would sleep serenely until noon…")

(Zolotow, Maurice. "MM's Psychiatrist a Troubled Man." *San Antonio Light.* [San Antonio, TX] 13 October 1973, p. 9-A: Ralph Greenson said, "She resented the fact that Pat Newcomb had taken some pills . . .")

(CONFIDENTIAL SOURCE: Greenson wrote to Dr. Kris on August 20, 1962, "She was still angry with her girlfriend who had slept 15 hours that night and Marilyn was furious because she had such a poor sleep." The complete letter is located in Greenson Papers, Special Collections, UCLA, sealed from the public until January 1, 2039.)

(CONFIDENTIAL SOURCE: Greenson wrote to Dr. Kris on August 20, 1962, "I finally asked the girlfriend to leave because this was Marilyn's request, and I asked the housekeeper to stay overnight . . ." The complete letter is located in Greenson Papers, Special Collections, UCLA, sealed from the public until January 1, 2039.)

(SLATZER 1975, p. 225: Mrs. Murray said, "Dr. Greenson asked me if I had planned on staying that night. He asked this in a rather offhand way . . .")

(*Say Goodbye to the President* documentary, 1985: Mrs. Murray conceded to Anthony Summers the real reason Marilyn was upset that last afternoon: her row over Bobby Kennedy.)

(WOLFE 1998, p. 90: "When Summers asked Murray why she hadn't told the truth to the police in 1962 . . .")

(SPOTO 1993, p. 566: Pat Newcomb claimed Marilyn was angry at her for getting more sleep but conceded "something else was behind it all.")

5   (Carpozi, George, Jr. "Was Marilyn Murdered? Shocking New Facts Uncovered About Her Death." *Motion Picture.* November 1975: "RFK made that statement in a deposition to Captain Edward [Michael] Davis.")

(MARTIN 1995, p. 383: Bobby Kennedy's deposition admitting his own presence at Marilyn's home on the afternoon of August 4, 1962.)

(RIESE AND HITCHENS 1990, p. 248)

(ROTHMILLER, MIKE. INTERVIEW WITH JAY MARGOLIS. 26 SEPTEMBER 2010: Rothmiller saw a copy of Marilyn's diary, not the original.)

(BROWN AND BARHAM 1993, p. 433: In 1978, former OCID detective Mike Rothmiller saw the deposition made by RFK, stored in the OCID building's secret filing rooms.)

(CONFIDENTIAL SOURCE: GREENSON, JOAN. UNTITLED 90-PAGE MARILYN MONROE MANUSCRIPT, p. 46: "Marilyn found out that the neighbor who you could see from her property was a professor at the university." The complete work is located in Greenson Papers, Special Collections, UCLA, sealed from the public until January 1, 2039.)

(WOLFE 2005, pp. 288–289: "In the course of researching my Marilyn Monroe biography, I learned from Vince Carter and other confirming sources that [Archie] Case and [James] Ahern had accompanied Robert Kennedy to Marilyn Monroe's house on the night she died . . .")

(ABBOTT, ALLAN. INTERVIEW WITH JAY MARGOLIS. 22 JULY 2012: "Noguchi admitted there was a needle mark under one of her armpits . . .")

(SLATZER 1975, pp. 251–252: A confidential source relayed, "Bobby said in his deposition that he and Peter Lawford went to Marilyn's house . . .")

(BARRIS, GEORGE. INTERVIEW WITH JAY MARGOLIS. 7 JANUARY 2011: "Gloria Steinem and I were signing the book we did together in Brentwood in a big book store . . .")

(BROWN AND BARHAM 1993, p. 335: "The Attorney General and another well-dressed man [Archie Case or James Ahern] came to the house sometime late in the afternoon . . .")

(SUMMERS 2000, pp. 469–470: "I tracked that story to its source, a woman called Betty Pollard . . .")

(MURRAY 1975, p. 128: Mrs. Murray explains how a Marilyn Monroe author "related sensational rumors about Bobby Kennedy's arriving at the house that afternoon with a physician, reportedly to sedate an hysterical Marilyn.")

(MURRAY 1975, p. 128: She continues to say how the "story stems from reports of a card party on Fifth Helena that afternoon at which the ladies were supposed to have looked out the window and seen Kennedy walking through Marilyn's gate with a man carrying a doctor's black bag.")

(SUMMERS 2000, pp. 520–522: "The source says both Marilyn's and Kennedy's voices were easily recognizable . . ." On their trip to Marilyn's home on August 4, 1962, Peter Lawford and Bobby Kennedy were looking, not for a listening device as Summers's source hypothesizes, but for Marilyn's red diary.)

(GRANDISON, JR., AND MUQADDIN 2012, p. 66: Deputy Coroner's Aide Lionel Grandison noted how Marilyn wrote in her red diary, "Bobby came back with Peter . . .")

(*Marilyn: The Last Word* documentary, 1993: Anthony Summers said it's very possible Bobby Kennedy was looking for Marilyn's red diary, not a listening device.)

(GRANDISON, JR., AND MUQADDIN 2012, p. 66: Marilyn wrote in her diary, "Bobby was really mad. Acted crazy and searched all my stuff . . .")

6   (SUMMERS 2000, p. 410: "During the morning Norman Jefferies, working on the kitchen floor, found himself looking at a pair of bare female feet. He looked up to see Marilyn wrapped in a huge bath towel, and was appalled.")

(WOLFE 1998, p. 455: Mrs. Murray relayed, "Oh sure, yes, I was in the living room when he [Bobby Kennedy] arrived. She was not dressed.")

(WOLFE 1998, p. 456: Norman Jefferies said, "Mr. Lawford made it very clear that he wanted Eunice and I [sic] out of there . . .")

(SUMMERS 2000, pp. 340, 410: "Murray's son-in-law, Norman Jefferies, was employed by Marilyn in 1962 to help with the remodeling of her house. Murray proved oddly reluctant to assist me in reaching Jefferies . . . There was indeed secrecy about the Robert Kennedy visit that he witnessed . . . In fact, Jefferies was still outside the house when Robert Kennedy arrived alone, driving a convertible.")

(SUMMERS 1994, p. 299: Assistant Director Cartha DeLoach said, "[William] Simon reported that Bobby was borrowing his [white] Cadillac convertible for the purpose of going to see Marilyn Monroe.")

(KESSLER 2012, p. 41: "[FBI agent] William Simon . . . headed the Los Angeles field office, just after the August [4], 1962, death of Marilyn Monroe . . . According to [Cartha] DeLoach, who saw the teletype, it said that then Attorney General Robert Kennedy had borrowed Simon's personal car to see Monroe just before her death.")

(KESSLER 2012, p. 41: William Simon's son Greg said, "My father said Robert Kennedy would borrow his white Lincoln convertible. That's why we didn't have it on many weekends.")

(SUMMERS 2000, p. 519: One of Otash's employees relayed, "Marilyn had done a turnabout. Lawford said Marilyn had called the White House, trying to reach the President . . .")

(Miner, John. "Marilyn Uncensored." *Playboy*. December 2005, p. 200: "I want someone else to tell him it's over. I tried to get the President to do it...")

(GUILAROFF 1996, p. 166: Marilyn recollected for Guilaroff: Bobby Kennedy told Marilyn, "It's over." Marilyn replied, "But you promised to divorce Ethel and marry me.")

(SUMMERS 2000, p. 512: Otash said he heard Marilyn say to Bobby Kennedy on that last day, "I feel passed around—like a piece of meat. You've lied to me. Get out of here. I'm tired. Leave me alone.")

(SUMMERS 2000, p. 519: After Bobby Kennedy's visit in the afternoon on August 4, "Otash insists that from then on, rather than Marilyn reaching out to Kennedy that evening, *he* tried to get her to come to the Lawford beach house. Marilyn's response, Otash says, was 'Stop bothering me. Stay away from me.'")

(SELSMAN, MICHAEL. INTERVIEW WITH JAY MARGOLIS. 28 MARCH 2011: "She was convinced that not Jack but Bobby would leave Ethel and all their kids . . .")

(WOLFE 1998, pp. 456–457: Sydney Guilaroff relayed, "She said, 'Bobby Kennedy was here, and he threatened me, screamed at me, and pushed me around! . . . ' She told me she had an affair with Bobby as well as Jack, and everything had gone wrong. Now she was afraid and felt she was in terrible danger. Bobby felt she had become a problem and had said to her, 'If you threaten me, Marilyn, there's more than one way to keep you quiet.'")

(GUILAROFF 1996, pp. 165–167: "What's the matter, dear? . . .")

(GUILAROFF 1996, p. 170: "Then and now I believe that there was a conspiracy between the Kennedys and Dr. Greenson . . . As far as I am concerned, John and Robert Kennedy, aided by Dr. Greenson, murdered Marilyn Monroe just as surely as if they had shot her in the head.")

(SUMMERS 2000, p. 513: Otash relayed how Peter's friend "Bullets" Durgom told him, "Bobby was very worried about Monroe getting spaced out and shooting her mouth off. He told Peter, 'Get her to your place. She won't talk to me now, you get her to the beach.'")

(WOLFE 1998, p. 460: According to Guilaroff, after Greenson's visit, Marilyn was in a better frame of mind and called Guilaroff one last time in the evening.)

(SUMMERS 2000, pp. 415–416: "At about 9:30 P.M., Marilyn called Sydney Guilaroff, a prominent Hollywood hairdresser who knew her well . . .")

(WILSON 1973, pp. 320–321: Monroe–Guilaroff phone call on the night of August 4, 1962)

(ENGELBERG 2004, pp. 281–282: Joe DiMaggio relayed to Engelberg: "The Kennedys killed her . . . Something the world should know about is in there . . .")

(ENGELBERG 2004, p. 282: "After his father's funeral, I asked him about that envelope . . .")

7   (WOLFE 1998, p. 459: "At Murray's request, Norman Jefferies stayed on into the evening.")

(WOLFE 1998, p. 461: "Norman Jefferies recalled that between 9:30 and 10:00 p.m., Robert Kennedy, accompanied by two men [Case and Ahern], appeared at the door. They ordered Jefferies and Murray from the house.")

(*Say Goodbye to the President* documentary, 1985: Mrs. Murray stated, "It became so sticky that the protectors of Robert Kennedy, you know, had to step in there and protect *him*.")

(SUMMERS 2000, p. 518: Mrs. Murray said, "It became so sticky that the protectors of Robert Kennedy, you know, had to step in there and protect *him*. Doesn't that sound logical?")

(WOLFE 2005, pp. 288–289: "In the course of researching my Marilyn Monroe biography, I learned from Vince Carter and other confirming sources that Case and Ahern had accompanied Robert Kennedy to Marilyn Monroe's house on the night she died.")

(HODEL 2004, p. 376: Names of Gangster Squad members.)

(OTASH, FRED. INTERVIEW WITH JAMES SPADA. 15 NOVEMBER 1988: "I worked undercover in Hollywood. I worked Vice. I first met Peter Lawford when I was on the LAPD in 1949 . . .")

(GATES 1993, p. 170: "I think Bobby always had an affection for LAPD . . .")

(WOLFE 1998, p. 461: Norman Jefferies said, "They made it clear we were to be gone . . .")

(WOLFE 1998, p. 460: After interviewing Sgt. Jack Clemmons in 1993 and 1997, Wolfe learned that days after Marilyn died, Clemmons got the opportunity to interview Marilyn's next-door neighbor to the east, Mary W. Goodykoontz Barnes. Incorrectly identifying the neighbor as Elizabeth Pollard who was actually a guest at that bridge party, Wolfe relayed Mrs. Barnes' observations as relayed to Sgt. Clemmons regarding that same night, "Three men [Kennedy, Case, and Ahern] walked down Fifth Helena Drive. One was carrying a small black satchel similar to a medical bag.")

(*The Marilyn Files* documentary, 1991: Sgt. Jack Clemmons relayed, "The neighbor [at 12304 Fifth Helena Drive Mary W. Goodykoontz Barnes] said, 'I've seen Bobby Kennedy go into that house a dozen times. That definitely was him. I don't know who the other two men were.'")

(CONFIDENTIAL SOURCE. INTERVIEW WITH JAY MARGOLIS: "Two of my brothers were FBI agents . . . I had heard that my brother John Anderson had seen Robert Kennedy and two men enter Marilyn Monroe's home. Hours later it was reported that Marilyn Monroe had died.")

(Turner, Dave. *Society of Former Special Agents of the FBI*. Kentucky: Turner Publishing Company, 1996, p. 235: "Anderson, John K. 1952–1977, membership number 000121")

(SUMMERS 2000, p. 537: "Bolaños . . . said that—in a telephone call on the night she died—Marilyn told him 'something that will one day shock the whole world . . . '")

(SUMMERS 2000, p. 416: "José Bolaños says he telephoned Marilyn from the Ships Restaurant, not far from her home, between nine-thirty and ten o'clock . . . He does say Marilyn ended the conversation by simply laying down the phone—she did not hang up while he was on the line.")

(WOLFE 1998, p. 461: "There was a commotion at the door, and Marilyn went to see what it was." José Bolaños said Marilyn put the phone down and never came back on the line. Marilyn left the room and went into the guest cottage to investigate a noise.)

(BROWN AND BARHAM 1993, pp. 456–458: Via a transcript edited by Otash, Schwarz read the sanitized version of the tape versus Strait's firsthand listening of the actual tapes that indicated murder and multiple persons in the room.)

(STRAIT, RAYMOND. INTERVIEW WITH JAY MARGOLIS. 13 DECEMBER 2010: On how Noguchi never believed suicide but didn't rock the boat.)

(STRAIT, RAYMOND. INTERVIEW WITH JAY MARGOLIS. 18 NOVEMBER 2010: "I had all those tapes in my garage . . .")

(BROWN AND BARHAM 1993, p. 457: Raymond Strait said, "Fred was afraid of the tapes... It was obvious that she was subdued . . .")

(Galloway, Stephen. "Taping Marilyn Monroe." The *Hollywood Reporter*. 6 June 2013: Fred Otash wrote in his notes, "I listened to Marilyn Monroe die . . .")

(HASPIEL 1993, pp. 199–200: "Suddenly without thinking further, the politician [Robert Kennedy] grabbed for a pillow across the bed and placed it over her tear-stained face.")

(VICTOR 1999, p. 137: "It is Haspiel's opinion that Marilyn was murdered as part of a conspiracy reaching up to the highest echelons of government, an opinion based upon tapes reputedly recorded by wiretapper Bernie Spindel.")

(GRANDISON, JR., AND MUQADDIN 2012, p. 193: Bobby Kennedy had ordered LAPD Gangster Squad partners Case and Ahern to "Give her something to calm her down.")

(CONFIDENTIAL SOURCE. INTERVIEW WITH JAY MARGOLIS: "I don't know if she was injected merely to subdue her or . . .")

(GRANDISON, JR., AND MUQADDIN 2012, pp. 60–61: Lionel Grandison wrote, "Miner and Noguchi were looking at some bruises on her leg . . .")

N, JR., AND MUQADDIN 2012, pp. 61–62:
on wrote, "My first thought was needle mark, but
Noguchi didn't concur . . .")

IAL SOURCE. INTERVIEW WITH JAY
JOLIS: "My friend Marty George was a Los Angeles photographer. He had a job where once a year, he would go down to
the Coroner's Office . . .")

(HALL, JAMES. INTERVIEW WITH MICHELLE MORGAN.
OCTOBER 1997: "On the autopsy report, Noguchi wrote, 'No
needle mark . . .' ")

(ABRAMS, ARNOLD, M.D. INTERVIEW WITH DONALD
SPOTO. 2 NOVEMBER 1992: "The odds that she took pills and
died from them are astronomically unlikely . . . I have never seen
anything like this in an autopsy. There was something crazy going
on in this woman's colon . . .")

(Rebello, Stephen. "Somebody Killed Her." *Playboy*. December 2005,
p. 188: Concurring with Spoto's medical professional Dr. Arnold
Abrams, John Miner maintains Marilyn couldn't have given herself
the enema that killed her. Miner explained, "If she administered
it... she would have been unconscious with all this stuff running out
of her before enough of it was absorbed to kill her.")

(AMADOR, ELIAS, M.D. INTERVIEW WITH JAY MARGOLIS.
11 JANUARY 2011: Marilyn was given an enema containing a total of
thirteen to nineteen 100-mg Nembutals and seventeen 500-mg chloral
hydrates. Dr. Amador originally estimated between 15–20 Nembutals;
however, 13–19 was the amount of Nembutal left in Marilyn's bottle
at the time the enema was given to her. The autopsy report noted that
10 chloral hydrates were remaining from a bottle of 50.)

(SPOTO 1993, pp. 585, 587: ". . . an enema—something on
which Marilyn often relied for other purposes.")

(VITACCO-ROBLES 1999, p. 106: The guest cottage had a
bath directly adjacent to it so water was indeed easily accessible
for an enema.)

(ROBERTS, RALPH. INTERVIEW WITH DONALD SPOTO. 2 MARCH 1992: Roberts said he learned from Marilyn's secretary May Reis that Marilyn often took about 6 Nembutals in one day.)

(SUMMERS 2000, p. 433: Peter Lawford's third wife Deborah Gould explained how Lawford told her, "Marilyn took her last big enema.")

(ABBOTT, ALLAN. INTERVIEW WITH JAY MARGOLIS. 7 JUNE 2012: "The pathologist never signs the death certificate...")

(Carroll, Ronald H., and Alan B. Tomich. "The Death of Marilyn Monroe—Report to the District Attorney." December 1982, p. 3: Concentrations of chloral hydrate and pentobarbital found in Marilyn's body at the time of her death.)

(Plant, Tony. "How Marilyn Died," n.d.: "Marilyn was taking 500 mg capsules of CH [chloral hydrate]. A normal dose of CH is between 500—1000 mg. The lethal dose is considered to be 10 grams, which is 20 capsules. Marilyn had roughly 80% of the lethal dose of 20 capsule amount in her blood so she would have had to take 17 capsules.")

(LITMAN, ROBERT, M.D. INTERVIEW WITH DONALD SPOTO. 23 APRIL 1992: "High content in the liver just means she died slowly.")

(AMADOR, ELIAS, M.D. INTERVIEW WITH JAY MARGOLIS. 11 JANUARY 2011)

(SLATZER 1992, p. 137: John Miner said as for the 13 mg. percent of Nembutal in the liver, "It indicates that however the drugs were administered, hours and not minutes were involved before she died.")

(SPOTO 1993, pp. 581, 583–585: Dr. Abrams estimated that the 4.5 mg. percent of Nembutal in the blood is equivalent to 40–50 pills.)

(WOLFE 1998, p. 36: "Norman Jefferies verified the existence of the diary. He recalled that Marilyn kept her red diary either in her bedroom or locked in the file cabinet located in the guest cottage.

Jefferies said that on the night she died, [one of] her [two] filing cabinet[s] was broken into and many of the contents were removed.")

(SUMMERS 2000, p. 416: "At about ten o'clock, Ralph Roberts learned the next day, a woman with a 'slurred voice' called his answering service. Told Roberts was out, the caller hung up.")

(AMADOR, ELIAS, M.D. INTERVIEW WITH JAY MARGOLIS. 11 JANUARY 2011: "Chloral hydrate will put a person to sleep.")

(SUMMERS 2000, p. 469: "Two fragmentary reports, one from a police source, one from a former member of the Twentieth Century-Fox staff, Frank Neill, suggest Kennedy arrived in the city by helicopter, putting down near the studio's Stage 18, in an open space then used by helicopters serving the area near the Beverly Hilton.")

(BROWN AND BARHAM 1993, p. 328: "The chopper had been approved to land at just after 11:00 a.m., as duly noted in the studio's security log... Neill later noted that Kennedy was preoccupied, gazing from side to side before sliding into the backseat. Through the open door, Neill caught a glimpse of the carefully tanned face of Peter Lawford.")

(SLATZER 1975, p. 232: Mrs. Murray related, "I saw that the telephone was under her. She was lying on it.")

(WOLFE 1998, pp. 461–462: Norman Jefferies relayed when he and Mrs. Murray returned, they discovered Marilyn in the guest cottage. Jefferies also noted that the phone was under her. Norman Jefferies said, "I thought she was dead. She was facedown, her hand kind of holding the phone . . .")

(WOLFE 1998, pp. 461–462: Norman Jeffries said, "Eunice took the phone and called an ambulance. Then she put through an emergency call to Dr. Greenson, who was someplace nearby and said he would be right over . . .")

(SUMMERS 2000, p. 515: Mrs. Murray blurted out to Anthony Summers, "Why, at my age, do I still have to cover this thing up? . . .")

(*Say Goodbye to the President*, 1985: Mrs. Murray told Anthony Summers, "When he [Dr. Greenson] arrived, she was not dead because I was there then in the living room.")

(Bryan, C. D. B. "Say Goodbye to Camelot." *Rolling Stone.* 5 December 1985, p. 74: Anthony Summers asked, "Marilyn was not dead when the first doctor arrived, is that what you're saying?" Mrs. Murray replied, "That's what I'm saying.")

(WOLFE 1998, pp. 461–462: Norman Jefferies said, "I went to the gates to wait for the ambulance, but before the ambulance got there Peter Lawford and Pat Newcomb arrived . . .")

(SUMMERS 2000, p. 516: Detective Sgt. Byron said, "Engelberg told me he'd had a call from the housekeeper . . .")

(SUMMERS 2000, p. 425: Helen Parker recalled her husband telling her regarding Marilyn's death, "This thing has to be straightened out in more ways than one.")

(*The Marilyn Files* documentary, 1991: Jack Clemmons and Sam Yorty's comments about Police Chief William Parker.)

(WOLFE 1998, p. 49: Former mayor Sam Yorty said, "Hamilton's Intelligence Division was Parker's version of the FBI. Parker believed that he was the man who would one day succeed J. Edgar Hoover, and Bobby and Jack Kennedy led Parker to believe he was their choice.")

(SUMMERS 2000, p. 425: Helen Parker on her husband drawing a question mark in the air regarding the Marilyn Monroe case.)

(DOUGHERTY 2001, p. 179: Marilyn's first husband Jim wrote, "Did someone know she was in trouble? . . .")

(BROWN AND BARHAM 1993, p. 455: Ted Schwarz, author of *Candy Barr*, reported how Otash told him that he heard over surveillance that Bobby Kennedy and Peter Lawford knew Marilyn was in trouble but let her die instead. However, Raymond Strait made it clear to Margolis that Otash was also present in the home as Marilyn was dying before Dr. Greenson injected her in the heart.)

(Carroll, Donald. "Conversation with Dr. Thomas Noguchi." *Oui*. February 1976, p. 74: Dr. Thomas Noguchi said, "Our examination was coupled with what we call a psychological autopsy . . .")

(ABBOTT, ALLAN. INTERVIEW WITH JAY MARGOLIS. 22 JULY 2012: "They had this first-time autopsy called the 'psychological autopsy . . .' ")

(ABBOTT, ALLAN. INTERVIEW WITH JAY MARGOLIS. 19 AUGUST 2012: "Noguchi seemed to be very cooperative with everyone involved . . .")

(Carroll, Donald. "Conversation with Dr. Thomas Noguchi." *Oui*. February 1976: Dr. Thomas Noguchi relayed, "When the case was assigned to me—I was only a deputy coroner then.")

(NOGUCHI 1984, pp. 80–81: Noguchi believed an oral accidental overdose of that many pills was highly improbable. Noguchi also asked Suicide Team member Dr. Robert Litman if he thought the actress had been murdered.)

(SMITH 2005, p. 55: Official Statement by Dr. Theodore J. Curphey dated August 17, 1962.)

(SLATZER 1975, p. 268: Q & A with Dr. Curphey.)

(BROWN AND BARHAM 1993, pp. 368–369: "[Police Chief William] Parker . . . told his force to investigate it as a suicide, and gave the coroner similar guidelines... He turned the case over to the new Suicide Prevention Team, which . . . could only determine *why* Monroe had killed herself. The team was not allowed to investigate *how* she had died.")

(SPOTO 1993, p. 582: "Litman and his colleagues submitted a verdict of suicide because that had been Curphey's initial judgment.")

(LITMAN, ROBERT, M.D. INTERVIEW WITH DONALD SPOTO. 23 APRIL 1992: "How do you explain how these pills got into her? . . . The coroner says we got a case here, which looks like they took fifty Nembutals and chloral hydrates and died . . . We want you to evaluate the mental state of the person from the stand-point, were these ingested intentionally or not intentionally?")

("In Search of . . ." *The Death of Marilyn Monroe,* History Channel documentary, 1980: Dr. Robert Litman said, "At the autopsy, her stomach was empty . . .")

(AMADOR, ELIAS, M.D. INTERVIEW WITH JAY MARGOLIS. 11 JANUARY 2011: "I am surprised that there are no capsules in the stomach . . .")

(SUMMERS 2000, p. 338: Farberow admitted the Kennedys were not questioned.)

(SUMMERS 2000, p. 455: Farberow and Pat Newcomb)

(FARBEROW, NORMAN, PhD. INTERVIEW WITH JAY MARGOLIS. 17 JANUARY 2011)

(NOGUCHI 1984, pp. 80–81: "An accidental overdose of that magnitude was extremely unlikely . . .")

(NOGUCHI 1984, p. 68: "I found absolutely no visual evidence of pills in the stomach or the small intestine . . .")

8   (NOGUCHI 1984, p. 73: "The most prevalent of [the theories] called Monroe's death murder, done to silence her and prevent her from destroying Robert Kennedy's political career . . .")

(WOLFE 1998, p. 14: Undertaker Guy Hockett said rigor mortis places the death sometime before midnight between 9:30 and 11:30 p.m.)

(NOGUCHI 1984, p. 77: Hall had described the killer doctor as having had "a mustache, longish sideburns, and a pockmarked face. Not me.")

(SLATZER 1992, p. 259: "Dr. J. DeWitt Fox shares Jack Clemmons' view that Marilyn was killed by a combination of two different drugs, but believes they were administered in a different way.")

(SLATZER 1975, p. 315: Noguchi's autopsy report read: "The stomach is almost completely empty . . .")

(*Marilyn Monroe: A Case for Murder* documentary, 1988—Interview with medical expert Dr. Sidney Weinberg: "Let me tell you about the doubts that were raised in my mind . . .")

(SUMMERS 2000, pp. 541–542: Noguchi's consideration of murder: "She had a bruise, on her back or near the hip, that has never been fully explained . . .")

(EBBINS, MILTON. INTERVIEW WITH DONALD SPOTO. 6 AUGUST 1992: "When there's an overdose of drugs, the first thing the doctor would give her was a shot of adrenaline.")

(Carroll, Ronald H., and Alan B. Tomich. "The Death of Marilyn Monroe—Report to the District Attorney." December 1982, p. 13: "In the November 23, 1982 edition of the *Globe*, a weekly tabloid published in West Palm Beach, Florida, the headline article states that a former ambulance driver by the name of James Hall alleges that he saw Marilyn Monroe murdered.")

(Carroll, Ronald H., and Alan B. Tomich. "The Death of Marilyn Monroe—Report to the District Attorney." December 1982, p. 13: "Mr. Hall first contacted the Los Angeles District Attorney's Office on 8/11/82. Thereafter, under a code name 'Rick Stone,' he telephonically contacted this office several times.")

(Blackburn, John, Chuck Orman, and Dan McDonald. "I Saw Marilyn Murdered." *Globe*. 23 November 1982, Volume 29, Number 47, p. 4: Hall said he arrived at Marilyn Monroe's "between three and four in the morning.")

(CONFIDENTIAL SOURCE: In a recorded phone call sometime after August 11, 1982, Carroll told Hall, "One of the things I'm concerned about. You mentioned the man in the business suit used a needle in the heart . . .")

(WOLFE 1998, p. 77: "The time discrepancy is perhaps explained by Hall's disclosure that he worked a twenty-four-hour shift . . .")

(CARLSON, MIKE. INTERVIEW WITH JAY MARGOLIS. 19 DECEMBER 2011: "Jim was working nearly twenty-four hours a day . . .")

(SUMMERS 2000, pp. 514–515, 604: Including Joe Tarnowski and Tom Fears, "No less than seven former employees of Schaefer's, one now a company vice president [Carl Bellonzi] recall hearing about the call in 1962.")

(CONFIDENTIAL SOURCE: In a recorded call sometime after August 11, 1982, Hall told investigator Alan Tomich, "You go in and you turn to the left and the bed was facing longways as you're looking at it . . .")

(Blackburn, John, Chuck Orman, and Dan McDonald. "I Saw Marilyn Murdered." *Globe.* 23 November 1982, Volume 29, Number 47, p. 5: "Private investigator John Harrison, who had been conducting polygraph examinations for 40 years, reports: 'When I was first brought into this, I thought the whole thing was a fairy tale . . .'")

(Blackburn, John, Chuck Orman, and Dan McDonald. "I Saw Marilyn Murdered." *Globe.* 23 November 1982, Volume 29, Number 47, p. 5: "Hall was interviewed while under hypnosis by Henry Koder, a professional forensic hypnotist with more than 20 years of law-enforcement experience and veteran of hundreds of major crime investigations . . .")

(WOLFE 1998, pp. 80–81: In 1992, polygraph examiner Donald E. Fraser relayed to Wolfe that he tested Hall ten years after the release of the article from *Globe*, "There's no question that James Hall is telling the truth . . .")

(*The Marilyn Files* Live TV Special, 1992: Fraser gave Hall polygraphs on August 10, 1992.)

(SPADA 1991, p. 326: Danny Greenson said, "I hate all this speculation, and especially that guy who says he saw my father plunge a needle into Marilyn's heart. That's ridiculous . . .")

(GREENSON, HILDI. INTERVIEW WITH CATHY GRIFFIN. 4 JUNE 1991: "I sometimes have a feeling that this ambulance driver went on a call that night somewhere else . . .")

(HALL, JAMES. INTERVIEW WITH MICHELLE MORGAN. OCTOBER 1997: "I told everyone I knew and everyone who showed even a casual curiosity . . .")

(HALL, JAMES. INTERVIEW WITH MICHELLE MORGAN. SEPTEMBER 1997: "It was definitely Dr. Greenson at Marilyn's house.")

(Flynt, Larry. "Marilyn Was Murdered: Eyewitness Account by James E. Hall." *Hustler*, May 1986, p. 84: James Hall said, "I thought that a doctor had futilely given her adrenaline . . .")

(CARLSON, MIKE. INTERVIEW WITH JAY MARGOLIS. 3 FEBRUARY 2012: "Days or weeks right after it happened . . .")

(CARLSON, MIKE. INTERVIEW WITH JAY MARGOLIS. 19 DECEMBER 2011: "He had no reason to tell me a story...")

(CARLSON, MIKE. INTERVIEW WITH JAY MARGOLIS. 19 DECEMBER 2011: "That's what he told me . . .")

(WOLFE 1998, p. 80: "Interviews with Hall's father [George], his former wife [Kitty], his sister [Lynn], and his longtime friend Mike Carlson confirm that Hall told them his story shortly after Marilyn's death.")

(SUMMERS 2000, p. 514: "Hall's story receives some corroboration from his family. His father, Dr. George Hall, a retired police surgeon, says his son told him of the incident at the time. Hall's former wife and sister say the same.")

9   (*The Marilyn Files* documentary, 1991: James Hall said, "She was naked. She had no sheet, no blanket . . . There was no water glass. No alcohol.")

(*Marilyn Monroe: A Case for Murder* documentary, 1988: James Hall said, "We ascertained that her breathing was very shallow . . .")

(MURRAY 1975, pp. 125–126: "Sometime during the earlier part of the day, the bedside table [for the guest cottage] was delivered and Marilyn wrote a check for it.")

(Flynt, Larry. "Marilyn Was Murdered: Eyewitness Account by James E. Hall." *Hustler*, May 1986, p. 82: James Hall said, "I remember noticing she had a fairly fresh scar there.")

("Marilyn Monroe Rests Well After Gall Bladder Removal: 7 Doctors in Attendance at Surgery in New York; DiMaggio Standing By." *The Blade* [Toledo, Ohio] 30 June 1961: The removal of Marilyn's gall bladder occurred the previous day, June 29, 1961.)

(HALL, JAMES. INTERVIEW WITH MICHELLE MORGAN. SEPTEMBER 1997: "No one ever said that Marilyn was in the guest bedroom except myself until now . . .")

(WOLFE 1998, p. 81: "In 1993, Liebowitz was located in a Los Angeles suburb living under the name Murray Leib. He admitted, after thirty years of denial, that he had been with Hall on the call to Monroe's residence. Stating that Hall's account was accurate, he then confirmed that Marilyn Monroe had died in the guest cottage.")

(HALL, JAMES. INTERVIEW WITH MICHELLE MORGAN. OCTOBER 1997: "As some of my credentials, I would like to offer the following . . .")

(HALL, JAMES. INTERVIEW WITH MICHELLE MORGAN. AUGUST 1997: "I am a big fan of Marilyn. I have been a fan since I was a young man . . .")

(SPADA 1991, p. 325: "According to Hall, when he arrived with his partner, Marilyn was in the guest bedroom . . .")

(NEWCOMB, PATRICIA. INTERVIEW WITH DONALD SPOTO. 3 AUGUST 1992: "Whoever the writer was who said I leaned over the body screaming, 'She's dead! She's dead!' I never saw the body. So what is he talking about, this ambulance driver? . . .")

(SUMMERS 2000, p. 514: Hall "says Marilyn's assistant, Pat Newcomb, was distraught, and already there when he arrived, and that Marilyn was not yet dead.")

(GUILES 1969, p. 326: "Pat was awakened by a phone call at 4 a.m. It was lawyer Mickey Rudin. 'Something's happened to Marilyn,' he told her; then added, 'She's dead.' When she recovered from the initial shock, Pat got dressed and drove to the Brentwood house . . .")

(HALL, JAMES. INTERVIEW WITH MICHELLE MORGAN. AUGUST 1997: " 'Oh my God, it's Marilyn Monroe,' I said. She lay unconscious . . .")

(HALL, JAMES. INTERVIEW WITH JAMES SPADA. 3 JUNE 1990: "They [Lawford and Iannone] walked in at the time he [Ralph Greenson] was injecting her . . .")

(FRANKLIN 2002, p. 112: Referring to the year 1992, Franklin wrote, "James Hall . . . told me that Sgt. Iannone and Peter Lawford had been present in the home . . . when Dr. Greenson injected Marilyn with the fatal heart needle.")

(WOLFE 1998, p. 77: "Hall later identified the hysterical woman as Pat Newcomb, the man in the jumpsuit as Peter Lawford, the doctor as Ralph Greenson, and the police officer as Sergeant Marvin Iannone.")

(HALL, JAMES. INTERVIEW WITH MICHELLE MORGAN. AUGUST 1997: "At that time, two men who I assumed were Los Angeles Police officers came in . . .")

(Flynt, Larry. "Marilyn Was Murdered: Eyewitness Account by James E. Hall." *Hustler*, May 1986, p. 82: James Hall relayed, "He [Noguchi] said he looked over the whole body with a magnifying glass and didn't find any needle marks, including under the tongue . . .")

(SLATZER 1975, p. 312: In the original autopsy report, Noguchi noted only two bruises, "A slight ecchymotic area is noted in the left hip and left side of lower back.")

(BROWN AND BARHAM 1993, pp. 382–383: Noguchi mentioned for the first time there were bruises on Marilyn's arms, not included in the original autopsy report!)

(SLATZER 1992, p. 207: Hall took credit for bruises on Marilyn's arms that Noguchi a year later mentioned to Brown and Barham. Hall stated, "One was on her upper arm—that's my fingerprints. One was on her fanny—that's where we dropped her.")

(CONFIDENTIAL SOURCE: District attorney's report dated September 27, 1982. Investigator Al Tomich interviewed Marilyn's physician Dr. Hyman Engelberg who said he didn't see any needle marks from an injection to Marilyn's chest, "I would have noticed any gross things. I didn't notice any such thing.")

(WOLFE 1998, p. 75: "Her body exhibited signs of cyanosis—the classic indication of rapid death. In cyanosis the body takes on a bluish cast due to the rapid depletion of oxygen and reduced levels of hemoglobin . . .")

(From the collection of YouTube member TVOsnam: Leigh Wiener said in a 1987 documentary, "They'll look like a frozen cube of ice... I took a picture of her toe with a tag on it . . .")

(WIENER, DEVIK. INTERVIEW WITH JAY MARGOLIS. 7 JUNE 2012: "In 1982, a couple of deputy D.A.'s knocked on the door . . .")

(WOLFE 1998, p. 10: James Bacon said, "I stayed there long enough to get a good view of the body . . .")

(*Marilyn Monroe: A Case for Murder* documentary, 1988: John Miner's account: "Her body was examined minutely by both of us under magnification to see if we could find any needle mark . . .")

(SLATZER 1992, pp. 134–136: John Miner related, "We both examined the body very carefully with a magnifying glass for needle marks... The duodenum was felt all the way down to the ileum, which is at the end of the small intestine but there was nothing obstructive.")

(NOGUCHI 1984, p. 67: "I found no needle marks, and so indicated on the body diagram in the autopsy report . . . On Monroe's lower left back was an area of slight ecchymosis, a dark reddish-blue bruise that results from bleeding into the tissues through injury. And the color of the bruise indicated that it was fresh rather than old," which supported James Hall's account of dropping her.)

(NOGUCHI 1984, p. 221: In the John Belushi case, Noguchi wrote, "The very fact that the fresh punctures had been so difficult to discover worried me . . .")

(WOLFE 1998, p. 28)

(SLATZER 1992, p. 258: Dr. J. DeWitt Fox explains how blue postmortem lividity could have hidden a needle injection on Marilyn's chest. Sgt. Clemmons agreed with Fox and James Hall. Hall told Melvin B. Bergman for *The Marilyn Files* that since he and Liebowitz discovered Marilyn in the guest cottage, she later must have been moved from the guest cottage to the main bedroom where Sgt. Clemmons officially discovered her. Marilyn's body was then placed facedown on the bed to hide the needle mark in her heart from Greenson's injection of pentobarbital.)

(WOLFE 1998, p. 29: "The faint lividity noted on her posterior must have occurred immediately after death, when Monroe's body was on its back for a period of time before being placed facedown . . .")

(Carroll, Ronald H., and Alan B. Tomich. "The Death of Marilyn Monroe—Report to the District Attorney." December 1982, p. 15: "Lividity, as described to our investigators, is a process by which blood drains . . .")

(SLATZER 1975, p. 311: Under the heading EXTERNAL EXAMINATION, Noguchi noted in his autopsy report, "Lavidity [sic] of face and chest . . .")

(SLATZER 1992, p. 258: Sgt. Jack Clemmons said, "It was obvious to me, apparent to me . . .")

(BROWN AND BARHAM 1993, p. 373: John Miner's admission that since the kidneys appeared to be clean of the barbiturates then an injection would have bypassed the stomach.)

(Carroll, Ronald H., and Alan B. Tomich. "The Death of Marilyn Monroe—Report to the District Attorney." December 1982, pp. 13, 15–16: "According to Hall, the doctor ultimately plunged a giant syringe filled with a brownish fluid into her heart, after which she quickly died while on her back on the floor...")

(NOGUCHI 1984, p. 84: "My involvement in the Marilyn Monroe case had caused me to study the young Senator [Bobby Kennedy], and I admired him very much. To me, he and his late brother [John Kennedy] represented what I called the 'Great America.' I respected everything about them . . . [including] their instinctive reaching out to all ethnic groups . . .")

(Carroll, Donald. "Conversation with Dr. Thomas Noguchi." *Oui*. February 1976: Noguchi said, "I was very fond of [Bobby] Kennedy.")

(SUMMERS 2000, p. 542: Noguchi on not eliminating death by injection in Marilyn's case.)

(SLATZER 1992, p. 137: John Miner said as for the 13 mg. percent of Nembutal, "It indicates that however the drugs were adminis-tered, hours and not minutes were involved before she died.")

(LITMAN, ROBERT, M.D. INTERVIEW WITH DONALD SPOTO. 23 APRIL 1992: "High content in the liver just means she died slowly . . .")

(MINER, JOHN. INTERVIEW WITH DONALD SPOTO. 11 JUNE 1992: "Dr. Curphey in one of his more exuberant moments said, 'Oh, she gobbled 40 pills all at one time.' That's not possible . . .")

(AMADOR, ELIAS, M.D. INTERVIEW WITH JAY MARGOLIS. 11 JANUARY 2011: An undiluted injection will kill someone regardless of the substance in the syringe and the amount injected into the body, therefore, this action by Ralph Greenson was murder, not adrenaline.)

(BROWN AND BARHAM 1993, p. 340: Clemmons related that Greenson was "cocky, almost challenging me to accuse him of something.")

(LAWFORD, PETER. INTERVIEW WITH C. DAVID HEYMANN. 1983. Transcript located at the State University of New York at Stony Brook: " 'Marilyn has got to be silenced,' Bobby told Greenson or something to that effect. Greenson had thus been set up by Bobby to 'take care' of Marilyn.")

(HEYMANN 1998, p. 322)

(WOLFE 1998, p. 81: "In 1993, Liebowitz was located in a Los Angeles suburb living under the name Murray Leib. He admit-ted, after thirty years of denial, that he had been with Hall on the call to Monroe's residence. Stating that Hall's account was accurate, he then confirmed that Marilyn Monroe had died in the guest cottage.")

(Flynt, Larry. "Marilyn Was Murdered: Eyewitness Account by James E. Hall." *Hustler*, May 1986, p. 86: James Hall relayed regarding Ralph Greenson's shot to the heart, "I say, 'Yes, I saw her get that injection.' So did Pat Newcomb...")

(*Say Goodbye to the President* documentary, 1985: Dr. Ralph Greenson relayed to William Woodfield on a taped phone conversation: "I can't explain myself or defend myself without revealing things that I don't...")

(Blackburn, John, Chuck Orman, and Dan McDonald. "I Saw Marilyn Murdered." *Globe*. 23 November 1982, Volume 29, Number 47, p. 5: On Greenson, James Hall related, "Strange, but when he was trying to find her heart, he had to count down her ribs—like he was still in premed school and had really never done this before.")

(Blackburn, John, Chuck Orman, and Dan McDonald. "I Saw Marilyn Murdered." *Globe*. 23 November 1982, Volume 29, Number 47, pp. 5, 7: Dr. Sidney Weinberg stated, "Knowing the results of the toxicology examination and the negative findings in the stomach...")

(WOLFE 1998, p. 463: Wolfe incorrectly surmised, "In the presence of Bobby Kennedy, she was injected with enough barbiturate to kill fifteen people.")

(SLATZER 1992, pp. 257–258: John Miner said, "The amount of drugs found in Marilyn's body was so large that had it been administered by injection [containing high dosages of Nembutal and chloral hydrate], the star would have died almost immediately . . .")

(Blackburn, John, Chuck Orman, and Dan McDonald. "I Saw Marilyn Murdered." *Globe*. 23 November 1982, Volume 29, Number 47, pp. 4–5: James Hall said Greenson had "pulled out a syringe with a long heart needle . . . filled it with a brownish fluid and injected it into Miss Monroe's heart.")

10   (CONFIDENTIAL SOURCE. INTERVIEW WITH JAY MARGOLIS: Fred Otash's soundman arrived at Marilyn's house *before* she was murdered by Dr. Ralph Greenson in the guest cottage with the undiluted Nembutal injection to the heart.)

(STRAIT, RAYMOND. INTERVIEW WITH JAY MARGOLIS. 28 JULY 2013: "Otash knew conversations between me and Jayne . . .")

(STRAIT, RAYMOND. INTERVIEW WITH JAY MARGOLIS. 13 DECEMBER 2010: "I knew Peter [Lawford] was there . . .")

(STRAIT, RAYMOND. INTERVIEW WITH JAY MARGOLIS. 18 NOVEMBER 2010: "Peter was drunk and hysterical . . .")

(STRAIT, RAYMOND. INTERVIEW WITH JAY MARGOLIS. 18 NOVEMBER 2010: "Fred was there in the house as she was dying.")

(STRAIT, RAYMOND. INTERVIEW WITH JAY MARGOLIS. 13 DECEMBER 2010: "Peter got scared and hysterical so he called Fred.")

(STRAIT, RAYMOND. INTERVIEW WITH JAY MARGOLIS. 18 NOVEMBER 2010: "Fred says, 'You meet me at Marilyn's house.' And Fred showed up with his soundman . . .")

11   (HALL, JAMES. INTERVIEW WITH MICHELLE MORGAN. SEPTEMBER 1997: "In 1985, I was contacted by the Flynt Distributing Co . . .")

(Flynt, Larry. "Marilyn Was Murdered: Eyewitness Account by James E. Hall." *Hustler*, May 1986: Larry Flynt wrote: "It's been a long time, but Hall wasn't simply another set of hands at the wheel . . .")

(*The Marilyn Files* live TV special, 1992: James Hall said, "Back in 1962, I rented an apartment, my wife and I, and my regular partner Rick [Charles Greider] . . .")

12   (Carroll, Ronald H., and Alan B. Tomich. "The Death of Marilyn Monroe—Report to the District Attorney." December 1982, p. 16: "Since Mr. Hall's statements . . . a Mr. Ken Hunter, has been located who claims to have been an ambulance driver who responded to the Monroe residence in the early morning hours of August 5, 1962 . . . with his partner, whom he believes with reasonable certainty to have been a Mr. Murray Liebowitz . . .")

(SUMMERS 2000, pp. 462–463: "In 1985, I talked on several occasions to the late Walter Schaefer, who was then still running the ambulance company he founded . . .")

(CONFIDENTIAL SOURCE: December 14, 1982 tape-recording of investigator Al Tomich interviewing Ken Hunter.)

(*Marilyn Monroe: A Case for Murder* documentary, 1988: The narrator mentioned a "mysterious midnight traffic jam in front of Marilyn's house the night she died." Marilyn's next-door neighbor to the west Abe Charles Landau relayed, "We had been out to a party. We came home and the place was like Grand Central Station. The cars were all the way up the alley . . . Some limousine was here. I don't know who it was. And of course, police cars and the ambulance.")

(CONFIDENTIAL SOURCE: December 14, 1982, tape-recording of investigator Al Tomich interviewing Ken Hunter. Hunter stated, "I know that Hall wasn't there. Period . . .")

(BELLONZI, CARL. INTERVIEW WITH DONALD WOLFE. 11 SEPTEMBER 1993)

(WOLFE 1998, p. 79: "Ken Hunter didn't work for Schaefer in 1962. Carl Bellonzi, Vice President of the Schaefer Ambulance Service . . . stated in 1993 that Ken Hunter wasn't employed by Schaefer until the mid-1970s, and that Hunter never worked the West Los Angeles area [but] in the 1970s and 1980s in the Orange County office.")

(BELLONZI, CARL. INTERVIEW WITH JAY MARGOLIS. 20 JANUARY 2012: "Hunter wore glasses and he was kind of heavyset . . .")

(*The Marilyn Files* documentary, 1991: James E. Hall's social security number and employment records prove that he did indeed work for Schaefer Ambulance in August 1962.)

(WOLFE 1998, p. 80: "Hall's social security records and Schaefer's payroll deductions indicate that Schaefer wrongfully denied that Hall was his employee. Dated October 4, 1962, a photo in the *Santa Monica Evening Outlook* shows James Hall transporting a crime victim for Schaefer Ambulance Service.")

13   (ABBOTT, ALLAN. INTERVIEW WITH JAY MARGOLIS. 7 JUNE 2012: "I knew Schaefer. We both bought our cars from the same place . . .")

(VILLALOBOS, EDGARDO. INTERVIEW WITH JAY MARGOLIS. 30 JANUARY 2013: Schaefer was born Schaeffer before he changed his name. Also, Mae West was Schaefer's cousin.)

(VILLALOBOS, EDGARDO. INTERVIEW WITH JAY MARGOLIS. 20 JANUARY 2012: "Mr. Schaefer was involved with all these people, including celebrities…")

(BELLONZI, CARL. INTERVIEW WITH JAY MARGOLIS. 20 JANUARY 2012: "Villalobos was one I trained…")

(BELLONZI, CARL. INTERVIEW WITH JAY MARGOLIS. 20 JANUARY 2012: "I picked up Marie McDonald…")

(VILLALOBOS, EDGARDO. INTERVIEW WITH JAY MARGOLIS. 14 JANUARY 2013: "In Santa Monica, everybody used to get all the celebrities…")

("Barbara Hutton Breaks Thigh Bone." *Evening Independent.* [St. Petersburg, Florida] 12 June 1971: "LOS ANGELES— Woolworth heiress Barbara Hutton was taken in an ambulance to unknown hospital after arriving here from London for treatment of a fractured thigh bone. Miss Hutton, 58, was put into the ambulance on a stretcher yesterday but ambulance officials would not tell newsmen where she was being taken. The heiress was flown to London from Rome after she reportedly broke her femur—by tripping over a carpet in the Italian city.")

(LEIB, SYLVIA. INTERVIEW WITH JAY MARGOLIS. 25 APRIL 2012: "Murray knew an awful lot of movie people . . .")

(LEIB, SYLVIA. INTERVIEW WITH JAY MARGOLIS. 11 MARCH 2012: "It was not until a few years before he died that he told me about Marilyn . . .")

(LEIB, SYLVIA. INTERVIEW WITH JAY MARGOLIS. 25 APRIL 2012: "Murray said, 'Nobody murdered her. Nobody killed her. It was just an overdose. There was an empty bottle and the place reeked of alcohol . . .'")

(Flynt, Larry. "Marilyn Was Murdered: Eyewitness Account by James E. Hall." *Hustler*, May 1986, p. 38: James Hall said, "Dr. George E. Hall, was a Beverly Hills surgeon and former chief of staff of Los Angeles receiving hospitals . . .")

(CARLSON, MIKE. INTERVIEW WITH JAY MARGOLIS. 19 DECEMBER 2011: "When Jim was fourteen-years-old, he was swinging on rings doing doubles and triples . . .")

(Flynt, Larry. "Marilyn Was Murdered: Eyewitness Account by James E. Hall." *Hustler*, May 1986, p. 40: James Hall said, "In 1961 I started with Walt Schaefer's California Ambulance Service . . .")

(Flynt, Larry. "Marilyn Was Murdered: Eyewitness Account by James E. Hall." *Hustler*, May 1986, p. 48: James Hall said, "I picked up Betty Hutton . . .")

(Flynt, Larry. "Marilyn Was Murdered: Eyewitness Account by James E. Hall." *Hustler*, May 1986, p. 48: James Hall said, "We took her to Cedars of Lebanon Hospital, to the Pavilion . . .")

14 (CONWAY, D. INTERVIEW WITH JAY MARGOLIS. 17 APRIL 2013: "I was Larry [Telling]'s neighbor. He died two or three years ago. He was a very big man, real heavyset. His wife Debra went to a bingo game and never did come back. He thought she would come home that night. She left him and just kept on driving. The neighbors there said she did give him a call and said, 'I'm not coming back. I've had it with you.' He was kind of rough on her. Then her brother had come to serve him with divorce papers and found him laying dead in the bed. He died of a heart attack. It's very sad.

Larry died of a broken heart because she wouldn't come home. Sure as luck, she inherited everything and sold the property all off. She was a lucky, lucky person.")

(SUMMERS 2000, p. 604: "Seven employees: int. Joe Zilinkski [sic], Carl Bellonzi, Tom Fears, Sean [sic] O'Bligh, Joe Tarnowski, Edgardo Villalobos, Murray Leib, 1985–6.")

(ZIELINSKI, LESLIE. INTERVIEW WITH JAY MARGOLIS. 15 JANUARY 2013: "Joe was seventy-five when he passed away in December 2008… When I met my husband, Joe was working for one of the mortuaries there in Inglewood. Then he worked at Schaefer's and then Goodhue. We were married in 1961. I think he started Schaefer's in 1961 or 1962. By the time we married, he was no longer working at the mortuary. Joe was six feet and at the time relatively thin, dark hair in a crew cut. Joe used to watch any documentaries on Marilyn and there were things there that he knew were different than what they were portraying. As far as Marilyn, I know that he remembered that night very well.")

(VILLALOBOS, EDGARDO. INTERVIEW WITH JAY MARGOLIS. 14 JANUARY 2013: "I used to call Joe Zielinski every week . . .")

(VILLALOBOS, EDGARDO. INTERVIEW WITH JAY MARGOLIS. 5 OCTOBER 2013: Rick Staffer, Donald Altrock, and Richard "Dick" Williams remember the ambulance call to Marilyn's home.)

(TARNOWSKI, RUTH. INTERVIEW WITH JAY MARGOLIS. 4 OCTOBER 2013: Rick Staffer, Donald Altrock, and Richard "Dick" Williams remember the ambulance call to Marilyn's home.)

(VILLALOBOS, EDGARDO. INTERVIEW WITH JAY MARGOLIS. 14 JANUARY 2013: "Hugh Patrick O'Bligh was the Vice President of Schaefer . . .")

(VILLALOBOS, EDGARDO. INTERVIEW WITH JAY MARGOLIS. 23 FEBRUARY 2014: "Mr. Schaefer called him Irish . . .")

(VILLALOBOS, EDGARDO. INTERVIEW WITH JAY MARGOLIS. 14 JANUARY 2013: "Because Carl was like a son to Mr. Schaefer . . .")

(VILLALOBOS, EDGARDO. INTERVIEW WITH JAY MARGOLIS. 20 JANUARY 2012: "The other guy was Larry Telling, my partner . . .")

(VILLALOBOS, EDGARDO. INTERVIEW WITH JAY MARGOLIS. 27 APRIL 2012: "Murray was a very nice person . . .")

(VILLALOBOS, EDGARDO. INTERVIEW WITH JAY MARGOLIS. 20 JANUARY 2012: "The psychiatrist is not supposed to inject . . .")

(VILLALOBOS, EDGARDO. INTERVIEW WITH JAY MARGOLIS. 14 JANUARY 2013: "Many times, we witness [an adrenaline shot] when the doctor comes in . . .")

(VILLALOBOS, EDGARDO. INTERVIEW WITH JAY MARGOLIS. 20 JANUARY 2012: "One time [about a year after Marilyn's death], I was in an ambulance in one of the intensive care units and there was a strange nurse . . .")

(VILLALOBOS, EDGARDO. INTERVIEW WITH JAY MARGOLIS. 14 JANUARY 2013: "That girl was sizing me up a lot . . .")

(VILLALOBOS, EDGARDO. INTERVIEW WITH JAY MARGOLIS. 14 JANUARY 2013: "Look what happened to Murray's partner Ryan . . .")

(VILLALOBOS, EDGARDO. INTERVIEW WITH JAY MARGOLIS. 27 APRIL 2012)

(VILLALOBOS, EDGARDO. INTERVIEW WITH JAY MARGOLIS. 20 JANUARY 2012: "You have to listen to a doctor . . .")

(VILLALOBOS, EDGARDO. INTERVIEW WITH JAY MARGOLIS. 20 JANUARY 2012: "Joe Tarnowski was a driver but then he became a dispatcher . . .")

(VILLALOBOS, EDGARDO. INTERVIEW WITH JAY MARGOLIS. 7 MARCH 2012: "Joe Tarnowski was the dispatcher.")

(BELLONZI, CARL. INTERVIEW WITH JAY MARGOLIS. 20 JANUARY 2012: "I know who the dispatcher was at that time, and that was Tarnowski . . .")

(VILLALOBOS, EDGARDO. INTERVIEW WITH JAY MARGOLIS. 14 JANUARY 2013: "Ruth Tarnowski was a nurse for Schaefer in the Santa Monica area . . .")

(TARNOWSKI, RUTH. INTERVIEW WITH JAY MARGOLIS. 4 OCTOBER 2013: "At the time Marilyn died, Joe and I were married and living in West LA . . .")

(VILLALOBOS, EDGARDO. INTERVIEW WITH JAY MARGOLIS. 27 APRIL 2012: "I used to fight. Amateur boxing. There were five of us . . .")

15 (*Marilyn Monroe: A Case for Murder* documentary, 1988: Female reporter said Walt Schaefer "is now dead but in a 1985 interview, he said an ambulance did go to the scene that night but it was *not* driven by James Hall." Walt Schaefer relayed, "We took Marilyn Monroe in on an overdose . . .")

(SLATZER 1992, p. 185: Walt Schaefer relayed, "I came in the next morning and found on the log sheet we had transported Marilyn Monroe... Anything can happen in Hollywood." Schaefer "did admit that Hunter had worked for him. He also admitted that Liebowitz had been Hunter's partner.")

(LEIB, SYLVIA. INTERVIEW WITH JAY MARGOLIS. 3 FEBRUARY 2011: James Hall *was* Murray Liebowitz's partner and they both went to Marilyn's house that night.)

(From the collection of YouTube member SGTG77: 1992 *Hard Copy* documentary with Anthony Summers where John Sherlock said Greenson relayed to him that Marilyn had been taken to the hospital and then brought back to her home after she was dead.)

(SLATZER 1992, pp. 185, 187: Walt Schaefer first reported that Marilyn died at Santa Monica Hospital then later told Slatzer he lied due to political pressure from the Kennedys that could ruin his business.)

(LEIB, SYLVIA. INTERVIEW WITH JAY MARGOLIS. 25 APRIL 2012: "Murray didn't like the owner who owned the ambulance. Schaefer lied . . .")

(SUMMERS 2000, p. 463: In 1985, contradicting his second wife Sylvia's statement to Margolis, Murray Leib related to Summers, "I wasn't on duty that night . . .")

16   (VILLALOBOS, EDGARDO. INTERVIEW WITH JAY MARGOLIS. 7 MARCH 2012: "Murray bought himself a carwash on Pico Boulevard . . .")

(SLATZER 1992, p. 186: Hall said that Murray Liebowitz has "been interviewed by numerous people and he won't talk. On a radio talk show, an attendant that rode with Liebowitz later . . .")

(SLATZER 1992, p. 186: Murray Liebowitz said, "Well, you remember I told you I'd tell you what happened to Marilyn . . .")

(SLATZER 1992, p. 186: Murray Liebowitz said, "After her funeral, I came into a very large sum of what you would call hush money and I bought these car washes . . .")

(LEIB, SYLVIA. INTERVIEW WITH JAY MARGOLIS. 25 APRIL 2012: "When we were watching that television program, Murray was laughing . . .")

(LEIB, SYLVIA. INTERVIEW WITH JAY MARGOLIS. 11 MARCH 2012: "He did nothing but tell lies . . .")

(LEIB, SYLVIA. INTERVIEW WITH JAY MARGOLIS. 3 FEBRUARY 2011: "He died after about seven years . . .")

(LEIB, SYLVIA. INTERVIEW WITH JAY MARGOLIS. 11 MARCH 2012: "That's how I met Murray; he was a customer at my car wash for a lot of years . . .")

(LEIB, SYLVIA. INTERVIEW WITH JAY MARGOLIS. 25 APRIL 2012: "The carwash is still there and fully in business . . .")

(ANNA, an employee of the LA County Assessor—Property Ownership. INTERVIEW WITH JAY MARGOLIS. 31 OCTOBER 2013: Via a phone call, Anna told Margolis as for the car wash located at 11166 Venice Boulevard, Culver City, CA 90232, that there was one recording date in the files listed in the year 1967 under "HLW CORP." When queried regarding the other car wash on 3131 West Pico Boulevard, Los Angeles, CA 90019, Anna told Margolis there was one recording date on file listed as September 6, 1991, under the name "MAP BUSINESS GROUP, INC." The entity number is C1697224 and the current owner is Moon Chong Kang. Interestingly, September 6, 1991, was the date when Pico Car Wash was recorded. Curiously, a little more than six months later *The Marilyn Files* (1991) was released to VHS on March 11, 1992, and *The Marilyn Files* TV documentary aired on August 12, 1992.)

(WATKINS, JOHN. INTERVIEW WITH JAY MARGOLIS. 12 DECEMBER 2013: "HLW Corporation is not owned by Sylvia Siegel and HLW Corporation wasn't listed as the owner of the car wash . . .")

(Complaint No. R4-2002-0032, Administrative Civil Liability for Violation of California Water Code, in the matter of: Mr. Kazuho Nishida and HLW Corporation: "HLW Corporation has owned the property at 11166 Venice Boulevard, in Culver City . . .")

(LEIB, SYLVIA. INTERVIEW WITH JAY MARGOLIS. 25 APRIL 2012: "Harry was born in 1913 and died at fifty-one years old . . .")

(LEIB, SYLVIA. INTERVIEW WITH JAY MARGOLIS. 11 MARCH 2012: "Murray was in the service and was in two wars . . .")

(LEIB, SYLVIA. INTERVIEW WITH JAY MARGOLIS. 25 APRIL 2012: "I married Murray on October 5, 1968 . . .")

(VILLALOBOS, EDGARDO. INTERVIEW WITH JAY MARGOLIS. 14 JANUARY 2013: "Murray bought car washes, two of them that I know . . .")

(VILLALOBOS, EDGARDO. INTERVIEW WITH JAY MARGOLIS. 27 APRIL 2012: "Dick Williams was an ambulance driver . . .")

(VILLALOBOS, EDGARDO. INTERVIEW WITH JAY MARGOLIS. 14 JANUARY 2013: "The one in West LA they said was Murray's, too . . .")

(LEIB, SYLVIA. INTERVIEW WITH JAY MARGOLIS. 25 APRIL 2012: "All the people that worked on the ambulance with Murray came to the car wash . . .")

(LEIB, SYLVIA. INTERVIEW WITH JAY MARGOLIS. 25 APRIL 2012: "The only thing that upsets me about the whole thing is that the Kennedys would get away with this . . .")

17 (*Say Goodbye to the President* documentary, 1985: Former Mayor Sam Yorty recalled, "Chief Parker told me confidentially that Bobby Kennedy was supposed to be north of Los Angeles . . .")

(WOLFE 1998, pp. 51–52: "In the process of his investigation, however, [Chief of Detectives] Thad Brown discovered something startling—the Attorney General *had* been in Los Angeles on Saturday, August 4. Thad's brother, detective Finis Brown, related [to Anthony Summers], 'I talked to contacts who had seen Kennedy and Lawford at the Beverly Hilton Hotel the day she took the overdose.'")

(FRANKLIN 2002, pp. 108–113: Detective Franklin pulled over Peter Lawford, Bobby Kennedy, and Dr. Ralph Greenson all in the same car at 12:10 a.m. on August 5, 1962.)

(BROWN AND BARHAM 1993, pp. 445–448)

(*The Death of Marilyn Monroe* documentary, n.d. Beverly Hills police officer Lynn Franklin said, "Just as I approached Olympic Boulevard, a Lincoln Continental went through the intersection eastbound heading for Downtown Los Angeles at roughly 80 miles per hour. So I threw on the red light and went in pursuit. When I pulled the car over, the only one who I recognized immediately was Peter Lawford. And in the backseat, once I shined the light back there, I recognized Robert Kennedy, the Attorney General.")

(WOLFE 1998, p. 463: Wolfe incorrectly stated that the car Lawford was driving was a black Mercedes. As Detective Franklin has always stated, it was a Lincoln Continental.)

(HEYMANN, C. DAVID. INTERVIEW WITH JAY MARGOLIS. 13 JULY 2010: Heymann was surprised when told that Lawford, Kennedy, and Greenson were pulled over in the same car by Detective Lynn Franklin.)

(FRANKLIN 2002, p. 109: "The significant thing that might be related to the hit attack on me . . .")

(FRANKLIN 2002, p. 111: "I'm not trying to cover the case here, but for my money, she was murdered and Robert Kennedy at least knew about it, maybe ordered the killing . . .")

(ROTHMILLER, MIKE. INTERVIEW WITH JAY MARGOLIS. 26 SEPTEMBER 2010)

(NAAR, JOSEPH. INTERVIEW WITH JAMES SPADA. 31 AUGUST 1988: "Peter wouldn't dare go over there. He made sure it was me . . .")

(NAAR, JOSEPH. INTERVIEW WITH DONALD SPOTO. 22 JULY 1992)

(NAAR, JOSEPH. INTERVIEW WITH JAY MARGOLIS. 2 SEPTEMBER 2010: "He is so full of shit. That is the most insane thing I have ever heard. I've *never* heard that one. Bobby was in the back seat? Peter was driving? . . . If you're the highest decorated officer, you don't need that kind of publicity . . . People like Warren Beatty think I know exactly what happened. That I'm covering it up . . .")

(SLATZER 1975, pp. 238–239: Sgt. Jack Clemmons relayed, "I heard that Marilyn and Bobby Kennedy were having an affair. But a friend of mine, who had been in the movie industry . . . said it was going around that Bobby Kennedy had Marilyn done away with, and he said, 'I'll tell you one thing, everybody in the business believes it.' ")

(FRANKLIN 2002, p. 127: "At a Beverly Wilshire Hotel Chamber of Commerce Breakfast, Chief B.L. Cork presents Det. Lynn Franklin the CHA Award. The highest Honor ever bestowed upon a Beverly Hills Cop.")

(BROWN AND BARHAM 1993, p. 446: Detective Franklin related that Peter "appeared drunk, terrified, and coming apart at the seams.")

(SCHWARZ 2009, p. 624: Otash recalled that Peter "looked like hell, trembling in the manner of a junkie going through cold turkey withdrawal.")

(SPADA 1991, p. 328: Milt Ebbins said, "I spoke to Peter at his house at one-thirty that night . . .")

(EBBINS, MILTON. INTERVIEW WITH DONALD SPOTO. 6 AUGUST 1992: "Peter was getting drunker by the minute . . . He'd be coughing then be silent.")

18 (*Marilyn Monroe: A Case for Murder* documentary, 1988: Abe Landau's "Grand Central Station" account in which the narrator mentioned a "mysterious midnight traffic jam in front of Marilyn's house the night she died.")

(FRANKLIN 2002, pp. 111–112: Detective Lynn Franklin, through correspondence with Fred Otash and James Hall, placed Sgt. Marvin Iannone and Peter Lawford on the scene at 11:45 p.m. and Fred Otash agreed that at this time an ambulance was present.)

(BROWN AND BARHAM 1993, pp. 447–448: At 12:10 a.m. on August 5, 1962, Detective Lynn Franklin pulls over Peter Lawford for speeding with Kennedy and Greenson in tow.)

(*The Marilyn Files* documentary, 1991: As Greenson injected Marilyn in the heart, James Hall observed, "At about this time, two men came in. The one man [Sergeant Marvin Iannone] was wearing a Los Angeles police officer's uniform . . . The guy in the civilian clothes went up to Patricia Newcomb, put his arm around her and calmed her right down . . . Subsequently, I've identified him, too and that was Peter Lawford.")

(WOLFE 1998, p. 77: "The officer went into the main house before returning to sign Hall's EPA call slip. Hall later identified the hysterical woman as Pat Newcomb, the man in the jumpsuit as Peter Lawford, the doctor as Ralph Greenson, and the police officer as Sgt. Marvin Iannone.")

(WOLFE 1998, p. 64: "Before departing, Captain James Hamilton promoted Marvin Iannone to lieutenant and transferred him to the downtown office of the Intelligence Division.")

(WOLFE 1998, p. 61: "Iannone was known to work for Hamilton in Intelligence, and whenever the President or the Attorney General visited the Lawfords' . . .")

19   (BUCHTHAL AND COMMENT 2010, p. 213: While at Payne Whitney in New York, Marilyn wrote to Ralph Greenson on February 2, 1961, "Someone when I mentioned his name you used to frown with your moustache and look up at the ceiling . . . He has been (secretly) a very tender friend . . . It was sort of a fling on the wing . . . but he is very unselfish in bed. From Yves I have heard nothing . . .")

(GREENSON, HILDI. INTERVIEW WITH CATHY GRIFFIN. 4 JUNE 1991: "It's just ludicrous . . .")

(HEYMANN 1998, p. 322)

(LAWFORD, PETER. INTERVIEW WITH C. DAVID HEYMANN. 1983. Transcript located at the State University of New York at Stony Brook: "I suppose the most surprising revelation in Marilyn's own tapes was the fact that not only did Marilyn have an affair with both Kennedys, she was also sleeping with Dr. Greenson, who appeared to be deeply in love with her . . .")

(HEYMANN 1998, p. 322: Peter Lawford said, "I also got hold of portions of the [Mafia-Teamster] tapes, and heard what seemed to be sounds of their lovemaking . . .")

(CONFIDENTIAL SOURCE: Ralph Greenson relayed, "I always had a weak spot in my heart to rescue damsels in distress . . .")

(LEAMING 1998, p. 391: Greenson and "damsels in distress.")

(GILMORE 2007, p. 198: "Like a jealous lover, Greenson manipulated Marilyn's thinking and her choices . . .")

(GILMORE 2007, p. 198: Ralph Roberts relayed, "He was having her get rid of the people who loved her and were devoted to her . . .")

(CONFIDENTIAL SOURCE: GREENSON, JOAN. UNTITLED 90-PAGE MARILYN MONROE MANUSCRIPT, pp. 23–25, 29–30, 32: "Why was it that no matter what she did she was striking? . . ." The complete work is located in Greenson Papers, Special Collections, UCLA, sealed from the public until January 1, 2039.)

(STRAIT, RAYMOND. INTERVIEW WITH JAY MARGOLIS. 18 NOVEMBER 2010: "Women like that who are very lonesome and feel like they've been abandoned . . .")

(JAFFE 2004, p. 171: Greenson said to a candidate in training, "There is the problem of a change in motivation that happens when, for example, the patient develops an acute sexual transference . . .")

(FARBER AND GREEN 1993, p. 109: Accounts of Drs. Leo Rangell and Melvin Mandel.)

20 (LAWFORD, PETER. INTERVIEW WITH C. DAVID HEYMANN. 1983. Transcript located at the State University of New York at Stony Brook: "I suppose the most surprising revelation in Marilyn's own tapes was the fact that not only did Marilyn have an affair with both Kennedys, she was also sleeping with Dr. Greenson, who appeared to be deeply in love with her . . .")

(HEYMANN 1998, p. 322: Peter Lawford said, "I also got hold of portions of the [Mafia-Teamster] tapes, and heard what seemed to be sounds of their lovemaking . . .")

(SPOTO 1993, p. 658: "The only five-week summer vacation [Greenson] took from 1959 to his death in 1979 was in 1962. With no other woman patient was he so involved, and the language of this passage is virtually a copy of his descriptions of MM in his August 20 letter to Marianne Kris.")

(GREENSON 1964, pp. 202–203: "Sometimes all that is necessary is time . . ." The complete work is located in Greenson Papers, Special Collections, UCLA.)

(SUMMERS 2000, p. 254: "Dr. Greenson listened to Marilyn's 'venomous resentment' toward Arthur Miller. She claimed her husband was 'cold and unresponsive' to her problems, attracted to other women, and dominated by his mother. She accused Miller of neglecting his father and not being 'nice' to his children.")

(GREENSON 1964, pp. 203–206: "The above incident occurred during the fourth month of her analysis with me . . ." The complete work is located in Greenson Papers, Special Collections, UCLA.)

(SUGARMAN 2000, pp. 279–282: In a paper entitled, "Countertransference," Greenson wrote, "Countertransference . . . is an inappropriate reaction of the therapist to his patient . . .")

(GREENSON 1967, p. 171: "Transference is the experiencing of feelings, drives, attitudes, fantasies, and defenses toward a person in the present," often the analyst, "which do not befit that person but are a repetition of reactions originating in regard to significant persons of early childhood, unconsciously displaced onto figures in the present.")

(GREENSON 1967, p. 155: "All people have transference reactions; the analytic situation only facilitates their development and utilizes them for interpretation and reconstruction . . . The two outstanding characteristics are: it is a repetition and it is inappropriate.")

(GREENSON 1967, pp. 52, 172: "Most psychoanalysts, however, are of the opinion that narcissistically fixated patients [as Greenson termed Monroe] require deviations from the standard psychoanalytic procedure.")

(GREENSON 1967, pp. 173–174, 184: "People who are essentially narcissistic will not be able to maintain a consistently analyzable transference relationship. Their relationship to the therapist will abound with fusions of self and object images, primitive forerunners of identification.")

(GREENSON 1967, p. 343: "borderline cases" and "their propensity for intractable transference reactions.")

(CONFIDENTIAL SOURCE: Greenson wrote to Dr. Kris on August 20, 1962, "If I behaved in a way which hurt her she reacted as though it was the end of the world . . ." The complete letter is located in Greenson Papers, Special Collections, UCLA, sealed from the public until January 1, 2039.)

(GUILES 1969, p. 315: "Clearly Dr. Greenson was concerned by her reliance upon the judgment of her hirelings.")

(CONFIDENTIAL SOURCE: Greenson wrote to Dr. Kris on August 20, 1962, "I have some misgivings about how correct was I in my form of treatment . . ." The complete letter is located in Greenson Papers, Special Collections, UCLA, sealed from the public until January 1, 2039.)

(KIRSNER 2007, pp. 479, 483: "Unfortunately, [Greenson's patient Lita] Hazen was miserable much of the time and was scarcely a clear case of being helped by psychotherapy . . . But it was probably not a coincidence that he said he had enough of her when she stopped providing cash to Anna Freud and the Foundation.")

(LITMAN, ROBERT, M.D. INTERVIEW WITH DONALD SPOTO. 23 APRIL 1992: "There was a real washing out of the usual doctor boundaries . . .")

(KIRSNER 2009, p. 153: "Greenson told his colleagues that he decided to offer his family as a substitute for the family Monroe never had . . .")

(SUMMERS 2000, p. 400: At Marilyn's insistence, her poet friend Norman Rosten became acquainted with Greenson during the spring of 1962. Greenson later wrote to Rosten on August 15, 1962, "I should have played it safe and put her in a sanitarium . . .")

(Turner, Christopher. "Marilyn Monroe on the Couch: To Dr. Ralph Greenson, Marilyn Monroe Was More Than Just a Patient. Now, for the First Time, His Family Recall Their Favourite

'Big Sister.'" *Telegraph*. 23 June 2010: Danny Greenson said, "He felt that therapy as he knew it wasn't working . . .")

(EBBINS, MILTON. INTERVIEW WITH DONALD SPOTO. 6 AUGUST 1992: "He made a statement that Marilyn was doomed and eventually . . .")

(RUDIN, MILTON. INTERVIEW WITH DONALD SPOTO. 31 OCTOBER 1992: "I think it helped kill him . . . 'Don't get yourself all emotionally involved' . . . should have been a rule for a psychoanalyst . . .")

(RUDIN, MILTON. INTERVIEW WITH DONALD SPOTO. 31 OCTOBER 1992: "When he went to Europe, I was delighted . . .")

("Marilyn Monroe Rests Well After Gall Bladder Removal: 7 Doctors in Attendance at Surgery in New York; DiMaggio Standing By." *The Blade* [Toledo, Ohio] 30 June 1961: The removal of Marilyn's gallbladder occurred the previous day, June 29, 1961.)

(CONFIDENTIAL SOURCE: Referring to July 1961, Greenson wrote to Dr. Kris on August 20, 1962, "At that time she was recovering from gall bladder surgery . . ." The complete letter is located in Greenson Papers, Special Collections, UCLA, sealed from the public until January 1, 2039.)

(TARABORRELLI 1997, p. 272: Rudin related, "She could have a crisis over what she was having for lunch . . .")

(RUDIN, MILTON. INTERVIEW WITH DONALD SPOTO. 31 OCTOBER 1992: "I wasn't impatient with her . . .")

(JACOBS 2004, p. 1: George Jacobs said, "Mr. S's lawyer Mickey Rudin . . . was a combination bag man, hit man, and Hollywood hustler.")

(STRAIT, RAYMOND. INTERVIEW WITH JAY MARGOLIS. 13 DECEMBER 2010: "He was a scumbag and everybody knew it. He was Sinatra's man . . .")

(RUDIN, MILTON. INTERVIEW WITH DONALD SPOTO. 31 OCTOBER 1992: "His wife was Swiss . . .")

(ROMANOFF, GLORIA. INTERVIEW WITH JAY MARGOLIS. 2 SEPTEMBER 2010: "She never had any real money. The house she died in was the first home she ever owned and it meant everything to her . . .")

21   (GREENSON, HILDI. INTERVIEW WITH CATHY GRIFFIN. 4 JUNE 1991: "She would have no plans whatsoever for an evening . . . I think at one point she asked the taxi driver to come in and have dinner with her . . .")

(SUMMERS 2000, p. 328: "As for his patient's attitude toward men, Dr. Greenson was to note Marilyn's increasing trend toward random promiscuity. In her last months she was to tell him she was having sex with one of the workmen remodeling her house. Once she invited in a taxi driver who brought her home.")

(FARBER AND GREEN 1993, pp. 95–98: Hildi said her husband found out about Marilyn's random promiscuity and "realized this wasn't healthy . . ." so he often allowed Marilyn to stay for supper like a family member and often attended Greenson's chamber music recitals. Also, Greenson discussed Marilyn with another actress, Celeste Holm.)

22   (FARBER AND GREEN 1993, p. 97: With dark glasses and a black wig, Marilyn joined Danny while he looked for an apartment. She would often use this disguise to attend many of Greenson's lectures.)

(CONFIDENTIAL SOURCE: GREENSON, JOAN. UNTITLED 90-PAGE MARILYN MONROE MANUSCRIPT, pp. 55–56: "Father liked to give lectures, and he was an excellent public speaker . . ." The complete work is located in Greenson Papers, Special Collections, UCLA, sealed from the public until January 1, 2039.)

(GREENSON, HILDI. INTERVIEW WITH CATHY GRIFFIN. 4 JUNE 1991: "When we'd have chamber music, my husband would invite her to come and listen . . .")

(FARBER AND GREEN 1993, p. 98: Janice Rule asked Greenson, "You knew I love music. How come you never invited me? . . .")

(CONFIDENTIAL SOURCE: GREENSON, JOAN. UNTITLED 90-PAGE MARILYN MONROE MANUSCRIPT, pp. 59–60: "She would sit in the living room in the big wing-backed chair . . ." The complete work is located in Greenson Papers, Special Collections, UCLA, sealed from the public until January 1, 2039.)

(ROSTEN 1973, pp. 99–100: "Finally, after coffee and cake and idle Sunday chatter, the other musicians showed up . . .")

(FREEMAN 1993, p. 27: A friend of Greenson's, Paul Moor, said, "Romi may have been the world's worst violinist . . .")

(GREENSON 1964, pp. 203–206: "When I left for a five week summer vacation . . ." The complete work is located in Greenson Papers, Special Collections, UCLA.)

23 (WEXLER 2002, pp. 241–242: "Greenson began to write more and more about the importance of the real relationship . . .")

(LAWFORD, PETER. INTERVIEW WITH C. DAVID HEYMANN. 1983. Transcript located at the State University of New York at Stony Brook: "I suppose the most surprising revelation in Marilyn's own tapes was the fact that not only did Marilyn have an affair with both Kennedys, she was also sleeping with Dr. Greenson, who appeared to be deeply in love with her . . .")

(HEYMANN 1998, p. 322: Peter Lawford said, "I also got hold of portions of the [Mafia-Teamster] tapes, and heard what seemed to be sounds of their lovemaking . . .")

(SUGARMAN 2000, p. 282: Greenson wrote, "One of the most frequent signals of countertransference reaction is . . . reacting sexually . . . to the transference manifestations . . .")

24 (GREENSON 1978, pp. 493–494: In a 1974 paper entitled, "On Transitional Objects and Transference," Ralph Greenson wrote, "I told an emotionally immature young woman patient, who had developed a very dependent transference to me, that I was going to attend an International Congress in Europe some three months hence . . .")

(GREENSON 1978, p. 494: In a 1974 paper entitled, "On Transitional Objects and Transference," Ralph Greenson wrote, "The situation changed dramatically when one day she announced… she had discovered something that would tide her over my absence . . .")

(GREENSON 1978, p. 494: "The evening before her announcement, as she looked at the set, through the sparkling light of a glass of champagne, it suddenly struck her that I looked like the white knight . . .")

(GREENSON 1978, p. 494: "The patient's major concern about . . . my absence was a public performance of great importance to her professionally . . .")

(CONFIDENTIAL SOURCE: GREENSON, JOAN. UNTITLED 90-PAGE MARILYN MONROE MANUSCRIPT, p. 52: "Father was to give a lecture in Israel . . ." The complete work is located in Greenson Papers, Special Collections, UCLA, sealed from the public until January 1, 2039.)

(GREENSON 1978, p. 494: In a 1974 paper entitled, "On Transitional Objects and Transference," Ralph Greenson wrote, "I was relieved and delighted to learn… that her performance . . .")

(MURRAY 1975, p. 103: Marilyn's housekeeper Mrs. Eunice Murray related, "Marilyn took a handsome chess piece from the set she had bought in Mexico—one knight to wrap in her handkerchief while she sang . . .")

(GREENSON, HILDI. INTERVIEW WITH CATHY GRIFFIN. 4 JUNE 1991: "That vacation we had, it was constant telephone calls . . .")

(HEYMANN 1998, p. 319)

(CONFIDENTIAL SOURCE: Greenson wrote to Dr. Kris on August 20, 1962, "I left Marilyn in the hands of a colleague whom she knew . . ." The complete letter is located in Greenson

Papers, Special Collections, UCLA, sealed from th
January 1, 2039.)

(CONFIDENTIAL SOURCE: GREENSON, JOAN. UN
90-PAGE MARILYN MONROE MANUSCRIPT, pp.
"Danny and I did get a call after her birthday. She had sounded
druggy. Her thick-tongued-ness . . ." The complete work is located in
Greenson Papers, Special Collections, UCLA, sealed from the public
until January 1, 2039.)

(FARBER AND GREEN 1993, p. 99: Hildi Greenson relayed,
"She was bright and lovely and interesting . . .")

(MURRAY 1975, p. 107: "Marilyn didn't want to interrupt the
psychiatrist's trip with her problems . . .")

(MURRAY 1975, p. 107: "A Dr. Wexler was on call for
Dr. Greenson's patients . . .")

(CONFIDENTIAL SOURCE: GREENSON, JOAN. UNTITLED
90-PAGE MARILYN MONROE MANUSCRIPT, pp. 74–75: "It
was clear that there was really no way Marilyn was going to make
it through that picture without my father here . . ." The complete
work is located in Greenson Papers, Special Collections, UCLA,
sealed from the public until January 1, 2039.)

(GREENSON 1978, p. 494: In a 1974 paper entitled, "On
Transitional Objects and Transference," Ralph Greenson wrote, "A
colleague of mine [Milton Wexler] who saw her [Marilyn Monroe]
in that interval said that all his interventions . . .")

(GREENSON 1978, p. 494: In a 1974 paper entitled, "On
Transitional Objects and Transference," Ralph Greenson wrote,
"Her anxiety and depression lifted . . .")

25 (SPOTO 1993, pp. 528–529: Greenson's angry letter postmarked
June 22, 1962, to friend Lucille Ostrow.)

(FARBER AND GREEN 1993, pp. 98, 106: "Janice Rule, who
was in analysis with Greenson at the time Marilyn died, remembers
how 'crucified' he felt by the press.")

(MEYERS 2010, p. 269: On June 22, 1962, Greenson wrote a letter to Anna Freud about Marilyn, a letter located in the Library of Congress. Greenson wrote, "This was a most frustrating experience, since now I was back home and she was feeling fine . . .")

(MEYERS 2010, p. 269: On July 2, 1962, Anna Freud wrote back to Greenson about Marilyn, a letter located in the Library of Congress. Anna Freud wrote, "I have tried to follow your fate in the newspapers . . .")

(BERTHELSEN 1987, pp. 152–153: Freud family maid Paula Fichtl relayed how Anna Freud told her she heard Ralph Greenson was the final person to phone Marilyn.)

(SPOTO 1993, p. 375: Marilyn's psychiatrist "Hohenberg had a suggestion for Marilyn, and forthwith whisked her off to meet her old friend Anna Freud, an analyst with a thriving London practice. Marilyn had several therapy sessions with Sigmund Freud's daughter.")

(GREENSON, HILDI. INTERVIEW WITH CATHY GRIFFIN. 4 JUNE 1991: "That felt very good, winning my suit . . .")

(SPOTO 1993, pp. 599–611: Capell, Mailer, Slatzer "started" the murder rumors.)

(*Oakland Tribune.* [Oakland, CA] 5 January 1964: "Following her death, Dr. Greenson was flooded with mail from haters . . .")

(CONFIDENTIAL SOURCE: Greenson wrote to Dr. Kris on August 20, 1962, "And on top of it all, the notoriety, the press all over the world writing about it and constantly linking my name . . ." The complete letter is located in Greenson Papers, Special Collections, UCLA, sealed from the public until January 1, 2039.)

26 (Shearer, Lloyd. "Marilyn Monroe—Why Won't They Let Her Rest in Peace?" *Parade.* 5 August 1973: Greenson and his alleged dinner engagement until around midnight. Greenson claimed that Mrs. Murray called him three hours later: "At 3 a.m. his phone rang . . .")

(CONFIDENTIAL SOURCE: On August 4, 1962, Greenson attended a dinner party at the home of actor Eddie Albert and his wife Margo.)

(*Say Goodbye to the President* documentary, 1985: Mrs. Murray said Marilyn was discovered "around midnight." Sgt. Clemmons agreed Mrs. Murray said midnight and Clemmons also stated that Greenson and Engelberg did not disagree with Mrs. Murray.)

(CONFIDENTIAL SOURCE: District attorney's report dated September 27, 1982. Investigator Al Tomich interviewed Marilyn's physician, Dr. Hyman Engelberg, regarding rumors that he arrived at midnight. Engelberg responded, "Nonsense. Absolute, utter nonsense.")

(SLATZER 1975, pp. 172–173: Picture 60 is a photograph of a man pointing at the broken window Greenson claimed he shattered to enter Marilyn's bedroom. One wonders how Greenson stuck his full hand into the window without cutting himself.)

(SMITH 2005, pp. 30–33: Police report #62-509 463 and follow-up police report show serious time discrepancies.)

(CONFIDENTIAL SOURCE: District attorney's report dated September 27, 1982. Investigator Al Tomich interviewed Marilyn's physician, Dr. Hyman Engelberg, who relayed, "The door was locked to the bedroom . . .")

(CONFIDENTIAL SOURCE: District attorney's report dated September 27, 1982. Investigator Al Tomich interviewed Marilyn's physician, Dr. Hyman Engelberg, who relayed, "I was parked in the basement of the parking area of a small apartment house and somebody parked in back of me . . .")

27 (SUMMERS 2000, pp. 416–417: "At about 3:30 a.m., at the Greenson home in Santa Monica, the psychiatrist's daughter, Joan, heard the telephone ring in her parents' bedroom . . .")

(CONFIDENTIAL SOURCE: GREENSON, JOAN. UNTITLED 90-PAGE MARILYN MONROE MANUSCRIPT, p. 82: "I went to bed around 8:00 . . ." The complete work is located in Greenson Papers, Special Collections, UCLA, sealed from the public until January 1, 2039.)

(GREENSON, HILDI. INTERVIEW WITH CATHY GRIFFIN. 4 JUNE 1991: "I was very worried, and my daughter was here and we immediately stayed up. We just went downstairs and sat around . . .")

(CONFIDENTIAL SOURCE: GREENSON, JOAN. UNTITLED 90-PAGE MARILYN MONROE MANUSCRIPT, p. 83: "I must have been in my bed for maybe five minutes when I heard the phone ring . . ." The complete work is located in Greenson Papers, Special Collections, UCLA, sealed from the public until January 1, 2039.)

28 (GREENSON, HILDI. INTERVIEW WITH CATHY GRIFFIN. 4 JUNE 1991: "Her room was locked and with a bolt lock . . .")

(GREENSON, HILDI. INTERVIEW WITH CATHY GRIFFIN. 4 JUNE 1991: "I don't think so, but it was locked that night.")

(SPOTO 1993, p. 486: Cherie Redmond wrote to Hedda Rosten, "There isn't one door in the place that locks.")

(MARSHALL 2005, p. 282: "Linda Nuñez . . . explained . . . that no one in her family ever had a key to any of the locks on any of the interior doors . . .")

(BROWN AND BARHAM 1993, p. 441: "We found out . . . that Monroe's housekeeper, Eunice Murray, had a skeleton key to Monroe's bedroom. It was attached to her own key ring. Greenson had insisted on it because Murray was often on suicide watch. Thus, there should have been no need to break in the movie star's bedroom window.")

(SPOTO 1993, pp. 575–576: "Between March 15 and June 30, according to their invoice # 7451, the A-1 Lock & Safe Company of 3114 Wilshire Boulevard, Santa Monica, installed only two locks in the house: a cabinet lock for Cherie Redmond's files, and a replacement lock for the front door of the house . . .")

(TURNER, ROY. INTERVIEW WITH JAY MARGOLIS. 19 JUNE 2012: "I never felt Marilyn killed herself . . .")

(SUMMERS 2000, p. 515: "In 1982, in a conversation with researcher Justin Clayton, she [Mrs. Murray] said she had 'found Marilyn's door ajar' at about midnight. As Clayton vividly recalls, Mrs. Murray then stopped dead, suddenly raising her hand to her mouth, and said, 'I mean, I found the door locked.' ")

(TARABORRELLI 2009, p. 474: "More intriguingly, Eunice would later say that there was no lock on Marilyn's door. If that's the case, then the entire story of how she was found seems to fall apart.")

(SLATZER 1975, pp. 289–290: see for the A-1 Lock & Safe Company Creditor's Claim and Invoices)

29 (SPOTO 1993, p. 570: Determining the exact time of Joe DiMaggio, Jr.'s call to be 7:00 p.m.)

(WOLFE 1998, p. 460: According to DiMaggio, Sr., Joe Jr.'s call with Marilyn lasted 15 minutes.)

(CONFIDENTIAL SOURCE: Greenson wrote to Dr. Kris on August 20, 1962, "When I left at 7:15, she seemed somewhat depressed . . ." The complete letter is located in Greenson Papers, Special Collections, UCLA, sealed from the public until January 1, 2039.)

(Shearer, Lloyd. "Marilyn Monroe—Why Won't They Let Her Rest in Peace" Parade. 5 August 1973: "That was the last conversation Greenson had with Marilyn Monroe. It was Saturday Aug. 4, 7:30 p.m. After dinner with the Alberts [Eddie and Margo], Dr. Greenson returned to his home . . . around midnight . . . He was tempted to phone Marilyn but didn't want to wake her . . . At 3 a.m. his phone rang. It was Mrs. Murray.")

(CONFIDENTIAL SOURCE: Greenson wrote to Dr. Kris on August 20, 1962, "About an hour later, someone [Mickey Rudin] called the housekeeper . . ." The complete letter is located in Greenson Papers, Special Collections, UCLA, sealed from the public until January 1, 2039.)

(CONFIDENTIAL SOURCE: Greenson wrote to Dr. Kris on August 20, 1962, "At midnight, the housekeeper awakened and saw that there was a light on in Marilyn's room . . ." The complete letter is located in Greenson Papers, Special Collections, UCLA, sealed from the public until January 1, 2039.)

(MURRAY 1975, p. 135: "I knew that the new white wool carpet filled the space under the door . . .")

(GREENSON, HILDI. INTERVIEW WITH CATHY GRIFFIN. 4 JUNE 1991: "People say that there were four hours before it was reported . . .")

(GREENSON, HILDI. INTERVIEW WITH CATHY GRIFFIN. 4 JUNE 1991: "Eunice Murray awakened at midnight and saw . . . the light under the door, and wondered about it, but fell asleep while wondering . . .")

(GREENSON, HILDI. INTERVIEW WITH CATHY GRIFFIN. 4 JUNE 1991: "The 'if' then was, *if* [Mrs. Murray] hadn't fallen asleep at midnight, [Marilyn] probably still could have been saved . . .")

(HEYMANN 1998, p. 323)

(CONFIDENTIAL SOURCE: GREENSON, JOAN. UNTITLED 90-PAGE MARILYN MONROE MANUSCRIPT, p. 84: "Her bedroom door was locked, there was a light, and a telephone cord under the door . . ." The complete work is located in Greenson Papers, Special Collections, UCLA, sealed from the public until January 1, 2039.)

(CONFIDENTIAL SOURCE: GREENSON, JOAN. UNTITLED 90-PAGE MARILYN MONROE MANUSCRIPT, p. 84: "He could see that she had been dead for some time . . ." The complete work is located in Greenson Papers, Special Collections, UCLA, sealed from the public until January 1, 2039.)

(CONFIDENTIAL SOURCE: District attorney's report dated September 27, 1982. Investigator Al Tomich interviewed Marilyn's physician, Dr. Hyman Engelberg, who relayed, "That particular line about being called at midnight, I remember Mrs. Murray telling us clearly that she went to sleep around midnight and she saw the light on . . .")

(CONFIDENTIAL SOURCE: Greenson wrote to Dr. Kris on August 20, 1962, "At 3:30 the housekeeper awakened and saw the light and phoned me . . ." The complete letter is located in Greenson Papers, Special Collections, UCLA, sealed from the public until January 1, 2039.)

(CONFIDENTIAL SOURCE: Greenson wrote to Dr. Kris on August 20, 1962, "It seems she had died around midnight . . ." The complete letter is located in Greenson Papers, Special Collections, UCLA, sealed from the public until January 1, 2039.)

(RUDIN, MILTON. INTERVIEW WITH DONALD SPOTO. 31 OCTOBER 1992: Rudin said he got a call from Greenson telling him Marilyn was dead and this was before midnight.)

30   (SMITH 2005, pp. 30–33: Police report # 62-509 463: Mickey Rudin claims he called Mrs. Murray at 9 p.m.)

(SUMMERS 2000, p. 458: "Eunice Murray agrees that Rudin called, but insists the lawyer said nothing about the troubling call Marilyn had supposedly had with Lawford. She assumed it was merely a casual inquiry and, without checking on Marilyn, said all was well.")

(SUMMERS 1994, p. 347: "Dr. Greenson confirmed privately, years later, that Robert Kennedy was present that night and that an ambulance was called.")

(SPOTO 1993, p. 575: On the morning of August 5, Mrs. Murray claimed she went outside Marilyn's house and used a fireplace poker to "part the draperies" of the only unbarred window.)

(NEWCOMB, PATRICIA. INTERVIEW WITH DONALD SPOTO. 3 AUGUST 1992: Newcomb recalled there was no "middle-divider" to the draperies Eunice Murray claimed she parted.)

31   (SUMMERS 2000, p. 516: Account of Detective Sgt. Robert E. Byron.)

(BYRON, DOROTHEA. INTERVIEW WITH JAY MARGOLIS. 13 SEPTEMBER 2010)

(SUMMERS 2000, pp. 424–425: Parker's wife Helen told Anthony Summers, her husband "wanted special attention paid to this particular case by the investigators . . .")

(BROWN AND BARHAM 1993, p. 440: "With the stroke of a pen, Chief Parker began the cover-up by refusing to assign a full-time detective team . . .")

(BROWN AND BARHAM 1993, p. 440: May Mann relayed, "He told me it would be bad for my health if I kept writing stories like that.")

(BROWN AND BARHAM 1993, p. 467: Rothmiller said, "It was this unit [the OCID] which had undertaken the clandestine probe of Monroe's death . . . Since nobody really ever investigated this death— they only covered up—all the trails were allowed to turn cold.")

(BROWN AND BARHAM 1993, p. 430: Rothmiller relayed, "This is precisely what they did with the Monroe investigation . . . they protected the name of the Kennedy dynasty . . ." "Intelligence chiefs" did this in 1962, 1975, and 1982.)

(From the collection of YouTube member SGTG77: 1992 *Hard Copy* documentary with Anthony Summers where Daniel Stewart discusses his knowledge that Robert Kennedy was in town at Marilyn's home before and after she died.)

(STRAIT, RAYMOND. INTERVIEW WITH JAY MARGOLIS. 18 NOVEMBER 2010: "Bobby skipped out of town and said he was never there but everybody knew he was there. You cover your tail as best you can . . .")

(BROWN AND BARHAM 1993, pp. 343, 503: Lady Lawford is adamant that neighbors saw Bobby Kennedy coming in and out of Peter's beach house that last Saturday.)

(BROWN AND BARHAM 1993, p. 330: Lawford's neighbor Ward Wood said, "It was Bobby all right . . .")

(*Say Goodbye to the President* documentary, 1985: Ward Wood's account.)

(SUMMERS 2000, p. 471: "As she [Lawford's third wife Deborah Gould] understood it from Lawford, 'He [Bobby Kennedy] left by helicopter to the airport.' Joe Hyams . . . and the former policeman both say they learned that a helicopter touched down on the beach, close to the Lawford house, late that night. They discovered this in separate interviews with Lawford's neighbors.")

(SUMMERS 2000, pp. 472–473: William Woodfield relayed, "The time in the log was sometime after midnight . . .")

(SUMMERS 2000, p. 517: James Zonlick remembered, "Hal had picked Robert Kennedy up at the beach house and left him at Los Angeles International Airport . . .")

(SUMMERS 2000, p. 517: Patricia Conners recalled, "Next morning, I remember saying, 'Did you hear that Marilyn Monroe died?'")

(SUMMERS 2000, p. 472: Bobby Kennedy's aide told Woodfield, "The Attorney General would appreciate it if you would not do the story.")

(SUMMERS 2000, p. 468: "Certainly the parish priest confirms, Kennedy was in Gilroy by 9:30 a.m. on Sunday, attending Mass at the church of St. Mary.")

(LAWFORD 1969, p. 36: Carmine S. Bellino and Bobby Kennedy's strict dedication to Mass.)

(STEWART, DANIEL K. INTERVIEW WITH JAY MARGOLIS. 14 JANUARY 2011)

(BROWN AND BARHAM 1993, pp. 437–438: Assumption of suicide tainted the Monroe investigation.)

(CARPOZI, GEORGE, JR. INTERVIEW WITH JOANNE GREEN-LEVINE. 21 JANUARY 1992: "They never conducted a criminal investigation . . .")

(GRANDISON, JR., AND MUQADDIN 2012, pp. 22–23, 26, 194: Account of Deputy Coroner's Aide Lionel Grandison from his memoirs.)

(DAMBACHER, ROBERT. INTERVIEW WITH JAY MARGOLIS. 9 MARCH 2011: "I was a Deputy Coroner at the time. My partner's name was Cletus Pace. So Cleet and I were dispatched at eight in the morning to go out to Westwood Village Mortuary to pick up her remains . . .")

(*The Death of Marilyn Monroe* documentary, n.d. *New York Herald Tribune* reporter Joe Hyams said, "I had a source at the telephone company. My source came back and said the Secret Service has already been here and taken our records . . .")

(SUMMERS 2000, p. 448: Joe Hyams contacted the telephone company "the morning after her death.")

(WOLFE 1998, p. 50: Florabel Muir wrote on August 8, 1962, how sources asserted, "Strange 'pressures' are being put on Los Angeles police . . .")

(SUMMERS 2000, p. 451: Jack Tobin said, "Hamilton told me he had the telephone history of the last day or two of Marilyn Monroe's life . . .")

(Carroll, Ronald H., and Alan B. Tomich. "The Death of Marilyn Monroe—Report to the District Attorney." December 1982, pp. 16–17: "Confidential LAPD records supplied to our office support the published media reports that toll records . . .")

(*The Death of Marilyn Monroe* documentary, n.d. Arthur Jacobs's employee Michael Selsman relayed, "I believe that the Kennedys were concerned that Pat, being a close friend of Marilyn's, would become very emotional and might at some point mention something to somebody about the extent of the relationship between the Kennedys and Marilyn.")

(*The Death of Marilyn Monroe* documentary, n.d. *New York Herald Tribune* reporter Joe Hyams said, "Eunice Murray, who was Marilyn's housekeeper and who had found the body, disappeared. And Pat

Newcomb disappeared but she reappeared very hastily working for the Kennedys in Washington. It just began to look like a vast cover-up.")

(BARRIS, GEORGE. INTERVIEW WITH JAY MARGOLIS. 7 JANUARY 2011: "I'll tell you about Pat Newcomb . . .")

32 (ABBOTT, ALLAN. INTERVIEW WITH JAY MARGOLIS. 13 JUNE 2012: "We had provided limousine service for JFK in Los Angeles for the Democratic Convention before he was elected . . .")

(ABBOTT, ALLAN. INTERVIEW WITH JAY MARGOLIS. 7 JUNE 2012: "I drove the limo on Clark Gable's service and the service for Ernie Kovacs . . .")

(ABBOTT, ALLAN. INTERVIEW WITH JAY MARGOLIS. 20 JUNE 2012: "Clarence Pierce, who was the younger of the two brothers, originally put out the call . . .")

(ABBOTT, ALLAN. INTERVIEW WITH JAY MARGOLIS. 7 JUNE 2012: "I actually stood at the door of the chapel . . .")

(Hast, Ron. "Just Conversation." October 2012—in the collection of Jay Margolis: "Founded in 1957 by my business partner Allan Abbott, and myself, our company . . .")

(ABBOTT, ALLAN. INTERVIEW WITH JAY MARGOLIS. 22 JULY 2012: "Joe DiMaggio left at eleven o'clock at night . . .")

(ABBOTT, ALLAN. INTERVIEW WITH JAY MARGOLIS. 13 JUNE 2012: "We stayed there until almost eleven . . .")

(ABBOTT, ALLAN. INTERVIEW WITH JAY MARGOLIS. 20 JUNE 2012: "In Leigh Wiener's book, it says we're employees of Westwood . . .")

(ABBOTT, ALLAN. INTERVIEW WITH JAY MARGOLIS. 13 AUGUST 2012: "I never met Noguchi until after Marilyn's funeral . . .")

(ABBOTT, ALLAN. INTERVIEW WITH JAY MARGOLIS. 21 JULY 2012: "Noguchi was a working fool. He would do six or eight or ten embalmings . . .")

(ABBOTT, ALLAN. INTERVIEW WITH JAY MARGOLIS. 7 JUNE 2012: "As Abbott & Hast, we provide funeral cars, hearses, limousines . . .")

(ABBOTT, ALLAN. INTERVIEW WITH JAY MARGOLIS. 21 JULY 2012: "Obviously when everyone found out that Westwood . . .")

(ABBOTT, ALLAN. INTERVIEW WITH JAY MARGOLIS. 7 JUNE 2012: "I get to the cemetery and there's about a hundred . . .")

(ABBOTT, ALLAN. INTERVIEW WITH JAY MARGOLIS. 13 JUNE 2012: "Marilyn's neck was bloated because I think Noguchi was in there . . .")

(ABBOTT, ALLAN. INTERVIEW WITH JAY MARGOLIS. 7 JUNE 2012: "Of course, she was already embalmed at the Coroner's Office . . .")

(ABBOTT, ALLAN. INTERVIEW WITH JAY MARGOLIS. 21 JULY 2012: "We had just finished dressing Marilyn. Charles Maxwell, the embalmer . . .")

(ABBOTT, ALLAN. INTERVIEW WITH JAY MARGOLIS. 7 JUNE 2012: "I kept thinking about those falsies . . .")

(ABBOTT, ALLAN. INTERVIEW WITH JAY MARGOLIS. 21 JULY 2012: "If Mrs. Hamrock hadn't come in, I would have never ended up with the falsies . . .")

(ABBOTT, ALLAN. INTERVIEW WITH JAY MARGOLIS. 7 JUNE 2012: "Then, when I got outside, I pulled them out of my pocket and some of the hair that was cut off of her was between the two falsies . . .")

("The Marilyn Tapes—Questions Still Remain About the Movie Star's Death." *48 Hours.* 20 April 2006: Peter Van Sant said, "Dr. Steven Karch is one of the nation's top forensic pathologists . . . All it would take are a few strands of that famously blonde hair . . . Dr. Karch says tests could be run to look for poisons or paralyzing drugs, not done back then.")

("The Marilyn Tapes—Questions Still Remain About the Movie Star's Death." *48 Hours.* 20 April 2006: Dr. Steven Karch said, "Somebody would have to open the crypt and take some hair and fingernails and analyze it.")

33   (BROWN AND BARHAM 1993, p. 338: Clemmons remembered a man with a European accent calling to notify him of the death of Marilyn Monroe.)

(Rebello, Stephen. "Somebody Killed Her." *Playboy.* December 2005, p. 187: According to John Miner, Greenson did call the police, contrary to the official police report that said Engelberg called instead.)

(Shearer, Lloyd. "Marilyn Monroe—Why Won't They Let Her Rest in Peace?" *Parade.* 5 August 1973: Greenson himself admitted it was he who called the police.)

(WOLFE 1998, p. 5: "Clemmons recalled, 'She was lying face-down in what I call the soldier's position. Her face was in a pillow, her arms were by her side, her right arm was slightly bent. Her legs were stretched out perfectly straight.'")

(BROWN AND BARHAM 1993, pp. 340–341: Clemmons said of Greenson and Engelberg, "Liars, both of them." Clemmons was not impressed when he felt Greenson was being fresh with him, "I strongly disliked Greenson's attitude . . .")

34   (SUMMERS 2000, p. 415: "Dr. Greenson would later say he had brought in Dr. Engelberg to try to wean Marilyn away from sleeping pills . . .")

(*Marilyn Monroe: The Final Days* TV documentary, 2001: Engelberg discussed Marilyn's last night and diagnosed his patient as bipolar.)

(HEYMANN 1998, p. 320: Peter Lawford mentioned Marilyn's "manic-depressive tendencies.")

(CONFIDENTIAL SOURCE: District Attorney's report dated September 27, 1982. Investigator Al Tomich interviewed Marilyn's physician, Dr. Hyman Engelberg, who relayed, "I saw her Friday evening . . .")

(HEYMANN 1998, p. 324)

(CAPELL 1964, p. 32: Engelberg's Creditor's Claim for giving Marilyn an injection on August 3, 1962.)

(CONFIDENTIAL SOURCE: Greenson wrote to Dr. Kris on August 20, 1962, "I had an internist [Hyman Engelberg] who would prescribe medication for her and to give her vitamin injections and liver injections . . ." The complete letter is located in Greenson Papers, Special Collections, UCLA, sealed from the public until January 1, 2039.)

(MALTZ, ESTHER ENGELBERG. INTERVIEW WITH DONALD SPOTO. 23 OCTOBER 1992: "Dr. Greenson used Hy to sedate [Marilyn].")

(SPOTO 1993, p. 661: "Regarding the so-called 'liver and vitamin injections,' the first Mrs. Hyman Engelberg told DS [Donald Spoto] that she never heard of them.")

(SPOTO 1993, p. 586: "Chloral hydrate interferes with the body's production of enzymes that metabolize Nembutal.")

(*Marilyn Monroe: The Final Days* TV documentary, 2001: Engelberg related, "The autopsy showed . . . a lot of chloral hydrate. I never gave her chloral hydrate and I don't think any doctor in the United States gave it to her. She must have bought it in Tijuana.")

(TARABORRELLI 2009, p. 378: "She was taking chloral hydrate to sleep, and Dr. Engelberg emphatically states that he never prescribed it to her, nor did Dr. Greenson. In fact, Engelberg would say . . . he now presumes she bought when she was in Mexico just before her death.")

(GRAY, MARIJANE. INTERVIEW WITH JAY MARGOLIS. 17 MAY 2012: Physician Dr. Hyman Engelberg wrote chloral hydrate prescriptions for Marilyn including one dated June 7, 1962, one day before Marilyn was fired. This prescription was sold at Julien's Auctions on May 7, 2011, for $1,664. Therefore,

Engelberg lied when he claimed ignorance of Marilyn's chloral hydrate prescriptions.)

(SPOTO 1993, pp. 497–498, 506, 581–582, 585–586, 590, 663: Greenson told biographer Maurice Zolotow and photographer William Woodfield that he was in fact aware of chloral hydrate prescriptions for Marilyn.)

(SPOTO 1993, p. 581: "100-milligram Nembutal capsules" and "500-milligram chloral hydrate capsules.")

(SPERIGLIO 1986, p. 19: "The Hocketts arrived . . . Father and son first collected the pill bottles, establishing that there were fifteen.")

(MURRAY 1975, p. 42: Mrs. Murray relayed, "Under Dr. Greenson's guidance, she was taking only chloral hydrate pills for sleep.")

(Zolotow, Maurice. "Monroe's Last Days: Drowsy Death in a Barbiturate Darkness." *Chicago Tribune*. 14 September 1973, sec. 2, p. 4: "Her psychiatrist, Dr. Ralph Greenson, was attempting to cut down her dependence on Nembutal by switching her to chloral hydrate as a sleep-inducer.")

(SPOTO 1993, p. 590: Greenson to Woodfield regarding the large chloral hydrate prescriptions written by Engelberg, "Well, I've made a number of mistakes in my time.")

(CONFIDENTIAL SOURCE: District attorney's report dated September 27, 1982. Investigator Alan B. Tomich interviewed Marilyn's physician, Dr. Hyman Engelberg, who relayed, "I don't know of anything Dr. Greenson gave her. Maybe he did. I cannot answer for him . . .")

(From the collection of CBS News: September 27, 1982, recorded interview for the District Attorney's Office with Marilyn's physician, Dr. Hyman Engelberg, conducted by investigator Alan B. Tomich:

TOMICH: Was there a reason there was a delay of half hour or do you consider it was a delay?

ENGELBERG: We were stunned. We were talking over what happened, what she had said. Ordinarily, when you pronounce somebody dead, you don't call the police, you call the mortician. I was the one who I guess eventually said, gee, I think in this case, we'd better call the police.)

(Zolotow, Maurice. "Monroe's Last Days: Drowsy Death in a Barbiturate Darkness." *Chicago Tribune*. 14 September 1973, sec. 2, p. 4: In an interview with Dr. Engelberg, Zolotow quoted him as saying, "The reason there was [a] delay [was because] normally you don't call the police. You call the mortuary to remove the body. Dr. Greenson and I discussed this back and forth. I strongly insisted that because of who she was and the possibility of suicide, we should call the police.")

(HEYMANN 1998, p. 312)

(GREENSON, HILDI. INTERVIEW WITH CATHY GRIFFIN. 4 JUNE 1991: "The idea was that she was never to be said no to when she wanted a prescription . . .")

(TARABORRELLI 2009, p. 377)

(CONFIDENTIAL SOURCE: GREENSON, JOAN. UNTITLED 90-PAGE MARILYN MONROE MANUSCRIPT, p. 84: "All she had to do was call her doctor and he would prescribe it to her . . ." The complete work is located in Greenson Papers, Special Collections, UCLA, sealed from the public until January 1, 2039.)

(WARNER 1991, pp. 582–583: "Part of improving the patient's environment is prescribing 'proper' medication that will magically solve problems. This medication is either what has recently been reported in newspapers or magazines as new and effective or what other affluent patients report as 'doing miracles.'")

(GREENSON 1964, p. 209: "The administering of a drug is a responsibility since it may cause physical side effects . . ." The complete work is located in Greenson Papers, Special Collections, UCLA.)

(CONFIDENTIAL SOURCE: Greenson wrote to Dr. Kris on August 20, 1962, "I later found out that on Friday night she had told the internist [Engelberg] that I had said it was all right for her to take some Nembutal . . ." The complete letter is located in

Greenson Papers, Special Collections, UCLA, sealed from the public until January 1, 2039.)

(SPOTO 1993, p. 586: How Greenson knew his star patient well enough to know on what prescription she was "somewhat drugged.")

(CONFIDENTIAL SOURCE: Greenson wrote to Dr. Kris on August 20, 1962, "I received a call from Marilyn at 4:30 in the afternoon. She seemed somewhat depressed and somewhat drugged." The complete letter is located in Greenson Papers, Special Collections, UCLA, sealed from the public until January 1, 2039.)

(GUILES 1969, p. 321: "She asked him to give her a new sleeping pill prescription. After he [Engelberg] was convinced that the drug she was taking—chloral hydrate—was not working, he agreed to prescribe twenty-five tablets of Nembutal.")

(MIRACLE 1994, p. 197: "Friday evening Pat Newcomb arrives at Marilyn's house to spend the night. Dr. Engelberg stops in, gives Marilyn an injection to help her sleep and, because the chloral hydrate has apparently not been working, writes her a prescription for twenty-five Nembutal capsules.")

(GREENSON, HILDI. INTERVIEW WITH CATHY GRIFFIN. 4 JUNE 1991: "In trying to help Marilyn get off the barbiturates she was on he was giving her a different kind of medication that is not quite as addictive . . .")

(MURRAY 1975, p. 42: Marilyn told Mrs. Murray regarding chloral hydrate: "You know they used to give these to the soldiers in the war for sleeping. They're really very mild.")

(From the collection of YouTube member wksufreshair: KNBC *Hard Copy,* April 20, 1992, Part 2 of 4 Marilyn Monroe: For *Hard Copy*'s reenactment of Marilyn's last day, Mrs. Murray's recollection of Marilyn taking chloral hydrate and how mild Marilyn thought it was.)

(CONFIDENTIAL SOURCE: On August 20, 1962, Greenson wrote to Dr. Kris, "At the end of the conversation she asked me whether I had taken away her Nembutal bottle . . ." The complete letter is located in Greenson Papers, Special Collections, UCLA, sealed from the public until January 1, 2039.)

(BROWN AND BARHAM 1993, p. 423: Joan Greenson said Engelberg didn't tell her father about the Nembutal prescription the day before Marilyn died because his wife was kicking him out of the house that day and he had a lot on his mind. However, this does not explain a bigger problem: Engelberg's original Nembutal prescription on July 25 just days before.)

(CONFIDENTIAL SOURCE: GREENSON, JOAN. UNTITLED 90-PAGE MARILYN MONROE MANUSCRIPT, p. 85: "That Saturday he had checked her medication . . ." The complete work is located in Greenson Papers, Special Collections, UCLA, sealed from the public until January 1, 2039.)

(GREENSON, HILDI. INTERVIEW WITH CATHY GRIFFIN. 4 JUNE 1991: "It happened on a bad day. A divorce either became final or he was moving out of his house . . .")

(SUMMERS 2000, p. 414: "An empty bottle, with a label indicating it had contained twenty-five Nembutal pills, would be among the medicines retrieved from Marilyn's room after her death. The label showed it had been prescribed on Friday, the day before her death.")

(SUMMERS 2000, pp. 432–433: A photograph in Summers's book proved Engelberg wrote an original Nembutal prescription for Marilyn on July 25, 1962, which was subsequently refilled days later on August 3. Summers incorrectly assumed this was for chloral hydrate.)

(SMITH 2005, p. 31: Quoting from the official police report #62-509 463: "Dr. Engelberg made the statement that he prescribed a refill for this about two days ago and he further stated there probably should have been about 50 capsules at the time this was refilled by the pharmacist.")

(NEWCOMB, PATRICIA. INTERVIEW WITH DONALD SPOTO. 3 AUGUST 1992: "She asked for some Nembutals. Engelberg was having problems with his wife . . .")

(LITMAN, ROBERT, M.D. INTERVIEW WITH DONALD SPOTO. 23 APRIL 1992: "I am stuck with the information that she went out and got pills from Siegel and Engelberg.")

(Carroll, Ronald H., and Alan B. Tomich. "The Death of Marilyn Monroe—Report to the District Attorney." December 1982, p. 25: Engelberg's refill and the alleged Nembutal prescriptions by Dr. Siegel.)

(SUMMERS 2000, p. 415: Dr. Lee Siegel from Twentieth Century-Fox denied seeing Marilyn in the last weeks leading to her death.)

35 ("Quiet services for Marilyn Monroe." *Redlands Daily Facts.* [Redlands, CA] 8 August 1962: Peter Lawford told a reporter he may have been the last person to speak to Marilyn on the phone.)

(CRAMER 2001, p. 419: "Peter Lawford came forward as the 'mystery caller'—he'd talked to Marilyn that Saturday night—and he quoted her last words to him (or maybe he wasn't really quoting): 'Say goodbye to Pat, say goodbye to the President, and say goodbye to yourself, because you're a nice guy.'")

(SUMMERS 2000, p. 457: Peter and the 7:30 p.m. call to Marilyn.)

(SUMMERS 2000, p. 421: Harry Hall said DiMaggio "held Bobby Kennedy responsible for her death.")

(SUMMERS 2000, p. 482: DiMaggio said to the funeral director, "Be sure that none of those damn Kennedys come to the funeral.")

(DePaulo, Lisa. "The Strange, Still Mysterious Death of Marilyn Monroe." *Playboy.* December 2005, pp. 194–195: DiMaggio's best friend Morris Engelberg relayed, "No woman in the world will ever be loved the way he loved her . . .")

(SUMMERS 2000, p. 482: Peter Lawford said, "It seems to be a concerted effort to keep some of Marilyn's old friends from attending.")

(SPADA 1991, p. 330: DiMaggio privately responded, "If it wasn't for her so-called friends, Marilyn would be alive today.")

(FANTA 1968, p. 37: On August 12, 1962, four days after Marilyn's funeral, "The President and his guests aboard the MANITOU on second day of Maine cruising," including Jack Kennedy, Peter Lawford, Pat Kennedy Lawford, and Pat Newcomb.)

(WOLFE 1998, pp. 244–245: Same *Manitou* photograph is located in the picture section between these two pages.)

(HEYMANN 1998, p. 325: "Three days after Marilyn's death, RFK left San Francisco on a camping trip to Oregon . . .")

(SLATZER 1992, p. 349: Quoting from the official police report # 62-509 463: "An attempt was made to contact Mr. Lawford . . .")

(LITMAN, ROBERT, M.D. INTERVIEW WITH DONALD SPOTO. 23 APRIL 1992: "Probable suicide" based on the "physical evidence" and "past history of having made overdoses.")

(SPOTO 1993, p. 582: Dr. Robert Litman related, "It was obvious to us, after speaking with Dr. Greenson about Marilyn's psychiatric history, that the only conclusion we could reach was suicide, or at least a gamble with death . . .")

(Rebello, Stephen. "Somebody Killed Her." *Playboy*. December 2005, p. 187: Miner discussed how Marilyn would have been unconscious before she could finish taking 30–40 pills.)

(Rebello, Stephen. "Somebody Killed Her." *Playboy*. December 2005, p. 187: Miner related, "I was called on a Sunday, and the techs wouldn't even have gotten to the specimens until the following day . . .")

(SUMMERS 2000, p. 432: Noguchi said, "For some reason I felt uncomfortable and shortly after the case was formally closed I called Toxicology . . .")

(History's Mysteries: *The Death of Marilyn Monroe* documentary, 2000: Noguchi said of Coroner Curphey, "He certified the manner of death to be 'probable suicide . . .'")

(History's Mysteries: *The Death of Marilyn Monroe* documentary, 2000: John Miner vehemently discounted the "probable suicide" verdict by Dr. Curphey: "What we really have is a coroner chief medical examiner . . .")

36 (Zolotow, Maurice. "MM's Psychiatrist a Troubled Man." *San Antonio Light*. [San Antonio, TX] 13 October 1973, p. 9-A: Ralph Greenson said, "I will always believe it was an accidental suicide, because her hand was on the receiver, her finger still in the dial . . .")

(MAILER 1975, p. 341: "Dr. Thomas Noguchi stated for *Time* magazine that 'no stomach pump was used on Marilyn.'")

("Two Myths Converge: NM Discovers MM." *Time*. 16 July 1973, p. 70)

("Psychiatrist Breaks Silence in Defense of Marilyn Monroe." *Yuma Daily Sun*. [Yuma, AZ] 23 October 1973: Ralph Greenson said, "I've decided that all I can do I've tried to do . . .")

(SUMMERS 2000, p. 337: "Dr. Litman says today that Greenson spoke to him of a 'close relationship with extremely important men in government,' that the relationship was 'sexual,' and that the men concerned were 'at the highest level.' Dr. Litman says . . . he had 'no real doubt' whom he meant by 'important men in government.'")

37   (MURRAY 1975, p. 156: Mrs. Murray said, "It's well known that Marilyn had a history of attempts at suicide. But at this particular time, she didn't seem to have a desperate need to end it all. Plans were being resolved and there were many promising, exciting possibilities for the future.")

(WIENER 1990, p. 11: "Years later, in an interview, Mrs. Murray would change parts of her story, but not the belief that Marilyn's death was probably accidental.")

(SLATZER 1992, p. 184: Marilyn's neighbor Abe Landau was told by Mrs. Murray how Marilyn took too many pills because she forgot that she had taken some earlier then died.)

("Two Myths Converge: NM Discovers MM." *Time*. 16 July 1973, p. 70: "It was not a case, says Noguchi, of 'automatism'—that gray area . . .")

38   (BROWN AND BARHAM 1993, p. 345: "To Allan, the master publicist, Lawford's story sounded as though it had been written for him by a public relations expert . . .")

(EBBINS, MILTON. INTERVIEW WITH DONALD SPOTO. 6 AUGUST 1992: "I was a confidant of Peter's . . .")

(EBBINS, MILTON. INTERVIEW WITH DONALD SPOTO. 6 AUGUST 1992: "I called and got a busy signal . . .")

(EBBINS, MILTON. INTERVIEW WITH DONALD SPOTO. 6 AUGUST 1992: "Peter Lawford wanted to go badly . . .")

(EBBINS, MILTON. INTERVIEW WITH DONALD SPOTO. 6 AUGUST 1992: "Peter was getting drunker by the minute . . . He'd be coughing then be silent . . .")

(EBBINS, MILTON. INTERVIEW WITH JAMES SPADA. 13 DECEMBER 1988: "I know the way this story may go and I'm prepared for it. I can't dispute you because you're liable to have proof . . .")

(EBBINS, MILTON. INTERVIEW WITH DONALD SPOTO. 6 AUGUST 1992: "That's a lot of crap . . .")

(EBBINS, MILTON. INTERVIEW WITH DONALD SPOTO. 6 AUGUST 1992: "How's Marilyn? . . .")

(EBBINS, MILTON. INTERVIEW WITH DONALD SPOTO. 22 SEPTEMBER 1992: "Come on! Bobby Kennedy had more ways. He could've gotten rid of Marilyn Monroe with a phone call to Peter Lawford . . .")

(EBBINS, MILTON. INTERVIEW WITH JAMES SPADA. 8 NOVEMBER 1988: "Marilyn was destined to die. She'd tried suicide four times. Peter felt guilty about not going over to save her, but Dr. Greenson told him . . .")

(EBBINS, MILTON. INTERVIEW WITH JAMES SPADA. 13 DECEMBER 1988: "Greenson told Peter that Marilyn had tried to commit suicide four or five times...")

(EBBINS, MILTON. INTERVIEW WITH JAMES SPADA. 8 NOVEMBER 1988: "I was on the phone to Peter all night the night Marilyn died . . .")

(ASHER, WILLIAM. INTERVIEW WITH DONALD SPOTO. 25 SEPTEMBER 1992: "I heard from Peter at eight or nine . . .")

(*Say Goodbye to the President* documentary, 1985: George "Bullets" Durgom relayed, "He [Peter Lawford] mentions maybe I ought to go up there and see if she's okay . . .")

(EBBINS, MILTON. INTERVIEW WITH DONALD SPOTO. 6 AUGUST 1992: "There were two numbers. Peter didn't have the other number . . .")

(RUDIN, MILTON. INTERVIEW WITH DONALD SPOTO. 31 OCTOBER 1992: "I did not call [Greenson]. He had had enough quite frankly . . .")

("Peter Lawford Phoned MM on Her Last Night." *San Antonio Express.* [San Antonio, Texas] 9 August 1962: Milton Ebbins relayed, "He [Lawford] said Miss Monroe told him she would like to come but that she was tired and was going to bed early . . .")

39   (LAWFORD 1992, pp. 77–80: Lady May Lawford, Peter Lawford's mother, suspects her son of foul play on August 4, 1962.)

40   (Scott, Vernon. "Debunking MM Murder Rumors Latest Hollywood Industry." *European Stars and Stripes.* [Darmstadt, Germany] 7 October 1985: Milt Ebbins related, "I talked to Peter on the telephone several times that night . . . I suggested we call Mickey Rudin, Marilyn's attorney, and her psychiatrist, Dr. Ralph Greenson, Mickey's brother-in-law . . .")

(Boyes, Malcolm. "The Passing of Peter Lawford Rekindles Memories of the Joys and Sadness of a Camelot Lost." *People.* 14 January 1985, Volume 23, Number 2: Peter Lawford remained "on good terms with the Kennedys. In fact, presidential candidate Robert Kennedy, after winning the California primary in 1968, was headed for a Lawford-hosted party when he, too, was killed by an assassin's bullets.")

(NAAR, DOLORES. INTERVIEW WITH JAMES SPADA. 5 JANUARY 1989: "We were all to go to that. Pat would have been there . . .")

(ROMANOFF, GLORIA. INTERVIEW WITH JAY MARGOLIS. 2 SEPTEMBER 2010: "I don't think there was a lot of affection between Bobby Kennedy and Peter Lawford . . .")

(FRANKLIN 2002, p. 109: On Bobby Kennedy snapping at Peter, "Lawford didn't react; apparently he was used to verbal whippings.")

41   (ASHER, WILLIAM. INTERVIEW WITH DONALD SPOTO. 25 SEPTEMBER 1992)

42   (NAAR, DOLORES. INTERVIEW WITH JAY MARGOLIS. 4 NOVEMBER 2010: "Peter called our house and said, 'Don't pick up Marilyn. She's not coming.'")

(SPADA 1991, p. 321: "Around seven-thirty, just as the Naars were leaving the house, they got another call from Peter. Marilyn wasn't feeling well, he told them, and wouldn't be coming.")

(NAAR, DOLORES. INTERVIEW WITH JAMES SPADA. 6 JANUARY 1989: "I read in one of the books that Bobby was upstairs . . .")

(NAAR, JOSEPH. INTERVIEW WITH DONALD SPOTO. 22 JULY 1992: Joe Naar claims Lawford told him, "I just talked to Marilyn and I'm scared. I don't like the way she sounds. I think she's taken some pills . . .")

(NAAR, JOSEPH. INTERVIEW WITH JAY MARGOLIS. 2 SEPTEMBER 2010: "I was on the phone with Peter most of that night . . . That's one-on-one with me at 11:30 at night . . .")

(SPADA 1991, p. 323: Dolores Naar stated that to her husband Joe, Lawford "said that he'd spoken to Marilyn's doctor and [Dr. Greenson] had said that he had given her sedatives because she had been disturbed earlier . . .")

(SPADA 1991, p. 323: During Peter's party, Dolores Naar recalled, "I picked up on nothing. Except that during the evening there was a call and Peter said, 'Oh, it's Marilyn again'—like she does this all the time. His attitude didn't change. It was very light, up evening." Erma Lee Riley, Peter's maid, agreed: "There wasn't a word of worry about Marilyn.")

(NAAR, DOLORES. INTERVIEW WITH JAY MARGOLIS. 3 NOVEMBER 2010: "I was in the room.")

(NAAR, DOLORES. INTERVIEW WITH JAY MARGOLIS. 4 NOVEMBER 2010: "So you don't need to go.")

(SMITH 2005, p. 180: "Peter Lawford telephoned to say that Marilyn had taken too many pills . . . Joe Naar . . . dressed in readiness, but Lawford called again before he set off. He said it was unnecessary to go . . . Dolores Naar recalls Lawford telling them that Marilyn's doctor had given her a sedative and she was resting.")

(SUMMERS 2000, p. 514: "Lawford phoned soon after that to say 'Marilyn's doctor' had given her a sedative, and she was resting.")

(SPADA 1991, p. 324: Dolores Naar said, "Peter probably called Jack or Bobby and was told to take care of things . . .")

(SPADA 1991, p. 323: "These were an odd pair of telephone calls in an evening replete with oddities . . .")

(SPADA 1991, p. 323: Dolores Naar had a hunch that Lawford's two calls were "calculated to mislead us . . .")

43   (LEAMER 1996, p. 569: Joe Naar said, "I blame the changes in Peter and his final decline into the bottle on Marilyn's death . . .")

(NAAR, JOSEPH. INTERVIEW WITH JAY MARGOLIS. 2 SEPTEMBER 2010: "You're trying to sort out the truth and put a puzzle together, but at this late date it's going to be extremely difficult . . .")

(*Marilyn Monroe: A Case for Murder* documentary, 1988: Former FBI agent Bill Roemer stated, "I would, yeah. I think there have been so many questions now and there's so much conjecturing . . .")

(MECACCI 2009, p. 29: "Marilyn's death was in the end a relief for everyone: for the Kennedys, who had been freed from the nightmare of a scandal; for the CIA and the FBI . . .")

(CONFIDENTIAL SOURCE. INTERVIEW WITH JAY MARGOLIS: "Two of my brothers were FBI agents . . . I had heard that my brother John Anderson had seen Robert Kennedy and two men enter Marilyn Monroe's home. Hours later it was reported that Marilyn Monroe had died.")

(Turner, Dave. *Society of Former Special Agents of the FBI*. Kentucky: Turner Publishing Company, 1996, p. 235: "Anderson, John K. 1952–1977, membership number 000121")

(SUMMERS 2000, p. 528: On July 8, 1964, Hoover wrote to Bobby, "His book will make reference to your alleged friendship with the late Miss Marilyn Monroe. Mr. Capell stated that he will indicate . . .")

(SUMMERS 1994, p. 350: Hoover's then-teenage neighbor Anthony Calomaris relayed, "He said she was murdered, that it wasn't a suicide, that the Kennedys were involved.")

(SUMMERS 1994, pp. 344, 349: When Marilyn and Bobby Kennedy saw each other at the Lawford mansion on February 1, 1962, Hoover was listening in over wiretaps: "For Edgar, reading the transcript in Washington, Kennedy's words must have held some comfort . . .")

(THOMAS 2007, p. 117: Ethel Kennedy and the anonymous recommendation of Police Chief William Parker to the head of the FBI.)

(THOMAS 2007, pp. 194, 429: *Seattle Intelligencer*. 7 August 1962: Bobby Kennedy publicly stated, "I hope Hoover will continue to serve the country for many, many years to come.")

(Taylor, Gene. "Will Marilyn Monroe's Secret Love Letters Burn Bobby Kennedy?" *Confidential.* October 1967, p. 72: Gay Talese of *Esquire* magazine wrote: "Mantle stepped forward. He stood with his wife and children, posed for the photographers . . .")

(Taylor, Gene. "Will Marilyn Monroe's Secret Love Letters Burn Bobby Kennedy?" *Confidential.* October 1967, p. 72: Gay Talese of *Esquire* magazine wrote: "Kennedy posed with Mantle for a photographer...")

(SUMMERS 2000, pp. 484–485: "Three years after Marilyn's death, in 1965, Joe DiMaggio stood in a ceremonial lineup for baseball hero Mickey Mantle at New York's Yankee Stadium. Robert Kennedy came along the line, smiling and shaking hands. Rather than shake Kennedy's hand, DiMaggio quickly backed away.")

(HEYMANN 2009, p. 77: "DiMaggio refused to shake Bobby's hand that day, giving rise to a *New York Daily News* sports page headline: 'Joltin' Joe—No Fan of RFK's!'")

(SUMMERS 2000, p. 421: Harry Hall said DiMaggio "held Bobby Kennedy responsible for her death. He said that right there in the Miramar.")

(HAYS 2005, p. 8: "In 1966, Chief Parker died of a heart attack during an engagement as a guest speaker at a military banquet.")

(LAWFORD, PETER. INTERVIEW WITH C. DAVID HEYMANN. 1983. Transcript located at the State University of New York at Stony Brook: "MM's affair with Greenson took on a far greater meaning at the time of her death . . .")

(LAWFORD, PETER. INTERVIEW WITH C. DAVID HEYMANN. 1983. Transcript located at the State University of New York at Stony Brook: " 'Marilyn has got to be silenced,' Bobby told Greenson or something to that effect. Greenson had thus been set up by Bobby to 'take care' of Marilyn.")

(HEYMANN 1998, p. 322)

(LAWFORD, PETER. INTERVIEW WITH C. DAVID HEYMANN. 1983. Transcript located at the State University of New York at Stony Brook: "I suppose the most surprising revelation in Marilyn's own tapes was the fact that not only did Marilyn have an affair with both Kennedys, she was also sleeping with Dr. Greenson, who appeared to be deeply in love with her . . .")

(HEYMANN 1998, p. 322: Peter Lawford said, "I also got hold of portions of the [Mafia-Teamster] tapes, and heard what seemed to be sounds of their [Monroe and Greenson's] lovemaking . . .")

(*Say Goodbye to the President* documentary, 1985: Ralph Greenson relayed, "I can't explain myself or defend myself without revealing things that I don't want to reveal... Listen, you know, talk to Bobby Kennedy.")

(CONFIDENTIAL SOURCE: Greenson wrote to Dr. Kris on August 20, 1962, "The ending at this particular time seemed so unfair and in a way unnecessary . . ." The complete letter is located in Greenson Papers, Special Collections, UCLA, sealed from the public until January 1, 2039.)

(SUMMERS 2000, p. 422: Ralph Greenson said, "She was a poor creature, whom I tried to help and ending up hurting.")

(LAWFORD, PETER. INTERVIEW WITH C. DAVID HEYMANN. 1983. Transcript located at the State University of New York at Stony Brook: "After Marilyn's death, the Kennedys gave Pat a job in Washington and soon sent her off to Europe . . .")

(CONFIDENTIAL SOURCE: Greenson wrote to Dr. Kris on August 20, 1962, "I had become a prisoner now of a form of treatment which I thought was correct for her but almost impossible for me . . ." The complete letter is located in Greenson Papers, Special Collections, UCLA, sealed from the public until January 1, 2039.)

(CONFIDENTIAL SOURCE: Greenson wrote to Dr. Kris on August 20, 1962, "She was making progress, but at times I felt I couldn't go on with this..." The complete letter is located in Greenson Papers, Special Collections, UCLA, sealed from the public until January 1, 2039.)

(CONFIDENTIAL SOURCE: Greenson wrote to Dr. Kris on August 20, 1962, "I had become the most important person in her life and there was nothing I could do except hope that as she improved still more . . ." The complete letter is located in Greenson Papers, Special Collections, UCLA, sealed from the public until January 1, 2039.)

(Hartford, Bob. "Marilyn Monroe's Bitter Battle Against Sex." *The National Police Gazette*. January 1960: Marilyn Monroe said, "I'm tired of playing sex kittens . . .")

(ROLLYSON 1993, p. 211: Marilyn to Richard Meryman, "I never quite understood it—this sex symbol—I always thought symbols were . . .")

POSTSCRIPT ENDNOTES

(JOLING AND VAN PRAAG 2008, p. 235: "The shooting within the pantry began at 12:15:59 a.m. and ceased at 12:16:04.")

(MOLDEA 1995, p. 312: Dr. Thomas Noguchi said, "The [rear of the right] shoulder pad shot as he was raising his arm…")

(*The Second Gun* documentary, 1973: Directed by Theodore Charach and co-produced by Theodore Charach and Gérard Alcan: When he was interviewed in 1971, Don Schulman asserted how Ace Security guard Thane Eugene Cesar was "standing directly to the side and back of Kennedy… He was standing on the right-hand side.")

(*The Second Gun* documentary, 1973: Directed by Theodore Charach and co-produced by Theodore Charach and Gérard Alcan: KNXT's Jerry Dunphy reported soon after the shooting while Sirhan Sirhan had not yet been taken out of the Ambassador Hotel: "Don Schulman of KNXT tells us that Kennedy was shot three times…")

("Robert F. Kennedy Assassination: The FBI Files." Filiquarian Publishing, LLC. 2007, Second Section, p. 8: Don Schulman said he witnessed "Kennedy being shot three times. The guard definitely pulled out his gun and fired.")

(MELANSON 1994, p. 78: "For days after the assassination the press and public assumed he was hit twice. Only Don Schulman correctly insisted Kennedy had been shot three times…")

(*The Second Gun* documentary, 1973: Directed by Theodore Charach and co-produced by Theodore Charach and Gérard Alcan:

In 1971, Don Schulman said Sirhan Sirhan was "from three to six feet" from RFK during the shooting.)

(*RFK Must Die: The Assassination of Bobby Kennedy* (An Investigative Documentary by Shane O'Sullivan). E2 Films, 2007: Karl Uecker stated, "That bullet which killed Kennedy, it was an inch away from his head...")

("Summaries of Interviews with Crime Scene Witnesses Concerning Distance of Sirhan from Senator Kennedy." Karl Uecker stated on February 20, 1975, p. 688 of 809: "There is no way that the shots described in the autopsy could have come from Sirhan's gun... Sirhan never got close enough for a point-blank shot, never.")

(JOLING AND VAN PRAAG 2008, p. 267: "Therefore, bent over the steam table, with his neck and gun-hand restrained [by Karl Uecker], Sirhan was never in a position to fire any shots from the rear of RFK. Kennedy received no frontal wounds.")

(SCHULMAN, DON. INTERVIEW WITH JAY MARGOLIS. 25 FEBRUARY 2014: "One was Sirhan Sirhan and the other one was the security guard...")

(*The Second Gun* documentary, 1973: Directed by Theodore Charach and co-produced by Theodore Charach and Gérard Alcan: In 1971, Don Schulman asserted, "Another man [Sirhan Sirhan] stepped out and he shot just as the guard [Thane Eugene Cesar] who was standing behind Kennedy took out his gun and he fired also. The next thing I knew is that Kennedy was shot three times.")

(Goldberg, Jerry. "Robert F. Kennedy Is Dead." *Valley Times* [San Fernando Valley, CA]. 6 June 1968: "He died at 1:44 a.m. today in the intensive care center of Good Samaritan Hospital. Death came a little more than twenty-four hours after an assassin's bullets... An autopsy team headed by Dr. Thomas T. Noguchi, Los Angeles County coroner-chief medical examiner, arrived at the hospital about 3:30 a.m. and conducted a post mortem on the body of the 42-year-old senator.")

(O'SULLIVAN 2008, pp. 131, 505: "Irene Gizzi was chairman of Youth for Kennedy in Panorama City and arrived at the hotel with six other girls [including Katherine 'Kathy' Lentine, Joan Wing Kies, and Edith Noonan, three names Ms. Gizzi relayed to Jay Margolis]. Around nine o'clock that night, Gizzi noticed a group of [five] people… 'who did not seem to fit with the exuberant crowd. Observed the female to be wearing a white dress with black polka-dots; the girl was standing with a male… [wearing a] gold-colored shirt, and light-colored pants…'" from "Irene Gizzi LAPD interview June 6 [1968]."

(GIZZI, IRENE. INTERVIEW WITH JAY MARGOLIS. 29 MARCH 2014: Jay Margolis asked, "The last person to actually interview you were LAPD?" Ms. Gizzi replied, "Yes, the police lieutenant that came to the house." "Back in [June 6] 1968?" "Yes.")

(GIZZI, IRENE. INTERVIEW WITH JAY MARGOLIS. 13 MARCH 2014: "First, Robert was speaking in the upper ballroom [the Embassy Room]…")

(O'SULLIVAN 2008, pp. 168-169: "After the speech [in the Embassy Room]… Kennedy didn't go downstairs to the Ambassador Room…")

(GIZZI, IRENE. INTERVIEW WITH JAY MARGOLIS. 12 MARCH 2014: To Jay Margolis, Irene Gizzi became the first person at the Ambassador Hotel on June 5, 1968 to identify both the polka-dot dress girl and her male accomplice via a photo line-up containing three males on the left and three females on the right. Margolis gave Ms. Gizzi a red pen to circle the man and woman she saw and to write defining characteristics for each person above their respective pictures. After circling her choices, she wrote "Medallion" above Tarrants's picture and for Ainsworth, she wrote "Polka-Dot Dress." After writing the defining characteristics, Ms. Gizzi initialed her own name below Tarrants's photo and Ainsworth's photo respectively. On the top of the page, she wrote, "Today is: March 12, 2014" and Ms. Gizzi also wrote on the bottom of the page: "I, Irene Gizzi, have identified these two individuals to Jay Margolis." In addition, Jay Margolis took a photograph of Ms. Gizzi holding the photo line-up diagram, both of which are in Margolis's collection. Jay Margolis took all the photos of Ms. Gizzi in this book.)

(TARRANTS III 1979, p. 72: "It was December 23 [1968]. Only three days earlier I had celebrated my twenty-second birthday on death row.")

(TARRANTS III 1979, p. 15: "In early spring [1968], I had been in California conferring with the West Coast coordinator of the Minutemen...")

(TARRANTS III 1979, p. 59: "I decided to take a trip to Los Angeles to deepen my ties with Dr. Wesley Swift, a leader in radical-Right circles.")

(NELSON 1993, p. 140: "Tarrants would later testify he bought a rifle from Swift with plans to use it to shoot Dr. Martin Luther King, Jr...")

(Mitchell, Jerry. "Book Probes MLK Killing: Authors Suggest White Knights of Ku Klux Klan May Have Played Role In Civil-Rights Leader's 1968 Slaying." The *Clarion-Ledger*. 30 December 2007: "On July 31, 1968, Margot Capomacchia, the mother of Jackson schoolteacher Kathy Ainsworth, told an FBI informant her late daughter... and four men [including Thomas Tarrants] were responsible for King's death and 'used radio equipment... in jamming police calls...' Eight years later, a similar allegation surfaced in Miami Magazine, in which reporter Dan Christensen cited 1968 Miami police reports [in which] police informant Willie Augustus Somersett mentions his conversations with a house painter [Sidney Barnes], described in one FBI report as being involved in a failed plot in 1963 to kill King... According to the Miami Magazine article, [Sidney Barnes] told Somersett the vehicle 'used to jam the police cars on relaying messages of the killing of King (that day)... was a car used by Thomas Tarrants.' [Sidney Barnes] also said Tarrants stayed at his house for a week or more after King's killing. This is 'the first I've heard of anything like this,' Tarrants responded. He called Barnes a 'head case...' Tarrants said he had nothing to do with King's assassination. At the time, he said, he was living in Franklin, N.C., staying with a couple who were followers of Swift. He wouldn't give their names but surmised they may be dead now because they were older then. As for the allegation the White

Knights jammed police radios at the scene, Tarrants remarked, 'I don't know they had people with the technical expertise to do that.' He said he certainly didn't do it. In Jack Nelson's book, *Terror in the Night: The Klan's Campaign Against the Jews*, Tarrants is quoted as saying, 'That was my ambition, to shoot Dr. King. I hated Dr. King.' Tarrants acknowledged having those views at the time but pointed out 'a lot of people in the South hated Martin Luther King.' According to *Terror in the Night*, Tarrants purchased a gun from Swift with plans to kill King. He acknowledged to the *Clarion-Ledger* that he bought a rifle from Swift.")

(GIZZI, IRENE. INTERVIEW WITH JAY MARGOLIS. 10 MARCH 2014: "The police interviewed me afterwards...")

(GIZZI, IRENE. INTERVIEW WITH JAY MARGOLIS. 25 MARCH 2014: Irene Gizzi identified to Jay Margolis two CIA agents George Joannides and David Sanchez Morales. Also, she saw Unidentified Man in Profile, who according to Ms. Gizzi, may or may not be the man with "blonde hair and horn-rimmed glasses" on page 452 of Shane O'Sullivan's book.)

(O'SULLIVAN 2008, pp. 442–443: "Joannides was born in Athens in 1922...")

(O'SULLIVAN 2008, pp. 446, 452: A possible identification for Unidentified Man in Profile witnessed by Irene Gizzi, Shane O'Sullivan wrote on page 446 how the bottom photograph on page 452 "showed a third man... with blonde hair and horn-rimmed glasses.")

(O'SULLIVAN 2008, p. 459: "The last leg of [David] Talbot and [Jefferson] Morley's journey took them to see Joannide's former station chief in Saigon, Tom Polgar. Word came back that before Talbot and Morley mentioned his name, Polgar identified Joannides in the photograph. Polgar also identified the blonde man in horn-rimmed glasses in the other ballroom photographs as James Critchfield, the CIA's chief in the Middle East at the time... When he was shown the ballroom photographs, Polgar told Talbot and Morley—and later confirmed to me—that the man at the Ambassador was 'not incompatible' with the Joannides he knew in Saigon, but he couldn't positively identify him. Polgar identified the third man [with blonde hair and horn-rimmed glasses] as 'not incompatible with James Critchfield.' ")

(GIZZI, IRENE. INTERVIEW WITH JAY MARGOLIS. 25 MARCH 2014: "When I saw them [Tarrants, Ainsworth, Joannides, Morales, and Unidentified Man in Profile], they were to the right of the entrance to the lower ballroom...")

(O'SULLIVAN 2008, p. 454: "Robert Kennedy and five others were shot in the pantry. Twenty-one seconds later, [David] Morales is first spotted in the footage... at the back of the Ambassador Room... This makes sense. Kennedy was due to go downstairs for another speech. If he wasn't diverted into the pantry and Plan B had to be activated, Morales was ready and waiting.")

(O'SULLIVAN 2008, p. 436: "[O'Sullivan] interviewed Robert Walton, a good friend of Morales's who had also acted as his lawyer during the seventies... [and Walton quotes David Morales as saying:] 'I was in Dallas when we got that motherfucker [JFK] and I was in Los Angeles when we got the little bastard [RFK].'")

(O'SULLIVAN 2008, p. 426: Robert Walton relayed, "[David Morales] started yelling about what a wimp Kennedy was, and talking about how [Morales] had worked on the Bay of Pigs and how he had to watch all the men he had recruited and trained...")

(O'SULLIVAN 2008, pp. 425–426: "David Sanchez Morales was a legendary CIA operative" who was employed at "JMWAVE in 1963. Morales was chief of operations.")

(O'SULLIVAN 2008, pp. 428, 526: Bradley Ayers said, "I transferred to South Florida, to JMWAVE...")

(TARRANTS III 1979, pp. 36-37: "Acquaintances in the Birchers told me of a mysterious figure involved in anti-Castro guerrilla activities...")

(O'SULLIVAN 2008, p. 470: "Michael D. Roman [a.k.a. CIA agent Gordon Campbell]... shared a birthday with Robert Kennedy—born on November 20, 1918, and died suddenly on December 22, 2002.")

(O'SULLIVAN 2008, pp. 469–471: "When I showed Bradley Ayers this footage, it reinforced his identification of Campbell…")

(O'SULLIVAN 2008, p. 428: Bradley Ayers said, "I met the assistant chief of station, a fellow by the name of Gordon Campbell…")

(O'SULLIVAN 2008, p. 473: "The Roman family recognized the figure of Joannides in the photographs…")

(O'SULLIVAN 2008, p. 473: Michael Roman's son relayed, "Both my sister and mother confirm the darker-haired man is Frank Owens [actually spelled Owen which was a cover name for Joannides]…")

(O'SULLIVAN 2008, p. 473: "Owens was a regional sales manager for Michael Roman, and seems to match a 'Frank S. Owen' from New York interviewed by the FBI on October 21…")

(O'SULLIVAN 2008, pp. 470–471: "Campbell [under the name Michael D. Roman] was working [as vice president of the Bulova Watch Company] for [Gen. Omar N. [Bradley], for a watch company that was having its sales conference at the hotel where Kennedy would be assassinated? It boggles the mind.")

(*RFK Must Die: The Assassination of Bobby Kennedy* (An Investigative Documentary by Shane O'Sullivan). E2 Films, 2007: Shane O'Sullivan stated, "Forty percent of Bulova's revenue came from the defense industry…")

(GIZZI, IRENE. INTERVIEW WITH JAY MARGOLIS. 12 MARCH 2014: "I still don't understand why the police kept trying to say that it was only Sirhan Sirhan…")

(GIZZI, IRENE. INTERVIEW WITH JAY MARGOLIS. 13 MARCH 2014: "Unless the cops got all the footage, there's a bunch of people that have footage because there were television crews…")

(MELANSON 1994, p. 69: "Three drawn guns were reported by witnesses…")

(MELANSON 1994, p. 68: Don Schulman told Special Counsel Thomas F. Kranz, "I had thought I saw three guns [but only witnessed Sirhan's and Cesar's actually being fired].")

(Pease, Lisa. "The Other Kennedy Conspiracy: The Assassination Of Robert Kennedy Never Received The Scrutiny It Deserves." *Salon*. 21 November 2011: "Fact: Donald Schulman, a young runner for a local TV station, claimed he saw security guard Cesar fire his gun. Schulman also told the LAPD he saw three guns in the pantry. (Some authors have mistakenly suggested Schulman wasn't in the pantry, but LAPD records confirm that he was.)")

(MELANSON 1994, p. 69: "Martha Raines asserts that a gun besides Sirhan's or Cesar's was fired... Martha Raines told the author of seeing a man fire a gun in the pantry.")

(MELANSON 1994, pp. 65–66: "According to Raines, the man fired a handgun of some kind... 'And, as I recall, one of them [the shots from Tarrants's gun] was high and should have gone into the ceiling...'")

(JOLING AND VAN PRAAG 2008, pp. 199–200: "[Ted] Charach states that Sirhan could not have shot the bullets that penetrated these [ceiling] panels. Rather, he states, someone behind Kennedy and facing in Sirhan's direction could have fired shots that would have hit those [ceiling] tiles.")

(TARRANTS III 1979, p. 33: Thomas Tarrants explained how he had "a dislike for John Kennedy and his policies on race and federal intervention...")

(TARRANTS III 1979, p. 81: "My defiance of authority began when authority placed itself on the side of federal intervention to integrate...")

(TARRANTS III 1979, p. 82: "As I saw it, America was being undermined by the communist-Jewish conspiracy.")

(*The Second Gun* documentary, 1973: Directed by Theodore Charach and co-produced by Theodore Charach and Gérard Alcan: In 1969, Thane Eugene Cesar said, "I definitely wouldn't have voted for Bobby Kennedy because he had the same ideas as John did...")

(Moldea, Dan E. "Who Really Killed Bobby Kennedy?" *Regardie's*. June 1987, p. 72: "The evidence to support Cesar's possible role in the shooting is extensive and clearly demonstrates means, opportunity, and motive.")

(JOLING AND VAN PRAAG 2008, p. 54: Sgt. Paul Sharaga relayed, "The woman stated that she and her husband were just outside the Embassy Room when a young couple, in their late teens or early twenties...")

(JOLING AND VAN PRAAG 2008, p. 55: Sgt. Paul Sharaga communicated on the LAPD logger tapes, "12:28:53 '2L30, description of the suspect; at 3400 Wilshire Boulevard; male Caucasian, 20 to 22, 6 ft. to 6 ft. 2, very thin...")

(NELSON 1993, p. 17: "It was evening, June 29, 1968... Thomas Albert Tarrants III was twenty-one years old... tall and trim— about six feet three and 170 pounds—with brown eyes and black hair combed straight back. Women were attracted to him.")

(NELSON 1993, p. 17: "It was evening, June 29, 1968... Kathy Ainsworth... was twenty-six years old, five feet four and buxom, with a pretty oval face and brown eyes that matched her thick brunette hair... [and was employed by] the Lorena Duling Elementary School" teaching fifth grade.)

(MELANSON 1994, p. 65: Noting Martha Raines's observations, Professor Philip Melanson wrote, "He [the third gunman] was approximately 6-feet 2-inches tall, Caucasian, with dark, wavy hair and wearing a suit (not a uniform).")

(*RFK Must Die: The Assassination of Bobby Kennedy* (An Investigative Documentary by Shane O'Sullivan). E2 Films, 2007: To NBC reporter Sander Vanocur, an hour-and-a-half after the shooting, Sandra Serrano relayed, "This girl came running down the stairs in the back and said, 'We've shot him! We've shot him!'...")

(O'SULLIVAN 2008, p. 21: "Campaign worker Sandra Serrano was still sitting on the fire escape below the southwest corner of the Embassy Room.")

(JOLING AND VAN PRAAG 2008, pp. 53–54: "Serrano's interview [with Sander Vanocur] occurred about 1 ½ hours after the shooting.")

(O'SULLIVAN 2008, p. 469: "As Kennedy left the stage, the crowd began to disperse, and a minute or so later, Kennedy was shot. As cries from the pantry ignited panic in the Embassy Room, we see Campbell walk forward from the back of the room toward the commotion. It's clear he was not coming from the pantry but had been watching the speech from the back of the ballroom. The Latin man with the mustache had also been watching the speech, a little closer to the stage. When I obtained a new, clean transfer of the original Campbell footage, it was also clear that he was holding his right hand across his chest as he walked through the room but his hands were empty. There was no container and no disguised weapon [because it was presumably hidden underneath his dress shirt as Campbell held it in place with his right hand across his chest]. Why he held his hand across his chest and why the Latin man was waving toward an exit remain a mystery.")

(*RFK Must Die: The Assassination of Bobby Kennedy* (An Investigative Documentary by Shane O'Sullivan). E2 Films, 2007: Shortly after the shooting of RFK, Ambassador Hotel footage shows CIA agent Gordon Campbell using his right hand to hold onto what may be Tarrants's murder weapon carefully hidden underneath his dress shirt as he is guided towards an exit by a Latin man.)

(O'SULLIVAN 2008, p. 405: "The two men [Enrique 'Hank' Hernandez and Manuel 'Manny' Pena] who had effective day-to-day control of the RFK investigation also had CIA connections.")

(*RFK Must Die: The Assassination of Bobby Kennedy* (An Investigative Documentary by Shane O'Sullivan). E2 Films, 2007: The late Larry Teeter, Sirhan's former attorney, stated, "The LAPD does have a history of ties with the CIA and we know that [from] two people who played a critical role in the investigation Manuel Pena and Enrique 'Hank' Hernandez.")

(*RFK Must Die: The Assassination of Bobby Kennedy* (An Investigative Documentary by Shane O'Sullivan). E2 Films, 2007: On a recording, Enrique Hernandez told Sandra Serrano, "I had been called to South America, to Vietnam, and Europe and I have administered tests. The last test I administered was to the dictator in Caracas, Venezuela. He was a big man, a dictator. Perez Jimenez was his last name. And this is when there was a transition in the government of Venezuela. And that's when President Betancourt came in... but this is all behind. But there was a great thing involved over there... and I tested the gentleman.")

(O'SULLIVAN 2008, p. 409: On a recorded 1992 interview, Manuel Pena explained to attorney Marilyn Barrett, "The way they've written it, it sounds like I was brought back [out of retirement] and put into the [RFK] case as a plant by the CIA...")

(JOLING AND VAN PRAAG 2008, p. 229: "In early November, 1967, Manny Pena officially retired from the Los Angeles Police Department. He had served the LAPD for 22 years... By January 17, 1968, however, Pena was back on duty with the LAPD... Following the assassination, Pena was appointed to the SUS [Special Unit Senator]... Both official and unofficial accounts credit Pena with a considerable role in the direction of the SUS's work and daily management. This role continued during the major period of the [RFK] investigation. In 1969, at some time following the conclusion of the Sirhan trial, Pena once again retired from active LAPD duty.")

(O'SULLIVAN 2008, pp. 405–406: "FBI agent Roger LaJeunesse had known Pena for years and was the FBI liaison to the LAPD during the RFK case. LaJeunesse said Pena left the LAPD for a 'special training unit' at CIA's Camp Peary base in Virginia... Pena had been doing special assignments for the CIA for a decade, mostly under AID [Agency for International Development] cover.")

(*The Second Gun* documentary, 1973: Directed by Theodore Charach and co-produced by Theodore Charach and Gérard Alcan:

Dr. Thomas Noguchi stated, "It is scientifically highly unlikely. In this case, there was an abundance of powder burn embedded deep in the tissue.")

(NOGUCHI 1984, p. 96: "Because of the soot in the hair...")

(NOGUCHI 1984, pp. 97, 102: "I now knew the precise location of the murder weapon at the moment it was fired... Thus I have never said that Sirhan Sirhan killed Robert Kennedy.")

(*The Second Gun* documentary, 1973: Directed by Theodore Charach and co-produced by Theodore Charach and Gérard Alcan: In 1969, Thane Eugene Cesar said, "When the shots were fired, I reached for my gun [and got it out of my holster]... I had it in my hand.")

(*The Second Gun* documentary, 1973: Directed by Theodore Charach and co-produced by Theodore Charach and Gérard Alcan: In 1969, Thane Eugene Cesar asserted he grabbed RFK's right elbow with his left hand, guiding him through the pantry and said, "I got powder in my eyes...")

(JOLING AND VAN PRAAG 2008, p. 213: "Gunpowder primarily blows back and to the sides from a fired gun, not forward. Powder residue is often found on the face and hands of the person firing the gun... Based on the locations of Senator Kennedy, Sirhan, and Cesar, however, the probability that powder from Sirhan's gun would have gotten into the eyes of the guard would be extremely unlikely.")

(MELANSON 1994, pp. 65, 69: "In addition to Sirhan's gun and that of security guard Cesar, Lisa Urso saw another one...")

(MELANSON 1994, p. 65: After the shooting was over, Lisa Urso said the man in the suit with a drawn gun was "by Kennedy.")

(Rosenthal, Harry F. "Testifies He Told RFK After The Shooting: You Can Make It!" The *Kokomo Tribune* [Kokomo, Indiana]. 16 February 1969, p. 20: Associated Press writer Harry Rosenthal wrote, "Shortly after midnight, Romero saw someone coming toward Kennedy." Juan Romero testified in court, "I thought it was a person who couldn't wait to shake his hand. I seen the guy put a hand at the Senator's head. And then I saw a gun." Asked if Sirhan Sirhan was the shooter, Romero replied, "I don't believe that's him.")

("Sirhan Trial: State Will Call 7 Eyewitnesses." The *Press-Courier* [Oxnard, California]. 16 February 1969, p. 17: United Press International wrote, "All except Romero were definite in their identification of Sirhan as the gunman seized at the scene of Kennedy's shooting. Sirhan stood up to give Romero a better view of him and the busboy said, 'I don't believe that's him.'")

(CHACON, RIGO. INTERVIEW WITH JAY MARGOLIS. 9 MARCH 2014: "I've known Juan Romero for more than twenty years...")

(Lopez, Steve. "Kneeling Again Next to RFK: Juan Romero Visits Kennedy's Grave at Arlington National Cemetery." *Los Angeles Times*. 21 November 2010: " 'Sorry,' he apologized to his daughter, Elda, and friend, Rigo Chacon, who had made the trip with him from California. 'If I can get it out of the way now...' Maybe a good cry would help him keep his composure, he said, when he finally stood at the grave.")

(NOGUCHI 1984, p. 95: Noguchi wrote that "the all-important bullet that had caused Kennedy's death" was from behind his head. "The bullet had entered the skull an inch to the left of Kennedy's right ear...")

(JOLING, ROBERT J. INTERVIEW WITH JAY MARGOLIS. 8 FEBRUARY 2012: Robert Joling told Jay Margolis he believed Cesar was Kennedy's assassin because Cesar was to the back-right of the Senator. While Cesar did fire and hit the Senator twice to his right armpit, it was Thomas Tarrants who was responsible for the fatal shot to the back of Kennedy's head. In fact, as Noguchi confirmed to Dan Moldea, the two shots to Kennedy's right armpit were nonfatal and they occurred *before* the fatal shot to the back of the head.)

(MELANSON 1994, p. 78: " 'Well,' Cesar replied, 'from where I could see, it looked like he was shot in the head, the chest and the shoulder.' 'How many shots did you hear?' 'Four.' This makes Cesar the only person besides Schulman to correctly state that Kennedy was hit three times. But Cesar even knew—or guessed—the approximate locations of the wounds. There were, of course, more than four shots fired, but four did impact on Kennedy (three wounds and the bullet that passed through [the rear of] his [right shoulder pad of the] suit coat).")

(TURNER AND CHRISTIAN 2006, p. 168: "It is also curious that Cesar's contemporaneous account locates the exact number and placement of shots and wounds in RFK's body—inflicted from the rear, his own conceded position—when no such identifications were possible until doctors examined the Senator at a nearby hospital some twenty minutes later.")

(Rosenthal, Harry F. "Testifies He Told RFK After The Shooting: You Can Make It!" The *Kokomo Tribune* [Kokomo, Indiana]. 16 February 1969, p. 20: Associated Press writer Harry Rosenthal wrote, "Shortly after midnight, Romero saw someone coming toward Kennedy." Juan Romero testified in court, "I thought it was a person who couldn't wait to shake his hand. I seen the guy put a hand at the Senator's head. And then I saw a gun." Asked if Sirhan Sirhan was the shooter, Romero replied, "I don't believe that's him.")

("Sirhan Trial: State Will Call 7 Eyewitnesses." The *Press-Courier* [Oxnard, California]. 16 February 1969, p. 17: United Press International wrote, "All except Romero were definite in their identification of Sirhan as the gunman seized at the scene of Kennedy's shooting. Sirhan stood up to give Romero a better view of him and the busboy said, 'I don't believe that's him.'")

(GIZZI, IRENE. INTERVIEW WITH JAY MARGOLIS. 10 MARCH 2014: Morales, Joannides, and Unidentified Man in Profile "were shorter than he [Tarrants] was because he was the tallest in the group.")

(MELANSON 1994, p. 65: Noting Martha Raines's observations, Professor Philip Melanson wrote, "He [the third gunman] was approximately 6-feet 2-inches tall, Caucasian, with dark, wavy hair and wearing a suit (not a uniform).")

(NELSON 1993, p. 17: "It was evening, June 29, 1968... Thomas Albert Tarrants III was twenty-one years old... tall and trim—about six feet three and 170 pounds—with brown eyes and black hair combed straight back. Women were attracted to him.")

(JOLING AND VAN PRAAG 2008, p. 55: Sgt. Paul Sharaga communicated on the LAPD logger tapes, "12:28:53 '2L30, description of the suspect; at 3400 Wilshire Boulevard; male Caucasian, 20 to 22, 6 ft. to 6 ft. 2, very thin...")

(TARRANTS III 1979, p. 37: "I developed a great fondness for firearms and marksmanship...")

(JOLING, ROBERT J. INTERVIEW WITH JAY MARGOLIS. 8 FEBRUARY 2012)

(JOLING AND VAN PRAAG 2008, p. 270: "As author Van Praag has scientifically demonstrated [regarding the Stanislaw Pruszynski recording], approximately 13 shots were fired within 5 ½ seconds...")

(JOLING AND VAN PRAAG 2008, p. 85: "Shouldn't there be some bullets on the scene that identify with Sirhan's gun?...")

(PEASE AND DIEUGENIO 2003, p. 557: "The serial number of the gun indicated did not match that of the Sirhan gun. The Sirhan gun had a serial number of H53725. The test bullets evidence envelope, however, bore the serial number of H18602... This gun had belonged, according to the LAPD's records, to a Jake Williams. It does not make sense that someone would look up the record of the Sirhan gun and come up with Jake Williams's gun number by mistake.")

(JOLING AND VAN PRAAG 2008, p. 159: "This exhibit [#55], related to the gun identified as a .22 caliber revolver bearing Serial

[Number] H18602 and belonging to Sirhan (actually it was not Sirhan's gun but a gun taken from LAPD Property).")

(JOLING AND VAN PRAAG 2008, p. 82: "[DeWayne] Wolfer testified that the Sirhan gun was in Grandy Jury evidence (having been admitted into evidence on June 7, 1968)… He also stated that he had removed revolver H18602, which was of the same make and model of the Sirhan gun, from the LAPD confiscated weapons collection on June 10… Wolfer further stated that through some inadvertent clerical error the serial number of H18602 had mistakenly been placed on the evidence envelope 'B.'")

(Moldea, Dan E. "Who Really Killed Bobby Kennedy?" Regardie's. June 1987, p. 69: "Wolfer testified at Sirhan's trial that he was able to match bullets from a test-firing of Sirhan's .22 with bullets taken out of the victims. Later, however, when the trial evidence was examined by outside parties, it was discovered that Wolfer may not have test-fired Sirhan's gun at all. Police records show that he test-fired an Iver Johnson Cadet .22 with the serial number H18602; Sirhan's gun was an Iver Johnson Cadet .22 with the serial number H53725.")

(JOLING AND VAN PRAAG 2008, p. 174: DeWayne Wolfer lied under oath at Sirhan's trial that the "Sirhan death weapon and no other gun in the world fired the fatal shot that killed Senator Kennedy.")

(Moldea, Dan E. "Who Really Killed Bobby Kennedy?" Regardie's. June 1987, p. 70: "That same year [1971] a formal complaint was filed against Wolfer by [Noguchi's] attorney Godfrey Isaac and journalist Theodore Charach who charged Wolfer with having made serious errors in several cases, including the Kennedy murder… [Former FBI agent Marshall Houts wrote:] 'Wolfer suffers from a great inferiority complex for which he compensates by giving the police exactly what they need to obtain a conviction…' In 1980… he was also cited by the state court of appeals for testimony in a major case 'bordering on perjury' and 'given with reckless disregard for the truth.'")

(JOLING AND VAN PRAAG 2008, pp. xxviii, 234-235: "One into Paul Schrade = 1; one into Ira Goldstein = 2; one into Irwin Stroll = 3; one into Elizabeth Evans = 4; one into William Weisel = 5; and four into Senator Kennedy and his suit jacket = 9.")

(Moldea, Dan E. "Who Really Killed Bobby Kennedy?" *Regardie's*. June 1987, p. 71: "DeWayne Wolfer's reconstruction of the eight shots fired from Sirhan's gun explains his theories nicely, but is not supported by the facts.")

("Robert F. Kennedy Assassination: The FBI Files." Filiquarian Publishing, LLC. 2007, Second Section, p. 9: "Cesar owned a .22 caliber revolver at the time of the shooting… at first telling investigating officers that he remembered selling the weapon in the spring of 1968 [months before the shooting], but [later] admitted that he had sold the weapon [on] September [6], 1968, to a friend [Jim Yoder] in Arkansas. This weapon… was a 9 shot cadet model .22 revolver.")

(JOLING AND VAN PRAAG 2008, p. 261: "While Cesar has claimed that he had the Ace Guard Service provided .38 gun with him that night, the police never checked his weapon and he initially told investigators (erroneously) that he had sold his .22 gun months before the shooting.")

(PEASE AND DIEUGENIO 2003, pp. 551–552: "The official autopsy report was not made available to the defense until after Sirhan's trial had commenced on January 7, 1969. The first mention of the autopsy report from the defense appears in a memo dated February 22, 1969 that [Robert Blair] Kaiser wrote to Sirhan's lead attorney, Grant Cooper… Kennedy had died on June 6, 1968, and the autopsy had been performed immediately upon his death. In the SUS card index, a card labeled only 'Medical' reports: 'Coroners protocol—Final Summary: 10 pages received 11-27-68…' What could possibly have kept the autopsy report from being delivered for nearly six months? Was it held back to keep the defense from figuring out that Kennedy was shot at a distance that could not be reconciled with the consistent reports of Sirhan's position relative to Kennedy's?")

(VILLALOBOS, EDGARDO. INTERVIEW WITH JAY MARGOLIS. 14 JANUARY 2013: "We got the call there at the Ambassador Hotel…")

(JOLING AND VAN PRAAG 2008, p. 235: "Robert Hulsman, an ambulance driver for the City of Los Angeles, together with Max Behrman, was dispatched to the assassination scene shortly thereafter. Their ambulance arrived at the front hotel entrance.")

(VILLALOBOS, EDGARDO. INTERVIEW WITH JAY MARGOLIS. 5 OCTOBER 2013: "They first took him to Central Receiving Hospital…")

(Rasmussen, Cecilia. "A Pioneering Public Hospital Checks Out." *Los Angeles Times*. 2 October 2005: "Perhaps the most famous of Central Receiving's patients arrived by ambulance in the early morning hours of June 5, 1968. Robert F. Kennedy had been shot at the nearby Ambassador Hotel after winning the California presidential primary.")

(Elliott, Osborn, ed. "Bobby's Last Longest Day." *Newsweek*. 17 June 1968, p. 30: "But Central Receiving has neither blood plasma nor X-ray equipment, and they had no choice but to send him on to 'Good Sam' – the Hospital of the Good Samaritan – four blocks away…")

(Stewart, Marilyn. "Former KKK Terrorist Cites C.S. Lewis' Faithful Obedience." *Baptist Press*. 9 August 2006: "As an operative for the White Knights, Tarrants was involved in some 30 bombings of synagogues, churches and homes before being apprehended in an FBI sting operation in Meridian, Miss [on June 30, 1968]. In the ensuing shootout between Tarrants and law enforcement officers, Tarrants's female accomplice [Kathy Ainsworth] was killed and he was shot 19 times, almost ending his life.")

(NELSON 1993, pp. 17–18, 21, 173–192, 200, 219–220, 233, 263: On June 30, 1968, in Meridian, Mississippi, the FBI opened fire killing Kathy Ainsworth and seriously injuring her partner-in-crime Thomas Albert Tarrants III.)

(TARRANTS III 1979, p. 14: "Ironically, Meridian was the home of one of the best orthopedic surgeons in the United States, Dr. Leslie Rush, who headed Rush Memorial Hospital in Meridian... My family talked to him about my situation, and after examining me, he volunteered to operate without charge.")

(TARRANTS III 1979, p. 95: Thomas Tarrants said how "there were too many for the extra cells on death row.")

(TARRANTS III 1979, p. 124: "On a bright, clear Monday morning, December 13, 1976, at about 8:30 a.m., a prison station wagon arrived at the pre-release center... I was packed and ready to leave.")

(TARRANTS III 1979, p. 109: "Nonetheless, some wouldn't be convinced. They no doubt still view my conversion as a gimmick for freedom.")

(TARRANTS III 1979, p. 119: "For one thing I was at one time labeled by the press and federal and state authorities as the most dangerous man in Mississippi. More importantly, I had shot a patrolman—an extremely serious offense in its own right.")